The Iota Story

*To Simon, who gave me the world
and the courage to accept it*

the iota story

Jenifer Simpson

The Iota Story

Copyright © 2010 Jenifer Simpson
jsimp@netspace.net.au

All rights reserved. No part of this publication may be reproduced, stored in a retrieval system or transmitted in any form or by any means, electronic, mechanical, photocopying, recording or otherwise, without the prior written permission of the author.

The information, views, opinions and visuals expressed in this publication are solely those of the author and do not reflect those of the publisher. The publisher disclaims any liabilities or responsibilities whatsoever for any damages, libel or liabilities arising directly or indirectly from the contents of this publication.

National Library of Australia Cataloguing-in-Publication entry

Author:	Simpson, Jenifer.
Title:	The Iota story / Jenifer Simpson.
ISBN:	9781921681752 (pbk.)
Subjects:	Simpson, Jenifer--Travel.
	Iota (Yacht)
	Yachting--Oceania.
	Yachting--Atlantic Ocean Region.
	Yachting--Pacific Area.
	Voyages and travels.
Dewey Number:	797.1246

Published by BookPal
www.bookpal.com.au
PO Box 3422
Sunnybank Hills LPO
QLD 4109

Edited by Helen Kershaw Editing Services
hvkershaw@bigpond.com

Typesetting by Myra Murtagh
myra_murtagh@yahoo.com.au

Cover illustration courtesy of Rod Lehmann

Acknowledgements

I would like to acknowledge the help and advice from my editor, Helen Kershaw and my typesetter, Myra Murtagh. I am grateful to all those who encouraged me in this endeavour, especially to Jenny Osten. Special thanks to Rod Lehmann, who so perfectly captured the character of *Iota* in the painting used for the cover illustration.

contents

Early Days	1
A Storm in the South Seas *1962*	21
Dwyn Wen, the Patron Saint of Lovers *1963*	47
If It's Worth Doing, It's Worth Doing Properly *1964*	71
The Majestic Marquesas and the Dangerous Archipelago *1965*	89
La Belle Martinique *1965-1966*	117
Trade Wind Sailing in the Lesser Antilles *1966*	141
Interlude in England *1966-1967*	167
The Bahamas – *Iota* in her Element *1967*	179
Homeward Bound *1967*	195
Rain and Shine in the Solomon Islands *1968*	215
Papua New Guinea – a Country of Contrasts *1968-1969*	245
To the Spice Islands in the Footsteps of Wallace and Darwin *1970*	279
Singapore – an Island State on the Move *1970-1971*	321
Singapore to Bangkok – Memories, Monkeys and Monks *1971*	345
Iota returns to the South Seas – Tonga and Fiji *1972*	379
Epilogue	413

early days

I was born in England with a travel bug. One of my earliest memories was when I was four. My brother, who had graduated to a two-wheeled bicycle, and I, on my tricycle, were pedalling along on the path outside our house. From inside we heard the sombre, grave voice of Prime Minister Neville Chamberlain on the radio saying the country was now at war.

'What's war?' I asked my brother.

'Don't know,' he said. 'Let's go and ask Mother.'

I don't recall her answer, but not long after she asked what we thought about going to Australia for the duration of the war. My father had an Australian friend who had offered to look after us in Sydney. My response was enthusiastic; my mother thought, probably correctly, that if I ever went to Australia I would never come back. I gave no thought at all as to whether I would miss my parents. In the end they decided against sending us, but a fascination with Australia, and a desire one day to meet a kangaroo, remained with me.

We survived the war. I can remember gas masks, ration books, air raid warnings and shrapnel falling in our garden. We could distinguish between the engines of Spitfires and Messerschmitts. Down in the air raid shelter where we slept each night in our fur-lined 'siren suits' the uneven buzzing of the German planes led my brother to diligently swat any invading mosquitoes. We took war for granted for we had no memories of peace.

I mostly enjoyed school. At the all-girls Edgbaston High School, where I started at age eight, we were fortunate in having a motivating headmistress. Miss Casswell was one of the first women to gain a degree in science and expected us all to aspire to gaining a university education. It was not a question of whether or not to go to university, but of which one, and what to read when we were there.

All through school and university my ambition to travel influenced my choice of subjects. At one stage the brighter members of the class were expected to take Latin as it was a requirement for entry to Oxford or Cambridge. I considered Geography more useful than a dead language so deliberately failed the Latin exam at the end of the year; I achieved a mark of 2%.

In Maths I was told that it was immoral to use the Pythagoras Theorem without being able to prove it. In Scripture class when I asked Miss Weller how *she* could prove what she was telling us, she said I should have faith. I argued and was sent out of the room. Next lesson I decided that, rather than argue, I would remove myself from the class before it began. I went and stood outside the Headmistress's study – the 'naughty corner'. 'Cass' came out of her room and asked me who had sent me. She was taken aback when I replied that I had sent myself. She wisely told me to spend Scripture classes in the library doing my Maths homework!

The two passions in my life were sailing and horses. Sailing won. My parents joined the sailing club because my brother was asthmatic and sailing was a sport he could take part in without having breathing difficulties. We sailed on a small reservoir just south of Birmingham – about as far away from the sea as one could be in England. We sailed Fireflies, the popular 12-foot dinghy designed by Uffa Fox. The Firefly was considered revolutionary at the time and, being mass-produced from hot moulded ply, was a true one-design. Winners won because they were better sailors rather than because they had a better boat. It was ideal for team racing; I was a member of our sailing club team, which gave me the opportunity to visit many other sailing clubs in the United Kingdom, all with their different challenges.

Compared to the sailing dinghies that existed at the time, the Firefly was a lively boat and taught us all we knew about sailing. We learned to make the most out of the fickle winds that were usual on the reservoir. We became sensitive to the boat, developing a sixth sense attuned to her needs; we could 'feel' if the boat was well trimmed and giving of her best. The highlight of each year was the Firefly Championships. We sailed on salt water and through waves; the current and tide had to be taken into account. The excitement of the start was almost unbearable – 150 or more identical boats were all attempting to be at the front at the windward end of the starting line at exactly the same time.

The feeling of elation from doing well, particularly in heavy weather, was addictive.

Having decided that a degree in science would be a useful asset when roaming around the world, I settled on reading chemistry at Birmingham, one of the original red-brick universities. I finished my degree and spent two years teaching chemistry and physics at Headington School in Oxford. I was only 20 when I graduated and fortunate to be teaching mainly seniors; a 19-year-old student who was about to take her Cambridge entrance exams addressed me as Miss Ashford, while I called her Elizabeth.

~

The Australian Government had a policy to 'populate or perish'. They made the English welcome, especially if we were qualified, and for £10 would get us there on condition we agreed to stay for two years. It seemed a good way to start on my travels – Australia was halfway around the world, I would get to meet a kangaroo and it had Sydney Harbour. When I gave my notice to the headmistress at Headington she reprimanded me: two years was far too short a time to stay in my first job; I had an unstable attitude that did not augur well for my future. She held up the commendable life style of Miss Bowen as an example I should strive to emulate. Miss Bowen had been at Headington from kindergarten to the sixth form and then spent two years at a college close by to qualify as a physical education teacher. She had returned to Headington and taught there ever since and was now in her fifties. I was not persuaded to change my mind.

Gordon Turnbull, Father's friend in Sydney, sent a young man to visit my family in England. His name was John Bleakley and he sailed his yacht *Gymea* on Sydney Harbour. He offered to sponsor me and look after me on my arrival. I jumped at the opportunity.

The Italian migrant ship took six eye-opening and pleasurable weeks to get to our destination. I savoured the footloose and fancy-free life and enjoyed being at sea, suspended in an isolated, self-contained world. I would have been happy if it had gone on forever. We stopped for a day in Aden where I went around with my eyes on stalks looking at such strange sights as dry, bare rocky hills, date palms and camels. Then it was non-stop to Australia.

We arrived in Melbourne at the weekend so I did what I would have done if I had been in an unfamiliar part of England – I looked for a sailing club. I expected a member to ask me if I was interested in boats and could I sail, and, that when I said 'yes', I would be invited to go out on the water. St Kilda Yacht Club fronted onto the bay so I wandered along the beach to where I could see their boats drawn up. They were familiar – Finns, the new single-handed Olympic class that I had sailed a few times. As I was looking at them, a man came up to me and said, 'Are you not aware that women are not allowed in the yacht club?'

'No,' I replied in amazement. 'Who sails them then?' It was not an auspicious start to life in Australia.

In Sydney, I stayed with John and his family and went sailing on *Gymea*, on the Harbour. It was my first experience of a larger boat, but I quickly discovered the principles were the same and had no difficulty in steering her. She whetted my appetite for more.

Before I left England John gave me the names of four schools similar to the one where I had taught in Oxford – private all-girls schools catering for both boarders and daygirls. I wrote to enquire if they were in need of a science teacher for the next school year. Three replied offering me a position so I had to make a decision. It was easy – I looked for the one that would give me the greatest access to sailing on the Harbour.

Abbotsleigh was at Wahroonga on Sydney's North Shore. I lived in residence so I could save enough money to buy a boat all the sooner.

The school's new headmistress, Betty Archdale, was a former captain of the UK Women's Cricket Team and principal of the Women's College at Sydney University. Her mother had been a leading suffragette and had spent several weeks in prison, much to the dismay of her traditional naval officer father. Betty's style and values were a shock for the more conservative members of the staff. She thought good discipline was self-control rather than control imposed from the outside. She favoured giving the girls more freedom and encouraged non-conformism. The older members of the staff expressed horror when she met the head of the Jervis Bay Naval College and arranged for a party of senior girls to visit the college for a weekend. It would be good experience; the girls and the naval cadets would learn how to behave in each other's company – an essential part of their education.

'You're coming,' she said to me. 'You can sail!'

As soon as I had enough money I answered an advertisement for a Gwen 12 skiff. I had never seen a Gwen 12, but it seemed to be as close to what I was used to sailing as I was going to find in Sydney. Kev, the owner, collected me from the train one Sunday morning and took me to the St George Yacht Club. The clubhouse had a boathouse behind it, built on piles over the water. The boathouse was also connected to the beach by a round telegraph pole covered in slimy green seaweed.

Kev stopped by the pole and said, pointing, 'She's in the boathouse. I'll meet you there.'

Light was dawning. 'You don't think I'm going to walk along that slippery round pole, do you? How are you going to get there?'

'Oh,' he said, 'I go through the clubhouse, but women aren't allowed in the clubhouse.'

I drew a deep breath. 'We seem to have a problem. I'm not going to buy your boat without first looking at it, and I'm not going to walk up that pole. So if you want to sell the boat to me, you're going to have to find a solution to the problem.'

'I suppose you'll have to come through the clubhouse, then,' he said, shrugging his shoulders.

He parked the car and walked quickly through the clubhouse, trying to pretend he had nothing to do with me. I followed. Four men were sitting at the bar leaning over their beers. They stared in outraged astonishment as I walked past. I could not have caused more of a stir had I walked naked into a men's toilet. They were equally astonished when I walked out again. I agreed to buy the boat.

I joined Mosman Sailing Club; female members were not a problem, however I was their only female boat owner. A phone call came from Ron, introducing himself as a member of Mosman Sailing Club. Was I in need of a crew? If so, could he please apply for the job? He could sail and wanted to experience the Gwen 12. I was delighted to have a competent crew who knew the harbour.

Like the Firefly, the Gwen 12 was 12 feet long and a one-design, but there the similarity ended. The Gwen was designed for Australian conditions and was considered one of the fastest 12-foot craft in the world. It was equipped with a spinnaker – or, more precisely, a 'shy kite' – and a trapeze. Typically, wind speed on the harbour was 20 to 25 knots. What a joy it was to have a brisk wind without bad weather – having wind and sun at the same time was a rare event in England.

In our first competitions we finished in the middle of the fleet of about fifteen skiffs, but we slowly improved our performance. We could hold our own on the beat to windward and in lighter airs, however the spinnaker was our undoing. The boat was exhilarating when she was flying out of the water, balanced by Ron stretched out on the trapeze, but she was also unstable. Ron's knowledge of the harbour was invaluable, especially if we were ever in the lead, for he always knew where we should be heading.

'Where's the next mark?' I asked one day.

'The buoy over there with the black-and-white striped thing on it,' he replied, pointing.

'Oh,' I said, 'I didn't know buoys came with black-and-white striped things.'

He never forgot the remark.

~

Living in residence, with its accompanying weekend duties, interfered with my sailing – I had to miss one in every four races. I thought about finding independent accommodation, but it would have taken a sizeable proportion of my income. I became aware that, as a teacher in a private school, I was paid less than a similar teacher in a state school and considerably less than a chemist working in industry. Perhaps I should change my employment; it would have the advantage of giving me a broader experience of life than a cloistered school. Maybe I would miss the school holidays, but what was the point of having holidays if I couldn't afford to enjoy them?

I was sitting in the staff room one morning marking books in my free period when Senior Mistress Miss Allen came to my desk. She was deceptively frail looking – both staff and students knew she must be instantly obeyed.

'There's a representative from the book store here, my dear,' she said. 'He has set up a table with books we might like to acquire for the library. You're the only science teacher free so would you mind, my dear, going to see if there are any we should be buying?'

'Of course, Miss Allen. At once, Miss Allen,' I replied, rising to my feet.

She put her hand on my arm. 'Will you be alright on your own, my dear? It's a man you know.'

Next day I gave notice that I would be leaving at the end of the year – it was bad enough that work interfered with my sailing, but it could not be allowed to get in the way of my social life.

I took a job as a quality-control chemist for Reckitts, a company making a wide range of household products. I gained the impression that the work would be varied and would take me into the real world. However, the factory was in an old area of Sydney, out towards the airport. The buildings were dark and depressing.

'There's absolutely nothing here that could be described as beautiful,' I thought.

The laboratory was basic and a tight squeeze for its three chemists and six lab assistants. In spite of these shortcomings, working for the company was enjoyable, with a cheerful relaxed atmosphere. Unlike teaching, I left work in the laboratory at the end of the day – it didn't demand my time and attention at home. One of the advantages was the variety of the work. The diverse and useful products the company made included analgesics, starch, laundry blue, silver and brass polishes, toilet cleanser, black metal polish, disinfectants, shampoo, denture cleaner and mustard. We never knew what product would be requiring our attention next.

Not long after I joined the company Chief Chemist Stan's wife died. The directors organised a visit for him to the parent company in the United Kingdom to distract him from his grief, but tragically while there he was killed in a road accident. The role of chief chemist fell to Maria, who had worked in the laboratory since her arrival in Australia from Yugoslavia two years before. An attractive redhead, she was a capable chemist, but her English was not yet quite up to the standard where she was confident writing official letters and reports. She frequently asked me to help her, which gave me inside knowledge of what was going on in the world of household products.

I took a room in a house in Mosman belonging to a Mrs Fulford. Two girls, Jan and Anne, shared the next room to mine. Our landlady enjoyed her lodgers and took a personal interest in our social lives, quizzing us about our various dates. She had a bad heart and frequently suffered pains, so we learned where she kept her pills.

At the end of my first season of sailing the Gwen 12, I slipped a disc in my back, no doubt as a result of lifting the boat in and out of the water. I ended up in hospital for a laminectomy. I returned to racing the Gwen, but with a new crew, John. He was not as able as Ron and irritated me by invariably being late. He would have preferred me to be his girlfriend rather than his skipper, but he couldn't sail well enough for me to be interested. Wary of taking risks with my fragile back I did not do as well as before.

Anchored in Mosman Bay was a 20-foot reverse sheer yacht called *Half Moon*, owned by a Dutchman, Albert. She was not a pretty boat, but performed well and took part in Junior Offshore Group racing – the 'Joggies'. The races were out at sea, to Botany Bay or Pittwater. Albert was looking for crew and invited John and me to sail with him. This was my first experience of racing offshore; the competition was keen and I was captivated.

A highlight of the season was a race to Pittwater starting in Rushcutters Bay after dark on a Friday evening. We were making good progress down the Harbour when we found ourselves on a collision course with a freighter. We hadn't seen her because her navigation lights were lost amid a host of much brighter lights on the shore. We just missed being cut in half by her bow, almost – but not quite – scraped along her ironclad hull and then were spun around in her wash. The yacht survived, but our nerves were shattered.

Through the night we beat into choppy seas along the coast and John was miserably seasick. He couldn't get off the boat fast enough and vowed never to sail at sea again. He would have to persuade me to give up this sailing nonsense and become a wife and mother.

The following weekend we were to bring the boat back to Sydney Harbour. John drove Albert and me to Pittwater, spent the night on board and left us at first light. We had all been invited to a party on a Harbour ferry to farewell friends who were off on their travels and Albert's wife and John were to meet us on the wharf. We should have had plenty of time for the trip, but shortly after rounding Barrenjoey, a brisk wind came up from the south. Although we pushed the yacht hard into the increasing headwind, by three in the afternoon we were not even half way.

'There's no way we're going to make it in time for the party,' I said. 'We'll have to go back and hope for a more favourable wind tomorrow.'

Albert agreed. 'We'll go into the Basin and pick up a mooring.'

To make a phone call to his wife Albert had to swim ashore as we had no dinghy. He returned with tins of food for a scratch meal and we then tried to sleep in *Half Moon*'s uncomfortable cabin. A bump and a clatter woke us just after midnight. We both shot up on deck to find a large motor cruiser alongside; the woman on her bow was armed with a boat hook. She had cast us adrift and attached her boat to the mooring. When she saw us she said, surprised, 'Oh, I didn't know there was anybody on board.'

We were speechless as we pulled up our sails and went looking for another mooring.

We made it back to Sydney the next day only to be accosted by Albert's displeased wife who had met John at the party and realised that her husband and I had spent the night together without John's chaperoning presence. Albert said it was John's fault, because he wouldn't come with us. It would be prudent of me to avoid sailing again with Albert, and what was the point of a boyfriend who was always late, not very keen on sailing – worse, prone to seasickness – and especially one with a desire to nest? It was time to move on.

A change of residence was also needed when, sadly, Mrs Fulford's ailing heart finally stopped beating. Her house was to be sold so we girls would have to move. Anne was about to get married so Jan and I agreed to share; we rented a small, basic yet delightful pad in Neutral Bay, looking on to an attractive garden.

It wasn't hard to find racing yachts that needed a crew. John Bleakley, my sponsor on arriving in Australia, frequently asked me to crew on *Gymea*, and Ron, now crewing on *Lass O'Luss*, knew if there was a crew wanted at the Cruising Yacht Club. I gained experience on several yachts, among them *Archina*, *Nimbus*, *Primavera*, *Jolly Roger* and *Wayfarer*, but most of the races were inside the harbour. It wasn't as exhilarating as sailing a skiff that could plane on top of the water rather than ploughing through it. Being a woman, I was expected to do the domestic jobs below decks – the cooking and washing up. I didn't get much of a chance to handle boat. However, though not in control or able to make the decisions, I was learning. While the basic principles of sailing are the same for any size of yacht there was still a lot to find out about the heavier gear needed to handle the bigger sails – winches, roller reefing, topping lifts – and steering with a wheel rather than a tiller.

Many of the races were organised by the Cruising Yacht Club – but it also lived up to its name by providing moorings for cruising yachts coming from overseas. I was fascinated by the thought that these yachts had sailed across the Pacific to get where they were. They were different from their racing sisters, being built for comfort rather than speed. One in particular caught my eye. She had character – this heavy, beamy ketch with a hull that gave an impression of resilience and strength. On her clipper bow was a figurehead – a voluptuous mermaid with abundant wavy hair, gazing soulfully into the future. Lazy jacks, ratlines and baggywrinkles cluttered her rigging. Her air of romance, freedom and adventure reflected her journeys – she had travelled for many months and many miles, braving waves, sun and salt. On her eternal quest she had explored the unknown and lingered in exotic tropical islands. Her name was *Dida* and she was the subject of gossip that added to her mystique.

An American couple searching for a yacht to sail around the world found her in the West Indies. They fitted her out, hired a crew, transited Panama Canal and sailed across the Pacific to Tahiti where their crew left them. A Tahitian lad took his place. Rumour had it that, even in the limited confines of the yacht, he had successfully seduced the owner's wife; the outraged husband had gone back to the States leaving the yacht to his unfaithful wife and her lover.

Dida made me think about where I was going to travel next. I had been in Australia for two years and the rest of the world was beckoning. Maybe I could sail back to the UK across the Indian Ocean. I started taking an interest in the larger yachts in the Harbour. I told myself that in Sydney there had to be somebody with a suitable boat who was looking for a crew.

An advertisement at the Yacht Club announced that Gordon Keeble, a former British naval officer, was holding navigation classes at the marina and boat yard he managed. Gordon, with his loud, commanding ultra-English voice, was an eccentric, but also an excellent teacher. With his help I unravelled the mysteries of coastal and celestial navigation. His marina was more than just somewhere where people kept their yachts – it was a social centre where an assortment of unconventional characters with alternative ideas gathered to philosophise about the meaning of life. It was the beginning of the hippie era and people were starting to question their values. Invariably, after the evening navigation class there would be an impromptu party and a lively discussion. We listened to the latest Beatles records.

It was my fellow Gwen sailor, Val, who introduced me to his boss, Simon, who had just bought himself a large ketch. Val described the yacht in glowing terms.

'You'd love to sail on her – she's one of the best looking boats on the Harbour,' he said. 'We're entertaining business clients on board next weekend – would you like to come? I'm sure I could arrange it.'

At 48 foot overall, with a 12-foot beam and an 8-foot draft, *Achernar* was an impressive, stylish yacht. A blue water cruising boat, she was well equipped and luxuriously appointed. She seemed to be ideally suited to her owner, Simon Simpson, whose presence and voice demanded recognition and immediate respect, even awe. He was an elegant, attractive man, tall with dark, curly hair and piercing eyes. He was not an experienced sailor – he had never sailed before he arrived in Australia from the UK. He had come under the spell of the glorious weather and magnificent harbour of Sydney and realised that, in order to fully appreciate and enjoy them, he needed to be able to sail.

Hans Erikson of Pittwater, known as 'The Skipper', ran a sailing school. He taught Simon the basics of sailing and persuaded him to buy *Achernar*; his client obviously needed an impressive yacht to reflect his position in life as the Managing Director in Australia of the prestigious Swiss pharmaceutical company, Roche.

We had a pleasant day social sailing. Simon asked me to take the helm while the sails were being set and I felt the yacht come to life as she responded to the firm but kindly wind. Like a well-bred horse, *Achernar* gave me the impression she was ready to go. Back on the mooring in the late afternoon, Simon ferried the visitors ashore in the dinghy. Over a sundowner in the cockpit, he suggested I might like to crew for him. It was a privilege to be asked and it seemed an ideal opportunity to learn how to look after and handle a larger yacht – something I had been looking for, but not finding. The Skipper kept a careful eye on his client's boat and I could benefit, too, from his knowledge and experience.

I was not, however, prepared to give up racing entirely so I agreed to sail on *Achernar* some weekends and certainly would be available if Simon planned to go out to sea overnight. It took a few weeks for me to get the hang of the boat and she needed a woman's touch to sort out the galley lockers. Simon was generous and willingly provided me with all I asked. He let me handle her, bringing her up to the mooring or alongside the jetty and was prepared to take the yacht out to sea, unless we had visitors aboard who might get seasick.

As well as learning about the yacht, over the next few months I slowly learned about the yacht's owner. Simon was born in Cairo, because, as he put it, 'My Mother was there at the time', his father being Director of Physical Education in the Egyptian Government. His birthday was on Anzac Day, 1920.

'Australia is the only country to declare a public holiday on the occasion of my birthday,' he boasted.

Simon went to boarding school in Edinburgh where he excelled at sports, being captain of the school's rugger, cricket and hockey teams. Together with his two brothers and a sister, he spent most school holidays with his eccentric aunt who had a farm on the border between Scotland and England, but he also travelled several times to join his parents for the longer summer holiday in Cairo. He had just started at Oxford University when war broke out. Immediately he volunteered to serve in the Arabian desert because of his proficiency in Arabic, but the War Office responded by sending him to Malaya. There he was a casualty of the Malayan campaign – he was one of the last to escape from Singapore when it fell to the Japanese and was actually in hospital at the time of the invasion. Friends escorted him in a partially conscious condition by sampan to Sumatra and thence to Java where they commandeered a riverboat to take them to Ceylon.

'A Japanese submarine surfaced not far away from us and fired a torpedo. We could see it coming through the water straight for us. But ours was a river boat with a shallow draft and it went underneath us, so we went with the bidding in our game of bridge.'

Simon was temporarily invalided out of the army and worked for a year in Northern Rhodesia as a district officer and magistrate in a remote area in the north of the province. He had many tales to tell of this time. He rejoined his regiment in India and then set sail for Malaya, where he witnessed the Japanese surrender in 1945. Following service as a military commander in the Pahang District of Malaya until demobilisation, he went back to university to finish his degree.

Simon's aunt expected him to manage her farm after he had graduated, promising him £200 a year and permission for his friends to dine at the family home on Sunday evenings. It was not to be, for at this time he wrote to F. Hoffman La Roche, the manufacturers of synthetic vitamins. He pointed out the social injustice of the distribution of the world's supplies – those who had the least need had most, but those who had the most need had least. Roche chairman Emil Barell responded with a challenge to Simon, to get himself out to India and indicate to Roche how they could help this country and, at the same time, earn a reasonable commercial return.

Subsequently he accepted the challenge of establishing Roche in Australia. By this time Simon had married. His wife, who could not stand being away from England, took their two children back home and she and Simon were subsequently divorced.

I envied Simon's experience of travelling to distant exotic places, the way he took it for granted and made it seem normal, easy and yet exciting. When I asked what were his future plans for his yacht I learned that he hadn't given it much thought. I told him of my longing to go cruising, on a long voyage across oceans to mysterious and glamorous lands; I must have struck a chord for he started talking about taking *Achernar* for a cruise through the Barrier Reef.

Most of our weekend sailing was from *Achernar*'s mooring at Church Point on Pittwater, around West Head and up the Hawkesbury River to Refuge Bay where we would pick up a mooring, have a swim and take a picnic ashore for lunch. They were pleasant occasions, often with interesting guests, many of whom were from overseas. Val, who had introduced us, was a frequent guest with Simon's other colleagues and their wives, their clients and the managers of other pharmaceutical companies.

Night made *Achernar* even more beautiful and enticing. The polished brass portholes and the varnish shone in the soft light of the oil lamps, creating a stimulating, sophisticated atmosphere for the guests.

Over the longer weekends, Easter and Christmas, we were more ambitious and went out to sea. My first Easter cruise on *Achernar* was memorable. We planned to sail northward along the coast as far as Nobbys Head and back again. The Skipper wanted to come with us, but was tied up with his sailing school. He clucked anxiously over us, not believing we would survive without him – or was it because his valued client was becoming less dependent on his services? We were determined to show him that we could manage on our own.

We left on Good Friday morning but, with light winds, did not sight Nobby's Head until Saturday afternoon. As we turned around, the wind, on the beam, increased to 20 knots. I relieved Simon on watch at midnight. *Achernar* was comfortably carrying full sail, just dipping her lee gunwale in the water, thrashing through the water at what seemed to be a tremendous speed, pushing the waves out of her way. Carefully I adjusted her four sails until she was balanced and light to steer. I came to realise the importance of having a mizzen properly trimmed for I was able to lash the helm and leave the yacht to look after herself.

I had the clear, warm night to myself with the full mysterious moon and stars that were fast becoming familiar friends. As I revelled in the fresh breeze and response from the powerful yacht, the words of John Masefield's poem *Sea Fever* came to me – 'And all I ask is a tall ship and a star to steer her by'.

Simon came on deck to join me and caught my mood of exhilaration. We sat together in the cockpit in the magic night imagining how awesome it would be to cruise the South Seas. We would be on a proud yacht sailing on the blue sea among incredibly beautiful islands – an earthly paradise with golden beaches and palm trees backed by majestic mountains. Simon was beginning to understand how the allure of cruising was captivating me, and he too was becoming a victim.

When the first rays of dawn challenged the moonlight, we awoke from our dream, but not before the magic of the night had cast its spell.

'Alas, the night is flown and cruel daylight comes.' Simon quoted. 'I'm hungry, let's have some breakfast!'

Gradually, I found myself spending more time on *Achernar* and less on other boats. At Christmas we headed out to sea; by now, even The

Skipper had given up worrying if the two of us could manage the big yacht without him.

'It seems a shame to have to turn around and go back and pick up the same mooring we've just left. It would be so much better to keep going and find out what's over the horizon,' I mused.

I voiced my thoughts, 'A boat like this needs to go on a voyage. She's wasted just sailing around the harbour. Why don't you sail her around the Pacific islands?'

'That would be good, but I have a job I like.' Simon replied. 'I'd have to give it up. And besides, yachts cost a lot of money to keep and if I didn't have a job, I wouldn't be able to afford to maintain her. I'm a wage-slave.'

I couldn't think of an answer to that dilemma. I tried another tack. 'Well, maybe you could ship her to Tahiti and we could go for a sail around the Society Islands during your holidays.'

'It would cost a fortune!' Simon dismissed the idea as impossible.

'How much?' I asked.

'I'll find out.'

Next time I saw him he told me what he had learned.

'The cost of shipping depends on the volume of the cargo. So, with a yacht like *Achernar*, you multiply the overall length by the maximum beam by the depth from the coach-house top to the bottom of the keel. It's called the shipper's cube. With a deep-keeled yacht like this, you'd be paying to ship a lot of air. She'd need an expensive cradle to hold her upright on the deck of the ship too.'

He told me the astronomical price.

'Good heavens!' I exclaimed. 'We could build a yacht for that amount of money.'

Simon thought for a while. 'That's not such a bad idea.'

'At least we'd have something to show for it,' I said.

The more we talked, the more we became convinced a portable yacht would be a viable answer to the yachtsman's dilemma of how he could go cruising without having to sacrifice his job.

Simon came back from his annual visit to the UK with a set of plans for *Yachting Monthly*'s Waterwitch. Her designer, Maurice Griffiths, described her as 'a sailing caravan', for her boxy and angular appearance provided the maximum accommodation for a yacht of her size.

One memorable weekend Simon told me he had made a decision – he was going to build the Waterwitch – he had already asked The Skipper to oversee the works. Next year we would ship her to Tahiti

Iota's frames show her hard chine and boxy shape.

and sail around the islands for eight weeks. My dream of going cruising suddenly became a real possibility – I wanted to shout it from the rooftops – but didn't dare in case something went wrong.

The Skipper's neighbour Neil Gale was an experienced carpenter and would be happy to get the project underway. We also appreciated Charlie, whose marine engineering works cleverly made to measure all manner of metal boat equipment including our water and fuel tanks and the cables by which the yacht was to be lifted.

The Waterwitch seemed ideal for our purpose: a barge yacht, hard chined and nearly flat bottomed with a long straight steel keel, taking maximum advantage of the shipper's cube. She was 30-foot overall and had an 8 ft 6 in beam. The leeboard version had a 2-foot draft so she could sit on the deck of a ship shored up with sawdust bags, thus avoiding the need for a cradle. But, although she was perfect for cheap shipping, I had doubts about her ability to go to windward – how could that blunt bow possibly cleave through the water against the wind and seas?

We soon had a hull – it did not take long to lay out the frames and fasten on the marine plywood – but fitting out the interior was a time-consuming painstaking process. Nothing was straight; every item had to be tailored to fit the curve of her hull. There was so much to think about and resolve, so much to make and buy: rigging, stores, life raft and flares, fishing gear, medicines and first aid, navigation equipment, charts and *Pilot Books* – the list seemed endless.

One important decision was her name.

'We'll call her *Iota*,' Simon decided. 'She's the smallest viable particle of ocean-going seaworthiness and comfort.'

Iota's shallow draft meant we did not have headroom in the cabin, but we reasoned we mostly went there to sit or lie down. Headroom was important in the galley – I needed to be able to stand up when cooking – so we put it under the hatch. The cabin had two settee bunks, one of which made into a double bed. Under the bunks was storage for food. There was a bookshelf and a table that folded out of the way against the mast. The forward cabin had a toilet, a hanging cupboard, a locker for clothes, open racks for vegetables and other items. Further forward again were the sail and chain lockers.

I was amazed how much could be stowed into such a small space. I quickly came to understand the meaning of the old adage 'have a place for everything, and keep everything in its place' – the problem was to remember where the place was!

Iota's main cabin looking aft   *Comfort was important.*

We made the cockpit as liveable as possible, and put a great deal of thought and discussion into choosing the engine; Simon wanted an outboard whereas I favoured an inboard diesel engine. I lost.

Simon booked a passage for *Iota* and me on the Messageries Maritimes ship *Tahitien* to take us to Tahiti in June when Simon would be taking his holiday. First he would go to Europe and then join me in Papeete for our cruise through the Society Islands. He wanted to sail northeast to one of the atolls in the Tuamotus and then return to Tahiti. This was an ambitious plan and indicative of our inexperience.

April arrived and Simon employed two full-time boat builders to meet our deadline. Slowly the hull turned into a viable, portable, cruising yacht. With a ketch rig, her main mast would not be much

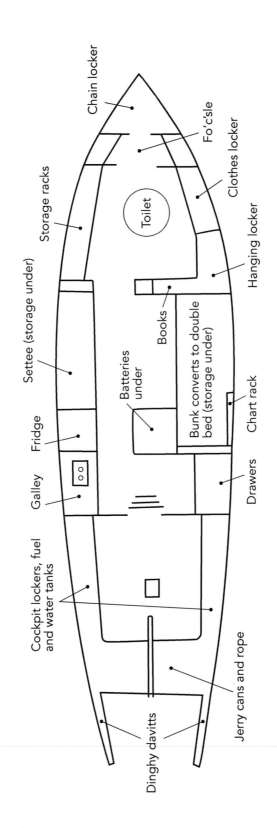

longer than the hull. The masts were stepped in tabernacles. We decided on twin forestays – as insurance and to make it easier when we were raising the main mast. Massive chain plates were to take her weight when she was being loaded.

We chose two anchors – CQRs – one 30 pounds and the other 60 pounds, the latter being our 'portable mooring'. In shallow water we could slide a weight down the chain to ensure that, when the strain came on the anchor, the pull was horizontal and the flukes would dig in. It was appropriately called 'Chum' and we were indebted to it on many occasions.

Iota was launched only three weeks before *Tahitien* was due to leave and, although Simon and I sailed her around Sydney Harbour, we had no time to take her outside the heads nor find out how well she went to windward.

Simon went off to Europe, leaving me with a long list of things to do. He thought of even more while on the plane and I received a long letter detailing all his concerns. Boat shed owner Max van Gelder was a tower of strength and completed all the tasks in time for me to invite my friends to see the new boat on the weekend before I left; more than forty turned up to have a look and to wish me well.

It would have been simpler and cheaper to have taken *Iota* down the harbour under her own power and load her from the water, but Simon had arranged for a crane and a truck to take her to *Tahitien*'s wharf at Darling Harbour, with Max supervising her loading. On the way across Sydney Harbour Bridge the toll collector exclaimed when he saw our beautiful cruising boat, 'Gorblimey, 'eres the Ark! Where's Noah?'

A crane lifted Iota *out of the water and placed her on a truck.*

Alongside Le Tahitien *ready to load*

a storm in the south seas

1962

The *Tahitien* was a 'combi-liner' – a freighter with passenger accommodation. Her role was to service French possessions in the Atlantic and Pacific, taking Government personnel to and from their posts together with their possessions. She carried freight for the islands on the way out and her back-loading was mostly copra. Jumbo jets, containerisation of cargo and the emancipation of the French colonial empire threatened this role. She could carry 70 first class passengers, 80 tourist class and 200 in her 'steerage' dormitory forward, but she was far from full.

Le Tahitien *(photo courtesy Commandant Charles Protat)*

An unlikely couple picked their way around the deck one morning as I went to check that *Iota* was travelling comfortably. A large flamboyant Polynesian and a small, mousy white girl stopped frequently to watch the waves go past and embrace.

'Bonjour,' I said.

The Polynesian responded immediately – in English. He told me his name was Eddie, and hers was Marjorie; he was Tahitian and she was Australian. They had met in Tulagi in the Solomon Islands where Marjorie was teaching at a mission school, fallen passionately in love and couldn't wait to get married. They had visited Marjorie's relations and now were going to Noumea to meet Eddie's friends and family. Eddie paused for breath and Marjorie nodded her agreement, but didn't speak; she seemed to be as introverted as he was extrovert.

Next time I saw them, we talked about *Iota* and boats and I told them I was going to Tahiti to cruise around the Society Islands. Eddie nodded his approval.

'I can sail,' he told me. 'I sailed my yacht from Tahiti to Sydney a couple of years ago. She's about 50 foot long, and very fast, a racing boat. She's called *Dida*.'

Eddie obviously had a tendency to stretch the truth. He sensed my disbelief, for my attempts to persuade him to tell me more about *Dida* were in vain. He changed the subject immediately! I thought there was no way I would trust him if I were Marjorie. A likeable and attractive rogue, but a rogue nonetheless.

They disembarked in Noumea and I saw them walking along the wharf carrying an assorted collection of untidy luggage. Eddie was dressed in a dinner suit too small for him with an outrageous red bow tie and Marjorie wore a long, shapeless, pink satin creation that would have looked more at home in a bedroom.

~

The crew of the *Tahitien* were interested in my portable boat. The Corsican bosco – bosun – bent over backwards to look after *Iota*, and me; he willingly provided sailors to assist with any task I was doing. He was a small, thin man with sad, dark eyes and his dearest possession was the one-stringed violin he bowed tenderly as an accompaniment to his croaking voice.

I quickly learned that the captain of a French ship is called 'commandant' and, confusingly, his first officer is the capitaine. The *Tahitien's* capitaine was André. When I told him I was *Iota's* navigator and had never taken a real sight on a real horizon, he suggested I bring my sextant and tables to the bridge and put in as much practice as I could while we were at sea. I took sun sights, including the noon sight, and graduated to morning and evening stars. It was relatively easy from the stable bridge of a ship, high above the water and in good weather; it was going to be much more of a challenge on *Iota*. The officer of the watch took sights at the same time so we were able to compare positions; after a few days I could navigate as well in French as I could in English.

'We'll pick you up on the way past,' André promised on one occasion when I was ahead of them.

I was surprised at how accurate the results were; islands appeared on the horizon at precisely the time and bearing predicted.

After Noumea we called at Port Vila in the New Hebrides. The islands had been administered jointly by the French and British condominium since 1906. It was more often called the Pandemonium because it was an inherently inefficient system, involving duplication to the point of absurdity. Each government, or residency, had an equal number of representatives, bureaucrats and administrators. There were French schools and British schools and two prison systems; the police force had two uniforms. There were even two sets of postage stamps and two National flags. All notices were in both languages, and translating from one to the other took up time and resources.

Two weeks after leaving Sydney the *Tahitien* came in to Papeete. As a parting gift, the Bosun gave me a cumbrous coil of coir rope, strong enough to tie up the ship. *Iota* was offloaded onto the quay.

Papeete from the main wharf

Picked up by two yellow cranes she was manoeuvred inelegantly and precariously just above the ground and lowered with a splash between the black stern of the *Tahitien* and the white one of the American cruise ship *Monterey*. A curious crowd collected. I climbed aboard and wondered what to do while waiting for clearance. I looked at the coil of rope, but it was too hard; I would start on an easy task – unpacking my clothes.

A voice hailed me from the shore. 'Are you disembarking here?' I looked out through the hatch; the voice belonged to a customs officer.

'Yes,' I said.

'Then I must see your suitcases.'

'I don't have any,' I replied.

'You must have. All passengers have suitcases.'

'I had two small bags, but I've unpacked them.'

'Bring them to the Customs,' he insisted.

'But they're empty,' I protested.

'Don't be difficult. Bring them to the Customs.'

I passed him up my two empty bags and followed him across to the shed. In silence he put them on the counter and, without looking inside, put a chalk cross on each.

'C'ést fini,' he grunted and handed them back to me.

Wondering, I took them back to the yacht.

'Will you be needing some help?' A lanky, redheaded officer hailed me from the stern of the *Monterey*.

'The pilot boat will be towing me to the quay when we're cleared. I'm still waiting for Customs to come up with the paper work,' I said.

'Well if you need anything, let me know. I've got plenty of sailors who would be happy to help. My name's Mike. Just ask for the First Officer if you need anything.'

'Thanks. Many thanks, indeed.'

Lunch time arrived and no sign of the customs agent; I went in search of food on the *Tahitien*. An hour later and still no sign of the papers, I went to the customs shed. Happily a different officer from the one I had encountered in the morning manned the counter. I tried out my dubious French.

'Est-ce qu'on a fini avec mon bateau?' I asked – Have you finished with my boat?

'Allez voir le monsieur là bas,' he mumbled pointing in the direction of the inner office.

I thought the name of the man I needed to see was Monsieur Labas, but he had actually said, 'Go and see the man over there.'

I went around the counter to a man who was rustling through an immense pile of papers.

'Etes-vous Monsieur Labas?' I asked.

He didn't look up. 'Peut être,' he replied – Maybe.

It was quite late in the afternoon when, at last, the clearance and the pilot boat arrived. I was free to join the other yachts tied to the Quai Bir Hakeim.

Two men jumped on board as the pilot boat took *Iota* in tow.

'The First Officer of the *Monterey* sent us to help you, ma'am,' they explained.

The pilot was in control. He told me when to drop the anchor, a surprisingly long way out from the quay. When we had closed with the quay, the two Americans pulled on either end of the coir line coiled on the stern and jumped ashore. In a trice the seemingly well-behaved coil was transformed into an unmanageable tangle of tight, snakelike knots. I hastily found two more lines to secure *Iota*'s stern. Satisfied that all was well, the pilot sped off across the harbour with a cheery wave and the roar of a powerful engine.

'The First Officer sends his compliments, ma'am. He said would you like a shower and dinner aboard this evening?' One of the American sailors delivered the invitation.

It was an offer too tempting to refuse. I put some clean clothes in a bag and walked back to the wharf with the sailors. They showed me to Mike's cabin where clean officers and elegant passengers were having a party. Mike briefly introduced me and then bundled me into a huge bathroom. I luxuriated in a torrent of hot water and all-enveloping fluffy towels. Half an hour later the guests had departed and I was hungry, ready to do justice to the six-course dinner served with a flourish in Mike's cabin. The chief engineer, Clint, joined us.

They were curious about *Iota* and what Simon and I intended to do. They asked penetrating questions for they were doubtful about such an outlandish idea as a portable yacht. When I told them that Simon wanted to cruise and, at the same time, keep a job that would enable him to afford it, they began to understand our objective.

'I've never met a girl travelling with a yacht before. It's a unique idea,' said Mike, 'but its success very much depends on you.'

'Not really,' I said. 'I need Simon's support. I keep thinking, I couldn't do that, but then I find myself doing it.'

I changed the subject, 'You've got it made – you not only get to experience paradise in luxury, you get paid to do it!'

They told me they enjoyed life cruising around the Polynesian Islands, but complained about their passengers.

'They're so elderly – they all have blue rinses,' grumbled Clint. 'Our sister ship the *Mariposa* is called the *Menopausa*. And they don't have a sense of humour.'

'Could I ask you a favour?' Mike smiled. 'I've got a new movie camera and would love to have you on record.'

It didn't seem possible to say anything but, 'Yes, of course', having been on the receiving end of such generosity. They set up the camera and seated me in a chair facing it. I put a smile on my face and said how much I appreciated their hospitality. Clint came into the picture, squatting by my chair. Suddenly I was flying through the air and landing in an undignified heap. Mike and Clint convulsed with laughter.

'Beauty!' exclaimed Mike. 'The best yet!'

They had electrified the chair. Then they showed me movies of their victims, sitting in the chair with a self-conscious grin and suddenly shooting out of it. Their surprise was followed by outraged, angry looks.

'You naughty boys!' I said. 'It's a wonder they didn't try to sue you.'

'Some did. You see, it's like we said – no sense of humour!'

Over the next few days I worked to make *Iota* shipshape and ready for her journey. I started by moving the embarrassing coil of rope ashore – surely some thief would take it away for me when I wasn't looking.

It was difficult to work without interruption; the fifteen yachts tied to the quay provided distraction. Mostly they were American so had endured a long downhill journey to reach Tahiti. *Seawind*, *Medley*, *Monsoon*, *Tangaroa*, *Driftwood*, *Maori* and *Enticer* had all come from California, *Ben Gunn* from Connecticut and *Makoa* from Honolulu. The Americans had met before – or at least knew of each other. *Maori* was sailed by the Taylor family; Howard's sister was the film actress Elizabeth Taylor and his two children both had her compelling violet eyes.

Iota's neighbour was a trim and pretty schooner, *Medley*. One of her crew, Jack, was minding the yacht while her owners were visiting the other islands. He spent most of his time lying on his back on cushions on deck. A hose was lashed in the rigging above his head and a trickle of water splashed onto his forehead.

My other neighbour was the diminutive *C'est la Vie*, from Sydney. She was just over 20 feet long and sailed by single-hander, John. John

Iota *took her place, stern to the Quai Bir Hakeim, Papeete.*

freely used his rich vocabulary of colourful Australian swear words. He had spent several months in Makemo in the Tuamotus.

Next-door-but-one was *Seawind*, a 38-foot Angelman ketch with a clipper bow and a distinctive aft rake to her masts. On board were Mac and Muff Graham who had set out from San Diego to sail around the world. Mac had a reputation as an experienced and accomplished sailor, and was highly respected by the other American yachts in Tahiti. He, too, was intrigued by the concept of a portable yacht and took an interest in *Iota*.

Mac offered to step *Iota*'s masts. I had intended to wait for Simon before attempting to do this, but his offer was too good to refuse. He enlisted the help of Kiwis Mal and David, brothers who were sailing on trimaran *Highlight*, and a workforce of local Tahitians and visiting yachties. Half an hour later both masts were upright and the rigging adjusted. It was great to feel like a proper yacht again.

A letter from Simon said he had met with Maurice Griffiths, the Waterwitch designer, in London, who strongly recommended putting lead in the bow. The likelihood of finding a suitable supply of lead in Tahiti seemed remote, but Mac learned one of the yachts had too much and was willing to let me have some. We did a deal and Mac helped to carry the heavy nuggets along the quay. I stacked them in the cockpit; tomorrow I would move them forward and securely imprison them under the floorboards.

A forest of cruising yacht masts on Papeete waterfront

Across the Quai Bir Hakeim was the Vaima café and bar. If you were looking for somebody, you would find them there – or somebody who knew where they were. It was the place where locals and visitors intermingled, where dates and deals were arranged, where friendships were forged. It was particularly convenient for the yacht crews, who appreciated an ice cold drink close by. The local Hinano beer was a favourite.

At the Vaima I met a group of American tourists who invited me to dine with them at their hotel. Included in the party was a soldier on leave from Vietnam. We had just finished our main course when a thunderstorm broke, accompanied by a strong wind from the west. The anchorage was exposed to the west and it would be a leeshore. I hastily excused myself and rushed back to the Quai.

Chaos reigned. Lightning and thunder flashed and crashed. Two yachts had dragged and had to motor out into the lagoon. Their anchors had become entwined and they were doing an intricate waltz around each other trying to disentangle them. The police were driving up and down the road blowing whistles; the objective of this was not entirely clear. I boarded *Iota* to find she was rubbing against her neighbour *Medley*, *Iota*'s armoured chainplates making frightful gouges in her neighbour's spotless topsides. Jack was nowhere to be seen so I put out more fenders and took down *Medley*'s awning. Back on *Iota*, I found she was dangerously close to the wall.

Just as I was wondering what to do, Mac – bless him – came to see if I needed any help. He took one look and called for the Kiwis, who came running. They managed to pull *Iota* away from the wall, and went ashore taking the gangplank with them. I was soaked to the skin and I had knocked a bar of lead off the pile in the cockpit onto my toe. It hurt. I went down below to change my wet clothes and recover my composure, only to discover the soldier who had been enjoying dinner at the hotel. He tried to grab me.

'What the hell are you doing here?' I pushed him away.

'I thought you might need some help,' he said.

I was outraged. 'How dare you! *Get!*' I shouted at him. 'Get off my boat. Get!'

My throbbing toe inflamed my fury.

'There's no gangplank,' he said.

'Do you think I care? Just get!' I screamed at him.

He got the message, jumped for the wall, missed and fell in the water. Mac, who was still checking on boats, fished him out. I didn't hear what he said to him.

~

A large Tahitian gendarme came to see me. He was in charge of entering the yachts and usually went out with the pilot boat to escort newly arrived yachts through the lagoon. He had a sixth sense and knew immediately if a boat would be a welcome visitor, with relationships in good order, or a potential troublemaker. His name was Gui Gui and he was to become a friend.

He told me of an English girl in the hospital who had developed appendicitis while on a migrant ship to New Zealand with her parents. The ship had put into Tahiti and she was whisked off to the hospital for the operation. She was about 18 years old. When I learned that neither of her parents had stayed with her and she couldn't speak French, I was astounded. Gui Gui said she was recovering well, but seemed lost and insecure. Please would I go and visit her.

The girl was now staying at the Hotel Tahiti to wait for the next migrant ship to take her on to New Zealand. I collected her from her hotel and we set off to replace her dreary skirt and blouse designed for an English winter. Sporting her new clothes in bright bold Tahitian designs, I took her to Vaima, where she immediately caught the eye of my Aussie neighbour, John of the colourful language, from *C'est La Vie*. The thought occurred to me that, when she eventually arrived in New Zealand, her parents would not recognise her as the girl they had left behind in Tahiti. Serve them right; I hoped she enjoyed her transformation.

During the fête drinking and singing continued all day and all night.

In France Bastille Day, le quatorze juillet – 14 July – is a public holiday, but in Tahiti Le Fête continues for more than a week. The Quai was transformed; stalls – les barracks – were erected all along the road and people thronged to them for food and drink all day and night. From the boats we could hear the throbbing sound of guitars and drums. As the days went by the smell of exhaust, sewage and sweat drifted across the Quai – scarcely the fragrance of paradise.

Simon arrived the day before it started. The first thing he noticed was the unruly coil of rope lying next to *Iota*'s gangplank.

'What's that?' he asked.

'It was a gift from the bosun of the *Tahitien*,' I said. 'I don't know what to do with it – I was hoping it might disappear. It's stiff and rough and unmanageable.'

'But it might come in handy. You shouldn't be so ungrateful. I'll stow it in the stern locker in the cockpit.' Simon's Scottish instincts came to the fore.

It took him all morning to persuade the uncooperative rope to disappear into the locker.

Le Fête was still going strong when we cleared from Tahiti and set off on our cruise. This was the first time we had sailed *Iota* in the open sea; we expected some teething troubles, but not quite so many. In

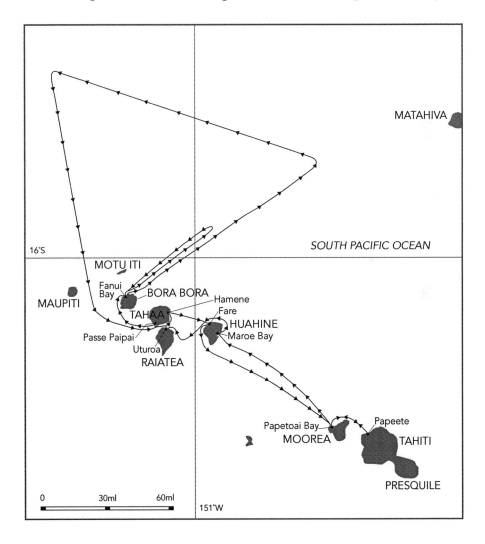

casting off from the quay we had to pull up our heavy anchor, all 60 pounds of it with its chain – hard work made more difficult because the bows of the cruise liner *Mariposa* were almost over the anchor, and her bowline tried hard to grab our mizzen mast.

Out at sea *Iota*'s leeboard bolts leaked badly so we had to bail frequently. With her flat bottom, even a little water in the bilge was a nuisance and it was difficult for the bilge pump to get hold of it as it raced from side to side with the motion of the boat. We decided to go into the next pass south of Papeete to see if we could fix the problem. There, the wind dropped, and we were close to the reef. We lowered the outboard on to its bracket and started it, but the fall of a halliard fell overboard and fouled the propeller. We hastily pulled it out, cut it free and put it back down again, all the time drifting closer to the reef. As we motored off, one of our forestays stripped its rigging screw. By the time we made repairs the wind had come up again so we set some sail. We pulled the outboard back on board but, as we did, it turned over, shrugged itself out of its safety harness and disappeared with a gurgle to the bottom of the Pacific Ocean. Could anything else go wrong?

We sailed away from Tahiti through the night and in the morning found ourselves conveniently close to Moorea, but with no wind – and no engine. It took a while to eventually drift into the spectacularly picturesque Papetoai Bay. Another yacht, *Ben Gunn*, with Hank and Elise on board was already anchored there.

Simon took the local ferryboat back to Papeete to buy another outboard. He returned with a 4 hp Seagull. We had to alter the bracket it sat on and I spliced three permanent lines on it – this engine was not going to escape us. We operated on the leeboard bolts and hoped we had reduced their leaks to manageable proportions.

Between times we watched the light changing on the mountains as the day progressed and wondered at the bounty of Mother Nature in this earthly paradise. The beauty of the valley was almost unreal – a fantastic stage setting. After the throbbing activity of *Le Fête* in Papeete, its peace and serenity were relaxing; for the first time we could hear a clock ticking.

The local villagers were amazingly generous, bringing us bananas and pawpaws. We collected limes and caught fish. We were introduced to the coconut and discovered which nuts were suitable for quenching our thirst – the coconut water in young nuts has a delicious spritzig. More mature nuts provide coconut milk and coconut cream; more mature again and the centre of the sprouting nut turns into a sweet foam. The dried kernel of the nut is called copra from which coconut oil is extracted, and other parts of the trees are also useful: palm wine can be made from the sap, superior charcoal from the shells and coir rope from the husks; the leaves may be plaited to make many useful articles including the walls of a house, while the trunks are excellent building material or can be hollowed out to make a small canoe.

For ten days we luxuriated in our surroundings. We waited until a northwest gale had passed and the wind had returned to the southeast before we set sail for Huahine.

This was a wonderful sail, all day and all night, with a fresh following wind. *Iota* behaved beautifully; she was surprisingly fast and we enjoyed her easy motion. As the new day grew lighter we made our landfall on Huahine and sailed through the pass to Maroe Bay. Here we spent two days before taking advantage of the favourable wind to go on to Raiatea. As we entered the Teavapitu pass we glimpsed the bright pink peaks of Bora Bora between the islands of Raiatea and Tahaa, reflecting the rays of the setting sun. We anchored in the nearest bay for the night before motoring next morning to the busy town of Uturoa.

It was market day and the main quay was swarming with little boats bringing villagers and their produce to town. Trading boats were loading and unloading every imaginable item. Pigs, chickens, bananas, fish and pawpaws had a place among an overload of laughing Polynesians.

Spectacular Papetoai Bay, Moorea

The peaks of Bora Bora

Raiatea and Tahaa are enclosed in the same lagoon so the crossing to Tahaa was a short, smooth and easy sail in contrast to the difficult passage out of the long narrow south-facing Passe Paipai, heading for Bora Bora. The wind had swung to the south and blown short, steep seas into it. We struggled with Seagull, but gave up as, alternately, the propeller raced out of the water or the engine was submerged so deeply its air intake was covered. It took us over half an hour to beat out the pass as *Iota* was reluctant to go about in the steep seas and we had to gybe around instead of tacking.

My doubts about *Iota*'s ability to sail to windward were well-founded when the waves were bunchy, but in smooth seas she far exceeded my expectations, perhaps not pointing as high as a more conventional yacht, but performing surprisingly well. We realised the wisdom of her designer in recommending lead in her bow to help her fight the waves.

Once we could bear away for Bora Bora we had an exhilarating sail, covering the thirteen-mile journey in just less than two hours.

~

During the war some 5000 American troops, considerably outnumbering the native population, were in Bora Bora together with their equipment. When they left, most of the buildings and the jeeps were pushed into the lagoon. In sheltered Fanui Bay a decaying quay was conveniently situated for visiting yachts. We tied alongside and luxuriated in fresh water from the nearby tap.

It was noticeable that most of the villagers of about 40 years or more could speak a little English, and many of the younger adults had fair hair and obviously European features. Occasionally we met a Polynesian with a distinctly Negro nose. One half-American lad spent most of his time sitting on the wharf gazing sombrely at us. His name was Terrance. He refused all invitations to come on board and appeared to speak no French, or English.

The French Governor and his family made a visit to the island – low-key, for the people of Bora Bora were more opposed to the French than other Society Islanders. Nobody was talking about this visit, but we were well aware that the cruise liner *Monterey* was expected on le onze août – 11 August. She was the topic of conversation for days beforehand. The local villagers were busy making souvenirs for the passengers to buy – wood carvings, grass skirts and shell leis.

Jec, the headman of the local village, invited us to a feast – a tamura. As the sun set in splendour over the motus we strolled to the village where his family, curious about who we were and where we had come from, welcomed us. A small boy climbed a coconut tree like a monkey and two choice drinking nuts fell to the ground with a rustle and a thud.

Iota *in Fanui Bay, Bora Bora*

The women served the dinner – a pig on a spit with breadfruit, banana poi, ia ota (fish marinated in lime juice) and salad – but did not eat with us. Dunking everything in coconut milk, we ate messily with our fingers, enjoying our food.

Jec's son had cut his leg on coral; it was inflamed, swollen and extremely painful. Our penicillin had an immediate and dramatic effect and in gratitude he made me a beautifully decorated grass skirt complete with bra, shell necklace and headdress, which I treasured.

Swept up by the enthusiasm for the visit of the *Monterey*, we went around to the jetty at the Hotel Bora Bora where much of the

Jec's son made me a grass skirt to treasure.

activity would take place. Precisely on schedule the elegant white liner appeared around the headland, made her way slowly through the pass and anchored in the lagoon. Liberty boats came bringing the loudly talking, brightly dressed passengers, to be greeted with a kiss on each cheek and a flower lei by their Polynesian hosts, finely dressed in clean new pareus. The tourists walked up to the hotel to be entertained to a native feast and dancing.

One of the *Monterey* sailors came over to *Iota*.

'The First Officer sends his compliments, ma'am. He said would you and your skipper like a shower and lunch aboard?'

'Thank you,' I said. 'Please tell the First Officer we're delighted to accept his invitation.'

Mike was his most hospitable self. Was there anything we needed? Yes, please – penicillin to replace our supply that we had given to Jec's son. He kindly obliged. He said the present bunch of tourists was worse than usual and he'd had to give up his electric chair joke; one of the passengers really meant it when she said she would sue the company.

As we left he said wistfully to Simon, 'I'm intrigued by your portable yacht and her talented crew. I'm envious of both of them!'

Impervious to the beauty of the island and its surrounding lagoon, the passengers returned to their ship in the afternoon, walking along the beach, still talking loudly. The price of their entertainment included as much rum punch as they could consume. Many were unsteady on their feet and reeled down the jetty, laughing drunkenly and singing. The cruise leader, a small extroverted man called Joey, had to be carried. The tolerant Purser steadied those stragglers in danger of joining the fish in the water. As they walked past *Iota*, the passengers and I looked at each other with mutual interest. They compared the little black yacht to their big white ship and felt sorry for me; in a short space of time, I was four pocketknives, ten packets of cigarettes and $5 better off.

The farewell blasts on the ship's siren signalled a return to normality on the island – but first there was a successful day to be celebrated. The dance in the hotel that evening was livelier than usual, and the carefree atmosphere radiated with fun and laughter. The band – guitar, ukulele and drums – happily accepted drinks and played faster and louder. The vahines in their best gay dresses with flowers around their necks and nestling in their hair, swung their hips provocatively. Bare feet beat out the rhythm. Terrance amazed us; tonight in a bold red shirt and a flower corona, he was a bundle of energy, his Twist an athletic feat, his body India rubber. He writhed, bounced and swayed with tireless enthusiasm, focussed even more on his dancing than on the pretty girl who was his partner.

The band needed little persuasion to play the Tamure; the urgent summons of the drum was greeted with cheers and a crowded floor. Restrained at first, then daring, Terrance followed his hip-wriggling partner around the floor, knees and hips keeping pace with the ever-faster music. The drumbeat was compelling; black hair gleamed and eyes flashed as the dance became more suggestive. The top parts of the dancers' bodies were temptingly still, their hips challenging. Suddenly, it ended; when the drums stopped abruptly, the dancers were poised, tensely motionless. Then laughter transformed the electric atmosphere and couples returned gaily to their tables.

Quietly leaving the hotel the following morning, we hoisted our red sails and slipped through the lagoon and out of the pass under an innocent clear blue sky. The sun reflected cheerfully off the water, through which we could see hundreds of colourful and fanciful fish basking and feeding in the coral. We were bound for the Tuamotus.

~

When we were out of the lee of the Society Islands, the moderate southeast breeze became stronger and the seas bigger. Going to windward in these conditions upset our leeboard bolts again so we decided to return to Bora Bora. Twenty-four hours after our departure, we were back beside the quay in Fanui Bay. This time we were in the company of Mac and Muff on *Seawind* and we came to know each other well – well enough to be impressed by their beautifully finished, impeccably outfitted ketch and to find that Muff's name was short for the endearment 'Muffin'.

Having enjoyed their company for two days, we set off again with the leeboard bolts fixed. For two days we made good progress to the northeast in a moderate southeast wind, almost laying Matahiva, the most westerly Tuamotuan atoll. On the third day the clouds gathered to windward and soon delivered heavy squalls with driving rain. They were local and we became adept at knowing which would pass and which would require action. This involved many sail changes and, at nightfall, we were reduced to a small jib and reefed main. By midnight, a howling wind and mountainous waves were assaulting us so we hove-to with just a tiny storm jib.

In the morning the conditions were worse.

'I think we should turn around and take it on our stern,' I suggested. 'That's what the books say you should do when you're in really bad weather. If we keep the storm jib up we'll have a bit of control and be able to keep the seas directly astern. We could stream some warps, too.'

Simon's eyes lit up. 'We have the coir line the bosun gave you; I knew it would come in handy! It'll reduce our drift to the east, too. Otherwise we'll be half way to Rarotonga and I'll be late for work!'

Turning was perilous as it exposed us to lying sideways to the seas, but we managed it without mishap. We pulled the coir line out of the stern locker and fastened it in a loop on either side to the arms of the davits. The line had a name – the Tahitien Line; it probably saved us.

Simon carefully went to check forward and we put an extra line around the dinghy. I found a stronger lifeline for the helmsman and secured it to a chain plate. We had already established the rule that the helmsman must be tied to the boat at all times, but especially when on deck alone. As darkness fell, the seas were getting even bigger so we streamed yet another warp. The leeboard bolts were leaking again, but not as badly. The boat seemed to be looking after herself so we went below, closed the hatch and tried to sleep. We lay tossing in our oilskins. *Iota*'s motion was violent, the noise was unbelievable and the claustrophobic cabin felt like a tiny prison cell. Eventually I dozed off.

At 3 am we were rudely awakened. *Iota* was laid flat by a breaking wave. Everything seemed to land on me, including Simon, who was gouged in the stomach by the top of the icebox. He lay gasping and I fought, almost in panic, to free myself. *Iota* quickly righted herself. No damage was done, but she could no longer manage alone; she needed help and we would have to steer.

For the next eighteen hours we battled to take the seas directly astern. Dawn revealed gigantic steep waves, towering like threatening fists, at least twice as high as *Iota* was long. We wondered as each approached whether *Iota* would rise to it or allow it to break over her. As her stern lifted, her bow seemed to point down to the centre of the earth and then gradually, as we slid off the back of the wave, it came up to point at the sky. On top of the waves we could see the stormy leaden sky and feel the full force of the wind and spray. Down in the troughs, in an ominous calm, we could see only water.

Gradually we gained confidence in the little boat as she kept us buoyantly out of trouble, but we were both becoming very tired; our watches were shorter and shorter, our minds were numb and we lost all sense of time. Sleep was elusive. Simon did more than his share of steering, but I did most of the pumping and bailing and managed to cook simple food – mugs of hot soup and coffee helped revive us. Everything below was wet.

Towards the end of the fifth day we detected a slight lessening of the conditions. The wind eased to about 40 or 50 knots, but the seas were relentless. Such was the strain on the Tahitien Line that it parted in the middle. All through another night we steered with the rain stinging our hands and faces. By morning, the wind had moved slightly into the north so we pulled in our warps, freed the storm jib and steered to the southeast in an attempt to return to the Society Islands. We had no idea where we were for the clouds and seas made taking sights impossible. When I did get a questionable fix it put us further to the southeast than we could have dared hope – we thought we would have been pushed much further to the west. The Tahitien Line must have done a good job.

We spent another night not knowing where we were. One consolation amidst the returning squalls and lightning and thunder was that the unbelievably heavy rain flattened the seas.

The next day was a bit clearer with an occasional patch of blue sky. I was determined to find out where we were. The time signal was not clear and the big seas made it difficult, but I managed to fix a position about thirteen miles WNW of Maupiti, a high island about 40 miles west of Bora Bora. From noon onwards we spent an anxious time hoping to make landfall before dark. The visibility was poor and we were apprehensive about Motu Iti, an atoll lying on our course that we couldn't hope to see until very close. I spent the whole afternoon wondering where my sight could be wrong when, at about 4 pm, there was Maupiti, exactly where I said it would be. Elated, we thought we were nearly home.

We washed in hot fresh water and Simon shaved off five days' growth of beard. We tidied up the boat and forgot about how tired we were. To fix definitely our position we closed Maupiti before dark, and, with the wind rapidly swinging to the northwest, decided to sail around Bora Bora through the night and make it to Raiatea the next day. Little did we know!

In the evening we shortened sail because of a squally sky, but left up our working jib. Suddenly about 11 pm a strong squall hit. Simon, rudely awoken from a deep sleep, struggled into the cockpit and went forward to drop the headsail. I joined him and in the meanwhile *Iota* sped through the water, spray flying everywhere. In the moonless night, we struggled together on the bow with the jib.

'Have you got the clew?' I asked.

'Clue? No, of course not – I've only just woken up.' Simon replied.

We clung together, giggling helplessly at this pathetic attempt at humour. The absurdity of two people standing on the foredeck of a miniscule yacht on a dark stormy night in the middle of the angry Pacific Ocean suddenly occurred to us and we giggled even more.

'Come on,' said Simon. 'Let's get this boat under control and have some sleep. We need it!'

Exhausted, it was easy to make the decision to heave-to for the rest of the night. It seemed reasonable at the time as the wind after our last storm experience in Moorea had stayed in the southwest for several days and we expected it to do the same.

By morning the wind had changed to the southeast and we had lost ground. We now faced a beat to Raiatea. All day the wind came and went from unfavourable directions and calms were interspersed with rainstorms, necessitating constant sail changes. Making progress in the right direction was hard work and frustrating. An aeroplane flew overhead – it would arrive at its distant destination long before we could reach Raiatea, just over the horizon. Its contrasting speed made it seem like a creature from another world.

By nightfall we had made up most of what we had lost during the previous night, but no more. With daylight we were better able to make use of the light wind with more sail; we made good progress and our spirits rose again.

We battled on for another two days and two nights with a failing wind. An increasing current made the boat uncontrollable and the sea was like a river with overfalls. Eventually the seas abated enough for us to use the Seagull outboard; we encouraged it to start by dousing its sparkplug with lighter fluid. Raiatea came into sight late in the afternoon. We motored through the night and, ten days after leaving Bora Bora, we tied up to the quay in Uturoa.

It took us while to realise we were, at last, secure. We looked around at the soggy chaos on board. Where to start? All our clothes and bedding were salty and wet, there was a mess in the galley, our batteries were flat, ropes needed coiling and stowing and Seagull needed attention from somebody who understood its problems.

'Let's get some sleep,' suggested Simon. 'It might not look so bad when we wake up.'

It was not to be, for we had visitors. Ahale was a jolly, king-sized

Polynesian who said he was the Guardien des Prisons and Jean, a Frenchman, was a schoolmaster at the high school. They wanted to talk – Ahale about his time in England during the war as a commando and Jean about the 200 children who were all becoming proficient welders under his watchful eye. Jean invited us to dinner and we met his delightful wife and several of his nine children, who danced the Tamure and Twist for us.

We slept like logs and woke to another hot, windless, humid day. Simon went ashore buy fresh food and to find Ah Tchoung, who was recommended as the finest fixer of outboard motors in the islands; no engine had ever dared to defy him. He lived in a large house, testament to his position in society as the only mechanic and owner of hire cars on the island. He was typical of the Chinese in the islands – always working and looking out for new ideas – in total contrast to the Polynesians. Ah Tchoung had a Tahitian wife and many remarkably attractive children who, I thought, benefited from the fine physique of their mother and refined features of their father.

I set to and started the clean up. By lunchtime I had made good progress, but Simon had not returned. When eventually he came along the quay he was looking pleased with himself.

'Where have you been?' I asked.

'I was looking for a garbage bin on the quay, but there didn't seem to be one. We're going to need one – we can't just throw our rubbish overboard,' he explained. 'On the way back from the market I came across the garbage truck doing its round. So I followed it all over town and, in due course, it came to the quay. There's a bin hiding behind the wall over there.'

I wondered what other people did on their holidays – whatever it was, it could not have been any more satisfying to them than following the rubbish truck had been to Simon.

With the boat in better order, we sailed across to Tahaa on the other side of the lagoon and found a snug anchorage behind a mountain off a village called Hamene. Two lads came in a pirogue with drinking nuts, and escorted us ashore through the reef. An elderly man solemnly greeted us and introduced us to his extended family. We shook hands with even the smallest children. Then we were at the head of a procession wandering around the village, and at each house went through the greeting ceremony. On arrival at la plus jolie baie de grandpère (grandfather's prettiest bay) the same old man greeted us; he had hastened across the reef in order to be at his house before us.

Hamene Bay

One of the boys gave me a shell, but a hermit crab was in residence. He took it back, held it close to his mouth and whistled.

Almost immediately the crab abandoned the shell.

In the evening men from the village came on board with guitars and ukuleles. It started to rain, and how we managed to fit seventeen people in the cabin I will never know. They played and sang happily and, when the rain stopped, went on deck. Strains of Vive l'Amour, Polly Wolly Doodle and At the Balalaika echoed around the bay. Around 11 pm their wives called from the beach. The party broke up and, obediently, the men returned ashore.

In the morning it was the women's turn. They brought us presents of fruit, shells, necklaces and vanilla beans. In return we took Polaroid photographs. The older ladies, kindly and comfortable mommas, wanted to have their photographs taken hugging me.

A crowd gathered to see us off. Fainter and sadder came the words of Bon Voyage as we drifted down the bay between the mountains towards the pass.

The sun was setting as we left the island. In the distance a yacht entering a pass in the reef further south was a white sail to us and we were a red sail to them. When Simon returned to Sydney he discovered the yacht was *Larapinta*, sailed by Peter and Lesley Mounsey, on the way home to complete their circumnavigation. They were to become good and lasting friends and Peter gave us much-valued advice from his wealth of experience of boats of all sorts and sizes.

The overnight sail took us to Huahine, where in brilliant sunlight we came through the pass off the main village of Fare into a magnificent lagoon, past idyllic white beaches with coconut palms leaning over them. Turquoise patches shaded to brown as the coral came closer to the surface in the lagoon, in contrast to the intense dark blue of the deep water.

We were puzzled when we came across an unusually large black buoy with a rope loop sticking up from it. Not for long – a seaplane appeared over the hills and landed quite close to *Iota*, giving us a fright. It taxied around us and picked up its mooring buoy while a small boat came out and transferred passengers. It then took off straight over our masts. It hadn't occurred to us to keep watch above our heads.

For four days we explored the idyllic bays on the western side of Huahine, wandering along the beach, swimming, snorkelling over the reef and exploring the hills and valleys. We could have taken a lifestyle like this forever, but all good things must come to an end. Reluctantly we set sail in light airs to Moorea and Papeete, accompanied by porpoises frolicking around us all day long. The headwind was fickle, requiring many sail changes over the four days it took us to reach Moorea. We spent one last night anchored in the comforting familiarity of beautiful Robinson's Cove.

On we sailed to Papeete. Our luck changed; an unusual gentle following wind came up from the west so we set all sail, wing and wing, and came through the pass as the sun set behind us. A large crowd gathered; cameras clicked. As we dropped our sails Mac rowed out to help with the anchor. People appeared from everywhere, taking our lines, helping us to tie up. They all wanted to know what had happened in the storm. They had not expected us to survive – an untried yacht with an inexperienced crew.

We ate on board *Seawind* with Mac and Muff and Peter and Jo and heard that the wind had gusted to over 100 knots while they rode out the gale in Bora Bora.

'You looked impressive coming in through the pass – red sails in the sunset,' said Muff. 'A grand way to come back from the dead!'

dwyn wen – the patron saint of lovers

1963

Simon had only two days back in Papeete before his plane left for Sydney. He was busy sorting out all the things he needed to take with him when there was a hail from the quay.

'Is that Simon Simpson's boat?' asked a tall Frenchman.

'Yes, come aboard,' I replied and called to Simon in the cabin.

His name was François Mautin and he and Simon had met in Honolulu, sitting on the beach on a night when the Americans tested an atomic bomb on Christmas Island. For 20 minutes the sky had lit up as bright as day. It was a catalyst that encouraged strangers to talk to each other, and Simon had told François about his yacht waiting for him in Tahiti.

'We should have a drink on this,' suggested Simon.

'Bon idée,' François agreed, 'Quinn's Bar is famous you know. Let's go there.'

The two men went ashore.

'I'll join you in ten minutes,' I said, for I wanted to finish what I was doing.

As I walked along the Quai I sensed I was being followed so increased my pace towards the notorious bar of 'disrepute' and joined Simon and François. An hour or so later the three of us wandered back along the Quai to the yacht. The next thing I knew François was lying on the ground with two men standing over him saying, 'You pinched our girl.'

Simon quickly moved to his defence and shouted at them. By some miraculous coincidence a gendarme appeared and restored order. François was shaken but not hurt. The gendarme told us the men were sailors from a British freighter in port. He shrugged his shoulders.

'C'est les Anglaises; c'est toujours les Anglaises.' – It's the English; it's always the English.

~

I went to the airport at Faaa to see Simon off. In the departure lounge a poetic looking individual with a wild thatch of hair came over and introduced himself.

'I'm Jack,' he said. 'I've noticed you two.' He turned to me, 'You're going to be lonely tomorrow.'

Jack was an author who wrote science fiction. He had come to Tahiti on a yacht from the West Indies two years ago and stayed.

'I met a couple in the Virgin Islands – they'd bought a boat and needed a crew.' Jack told us. 'They were aiming at sailing all the way around the world. When we got here I'd had enough of sailing for a while – it's a long way across the Pacific and the boat rolled all the way. They took on a big Tahitian lad after I left, heading for Sydney, but I lost touch with them. She was called *Dida* – perhaps you saw her in Sydney?'

'Indeed I did! I saw her – she was definitely distinctive – but I didn't meet her owners. I met Eddie, the fellow who took your place, on the *Tahitien*. He was going from Sydney to Noumea with a missionary lady from the Solomons – they were going to get married.'

Jack was amazed. 'It's a small world,' he said. 'Particularly the sailing world.'

Simon arranged for *Iota* to be shipped back to Sydney on a Messageries Maritimes freighter, the *Irrawaddy*. Before Mac and Muff left to continue their voyage around the world Mac helped me lower *Iota*'s masts and take her alongside the freighter for shipping back to Sydney. Loading went without drama except I had forgotten the lead we had put in the bow and *Iota* came out of the water at an alarming angle.

I moved on board a large schooner recently arrived from Honolulu – *Dwyn Wen*. She was looking for crew to take her back again and it seemed an opportunity too good to miss. The date of her departure was not yet decided; in the meantime I was free to savour life in Tahiti.

Jack came looking for me.

'I'll take you to meet some friends of mine on the other side of the island. They all came for a holiday and stayed. We'll start with John. He was an English spy in World War I and later lived for several years on his ranch in Argentina. He built himself a house by the beach in Punavia. Then there's Michel; he's an artist – not a very good one – but he enjoys his lifestyle and has wealthy doting parents to support him.'

At John's delightful house by the lagoon Jack and I joined other guests – a diverse and interesting collection. Apart from the locals,

Mac Graham helped me prepare Iota *for loading onto the* Irrawaddy.

around the table were Michel, the aspiring French artist, Paul, an American anthropologist using the excuse of studying the Polynesians to prolong his stay in the islands and Georges from Toulouse. Georges had come to Tahiti eight years ago. He'd panicked the day before he was due to get married and taken the first plane out of France. Bob, another American, had arrived only a month ago on a yacht from California – an incompatible crew and an abominably rolling yacht meant he was staying in Tahiti for as long as his visa permitted.

I never saw Jack again, but the others welcomed me into their circle. Michel and Georges were planning a trip to an island in the lagoon on the Presqu'ile, the peninsula protruding from the southeast corner of the main island. There they were to 'return to nature' for a few days, free of the trappings of civilisation. Bob and I were to join them on the chosen island, which seemed to offer all we needed: coconuts and pawpaw trees, and fish abounding in the lagoon.

What should we take with us? It couldn't be much because it all had to fit with us into a pirogue: a tent, blankets, snorkelling and spearfishing gear, matches. We each took one indulgence: Michel's essential was a pack of playing cards and Bob couldn't survive without his daily dose of coffee; both Georges and I opted for a bottle of wine and he remembered a corkscrew. We were going to be self-sufficient so took little food – just enough for the first night.

A Tahitien dance troupe in rehearsal

A dance troupe rehearsal greeted us at the island and put us in the mood for the exotic experiences of the next three days. We were in good spirits as we put up the tent, lit a fire and cooked our dinner, wrapping the meat in leaves and burying it in the hot embers. It was surprising how little it seemed to matter that Georges and Michel could not speak English and Bob had little French. We opened a bottle of wine and played bridge until it was time to pile together in a heap in the tent and hope for sleep.

Michel and Georges set off in the morning to catch our food for the day. They were both armed with spear guns. It was not long before they returned; Michel had mistaken Georges for a fish and shot at his arm! Fortunately it was not as serious as it might well have been – the spear only grazed his forearm – but we had no dressings for such an accident. A contrite Michel returned to the water and eventually speared a fish, not big enough to satisfy four hungry people. He had been in the salt water for so long his eyes were suffering – he looked as if he had conjunctivitis.

Bob tried to save the day by walking out on the reef to see if he could find a lobster. He made the painful mistake of going barefooted and soon had sea urchin spines embedded in the soles of his feet. Three down – I was the only one left to provide for tonight's dinner. I took a spear gun and went into the water. It was easier said than done to catch the fast moving fish, but I came across one more sluggish than the others and managed to spear it. I waded ashore to take it off the spear, but its dorsal fin spiked the fleshy part of my thumb; the agony was instant and long lasting. The boys all agreed the fish was most likely poisonous to eat.

It seemed like an eternity until the pirogue appeared to take us back to civilisation. Our forthcoming visits to doctors and hospitals were the only topic of conversation. Heavy rain added to our discomfort and floodwater cut off the Presqu'ile from the main island. We had no choice but to stay in the village for the night. The hard floor of somebody's kitchen did not encourage sleep so we gave up trying and spent the night playing bridge.

By morning the floods had subsided, Michel's eyes were no longer red, our attempts to dig the spines out of Bob's feet had been successful, Georges' arm was bandaged and healing satisfactorily and my throbbing thumb had ceased to dominate my thoughts. But nobody suggested going back to the island!

~

Life in Tahiti was so easy to take. Visitors emulated the relaxed lifestyle of their Polynesian hosts and hostesses. The catchcry was 'aita péa-péa' – it doesn't matter. The local sense of humour was bizarre; the bigger the disaster, the funnier it was. I was in a music shop where somebody was listening to a recording of the Tamure. A boy standing on top of a ladder cleaning windows started to sway his hips. He fell off and broke his leg – much to the vast amusement of the onlookers.

Another day a car came down the hill to the Quai Bir Hakeim, but failed to turn right or left. It went straight across the road and grass strip and into the water where, amazingly, there was a gap, for a yacht had just left. Passers-by pointed in disbelief and laughed; none thought the people in the car might need some help. The crew of a neighbouring yacht dived down and rescued the two occupants just in time.

~

The *Monterey* came in on her regular visit so I went to find Mike to tell him of our adventures. He greeted me with a warm embrace.

'I was worried about you,' he said. 'That was a nasty blow you were caught in. We were on the edge of it and it was bad enough – most of the passengers were seasick!'

'The other yachts didn't think we could possibly have survived and were surprised when we came sailing in to Papeete.' I told him how we had come back from the dead.

'What are you going to do now?' Mike asked.

'I'm sailing to Honolulu on that big schooner over there,' I replied. 'I haven't had enough of cruising yet. It's addictive!'

'What about Simon? Does he approve?'

'I don't know. We didn't discuss it,' I said.

Mike raised his eyebrows, but said nothing.

Dwyn Wen *in Papetee*

At the Hotel Tahiti we sat under the stars and looked out over the lagoon to Morea while sipping rum punches and allowing ourselves to be seduced by the throbbing music. The cool breeze was welcome as we caught our breath after a lively dance. The Twist had caught on in

Tahiti and was rivalling the Tamure in its popularity and the amount of energy to perform it. It seemed as if everyone there was a friend and had come to help me savour the last few hours of Paradise before my next journey. The party continued until the sky was getting light.

A large crowd gathered to see off the *Dwyn Wen*. It was an emotional farewell with kisses, hugs, tears and literally hundreds of heavy shell leis – my neck was scarcely long enough to accommodate my twenty or so necklaces. *Dwyn Wen* fitted comfortably into the Tahitian culture as a meeting point between the sailing world and the local Tahitians. She epitomised the good life and witnessed forging of friendships, dalliances and intrigues – even love affairs.

To everybody's surprise we left Papeete when Skipper Stan had decreed. Promptly at 11 am, with the last of our papers in order, the officials and visitors went ashore. We cast off our lines, pulled up the anchor and motored out of the lagoon.

It was believed that people leave behind their inhibitions and responsibilities on the motu – the island – on one side of the entrance to Papeete's lagoon. As we went through the pass and out into the deep Pacific I wondered if mine would come back. Maybe, but even my short time in Tahiti had been enough to change my views on life and the way it should be lived. I had always wondered about the importance of being conventional for the sake of conforming – I now knew the answer.

My gaze was wistful as I watched the island disappear below the horizon. Memories of the grandeur of her mountains, her lush vegetation, the seductive scent of her flowers and her carefree people would always tug at my heart.

Once out of the lee of the island a gentle wind encouraged us to set sails and I was brought back to reality by the shout, 'All hands on deck!' While the weather conditions were kind it was an opportunity for us to learn about flying headsails and how the big fisherman was set between the masts. Most of the crew were unfamiliar with the yacht; we had to learn to work together, for her canvas sails were heavy and she had no halliard winches. Skipper Stan allotted our tasks – mine was to take the helm during sail changes. *Dwyn Wen* responded to her sails by heeling to the wind and forging through the waves as if she were glad to shake off the torpor of life in Paradise and get back to the sea and the sky where she belonged.

The 105-foot schooner was built in Dartmouth in 1906 and named after the Welsh patron saint of lovers Saint Dwynwen. The pious

Dwynwen fell in love with a young prince called Maelon Dafodrill, but her love was unrequited. History is not clear about their problem – perhaps she loved against her father's wishes, or Maelon sought a less virtuous mate. Either way, she prayed that she should forget her love for Maelon. When an angel answered her prayers and turned Maelon into a block of ice she prayed again, requesting he be thawed. She also asked that, through her, God should look after all lovers. Her wishes were granted and in gratitude she spent the rest of her life forsaking love in a nunnery on a remote island off the coast of Anglesey.

Built for comfort rather than speed, *Dwyn Wen* had a graceful hull with a long bowsprit and flush decks. Below deck she was spacious – no doubt she had been a luxurious pleasure yacht in her younger days. Originally gaff-rigged, in the 1920s she was turned into a masthead schooner so her masts appeared short by modern standards. As a consequence she had lee helm; I never did get used to her unnatural, negative response to the wind.

In her early years she was based in Wales, but in 1923 her owner set out to sail her around the world. In Hong Kong he fell sick and died. *Dwyn Wen* languished on the slip for over a year. In run-down condition she was purchased by an American, who sailed her across the Pacific to Oregon. When he sold her, her new owner took her to Hawaii. From 1942 to 1944 she served in the US Navy and there are records of her visiting Polynesia and the Galapagos Islands in the 1950s.

Her present owner, Jim, was based in Hawaii. She had sailed from Honolulu to Tahiti with a crew of three and 25 young passengers who were paying for the experience. The three crew – Skipper Stan, First Mate Jerry and Roy the Cook – were still on board.

Stan, a Canadian, was an excellent skipper. He was a competent and experienced seaman but, perhaps more importantly, managed to strike a perfect balance between an easygoing attitude and sufficient discipline to ensure shipboard life ran safely and smoothly. We all liked and respected him.

Jerry was also very able; the ageing boat had no problem he could not manage. His dry wit was put to good effect in meting out more discipline than Stan, for he was the one who had to fix the results of our carelessness or incompetence.

Roy, like Jerry, hailed from California and did the formidable job of providing three meals a day for the five weeks we were at sea. We ate well, although our less adaptable crewmembers complained when his cooking became a little more adventurous. From Dave we heard the classic comment: 'I can't wait to get home to Mum's cooking – none of this fancy stuff like mashed potatoes!'

Dave was quickly nicknamed Dirty Dave by Stan because he found it inconvenient to wash in salt water. He was young and naive and missed his home, his family, his junk food, his comfortable bed and, particularly, his mother, who, obviously, was in the habit of waiting on his every whim. This was his first trip away from home; at first he thought it might be the last, but as the days went past he slowly adapted to life at sea and began to enjoy it.

Skipper Stan climbs Dwyn Wen's mast.

Life on board was very different from anything Ted had ever experienced. His main objective was to evade having to do anything resembling work. He did this by spending a great deal of time in his bunk, by being incompetent at any task allotted to him and avoiding anything requiring physical or mental effort or application.

In complete contrast was John – Big John we called him – a Kiwi. With a typical New Zealand rapport with nature he excelled at all outdoor activities. He was a competent sailor and always cheerful, willing and energetic. We were lucky to have him aboard.

Fred had sailed to Tahiti from California in one of the first catamarans to cross the Pacific. Those who had seen the boat were incredulous that she had made it, for she had some basic design problems. Those of us who sailed with Fred were even more incredulous because we noticed he had difficulty in concentrating on the task in hand. When it was his turn at the wheel he was frequently way off course, particularly at night. He was a man with many interests, but when occupied with one of them he was thinking about another.

Swiss Marcel was quiet and shy and further inhibited by the language problem, however he was transformed when he played the guitar and sang. He became confident and outgoing, protected from the world by his music. As the voyage progressed he grew more secure and we appreciated his company.

Dwyn Wen's crew (from left: Fred, Mike, Stan (hidden), Ted, Roy, John, Marcel, Dave and Jerry)

And there was Mike. It was a while before we realised we had Mike on board, because he was seasick and remained in his cabin.

Stan, Jerry and Roy did not stand watches. The rest of us were organised into three four-hour watches, each with two people – an experienced sailor and a beginner. One person was left over, to do the household chores. This duty rotated every third day, and I was the one who moved so I had the opportunity to be on watch with each of the others.

Our course was to take us northeast through the Tuamotu Archipelago to the Marquesas and then northwest across the equator to Hawaii. Stan planned to stop at Anaa, an atoll with a totally enclosed lagoon. We first saw the island about two in the morning on a clear moonless night and waited off until first light to investigate the possibilities of getting ashore. There was a new stone wharf and a narrow pass had been blasted through the reef. However, even in ideal conditions, waves were breaking against the wharf and Stan did not consider it worth the risk of sending in a boat. Disappointed, we set sail and made as much haste as the wind allowed in order to clear the dangerous low islands before dark.

On the fourth day at sea Mike appeared on deck, somewhat recovered from his seasickness. He was not a pretty sight – dishevelled, unshaven and clad only in his underpants. He was miserable; only two things in life were worth having – food and sex, the order depending on which desire had last been indulged. Food had no appeal and, as I was the only female aboard and found him singularly unattractive, sex might be hard to come by – not that he didn't try; he made his intentions so abundantly clear that I thought it wise to lock my cabin door. Sure enough, just after the change of watch that night the door rattled and Mike demanded to be let in. Happily the catch held, but trying to sleep in the unventilated cabin was almost impossible. I shouldn't have to put up with this, I thought. Next night I was on watch with John and confided to him my problem with Mike.

'He's a sex maniac,' I said, 'and what's more he's got lice – he's constantly scratching his groin.'

John thought I was exaggerating, but agreed to swap bunks with me, taking my place in my cabin while I crept into his bunk in the forecastle without waking the other boys. Just after the change of the next watch shouts came from my cabin – John was outraged.

Mike slunk off, thwarted and frustrated. 'Oh shit!' he said.

In the morning came the familiar call of 'All hands on deck!' Strange, there didn't seem to be any need for a sail change and Jerry was in control rather than Stan. He was carrying a large tub. He gave me an exaggerated wink as I went to take the wheel. Mike was going to get his lice fixed. The boys filled the tub with diesel fuel and manhandled their reluctant, struggling victim so he was sitting in it, no doubt wondering if his precious equipment would ever function again. The smell of the diesel didn't do much for his seasickness either.

Stan came aft with a crooked grin on his face. 'Well hung,' he said, 'but absolutely no couth.'

~

The Tuamotus were behind us and we sailed in beautiful warm, sunny weather. The wind was fitful and inclined to die away at night so progress was not rapid. *Dwyn Wen* was not the most efficient at sailing to windward so gaining our easting was a challenge and every mile achieved was a victory. By now nobody – except Mike – worried too much as this sort of life was easy to take.

After two weeks we reached Haakuti, a village on the island of Ua Pou. The day before we arrived the wind increased, and with it, our speed. We trolled, using a red feather lure; a bell was rigged up on the line so it rang when a fish was hooked. In answer to its clanging noise we pulled on the line to find we had a beautiful 30 kg yellow fin tuna. It was a timely gift for our hosts and fed the whole village and us for two days.

We anchored in 10 fathoms off the village with scarcely any protection from the northeast wind, still blowing quite hard. It was like anchoring at sea and, after a disturbed night spent dragging we laid a second anchor.

We caught a blue fin tuna just before we arrived in Haakuti.

Because of the difficult anchorage yachts rarely visited Haakuti. The villagers had enjoyed *Dwyn Wen*'s first visit on her way to Tahiti and were pleased to see her again. Their hospitality was overwhelming. After shaking hands with the reception committee, headed by Chiefy and involving just about everybody in the village, I was taken over by a cheerful, plump vahine called Tahia.

She gave me a toothless smile and took my hand, 'You come house me.'

Her family lived in a coconut-thatched bamboo house with an earth floor. The furniture was sparse – just a table and benches outside the house and one bed inside. I slept like a queen on the bed while father, mother, brothers, sisters and their children lay around me on mats on the floor.

I was made an honoured guest. Tahia and her family washed my clothes and pressed them to perfection with a charcoal iron. Incredibly, the village had piped water. The shower was screened on two sides up to waist level so I could stand under the tap and enjoy the fresh, cool water while looking out over the spectacular mountains. The toilet was behind big rocks at the end of the garden and it changed its location daily. There were unlimited quantities of coffee, bananas, oranges and pawpaws – we seemed to be eating all day long.

Their animals shared their lives and were all jumbled up together. The ducks raised chicks and the dogs suckled kids. The chickens didn't know whether to fly or swim, the piglets whether to bark or bleat. Tahia had a puppy we called Hotdog. One morning he was in the house losing a battle with a kid when an alarmed chicken flew up and knocked a saucepan off the shelf onto the puppy's head. He yelped and ran away, bumping into a furious goose. Fur flew – some days you just can't win.

Sunday was approaching and a feast was in order. Stan and John went hunting for wild goats with some of the boys from the village and returned with three. They had shot five, but the other two had fallen down the rocks so had to be retrieved in a canoe.

My shirt and shorts were not considered suitable for church and a feast so Tahia dressed me in some of her own clothes. I wore a bright red petticoat and over it, a full yellow dress just reaching to my knees. My hair was brushed and oiled and my lips anointed with lipstick. The boys were incredulous and not very polite, but fortunately Tahia didn't understand their remarks.

Everyone in the village filed into church wearing their best clothes. Led by the imposing pastor and his wonderfully rich bass voice they sang a himane, a Polynesian hymn. Groups of other chanting voices followed him and blended together; the effect was spellbinding. They harmonised naturally and obviously enjoyed this Sunday ritual. The pastor then made a speech of welcome to us, and the rest of the congregation took it in turns to add their greeting. It was all in Marquesan and seemed to go on forever. One dignified, elderly gentleman surreptitiously smoked rolled cigarettes and passed his matches to a small boy, about eight years old, who had no light for his own smokes.

After the service we gathered for a feast – and what a feast it was! The goats were roasted on the spit, along with pork, chicken, duck, gannet, fish and breadfruit. Local vegetables and wonderful tropical fruit accompanied them. Food was indeed abundant in this benevolent climate and rich soil.

John (centre) and Stan (right) joined the hunting party.

John had a narrow escape that night. He was paddling out to the *Dwyn Wen* in an outrigger canoe with Chiefy's son, Poko, to take his anchor watch. This was the canoe used to collect the goats that had fallen down the cliff and must have smelt of blood. A shark attacked them breaking one arm of the outrigger. Fortunately the other arm withstood the onslaught and Poko used his paddle to support the outrigger. The canoe was stable, but John and Poko were helpless and drifting out to sea. Happily, their plight was seen from the yacht and they were rescued in the dinghy.

As soon as he went ashore, Mike recovered his appetite for food and sex. He was quite sure he was going to find pretty, brown-eyed vahines, all willing to satisfy his desires. The village maidens were not impressed, but, heedless of their aversion, Mike romped around the village casting lecherous looks at anybody in a skirt regardless of their age.

We were in the village one morning when we heard a strange noise coming up the path. The boys of the village, about fifteen of them, had been organised and were each armed with an empty tin can and a stone. Mike was ashore, and his escort was sounding the alarm.

'Ooh la la – Mike!' exclaimed Tahia and she hurried her away, out of sight, with all the other women and girls.

The evening before our departure Chiefy organised a feast and a dance. We were embarrassed by Mike's behaviour so Stan made sure he was on anchor watch. Everybody in the village was there. The three guitarists, two ukulele players and drummer were joined by John and Marcel with their guitars. Marcel's yodelling made him an instant success, and his entranced audience would not allow him to stop.

The Twist had not yet reached the Marquesas, but was adopted with enthusiasm after we demonstrated the basics. Chiefy danced with me energetically, if not very skilfully, and it became a contest to see who could keep going longest. I won because he was drinking large quantities of alcohol. After a while he disappeared. Stan beckoned to me and, putting a finger to his lips, took me to Chiefy's house where we discovered him, a wild and drunken figure, immersed up to his waist in a barrel of water, singing and splashing happily in the moonlight.

~

We had a glorious sail across to Nuku Hiva, 27 miles away, with all sails set and a 20-knot wind behind us. Late in the afternoon we came into Taiohai, the main town in the Marquesas and the port of entry. The gendarme came out to us to clear us.

Roy and I spent a day riding up into the mountains. We climbed a rocky path past the foundations of old houses – a reminder that the population of the islands had been much larger before the white man came with religion and disease. The view from the top was magnificent, looking over spectacular, lush green mountains to the deep blue sea.

When we left Taiohai we were one crewmember less. Stan had had a long talk to Mike, who agreed to return to Tahiti on a copra trading boat. Mike had not enjoyed his time aboard *Dwyn Wen* and nor had we enjoyed having him!

For the first few days after we left the Marquesas we had a favourable wind and made excellent progress. The ocean seemed endless and time stood still as we settled into a happy routine. Stan, Jerry and I did the navigation. Creative Fred occupied himself carving and engraving wood, Marcel was learning Japanese, Roy was an expert at knotting and splicing and Stan made model ships. Dave spent many hours unsuccessfully looking for a carton of beer he was sure he had brought on board and equally sure he had not consumed. He cast accusing glances at us. We played chess, Scrabble and Monopoly and shot at balloons and tin cans with an airgun. Occasionally the fishing line bell rang, alerting us to a welcome fresh fish.

I was the ship's doctor. My patients were Dave, covered with septic sandfly bites on his back and legs, and Stan, with cuts to his feet from walking barefoot on the reef after a boating misadventure in Taiohai. Fortunately we were carrying some antibiotics.

As we approached the equator the sky became overcast and the wind dropped. Prolonged periods of torrential rain accompanied huge and confused blind swells. Eventually we had to take down the sails because they were thrashing themselves to shreds on the rigging. Without sails to steady her *Dwyn Wen* rolled wildly and unmercifully, digging alternate gunwales under the waves.

In spite of the difficult conditions Roy turned out his usual high standard of cooking. It wasn't easy, because any container not on the gimballed stove or main saloon table immediately went flying from side to side of the boat, spilling its contents. Food, drinks, plates, knives and spoons stayed miraculously in place on the saloon table and we were careful not to touch it.

One day at lunchtime, Ted, who had been on watch, came to eat after the rest of us had finished. His tactics to avoid doing any work were beginning to irritate us. He sat in the only chair in the saloon that was not tied down.

'You'd better fix that,' cautioned Stan.

'Oh, I'll be all right.' Anchoring the chair was too much trouble for Ted.

As soon as the words were out of his mouth his chair began to slide away from the table. We all knew what was going to happen next and yelled in unison, 'Don't touch the table, Ted!'

Then the inevitable: Ted slid back, his arms out-stretched. He grabbed the table and fell off his chair. The table tipped the remains of our lunch all over him. Without a word we all stood up and filed out on deck.

~

After what seemed an interminable number of days the wind came back and the skies cleared. The days were getting shorter and cooler. We could no longer see the Southern Cross, but the Pole Star, Polaris, appeared briefly in the North and Orion stood on his feet again. I realised I had not been in the northern hemisphere for five years.

On Christmas Day late in the afternoon we made our landfall on the big island of Hawaii. John climbed the ratlines and his shout of 'Land Ho!' brought us all scrambling on deck. We saw the distinctive shape of the volcano, Mauna Loa, floating above the clouds on the horizon. It was our Christmas present.

Life on board took on a new purpose as we prepared ourselves for arrival. In many ways we welcomed it because it brought a promise of hot showers, fresh food and the trappings of civilisation. In other ways we were sad because it signalled the end of this idyllic time of communion with the sea, the ship and each other.

Four days later, early in the morning, we hoisted our yellow quarantine flag and came into Honolulu. We tied up to the quarantine jetty and waited impatiently for police and customs clearance.

No marina berth was big enough for *Dwyn Wen* so we anchored in a corner of the harbour opposite the yacht club. The schooner's owner Jim came aboard to greet us.

'Just in time to take us on a honeymoon cruise. Aloha and I got married last week so I was hoping you'd be here in time to take us to Maui for the New Year.'

'Doesn't give us much time,' said Stan, 'but we'll see what we can do.'

The yacht became a hive of activity. Most of the boys left to spend the rest of the Christmas holiday with their families, leaving only four of the original crew on board – Stan, Jerry, John and me. I took all the sheets and towels to the launderette next to the yacht club and, while they were washing, I indulged in a long shower. I had the greatest difficulty in tearing myself away from the luxurious fresh, hot water. What bliss!

I cleaned all the cabins and saloon and then turned my attention to the forecastle. John came to help me.

'There's some loose boards under Dave's bunk – must have been really uncomfortable,' I said. 'Could you try to make them a bit more secure?'

John went to investigate. 'Look, there's a cardboard carton in here. Good heavens! It's Dave's lost beer! His head would have only been two feet away from it every night!'

'All that fuss!' I said. 'It's a good thing he's gone – we'd never have been able to tell him!'

Next day Stan and John went ashore to buy provisions, leaving Jerry and me on board. In the afternoon a thunderstorm descended on us with vicious squalls and torrential rain. I went up on deck to see what was happening and noticed the yacht was not lying head to wind. Strange, I thought, and then it dawned: the anchor wasn't holding – we were dragging. I shouted for Jerry to start the engine and ran to the wheel. I was soaked to the skin before I got there.

'I'll have to get the anchor up and put another one down,' called Jerry, his words torn from his mouth by the wind. 'There's a CQR in the forepeak. It should do the job, but it'll not be easy to get it up on deck. Keep heading into the wind and take the weight off the anchor.'

He went forward and, for what seemed an eternity, I held the yacht into the blustery wind and driving rain. Instantaneous lightning and thunder surrounded us. Controlling the yacht in the confines of the tiny harbour while Jerry pulled up the dragging anchor and laid the CQR demanded intense concentration; *Dwyn Wen* had suddenly become enormous, cumbersome and disobedient.

We had the yacht secure again just as the thunderstorm stopped, the rain eased off and the coastguards, their powerful launch at full speed, came to save us. They were disappointed we didn't need them, but came alongside anyway and shared a glass of Dave's Tahitian beer. We inspected the suspect anchor – the shaft was bent – no wonder it didn't hold!

Next day Jim and Aloha came on board with six of their friends. We sailed to Maui with a brisk quartering wind and rough seas, *Dwyn Wen* romping along. In calm water off Lahina we anchored in time to join the New Year celebrations, starting with a Japanese feast on the beach, continuing in the local hotel and ending up back on the yacht.

Jim and Aloha were going to hire a car and tour the island. They invited John and me to join them.

'We should be able to find some places to camp out,' said Jim. 'And there's a hut we can use in the crater of the Haleakala volcano. We can buy all we need in the way of food and drinks on the way round.'

Scenically Maui was beautiful and extraordinarily varied. We wound through coastal villages with lush tropical vegetation – waterfalls appeared around every corner. We picked our fill of guavas, wild raspberries and bananas and spent the night camped on the beach under pandanus trees, lulled to sleep by the sound of breaking surf.

Fine open grazing country greeted us on the following day and we saw many mongooses – weasel-like creatures that were imported to control rats, but preferred to eat birds and their eggs. The road was lined with eucalyptus and jacaranda trees. We stopped to swim in natural freshwater pools before reaching the rugged southern tip of the island and its magnificent coastline.

Outside the store in a small village we pulled up at the bowser to refuel the car and buy some food. John went inside and asked the owner, 'May we have some petrol, please?'

The owner looked puzzled and searched his shelves. Then he shouted to his wife out the back, 'We're out of petrol, aren't we dear?'

Jim was laughing. 'John, try asking for gas!'

A rough road snaked 60 kilometres from sea level up 3,000 metres to the rim of the Haleakala caldera, the vegetation changing from open country to rainforest as we climbed. At the summit a stark, dramatic scene of lunar-like desolation confronted us. The crater was about 30 kilometres across and contained rust-coloured cinder cones, some of which rose to 600 metres. We were above the clouds and the cold air was invigorating.

It was a lonely place, the only sign of human influence being the little cabin where we were to spend the night. We reached it at sundown by sliding down loose lava cinders and trekking across the crater, carrying our food and water. Jim and John attended to the fire while Aloha and I prepared the food. Then, with a glass of wine we sat outside the hut to watch the colours in the cliffs and cinder cones change and glow in the rays of the setting sun.

~

Back in Honolulu I met a Chinese-American professor of history who had written a book that had been turned into a musical stage show and a movie. It was a spectacular hit and he had acquired a windfall – more money than he could ever have imagined – like winning the lottery. He was in Hawaii looking for ways to spend it, investment in real estate being one, and had arranged to fly to the big island of Hawaii with an agent. There was a seat on the plane for another passenger and without hesitation I accepted his invitation to fill it, for volcanoes fascinated me and Kilauea was one of the most active volcanoes on earth.

On landing at Hilo I caught a bus to the Kilauea caldera. It was a quiet time for this active volcano – no spectacular eruptions or lava flows – but this meant a closer acquaintance was possible. I said goodbye to the bus when it stopped at the Volcano Inn and took a track through rich rainforest down into the crater where the vegetation gave way to a more forbidding scene. I spent the afternoon scrambling over the top of shining new lava flows and the darker older ones, wondering at their fascinating whirls and contortions. In this awesome landscape steam escaped from cracks in the hot rocks and lava pools boiled around sinister yellow deposits of sulphur.

I was hot, tired and dirty by the time I got back to the Volcano Inn. Few other guests were staying, but several locals were in the bar. My feet had suffered from walking on the rough lava so I enquired about a horse to hire.

'We've got mules,' said a woman. 'Could you manage a mule?'

Her husband was interested. 'I've got to round up some bulls tomorrow and I could do with some help.'

The couple invited me to stay with them. They were an interesting family: Alf was part Japanese and his wife, Mary, part Filipina. They had three rowdy kids, their modest home was spotlessly clean and they made me feel welcome. The volcano was an integral part of their lives; they ran cattle on its grassy slopes and were affected by its moods. Kilauea's activity was generally in the relatively safe form of lava flows; there were records of explosions, but none had happened in their lifetimes. They had witnessed many glowing lava flows and spectacular firework displays over the years and learned to live with the thought of a major catastrophe.

Alf saddled up a pale chestnut mule for me. She was called Pele after the Hawaiian goddess of fire who lived in the volcano. We set off up the mountain to find the cattle. Alf lassoed a big bull, remarkably quiet and obviously used to this sort of treatment. I was instructed to take him down through the trees to a new paddock. The bull was reluctant to leave his herd, but, after Alf shouted at him, he eventually agreed to follow the mule. If he came too close, Pele kicked at him; she seemed to have eyes in the back of her head and always knew where he was and what he was doing. All went well until we ended up on either side of a tree. We spent an interesting few minutes going round in circles disentangling ourselves. As the day wore on I learned to work with the mule and trust her so I became a little more proficient.

~

In a gale and pouring rain I flew back to Honolulu to a life that centred on the yacht club. Several of the yachts we had met in Tahiti were there and we had a happy time comparing notes. The yachts in the Transpac race had arrived a few weeks earlier and several were looking for crew to take them back to the States. I had numerous offers, including navigator on an exquisite 60-foot schooner, *Defiant*, heading for the West Indies.

Waikiki Yacht Club was celebrating an anniversary with a special race. The four of us from *Dwyn Wen* were invited to crew on *Defiant*. We won, easily, and I was even more impressed by the schooner for she was sea-kindly and comfortable as well as fast. After the race we dressed her with flags and joined the other colourful yachts parading the length of the Waikiki Beach and back again in time for the champagne lunch. The owner again offered me a trip to the West Indies, this time not just as navigator, but as paid skipper. Serious thought was needed. I was going to have to make a decision: keep travelling or go back to Australia? The Pole Star or the Southern Cross? I had not discussed with Simon what the future held in store for us, let alone our relationship. I wondered what his thoughts were about cruising after the ordeal of the storm; had it whetted his appetite for more or deterred him from wanting to go to sea again?

As if on cue a cable came from Simon. He said Maria at Reckitts wanted me to go back to my old job. The factory had moved and they were looking for somebody who had experience of their products.

That evening the four of us on board *Dwyn Wen* treated ourselves to more of Dave's beer and discussed our futures. Stan and Jerry knew what they were going to do – *Dwyn Wen* had already attracted interest from some potential charterers. For John and me it was decision time – our American visas were about to expire.

John was footloose and fancy-free. His ambition was to go to Europe, but he didn't mind how long it took him.

They turned their attention to me.

'I know what you're going to do,' Stan said. 'You'll go back to Australia and Simon – at any rate that's what you should do.'

Jerry turned to him. 'No, she won't, she's fallen in love with a schooner.'

'What do you think I should do, John?' I asked.

'You should do whatever your heart tells you to do,' he said wisely. 'Only you can determine that.'

~

I didn't have to think; I knew instinctively I was going to return to Simon and *Iota*. I enquired about a flight back to Sydney and discovered I had to go via Tahiti where the aircrew would have a two-day break before continuing to Fiji and thence to Sydney. A weekend in Tahiti sounded attractive so I made a booking and cabled Simon telling him I would be arriving on Monday.

I spent a memorable weekend saying hello and goodbye again to many of my friends in Tahiti. When I arrived in Sydney I learned it was a public holiday, Australia Day. There was no sign of Simon at the airport. I wondered what to do, for I had no idea where he was or how to contact him. I thought seriously about catching the next plane back to Honolulu!

I took a taxi to where I thought *Achernar* would be moored – at least I would have somewhere to stay while I was looking for her owner. I was right, but Max at the boatshed didn't know where Simon was – he had only his office address. I rang up Val – thank goodness he was at home. He also was not sure where Simon was, but thought he might be able to find him living in a house where Roche were set to build their new offices. He would come and pick me up and we would go looking.

He greeted me warmly. 'Simon didn't tell me you were coming, but I'm so pleased you're back.'

'Thanks. I sent a cable to the office telling him my flight number, but perhaps he didn't get it because today is a holiday.'

'Simon's been lost without you.' Val recounted a conversation he'd had with him. 'I asked him when you were coming home, but he said he didn't know. When I asked him if he had asked you to come back, he looked surprised and said, "No, do you think I should?" Of course, I said, she won't come back if she doesn't think she's wanted.'

'Hence his cable,' I said. 'It was thanks to you – and Maria!'

We drove to Dee Why and turned inland past paddocks previously used for market gardens, but now giving way to more lucrative development. We spotted *Iota* looking forlorn, propped up on blocks in a paddock full of old greenhouses behind a suburban cottage. Simon came out of the house when he heard the car.

'Just in time for a beer. Are you staying?'

'If you'll have me,' I replied.

Iota *looked forlorn in a paddock full of old greenhouses.*

If it's worth doing, it's worth doing properly

1964

The first thing we talked about was our future cruising in *Iota*. That Simon had already started planning the improvements *Iota* needed reassured me that he was as hooked on cruising as I was and wanted to continue. We were pleased with *Iota*'s performance; the idea of a portable yacht had worked well, but she had been built in a hurry and had much room for improvement. Her shortcomings could be fixed; we needed to learn from our experience and take our time to refit.

'I've written an article for the *Yachting Monthly* – they've published it and now they want more – so we'll just have to go again!' Simon showed me the article.

> *Iota is the answer to the yachtsman's dilemma of how to go cruising and keep a job in order to be able to afford it. She gives us a combination of pleasures – a taste of boundless freedom. She enables us to explore places that are accessible only by yacht. And it's the challenge of the forces of nature and exposure to the best and worst the weather can do.*

'And I heard from Messageries Maritime that they're going to call briefly at Nukuhiva in the Marquesas on their return journey to Europe. We could get *Iota* dropped off, explore the Marquesas and sail through the Tuamotus back to Tahiti.' Simon had not been deterred by our experience – indeed, it had whetted his appetite for more.

We then discussed our domestic arrangements. If we could survive amicably on a small boat in tough conditions we should be able to manage to live together on land.

'Coming back from the dead together is kind of binding,' I said. 'It's something special to share.' Simon nodded his agreement.

It seemed silly for us to have two separate establishments just to conform to convention. Simon did not want to get married – having one attempt ending in divorce he was once bitten, twice shy. To me, marriage was immaterial; if I had made a commitment a ceremony and a piece of paper did not make any difference. I did not want children, and Simon shared the responsibility for his two and had no desire for any more.

'What will your mother have to say about it?' asked Simon.

'I expect she'll be horrified,' I replied. 'Tradition and what other people think are very important to her, but she's on the other side of the world, and it's my life. What about your colleagues – would it make any difference at work?'

'It's nothing to do with them. They all know I go sailing with my crew. The Swiss might have more of a problem, but like your mother they're on the other side of the world.' Simon dismissed them.

He told me Maria had rung him because many of their employees had left and been replaced by new, inexperienced ones when Reckitts moved their factory to the west of Sydney, a fair distance away from the old one. They were looking for a chemist who was familiar with the products to sort out production problems.

'You can take the job if they give you a substantial rise in pay,' Simon advised. 'I'd never re-employ somebody who'd left me, but Maria sounded desperate so you have the whip hand. You wouldn't find it difficult to get another similar job and they know that.'

I went for an interview with Jim the Works Manager and Maria. Maria, who was as much a friend as a colleague, was willing to give me anything I asked for, but Jim was uncomfortable. He was well aware that my request for more pay was because of Simon's influence; I would not have been so bold without his backing. He felt threatened by my relationship. Maria prevailed – she was pleased to see me again and approved of Simon – so we agreed that I should return to my old job for a period of at least two years.

Simon's cottage, adjacent to the building site where the new Roche Building was under construction, was minimally but adequately furnished for the two of us. Loud thumps of the pile driver shook the walls so it was a relief to be away from it all day. One of Reckitts' directors, Alex Dix, lived at Collaroy and was able to give me a lift to and from work. As we set off each morning I thought how lucky I was – going to work into a stimulating world rather than staying at home all day like Alex's wife Ann who already had three children under five; another – it turned out to be twins – was on the way. During the journey we exchanged useful information about what was going on in our particular part of the organisation – he was responsible for the management of the warehouse. Alex had a sharp, enquiring mind and he and Ann were to become long lasting friends.

The new laboratory was modern, well equipped and there was plenty of bench space – so much easier to keep clean and in good order. We had a full-time staff member to wash the used glassware and a laboratory secretary; no longer did we have to use the office typists who were not familiar with laboratory terms.

I slipped back into my role of looking after household products, and added to it the evaluation of competitors' products. We were busy, for Reckitts had been taking over several companies; food products and floor finishes added to the variety and presented new challenges. The staff was increasing; new lab assistants had to be introduced to their tasks and supervised. There was a good rapport and ambience in the laboratory where the number of different nationalities represented reflected the Australian Government's policy of encouraging qualified migrants. Unusually the chief chemist – Maria – and three of her five senior chemists were women.

Simon's work and the new building were equally demanding. Several Swiss visitors – architects and construction experts – demanded his time during and after working hours. We took them sailing on *Achernar* – she was up for sale, but we might as well take advantage of her in the meantime. More came to attend the ceremonies on completion of the building – an eye-catching handsome creation ahead of its time. It offered excellent facilities for the staff, who were able to live conveniently close to work in beachside suburbs offering the best of Sydney's lifestyle.

My Mother, as predicted, was upset by my domestic arrangements, but no-one found it unusual when Simon introduced me as his crew. The woman I employed to come in once a week to clean the house resigned when she discovered that we were living together out of wedlock – she worked only for respectable people.

The pace of my life rapidly accelerated and the rat race seemed to be overtaking me; there was no time for reflection as I rushed from one undertaking to the next. The blissfully relaxed life style of Tahiti had become a remote dream after only a few weeks back in Sydney – but at least I had experienced it and knew it existed!

We made major improvements to *Iota* and needed help for Simon was not very dextrous – hands to him were for passing the ball out of a scrum – so Neil Gale who had started building *Iota* worked with us most weekends.

The decks were fibre-glassed to stop leaks and covered with non-slip Trakmark. A fundamental change to the mounting of the leeboard bolts ensured they could not possibly leak again. We obviously had to do something about a new engine. I was still in favour of spending a bit more money and having a water-cooled marine diesel. I lost again because Simon was concerned that the increase in weight would make loading onto a ship more hazardous. He decided on a small air-cooled 8 HP diesel designed with a lawnmower in mind. It was certainly better than the outboard, but was not easy to live with, being extremely hot and noisy.

The Skipper was no longer in Sydney; his marriage had broken up and he had gone north to Queensland to set up a sailing school. Peter Mounsey, whose yacht *Larapinta* we had seen entering Raiatea as we were leaving Tahaa, became a valued adviser; he had a wealth of experience and was full of practical tips to make life on board more efficient and safer. Particularly innovative was the system he devised for raising our main mast. Twin whisker poles formed a bipod bolted to the chainplates, which enabled me to raise the masts with the help of just one other (though the help of two people was better). The only heavy work was to move the mast into position in its tabernacle.

As soon as *Achernar* was sold we moved *Iota* back into the water and kept her on the marina at Max van Gelder's boat yard at Neutral Bay. There we prepared her for a four-week cruise through the Barrier Reef from Mackay to Cairns.

'We need to do a short cruise to make sure we've ironed out all her problems,' Simon said, recalling the eventful day when we first took *Iota* to sea out of Tahiti.

It was August in 1964 when we took *Iota* alongside the *Denman* bound for Mackay and were hoisted aboard. *Iota* travelled by herself, but Simon was there to meet her.

I was hoping that, when I arrived a day later, Simon would have stepped the masts. With the aid of Cyril the Pier Master he had succeeded only in splitting the tabernacle. Coming to our rescue was Harry, the owner of a nearby yacht. With his help we repaired the damage. He enlisted the skipper of a neighbouring boat and we raised the masts without further trouble.

Harry invited us home for a shower and dinner having warned us he didn't care much for his wife. When we arrived she did not speak to us. I made the mistake of thanking her for dinner. She told us she had to do it or she would be beaten and would be happy to show us the bruises next day. Harry, embarrassed, said later that he didn't beat her – which we believed – but I couldn't think why not. Apparently her problem had to do with it being Sunday; she had been deprived of going to church, which she liked to do twice on a Sunday, no doubt – in my mind – to learn how to behave as a Christian.

'I wonder why he doesn't sail away – his yacht's ready.' I commented. 'She certainly succeeded in embarrassing him and making us feel uncomfortable.'

Simon expressed his opinion. 'It just goes to show that if every dog can have his day, then so can every bitch.'

We had expected to have a headwind, a southeast trade wind, for our trip to Middle Percy Island, about 70 miles from Mackay. At dusk there was no wind and a calm sea. We powered through the clear moonlit night until dawn when a light breeze came up. With relief we stopped the noisy, hot engine. We anchored off a beautiful white beach, but, as *Iota* was rolling, moved her into a small, almost totally enclosed lagoon, taking advantage of her flat bottom so that she was relatively comfortable when she dried out at low tide.

We took advantage of Iota's *flat bottom to dry out at low tide.*

In this part of the ocean spring tides had a rise of about six metres and the current in the narrow channels ran at up to 6 knots. We entered the lagoon at half-tide and within the hour *Iota* was leaning comfortably on her starboard chine. At low tide great armies of little soldier crabs moved around in formation on the sand with their curious side-stepping gait. Their bright blue bulbous bodies would disappear into the sand in half a second if they were threatened; alternatively they curled up with their brown legs wrapped around themselves in the hope they wouldn't be noticed.

We wandered over to a shack on the beach with a big red sign reading 'Telephone'. On the rough-planked walls of the shack were painted the names of visiting yachts. I added *Iota*. Simon wound the handle of the ancient telephone and was soon chatting to Harry White, who lived with his brother and sister in the homestead on the windward side. We walked over the hill to visit this elderly trio, who still worked hard on their land and were remarkably self-sufficient. Harry showed us the thriving vegetable garden and the plots of bananas, pineapples and sugar cane. The pasture for their sheep and horses reached down the hillside to the front of their house.

Harry told us the history of the island. Matthew Flinders named the Percy Isles in 1802. In 1887 a Colonel Armitage bought the first lease and started a coffee plantation. The White family, from Canada, took over the lease in 1921, and Dolly and her brothers, Harold and Claude, had run the island as a sheep farm for 42 years. They had just decided to sell their lease – they were finding the amount of work more than their advanced years could manage. All three – particularly Dolly, who had not been to the mainland for fifteen years – had mixed feelings about their forthcoming change in lifestyle, and hoped the English group who were interested in the island as a site for a 'New Utopia' would look after it and continue the tradition of welcoming visiting yachts.

We walked back to the lagoon laden with fruit. *Iota* was afloat; we turned her around so when she dried out again during the night we would not roll out of our bunk. As we sat in the cockpit enjoying our 'sundowners' the screeching of hundreds of noisy, white cockatoos nearly deafened us.

As soon as *Iota* was afloat on the morning tide we sailed in a fresh wind the 70 miles to Skawfell. At midnight we hove-to off the island to wait for daylight to show us the way in to Refuge Bay. There we anchored in the company of five hospitable fishing boats who asked us to join their beach party. A feast of oysters collected from the rocks and steak cooked on an open fire was washed down with copious quantities of beer and rum, followed by the fruit we had been given in Middle Percy.

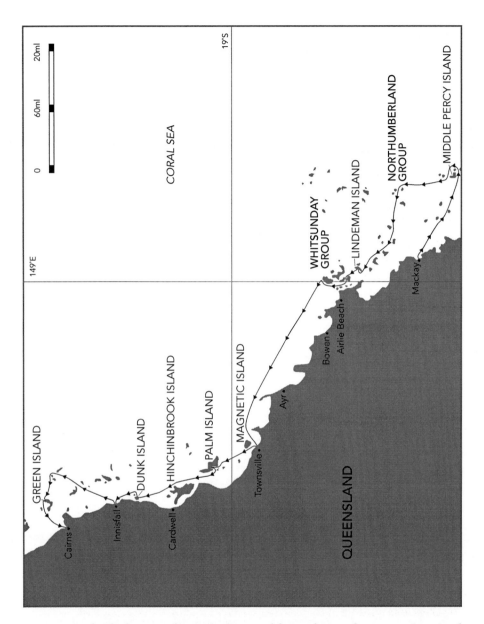

Les and Gladys on the *Wanderer* told us about their carefree and remunerative life. At this time of the year they were trolling for mackerel, following them north as far as Townsville and then heading to the outer reef for coral trout and sweetlip. Observing that our fishing gear was much too light for the conditions, they made us up a trolling line with two massive hooks attached by heavy wire to a large swivel on our braided nylon cord. They knew the islands well and gave us invaluable information on the anchorages.

'Make sure you don't miss Hamilton Island,' said Les. 'A couple has taken the lease and they're running sheep. They reckon the husband is having an affair with the governess and the wife with the farmhand. It's a queer set up.'

Simon dutifully noted 'queer set up' on the chart.

For the next three days after leaving Skawfell we had an easy and pleasant sail to the next island, arriving in time for a swim and a stroll along the beach. Most afternoons we caught a fish for our dinner. Brampton Island was a tourist resort, but Goldsmith and Shaw Islands were uninhabited. The anchorage at Goldsmith was uncomfortable as the yacht was lying to the tide rather than the wind, and rolling. Ashore the scrub was impenetrable. A notice told visitors to the island that this was a National Park. Despite a long list of things not allowed, the beach was littered with empty beer cans.

Shaw Island was pretty, featuring coconut trees along its beach. The fishing was easy – Simon caught our dinner when he threw the line overboard to wind it on to the reel, hooking a passing parrotfish in the head. We lit a fire on the beach and fried it quickly with a little butter and a squeeze of lemon juice. I cooked a green pawpaw to go with it.

'Exquisite! Such a feast deserves a bottle of wine.' Simon rowed back to the boat to fetch one.

The light southeast wind we had behind us for the run to Hamilton Island gradually increased in strength as the day wore on. We came into the bay on the northwest of the island, but had trouble finding a place free of coral to anchor. The chart showed a large sand patch, but Simon could not see it from the ratlines. People on the beach were waving to us so I rowed ashore. They told me of another bay on the other side of the headland – it had sand on which we could dry out. We rushed around, determined to beat the outgoing tide, our little air-cooled engine rattling and shaking. The water left us just 20 minutes after we arrived.

The sheep run lessees, Ron and his wife Jenny, came on board and we talked about the missing sand patch. I produced the chart for them to see. Simon noticed, fortunately before they did, the words 'queer set up'.

'No, not that one.' He swiftly changed the subject.

Iota was Ron and Jenny's first visiting yacht. They invited us to their house. I had not expected to find the trappings of suburbia on an island – they seemed a little out of place. I had a hot bath in a tiled bathroom decorated with mauve coral and artificial flowers. The kitchen was full of modern appliances and they had a pushbutton toilet, a radiogram and many records and books. The house was in a wonderful setting, looking out over a green lawn with palms, citrus trees and coconuts down to the bay and across the Whitsunday Passage and all the islands. They royally wined and dined us.

The evening radio session told Ron and Jenny that expected visitors had arrived in Shute Harbour: please come over and collect them. Until the midnight tide floated their boat and they could set off for the mainland they came on board *Iota*. We never found out if there indeed was 'a queer set up'.

Into the Whitsunday Islands

As soon as we were afloat the next day we took our anchor and lines on board and set off across the Whitsunday Passage, so named by Captain James Cook when he passed through it 'on the day the Church commemorates that festival'. The weather deteriorated and we crossed the shipping lane in poor visibility. Two warships were in the channel, quite close. We piled on more sail and rushed, in increasing seas, along the coast of South Molle and around the northeastern headland. Two tacks into the howling wind and rain took us into the bay close to the jetty. We put out our heavy anchor with our Chum weight on it to hold it down.

During the night the weather grew worse, the wind coming in bullets from both sides of the bay. *Iota* snatched at her anchor chain and rolled. We stayed at South Molle for three days, waiting for the weather to improve. Managing to get ashore we hoped the resort would cheer us up, but were disappointed. Inebriated members of a football team inhabited the squalid bar. For lunch we were served with tinned food; even the fish came out of a tin. We avoided the resort after that and went for pleasant, if wet, walks.

We set off for Hayman Island and its neighbour, Hook Island, as soon as the weather cleared, racing against the Hayman Island catamaran – and losing. The crew on the cat suggested picking up a mooring buoy, but the Hayman Island anchorage was an exposed lee shore. A cruise ship came into sight, heading for the island, and that decided us; we crossed over to Hook Island and had Butterfly Bay to ourselves. There we spent the afternoon collecting oysters. Small brown-winged terns perched cheekily on the boat; one tried to land on Simon's head.

~

It was difficult to tell the difference between mainland mountains rising from low, flat plains and the islands. Gloucester Island emphasised this, for it was cut off from the mainland by a narrow passage. Its long steep ridges generated bullets of wind down into the passage; the shore was stony and the anchorage poor so we stayed just long enough to have lunch before setting off for Townsville, sailing through the night.

We were in the shipping lane and were particularly troubled by ships coming up astern of us. They were not travelling much faster than we were so seemed to be stalking us for hours. It was difficult to orientate the ship's lights, which, by the time they materialised as red, green, high or low, were alarmingly close. On two occasions ships altered course to inspect us; when we shone a light on our sails they went away.

We came around Cape Cleveland late the next afternoon and anchored for the night before motoring into Townsville's crowded harbour. We tied *Iota* alongside a schooner, *Cimba*, at the city wharf and learned that her crew of three boys were on a sail-as-you-earn trip around the world. Bill had a job fitting a galvanised iron roof to the new sugar store, Charlie had one day's pay at the meat works before they went on strike and Dave was working on their boat.

After two days in Townsville and well stocked up with beer, ice, fresh vegetables and bread we sailed to Great Palm Island, a reserve for Aboriginal people. It was a self-supporting community boasting a sawmill and a cattle run. The 1500 Indigenous and 100 white residents mostly ignored us, but we were pounced upon by a strange man who was teaching boatbuilding. He was obsessed by barges and leeboards and could not believe his eyes when he saw *Iota*. He invited us to his house and regaled us with his theories about double prismatic cones. The superintendent of the island rescued us; he came to tell us we should have reported to him as soon as we came ashore, and invited us home for dinner.

~

We had a glorious sail along the coast of Hinchinbrook Island. It was spectacularly rugged and densely wooded, the trees clinging precariously to the steep rocky sides of the hills. Two fishing boats joined us when we anchored for the night and we shared a merry evening.

At Dunk Island we found a rundown hotel – the previous manager and his wife had consumed all the profits in the bar. Under new management it didn't seem to have changed much as we never saw any of the eleven guests in the bar; the staff were always there. However they cooked us a delicious dinner and we enjoyed the relaxed atmosphere.

Winding around the island through the thick tropical growth were well-kept paths, busy with Ulysses butterflies, swarming around like big blue flakes of snow. The ground under the trees was a blue carpet of the dead ones.

Dunk was the island home of Edmund J Banfield and his wife Bertha from 1898 to 1923. He was born in Liverpool in England in 1852 and his family brought him to Australia while he was still a boy. He became a journalist and went to North Queensland where he joined the staff of *The Townsville Daily Bulletin* and strongly supported the movement striving to achieve separate statehood for North Queensland. His health began to deteriorate. Diagnosed with pulmonary consumption he was given six months to live. Mindful of the advice of Henry Thoreau, whom he greatly admired – 'To the sick the doctors wisely recommend a change of air and scenery' – Banfield and his wife went to Dunk Island to spend the few remaining months of his life.

He survived for another 25 years during which time he wrote prolifically, documenting his break away from the pressures of city life and his life on a tropic island. He described the birds, plants and animals on Dunk down to the minutest detail.

A stone cairn marks his grave on the island with the words of Thoreau: 'If a man does not keep pace with his companions perhaps it is because he hears a different drummer. Let him step to the music which he hears'.

A stone cairn marks the grave of the Banfields.

After an early morning swim we left lovely Dunk Island and had a fast sail, goosewinged, in a brisk 25-knot wind to Innisfail. *Iota* handled easily, surfing down the waves. We had to stop twice when we hooked sharks on our trolling line. The first one was relatively small so we pulled it on board, but the second one was so big we cut it free. We thought better of fishing after that.

Bill, the skipper of a fishing trawler anchored off Dunk Island, warned us that the charts for Gladys Inlet that led into the Johnstone River, and for the river itself, were inaccurate. He gave us careful instructions, drew a mud map and cautioned us about crossing the bar at the river mouth at low tide.

As we entered the Inlet we had trouble distinguishing the leading marks. We were apprehensive for we were embarked on an irreversible course with a determined wind pushing us towards a lee shore. We identified Flying Fish Point and located the entrance to the river. The prospect did not look inviting as the ebb tide was running directly against the wind and kicking up short steep seas. An ominous line of breakers stretched out across the bay over the sand bar. It was three hours before low tide so we knew there was enough water for *Iota*'s shallow draft, but would she be able to ride the breakers?

We dropped our sails and firmly secured everything on deck, bolted the hatches and put the engine on full throttle. We surfed through three big breakers, fighting to keep the boat straight and suddenly found ourselves in calm water. We had taken a lot of water over the decks, but otherwise were unscathed. *Iota* did well.

We hooked and landed a small shark.

Innisfail was about three miles away up the Johnstone River. We followed Bill's directions carefully and were almost in sight of the town when Simon hesitated; instead of one island, as drawn on the scribbled chart, there were two. He chose the wrong one and we came gently to a halt on a muddy sand bank in the middle of the river. Fortunately it was approaching low tide.

I consulted the *Pilot Book* to find out what it said about the Johnstone River. It warned against swimming as it was 'infested with crocodiles that live their lives in a state of constant rage'. I looked carefully around for any suspicious submerged logs as Simon waded out with an anchor to ensure we would float free of the sand bank when the tide came up. We sat in the middle of the lovely river, being eaten by sandflies.

Next day we went on to the picturesque and tranquil town of Innisfail, to hire a car and drive through sugarcane country. We started along the coast and crossed the river on an old ferry to Flying Fish Point to survey the scene of our previous day's sailing. The weather had changed completely, there being only a slight swell and a light air. On the second day we went inland through tropical rainforests to Palmerston National Park and back along the Gillies Highway, admiring fabulous views. It felt strange to be in a car and two days were enough – the reef was calling.

Two fishing boats escorted us down the Johnstone River on the afternoon ebb tide. We planned to visit the outer reef that, in this area, is relatively close to the mainland. With no wind, we motored until we picked up Fitzroy Light and then drifted in a flat calm waiting for dawn.

At first light we set off in perfect conditions for approaching the reef. From the ratlines Simon picked up the outlying 'bombies' that arose abruptly from countless fathoms to the surface. We edged cautiously along the reef until we found a low-lying sand cay and dropped our heavy anchor in about four fathoms on a sandy patch.

We spent several peaceful days fishing, fossicking for shells on the small bare sand cay and snorkelling over the reef. The colour of the scene around us changed as the tide rose and fell. It was a strange and exhilarating sensation to be anchored in the middle of nowhere – completely alone except for the birds on the island.

Simon read about the plight of Captain Cook whose ship *Endeavour* had run on the reef north of Cairns. Although he knew he was sailing amongst coral islands, Cook was unaware he was behind a reef that stretched more than 2000 miles. A cautious sailor, he was proceeding slowly with all hands taking soundings, but the reef gave no warning of its presence. The *Endeavour* struck and was badly damaged.

We sailed to Green Island, about sixteen miles away. Each day about 300 tourists visited the island from Cairns so, after our few days of isolation, it was a startling contrast to find people everywhere. Both the undersea observatory and aquarium were well worth a visit.

Cairns was a fast close-hauled sail away. A buoyed channel and beacons led us into a muddy, crowded anchorage. Simon was due to return to Sydney; before he left helped me take down the masts, move the lead and ready *Iota* for shipping on a small freighter, the *Dalby*.

I had three days to wait before *Iota* was loaded and spent one of them on a Bush Pilot Cessna delivering mail to inland cattle stations, going up and down on short bumpy airstrips. I gained an impression of a brown countryside, scattered with eucalyptus.

I took *Iota* alongside the *Dalby* early in the morning; the sailors invited me to breakfast and then to morning coffee. The chief wharfie came onboard to look at our lifting gear and then it was time for beer with the captain and first mate, shortly followed by lunch. The first mate and the chief wharfie each had his own idea about loading the yacht so we ended up with an unsatisfactory compromise. The pulpit was nearly pulled off and the rudder only just missed a similar fate.

It was difficult to complain for the captain invited me to dinner and delayed the ship's sailing so I could indulge in the crayfish mayonnaise, grilled pork chops and strawberry flan. I flew back to Sydney next day.

~

Maria decided to take her skiing holiday at the same time as I was away from work – a couple of weeks with us both away should not have been a problem – but she had broken her leg and was off work for much longer than planned. They tried to find me to ask me to go back to Sydney, but I could not be contacted. It was an advantage not having a radio while travelling, but there was now a daunting backlog of tasks needing urgent attention.

The changes we made to *Iota* before her cruise through the Barrier Reef proved to be a big improvement – except for the hot and noisy engine. It was certainly better than an outboard, but 8 HP were not enough – Iota was underpowered.

We now had eight months before our next adventure back to the South Seas. At times it seemed as if it would never come, but often we wondered if we would ever be ready in time. The *Tahitien* and *Caledonien* regularly called in to Martinique on their way back to France so Simon came up with the idea of shipping *Iota* on to the West Indies instead of returning her to Sydney after the cruise. It was the first of many times when Simon's proposals provoked in me the thought, 'I couldn't do that!' only to find myself doing it.

We read every book we could find on the Marquesas and Tuamotus, particularly those relating the experiences of yachts cruising in the area. Few had fully explored the islands, partly because they had travelled a long way across the Pacific and were anxious to get to Tahiti and 'civilisation', but also because the anchorages in the Marquesas are relatively unprotected – they lack the fringe of coral that makes the

Society Islands seem more welcoming. The low atolls of the Tuamotus present difficult navigational problems.

Simon spent time in the Mitchell Library reading up on the history of the Pacific. He wanted to learn Tahitian so put an advertisement in the paper asking for somebody who spoke the language to contact us. Celestin Teretino Takoragi (call me Les) answered it, principally because he was curious to know who was interested in his native language. He worked as a washer-up at the Hotel Australia and was able to come sailing with us on his days off. Les was from the Raroira

Simon conning from the ratlines

in the Tuamotus and did not speak the same dialect as the Tahitians, but he could communicate with them as he had attended school in Tahiti – where he was taught in French! We learned to sing and dance like Tahitians, but did not learn a great deal of the language for he was a hopeless teacher. We picked up useful phrases, but were lost when it came to personal pronouns for there seemed to be a different word for each person in a family. We asked him to record a message in his own language for his relatives in case we came across them.

The time came closer to our departure. Provisions were on board, the compass had been swung, the charts bought and stowed away in the order in which we would need them; we were much better prepared than we had been when we set off for our first cruise in French Polynesia three years before. I fixed the date for quitting my job. Maria insisted on giving me a send-off party and persuaded me to wear my grass skirt for the occasion.

It was going to be the adventure of a lifetime and I couldn't wait for it to begin.

Lowering the masts to ready Iota *for her next adventure*

the majestic marquesas and the dangerous archipelago

1965

I left Sydney at the beginning of April, loading *Iota* onto the foredeck of the *Caledonien* early one morning. She had the company of four young bulls on their way to Noumea. Quite a crowd gathered to see me off; they boarded Max's 50-foot motor cruiser and escorted the *Caledonien* to the Heads.

At dinner I met my table companions. John, a young sheep farmer from New South Wales, was heading for Europe to broaden his horizons. Marshall and Daphne, from Melbourne, were setting off on the holiday of a lifetime equipped with a tent and camping gear to spend two or three months 'going native' in the Society Islands. They were celebrating Marshall's return to good health after being in hospital suffering from a gastric ulcer.

Our first stop was at Noumea in New Caledonia and from there we went on to Port Vila in the New Hebrides. On the morning of our arrival in Vila Daphne came to the table looking worried; Marshall was haemorrhaging again. The ship's doctor recommended hospital as he was not equipped to deal with a problem of this severity. The hospital was improbably situated on an island in the middle of the harbour. John and I went with them in the boat, Marshall pale and wan on a stretcher. I thought they might need somebody to translate and I was right because the doctor at the hospital could speak only French. Marshall needed a blood transfusion. He was of a negative blood group and by coincidence both Daphne and John were negative. However the New Hebridians were all positive; more negative type blood would be needed so I went back to the ship to seek donors.

The *Caledonien* had moved to the other side of the harbour alongside a barge to load copra. I went to check *Iota* late in the afternoon and discovered, to my horror, a large hole in her hull on the chine near the bow. The ship had been tied alongside a barge that was shorter than her, and rather than take a line from the bow they had passed the mooring cable through a block on the deck near *Iota* to give a straighter pull. With the whole weight of the ship on it, the block had given way and flown with tremendous force through *Iota*'s hull, on the chine, breaking a stringer and two frames. The repair was quite beyond the ship's carpenter, but, according to the bosun, at Espirito Santo, the next port of call, there lived M. Ouseaux, an excellent boat builder.

M. Ouseaux was a wizened but lively Frenchman who had lived in the New Hebrides for many years. When he saw *Iota* he brushed a tear from his eye. Working methodically and thoroughly without haste for the two days we were in port, he was a joy to watch.

On the evening before we left *Iota* was seaworthy, although there had been no time to restore her forward cabin, which was still in a still in a chaotic state. I went with M. Ouseaux and most of the ship's officers to the local watering hole, Mau's Bar, to celebrate. It was a dimly lit dingy establishment with canned music blaring from a jukebox. The crew of an island trading boat were also in the bar, stocking up on beer before their next trip.

One of her crew joined us. His name was Henk and he was Dutch. He asked what we were celebrating. When I told him about *Iota* he told me he had just bought a yacht in Port Vila. He was going to sail her back to Europe, and was working to save enough money to refit her – she had been neglected for a while and needed work.

'What's she like?' I asked.

'She's about 50 foot, a beamy, heavy ketch, built in the West Indies,' he said. 'I bought her from an American woman. Her name is *Dida*.'

'I don't believe it!' I said. '*Dida* keeps on turning up in my life. I first saw her in Sydney – there were rumours around about a scandal on board. And I met Eddie who said he had sailed on her from Tahiti to Sydney. That was three years ago on the *Tahitien* when he was going to Noumea with Marjorie whom he had met in the Solomons. *Dida*'s first crew, Jack, introduced himself to us in Tahiti. He writes science fiction. But I never knew what really happened – tell me about it.'

'I think the rumour was true,' said Henk. 'As far as I can make out Eddie couldn't resist the challenge to seduce Ellen, and by the time they reached Sydney she'd fallen for his charms. Pretty amazing when you think of the situation on the yacht – there's not much privacy! Her husband gave up and went back to the States.'

'Eddie seems to be "un homme fatal",' I commented.

'Indeed,' Henk continued. 'Eddie and Ellen sailed *Dida* from Sydney to Port Vila where Ellen opened a bar. Eddie got tired of Ellen and working so he made an excuse to sail *Dida* to the Solomons where he met Marjorie. Their affair didn't last long. He stayed in Noumea – heaven knows what happened to Marjorie. Ellen did quite well with her bar until it came time to renew her liquor license. She had an English licence, but the English authorities were reluctant to renew it because her establishment was rumoured to be a house of ill repute. It was easier for her to get a French licence as they don't have hang-ups about these things. She sent for Eddie and demanded that he married her so she had French nationality. He did as she asked – he needed some money – and she got her licence. She made him bring *Dida* back to Vila and then sent him back to Noumea to work in the mines.'

'I'm glad to hear *Dida* is going to be looked after again – she's such a character – the embodiment of freedom, romance and adventure!'

'I wonder if I'll become as eccentric as the others who've sailed on her?' Henk was aware of her appeal. 'She seems to have attracted some oddballs – or maybe she created them.'

Bad weather between the New Hebrides and Tahiti prevented me from working on the boat and a cable from Simon saying he was sick in hospital, suffering from a haemorrhaging gastric ulcer made me think the cruise was doomed. Things happen in threes – I hoped Marshall's problems were included in these three, but maybe not. I scarcely dared to leave my cabin in case something awful happened to me too.

I went to the bridge before dawn each day for morning star sights and I learned how to manage when the sun was directly overhead at noon. My tutors, the officers of the watch, Jean-Jacques and Pierre, were generous with their time; they realised the importance of my being able to navigate accurately in the Tuamotus. Morning star sights were taken as the watch was changing and before dawn I identified the stars before finding them with the sextant. I asked to be woken, and always received a phone call, even when it was to tell me 'Il n'y a pas des étoiles ce matin, Mam'selle' – There are no stars this morning.

~

Simon was in Tahiti when we arrived, looking like death warmed up but fiercely determined to keep going. He had discharged himself from hospital against the advice of his doctors. I wondered about the advisability of going away from medical help – but I knew better than to argue with him. We pushed on to the Marquesas.

Bosco Batty presented me with a bunch of artificial flowers.

Our farewell to the *Caledonien* at Taiohae was emotional. Everybody gathered on deck to say goodbye and the bosun, Bosco Batty, a large Corsican with a strong sense of humour, presented me with a big bunch of plastic flowers.

Off-loading was hazardous as the *Caledonien* was rolling, but the capitaine was careful to lower *Iota* quickly into the water as she swung away from the ship. We unshackled the cable, started the engine and took the yacht away from the ship's side without any damage. A good omen – maybe our luck was about to change!

A few hours later we waved goodbye to the *Caledonien* as she moved off, saluting us with a mighty blast on her foghorn. We felt very much on our own as we set about slowly sorting ourselves out and acclimatising to the new surroundings. Willie la Garde, the administrator's assistant, opened his house to us and was hospitable and helpful. Chef du District Stanislaus Taupotini, an elderly Marquesan with an equally elderly horse, made slow but dignified progress to and from his work, four times a day. He provided us with two strong men help us raise our masts. When they were up we felt much more like a yacht again and ready to begin the cruise.

We were over a week in Taiohae; Simon's health visibly improved and he gained strength with each day. We took the first part of the trip

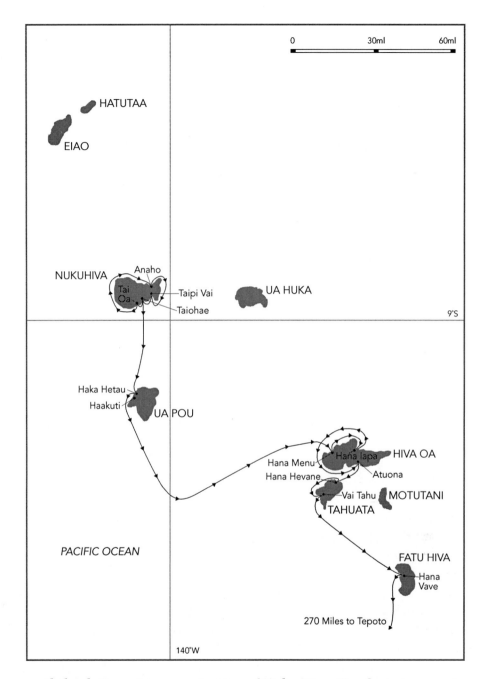

easily by doing a circumnavigation of Nuku Hiva. The first stop was in a valley called Tai Oa, only a few miles down the coast. With a narrow hidden entrance and an excellent sheltered anchorage inside, it was a stunningly attractive place – everywhere we looked a scene demanded to be photographed.

Chef du District Stanislaus Taupotini

One of Tai Oa's eight residents

Tai Oa's pretty church

Only eight people lived here whereas two centuries ago, before the days of whalers and missionaries, smallpox, measles and syphilis, the valley supported about 4000 Polynesians. The great stone foundations of their roads and buildings could still be seen in the thick undergrowth. There was a picturesque, little-used church. It was, despite its unworldly beauty, rather a sad place.

We borrowed horses and rode beside a fresh, sparkling stream up the valley to see a waterfall, reputed to be one of the highest single drops in the world. On one side towering cliffs rose to at least 300 metres. The misty waterfall appeared dramatically around a corner, cascading into thick green vegetation.

The spectacular waterfall in Tai Oa

We sailed around the awesome south coast of Nuku Hiva; the dark, silent mountains possessed an aura of violence as if an enraged sea had flung them out of the ocean.

In a tranquil bay called Anaho we anchored and met the two inhabitants – an elderly couple. Tei was crippled with elephantiasis, both his legs being enormously distended. He spent his days lying or sitting on a mat on the wooden floor of his shack, gazing nostalgically over the beautiful bay. His wife, old she was, rushed around collecting fruit for us.

We walked one day over the hill to the neighbouring prosperous village of Atiheu and were entertained to lunch by the chef du district, a knowledgeable man with a charming wife who was learning to be a schoolmistress. He was very much against the French 'bombe atomique' in the Tuamotus and did not encourage his villagers to volunteer to go away to work for the project. Because of this he had made himself unpopular with the administrator. He was a businessman, agitating for a wharf for cargo ships in Taiohae to save the cost of shipping copra to Tahiti and hence getting a better price in the Marquesas.

Anaho's well protected bay

On our way back to Taiohae we called in at the famous Taipi Vai, the valley where both Jack London and Herman Melville had lived and written with great enthusiasm about its wild beauty. Melville described mountains 'whose verdant sides, perforated with deep glens or diversified with smiling valleys, formed the loveliest view I ever beheld'.

On going ashore however, clouds of ferocious black sandflies, nonos, greeted us.

'Let's get the hell out of here!' Simon was wary of biting insects. We had seen other cruising folk covered from head to foot in running septic sores and had no desire to be in the same miserable state. We fled back to the boat.

In Taiohae *Iota* was fumigated against a coconut tree disease present in Nuku Hiva, but not in the other islands. We stocked up with fresh bread and salad and had a beer with Bob McKetterick, a

Scotsman who had arrived in the Marquesas more than 50 years ago and never left. He had opened the only bar in the Marquesas, now run by his son Maurice. It was a dingy, dirt-floored establishment. Bob was blind and muddled in his thoughts, but his yarns were fascinating and vividly told.

Anticipating having to tack into a southeast wind we had an unexpectedly easy and fast sail to Ua Pou, 40 miles to the south, in a fresh northeaster.

The Marquesas have no reef to protect the islands from seas built up over 4000 miles of the Pacific Ocean. Many of the anchorages offer minimal protection so, in some of them, we put out a stern anchor to hold the yacht's bow on to the swells. Hakehetau was a typically difficult anchorage with a challenging landing on rocks in the heavy swell.

Pretty breadfruit trees with twisted branches and large, floppy indented leaves like oversized oak leaves, shaded the village. We enquired whether it was possible for me to go over the hill to Haakuti where I had stayed for a week three years ago while travelling on the *Dwyn Wen*. Yes, they could find a horse for me. A vahiné, Veroni, accompanied me on a little mare with a young foal skipping along beside her. Veroni guided me along a steep path around the edge of the cliffs, high above the sea. I held on to the horse and left his head free, hoping he would not choose the wrong moment to stumble.

Veroni's mare had a foal.

Haakuti had changed – Tahia now had a baby and the villagers were constructing a school and a hospital just opposite her house. Several men had 'gone Mururoa' to work for the French 'bombe atomique'. The new Protestant church had been finished. The villagers greeted me like a long lost relative. Tahia cooked goat stew with rice, omelette, baked beans and pamplemousse and we talked about the *Dwyn Wen* and her well-remembered visits.

Next morning we set off for Hiva Oa, beating, well reefed down, into a strong east wind, pouring rain and a lumpy sea. Towards evening the wind swung to the southeast, the sky cleared and we made good progress until dawn. We came to a well-sheltered bay, Hana Menu, on the northeast coast of the island; it was the home of the Rohi family. Lucien Rohi was half French and half Marquesan and although he had lived in Tahiti as a boy, he had spent most of his life as a supercargo on a schooner and as a storekeeper in the Tuamotus. He inherited his land from his maternal grandmother and now worked it with his wife and son. There were six other children, all of whom were in Tahiti, either married or at school.

The Rohis' lifestyle was a lesson in self-sufficiency; they lived in the comfortable house they had built out of rosewood from the valley with walls of plaited coconut fronds; they used bamboo to pipe water to the house. The bountiful volcanic soil and balmy climate enabled them to grow an abundance of fruit and vegetables. Coconut palms and breadfruit trees were plentiful. Vanilla and coffee grew wild in the valley and the sea was full of fish. Pigs, goats and wild cattle roamed the hills above the valley. Their dog, Chocolat, was an implacable huntress whose eyes never ceased to scan the mountainside for any sign of an animal.

The valley was blessed with a spring of sparkling, clean, cold water coming out of the rocks in a series of little waterfalls through ferns and a profusion of trees and plants into a pool near the beach. Clean, white, cheerful ducks were swimming in it. We changed our muddy Taiohae water, did our laundry and bathed. What bliss!

The Rohis invited us to lunch on Sunday and afterwards entertained us with Marquesan and Tuamotian songs. They spoke fluent French and obviously enjoyed a visit from strangers from the outside world. Lucien spent several evenings on board *Iota* chatting about this and that, enthusiastic about the guesthouse he was building so they could invite their visitors to spend a night ashore. The valley was isolated as the track to the next bay was steep and difficult and their boat was seaworthy only in the best conditions.

Hana Menu was blessed with springs of pure fresh water.

We sadly said 'au revoir' to our friends and went on to Hana Iapa, ten miles further east. From the bay the village appeared deserted, but about 200 people lived there. In the middle of the village were a school, the usual two churches and a volleyball court. The Chinese/Tahitian schoolmaster, Jimi Timi Mopi, took charge of us and showed us around, giving us the impression he ran the whole village. We admired a profusion of flowers – bougainvillea, cannas, frangipani, tiare Tahiti, roses and hibiscus. Jimi Timi told us his pupils tended them after school. It was a prosperous village, well endowed with coconuts and coffee.

Two sturdy horses took us up the valley onto the plateau, through coconuts and fruit trees near the coast to more shaded vegetation where the coffee was growing. We passed bananas and wild grapes growing in the thick bush and, finally, came to more open country. The scents changed around every corner, from the sickly sweet smell of mangos to earthy aromas where the coffee grew and the strong, seductive perfume of ginger. On the plateau we could see a long way over the rolling green hills to Atuona on the other side of the island; other islands in the group were visible far away.

Jimi Timi spent a whole day organising everybody to prepare dinner for us. He detailed them to go fishing and prawning, to collect breadfruit, limes and watercress. The whole village came to the feast and joined in the singing and dancing to two ukuleles and a guitar. The Polaroid camera was an immediate success; Jimi Timi posed in various shirts and pareus in quick succession, with his radio and tape recorder.

~

While we sailing around the coast of Hiva Oa to Atuona there was an almost total eclipse of the sun. We first noticed sea birds flying back to the island, then the sky gradually became a dark blue. Shadows became intense, more prominent than the objects causing them. It was a weird experience; we could easily have believed the end of the world was nigh. We observed it through the sextant glasses; only a sliver of the sun was visible at its maximum.

Atuona, also known as Traitor's Bay, was once the administrative centre of the Marquesas, but its business was moved to Taiohae because of a better harbour. On our arrival the weather was good and we were pleased to find a smooth anchorage in reasonably shallow water quite close in. We landed on a little black beach in the corner of the bay and went into the village where the gendarme stamped our passports and took us to his house for a drink. He possessed the only vehicle in the village that worked, the other having had an unfortunate encounter with a tree. He transported fuel and stores back to the boat for us.

The artist Paul Gauguin's grave, an ugly brown rock in the Catholic cemetery, contrasted strongly with the elaborate tomb belonging to the Bishop with whom he fought so bitterly whilst he lived in Atuona. Gauguin annoyed the Bishop by painting portraits of the children in the village, giving them features strongly resembling those of the Bishop.

A schooner, the *Namoiata*, arrived while we were ashore. We met a Canadian tourist who was enjoying his trip although it was far from luxurious. His main complaint was that the toilet, a box suspended over the stern of the boat, was locked after dark.

In the afternoon it started to rain. A swell was coming into the bay and waves were breaking on the shore. The *Namoiata* was unloading cases of provisions into a whaleboat. The boat, powered by two huge men with oars and another equally large man steering with a sweep, crashed in through the surf. It was a perilous process.

When we returned to *Iota* waves were breaking on the black sand beach and the bay was stirred into froth as the swell met the current from the swollen river entering the bay. We had difficulty launching the dinghy. *Iota* was in imminent danger of being swamped so we moved her away from the shore. Being unable to retrieve her stern anchor we cast it off, buoying it so that we could find it when the conditions improved. We spent an extremely uncomfortable night tossing and rolling wildly as big waves bounced off rocks on one side of the bay and reflected off the other. We learned why the administrative centre of the Marquesas had been moved to Taiohae.

In the morning Simon went off in the dinghy to try to retrieve the stern anchor. I watched with apprehension. After an hour-long battle he heroically managed to recover it without capsizing. We had no choice but to leave the bay and try our luck at the neighbouring island of Tahuata.

Unloading cases of provisions from the Namoiata *was a perilous process.*

A small, shallow bay called Hana Hevane had been recommended to us. Unusually for the Marquesas it had a reef across its entrance with a narrow pass through it. When we arrived the swells had abated and the sun came out so it was easy to see the way in and wriggle around the rocks. *Iota* had an annoying leak so we careened her at low tide on soft sand and recaulked a seam near the damage she had suffered on the *Caledonien*.

For the next two days it poured with rain; waterfalls appeared in the hills and the path to the village became a raging torrent. Water collected in a large pool under the coconut trees. Suddenly the bank

We careened Iota *in Hana Hevane to fix a leak.*

gave way and muddy water spilled into the bay with a roar, threatening to build an island underneath *Iota*. When we left on the high tide the water was still muddy and it was impossible to see the rocks. We held our breaths and crossed our fingers – and made it safely.

It was a close-hauled sail to Fatu Hiva 50 miles away and we arrived in the afternoon at Hana Vave. The bay had a steeply sloping bottom – three to 30 fathoms in just a few metres – the holding was poor and it had a reputation for the strong 'bullets' coming down from the mountains. We anchored close in, laying out both our anchors.

Hana Vave was also called the Baie des Vierges because of a pinnacle of rock resembling the Virgin. Her moods changed; in the late afternoon she took on the threatening appearance of a clenched fist. The gorge was fantastic, with a narrow entrance between sheer rocks leading into a deep valley. At the end of this valley rose the vertical walls of high gloomy mountains. It was almost unreal, like a film set, elaborate and overpowering. Hana Vave was a prosperous village whose residents were industriously gathering coffee beans. The new season's price had just been announced; it was exceptionally high.

Hana Vave was also called the Baie des Vierges because of a pinnacle of rock resembling the Virgin.

In the evening we noticed the swells were getting larger and breaking in the corner just beyond *Iota*. The chef du district came to the beach and yelled at us, 'Go! Go! Go!' We hastily started the engine, pulled up our two anchors and retreated out to sea amid a great confusion of anchor gear, dinghy and half-cooked dinner. We pulled up the mainsail, hove-to and sorted ourselves out. We did not know whether the swells heralded bad weather or were just a sign of the changing wind so we kept watch all night and, when all was well in the morning, motored back and anchored way out in the middle of the bay – it seemed almost like the middle of the sea – in 20 fathoms.

Several people had urged us to visit an elderly Swiss gentleman who lived in the next valley to the south, Omoa. M. Grelet had known Paul Gauguin when he lived in the Marquesas. Omoa was a larger village than Hana Vave, but its anchorage was even worse. I had read in a book about the path between the two villages – 'flat and easy, taking about an hour and a half'. I hired a horse and set off early in the morning, leaving Simon on board. Horse had an uncomfortable wooden saddle and his bridle was a rope wrapped a couple of times around his nose.

The path followed the river between sheer rocks. The Virgin stared down at me with her grotesquely bulbous eye. The valley opened up and I rode through fertile country with an abundance of fruit trees and coffee bushes to the river. Horse took fright in the middle of the crossing when the water was up to his belly. There were men building a bridge and one of them pulled us out.

The track wound around the bottom of the valley, crossed the stream again and suddenly ended in a glade with two horses in it. They neighed in greeting – Horse had taken me to meet his friends. I found another track, but, about a kilometre further on, it ended abruptly in a dry river, full of big, impassable boulders. I retraced my steps and took what I thought to be yet another track only to arrive back in the glade with the neighing equine friends. Horse had fooled me again. This time a small boy appeared. Communication was difficult, but when I said, 'Omoa!' he pointed upwards. I had to go up the mountain along a path leading off further back. I had just located it when I discovered I had lost my camera. I retraced my steps and found it lying among the boulders.

The path zigzagged steeply upwards – nothing like the 'flat and easy' journey I had been led to believe – and a magnificent view opened up. On one side, so close I felt as if I could touch it, was the sheer cliff of the other side of the valley and, almost directly under my feet, was the village nestled among the coconut trees, the beach and *Iota* lying to her anchor way out in the bay.

The track along the ridge at the top of the mountain seemed endless, but eventually it abruptly divided. It was a toss-up; I chose the right-hand one and luckily, after another half-hour, Omoa appeared down in the valley below. The track descended rapidly, crossed the river and led to the middle of the village with its large church, school and football pitch. It was easy to find M. Grelet and, over a welcome bottle of icy Hinano beer, he told me about his life in the Marquesas.

M. Grelet had arrived in Omoa in 1900 with his brother. After a few years in the valley he had returned to Switzerland, while his brother had stayed and married a Marquesan; their son became chef du village. Many years later, after the death of his wife, M. Grelet had returned and joined his nephew, who later became ill and died in France. M. Grelet was a frail-looking man and spoke with a soft voice.

He had become well acquainted with Paul Gauguin before his death in 1903 and told me of the animosity between the artist and the French administration and the church. Although in bad health, Gauguin was a prolific worker and his years in Atuona were the most productive and

'Horse' and I crossed the plateau from Hana Vava to Omoa.

inspired time of his life. M. Grelet also spoke of Thor Hyerdahl of *Kon Tiki* fame, who had lived in Omoa with his new bride in 1937, seeking 'to return to nature' and finding it not as easy as he had imagined.

'He discovered that going back to nature wasn't the same as living in Paradise,' M. Grelet explained. 'They had only acknowledged the disadvantages of civilisation and ignored the benefits.'

At about three o'clock I started back at top speed to try to reach Hana Vave before dark. The journey started badly; when we plunged into the river at Omoa the tide had risen and Horse had to swim. We nearly capsized, but scrambled out the other side and shot off up the hill. I led him through the more difficult rocky places. We made rapid galloping progress along the plateau. Horse gained extra energy as he thought wild cattle were chasing him. We arrived at the descent into Hana Vave with about half an hour's daylight. It started to rain.

Horse stumbled and his girth broke. I landed on the edge of the track under the saddle and only just managed to stop rolling down the cliff into the valley below. I picked myself up and caught Horse who was staring at me with a rude, incredulous look on his face. It was safer to walk down the steep, slippery track. At the bottom it was quite dark and I was tired. The villagers were out looking for me and Simon was too – he had seen me winding my way down the ridge and had come ashore to meet me.

I woke stiff and sore in the morning so we spent a quiet day preparing for the next leg of our journey – 280 miles to Tepoto, one of the Disappointment Islands. Although in the Tuamotus, Tepoto is not an atoll; it is slightly higher than the other islands and does not have a lagoon. We would not be able to stop, but it would be an excellent navigation check two thirds of the way to our goal, Raroira.

On the morning of our departure dark clouds menaced Fatu Hiva. Our friends, with a parting gift of oranges, came out in their canoes to help us retrieve our heavy anchor and chain. We set off, close hauled, in a brisk ESE wind with frequent rainsqualls forcing us to reduce sail. The seas were not particularly big, but were moving fast and breaking. *Iota* was stiff and handled the conditions well; we were gaining confidence in her and in each other. Occasionally she fell off a wave, but always picked herself up again and charged onwards. Simon wrote:

> *I was woken up during the night by a loud crash. We seemed to be thumping through the seas at a tremendous pace. I looked through the open hatch at Jenifer dimly moonlit in the cockpit. She had the fall of the leeboard tackle hitched around the tiller to take the weight off the steering. I called to her but in all the din of the sea, she could not hear. Her hair was blowing in the wind and, from time to time, spray carried across the cockpit. She gazed for a moment at the compass, then up at the weather to windward and around the horizon. All seemed to be well. I looked at my watch, relaxed and went to sleep again.*

~

We made good progress, 112 miles the first day and 140 miles the next. I had just taken the morning sight on the second morning when Simon sighted Tepoto on the horizon dead ahead, confirming the results of my navigation. As we came closer we saw a trading schooner lying off. We recognised her; we had met *Namoiata* in Atuona. She was swarming with people, pigs and hens, all adding to the strong smell of copra. Our Canadian friend waved to us. We watched a boat going ashore to pick up yet more copra stacked on the beach in sacks. Close by two humpback whales frolicked in the sea.

The Namoiata *off Tepoto, one of the Disappointment Islands*

After an hour we set sail again with renewed confidence in our ability to find our way. Navigation in the Tuamotus, called variously the Dangerous Archipelago or the Graveyard of the Pacific, is not easy because the islands are only about two metres above sea level. The currents are unpredictable and often strong. The *Pilot Book* repeatedly warned of the currents, known to set vessels over 30 miles off course in a night.

There are 78 Tuamotu atolls in an area of 900 by 300 miles in the middle of the South Pacific. They typically consist of a circular ring of coral around a lagoon. The leeward (north and west) sides of the atolls have long narrow islands supporting coconut trees, but the weather (south and east) sides are usually just bare reefs. Waves travelling across the Pacific without interruption smash against the reef on the windward side of the atoll and fill up the lagoon. The only way out for the water is through the pass so the current is invariably running out, at up to ten knots. It was possible to predict the strength of the current according to the rising and setting of the moon, but not always possible to arrive at the pass at the optimum time.

Just before dark on the second day out from Tepoto Simon shouted, 'There's a collection of matchsticks on the horizon.'

He had seen the coconut trees on Takume, a coral atoll that, unlike

Raroira, had no pass into its lagoon. It was just where my sights and estimated position said it should be, about eight miles away. Raroira was ten miles further, and we had no hope of reaching it in time to enter the pass before dark. We sailed clear, hove-to and waited for dawn.

My morning sun sight put us about nine miles west off the northern tip of Takume. We sighted the island again and piled on sail to cross the turbulent channel between the islands. *Iota* sailed along the coast of Raroira for another ten miles before we easily spotted the pass; the current was rushing out in a tremendous watery commotion. We noticed a little less turbulence along the northern side of the pass so added the engine to our sail power and roared into the fray. Twenty minutes and 50 metres later we were inside the lagoon and confronted with patches of coral. We felt our way, Simon guiding me from up the mast, until we came to the village.

A pirogue came out to meet us; in it were a Polynesian boy and a French soldier. They took our lines and anchors and attached us securely to coral patches. At one stage the soldier was left alone in the pirogue and promptly overturned it. This caused tremendous mirth among the rest of the population who had come out to greet us. It had to be repeated. We were bustled ashore to meet the 50 residents and shook hands with them all. With the chef du village on one side and the mutoi – the policeman – on the other, we walked in procession around the village, admiring the fine coral stone church and school that had been built towards the end of the previous century. The school had not been used for many years and nobody could remember how long the rectory beside the church had lain empty. The mutoi told us the island had never recovered from the 1906 hurricane.

The elderly chef du village did not speak French and seemed weighed down with dignity. He lacked the ability to see the funny side of life, second nature to other Polynesians. When he came on board we asked him to sign the visitors' book and Simon noticed his name was Takoragi. We played him Les's taped message. He was astonished and overwhelmed; his face crumpled into a smile and tears appeared in his eyes.

The bombe atomique in Mururoa had had an impact on the village. Several houses were empty and the men who remained were busy helping the French army build a meteorological station on the island as part of the project. During the day the village appeared deserted, but in the evening we were invited ashore to Takoragi's house or welcomed guests on board with their guitars and ukuleles. We taped some of

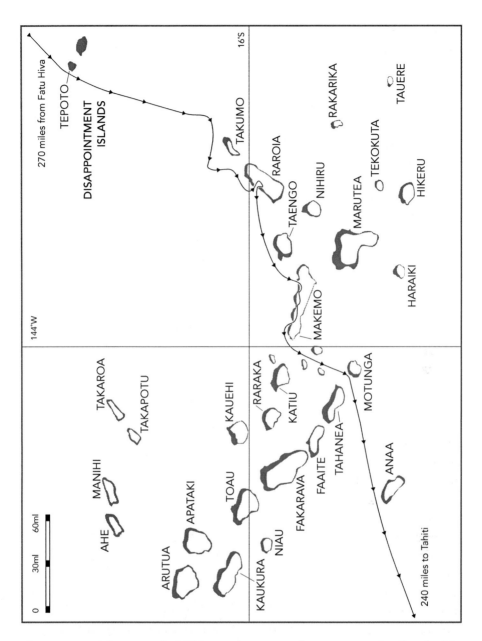

the songs and persuaded Takoragi to record a message for Les in his own language.

Thor Heyerdahl's raft *Kon Tiki* came ashore at Raroira. The villagers wanted to tell us about it. One of the crew, Bengt Danielsson, had returned several times and written a book about the 'Happy Island'. They called him 'the man with the upside down head' because he was bald but had an improbable bushy beard.

Simon observed brightly coloured fish gathering around the orange skins and pips he threw overboard when he squeezed our morning orange juice. He devised a way of threading a slice of orange onto a fishhook so the fish could not pull off the flesh without being caught. He was so proud of himself and delighted he could catch a fish as and when we wanted one. He even gave a demonstration to the villagers.

We gathered in our lines on the third day and set off for Makemo, laden with drinking nuts, specially baked bread and interesting shells. As we came to the pass we saw breakers right across so we circled around, watching. The current was going out but meeting waves pushed up by a northerly wind. On one side the confusion in the water was less so we secured everything on deck and went for it.

We approached, lost courage and tried to circle, but were sucked in. The current engulfed us and swept us bodily sideways into a gigantic whirlpool. It was terrifying. Poor *Iota*; she was still sliding down a wave at the same time as her bow was struggling to climb the next one. The hostile breaking crests roared at her as they poised way above her bow on top of sheer walls of menacing water. At times she seemed to be twisting, her bow rolling one way and her stern the other. All the time her engine roared back at full throttle. Our combined strength on the tiller held her straight and gradually, after what seemed to be an eternity, we were spat out into relatively calm water, bruised but otherwise intact.

Our nerves recovered during a pleasant afternoon sail. We sailed on through the night, taking care to keep well clear of Taenga, the island to the north of Makemo. At dawn we gybed, set more sail and took a sight to confirm our dead reckoning position. Surprisingly, the position line went exactly through our estimated position, indicating an absence of current. We soon sighted Taenga from up the mast and shortly afterwards Makemo – as the matchstick collection on the horizon that was becoming so familiar.

Makemo welcomed us with a quiet ingoing current in its pass and smooth water. We went with it and anchored off the village of Puheva. A pirogue came out with two men – a round, laughing mutoi, Jean, and the more serious storekeeper, Simeon. With our shallow draught, *Iota* could go alongside the village wharf so they piloted us around the coral heads and securely moored us.

A crowd was waiting to shake our hands. It was quite a large village with about 250 adults and 400 children. All the women were clutching small babies and most were pregnant again. The remarkably large, well-made stone buildings included a copra store, post office, government

With her shallow draught, Iota could go close to the village wharf in Makemo.

offices, an old Catholic church dating back to 1880 and, most astonishing of all, a new church of incredible size and height. The villagers had started building it ten years ago and it was still not finished. The hospital was just completed and they were building a new school, large enough to accommodate children from neighbouring islands.

From *Iota* we looked down the principal street to the lighthouse, about a kilometre away – the whole width of the island – on the ocean side. All the first day a stream of visitors came bearing gifts: a live hen, a few eggs, pawpaws, delicious fresh bread, fish and shells. The eggs promised to be a real treat until we opened them – they were full of chicks. In return we gave them oranges and Polaroid photographs.

Simeon came in the evening to reorganise anchors as he thought the wind might change. He was confident and capable with *Iota*, but managed to upset the dinghy and everybody in it. This again triggered the 'banana skin' Polynesian sense of humour and, as the performance was so funny, he had to do it again. He told us he could speak English. When we asked him what he could say he replied with a volley of swear words that could only have been learned from an Australian.

'I bet this was the island where *C'est La Vie* stayed!' I said.

Hearing the words *C'est La Vie*, the storekeeper nodded vigorously and smiled.

Storekeeper Simeon and his wife

Makemo was full of characters, just as varied as the houses in which they lived. The French schoolmaster, who also looked after the hospital and radio station, was a harassed plump figure who appeared every morning to do the routine radio schedule. At 7 am precisely his loud voice and motorbike could be heard coming down the road and he disappeared into the copra shed to start the engine to generate power for his transmitter. Instead of a carburettor the motor relied on a collection of dripping bottles and was inclined to splutter and stop. When it stopped, the schoolmaster emerged from the radio station, coaxed it back into life and returned to his radio just as it stopped again. We thought it rather amusing, but he didn't.

The woman who organised the local women's association spoke excellent French. She darted busily about getting her flock to make cakes and sew – anything to raise money for the new church. She was so like her counterpart in other parts of the world it was difficult to think of her as Polynesian. I dutifully contributed.

In the evening we went to Simeon's house and watched a game of snooker played with great concentration but not much skill. After the game the players produced their guitars and ukuleles fashioned from coconut shells and sang Tuamotuan songs. We taped them and they enjoyed hearing themselves when we played it back.

Simeon told us a story about the infamous Pisco treasure stolen from a church in Peru in 1850 by four European mercenaries serving in the Peruvian army. They had loaded fourteen tons of gold and many diamonds onto a ship and, once out to sea, murdered the captain and the rest of the crew. In the Tuamotus they had off-loaded the treasure and buried it on an atoll whose name they did not know. They had drawn a map and sailed on to Australia, scuttled the ship and claimed to have been shipwrecked. It is not clear if the treasure was recovered, but Simeon believed most of it had been found except for the diamonds, which – the story has it – had been reburied on Makemo. Looking around to make sure nobody was listening, Simeon asked if we could send him a Geiger counter to help him find it. He was genuinely disappointed when we explained a Geiger counter could not detect diamonds, only metals.

Makemo atoll is about 70 km long and has two passes into the ocean, the one we entered by and the other, Tapuhiria, at the western tip. We made our way to it in easy stages through the lagoon.

The weather was perfect – sunny and calm with a zephyr of a southeaster to ruffle the surface of the lagoon. Although the conditions were ideal it required concentration to avoid hitting the patches of coral. Simon stayed in the ratlines conning while I steered. By midday the heat from the engine was becoming unbearable and the sun was too far ahead to see the reefs so we anchored off a pleasant yellow beach to swim and explore the reef. The coral here was a profusion of yellow and orange; we saw clams with vivid mantles and lovely stag coral with delicate white branches.

The Tuamotus supported coconut palms, but little else.

Onshore was a narrow belt of coconut trees then large boulders of coral rock and reef falling off into the deep blue ocean. Waves were breaking gently on the reef making a line of sparkling surf. The old copra collector's house had fallen down and the coconuts had been neglected. Each fallen nut had a small round hole where rats had gnawed through to get the meat. We stayed for two days revelling in the remoteness and loneliness of the island.

Iota needed ideal conditions for the next leg of our journey, as we had to pass through the main part of Tuamotu group – the Graveyard. We hoped to stop at Motutunga, an uninhabited atoll with two passes. We waited for a clear day and a 15-knot easterly before pulling up our anchor and allowing the current to take us out of the pass. We set the main, mizzen and big genoa and made rapid progress, sighting Hiti, Tuanake and Tepoto as we sailed past, arriving off Motutunga by noon. We identified the pass. Although the *Pilot Book* described it as deep, it was narrow and shallow – the colours of coral were clearly visible and water was running out of it with a roar.

'It's like Niagara Falls,' shouted Simon over the noise. 'We'll never make it!'

'It's like Niagara Falls!' The current in the pass at Motutunga prevented us from entering the lagoon.

We didn't. We battled with the current, but gave up after struggling for nearly an hour. We'd worked the engine harder than was good for its health – and we might need it again. We plotted a zigzag course to keep well clear of Tahanea and Anaa through the night and in the morning identified Anaa, a large atoll with no pass into its lagoon. Reflected onto the clouds that formed over the island was the green of the shallow lagoon. We saw these clouds from a considerable distance, although we did not see the atoll until we were eight miles away.

The wind was now behind us, but it dropped and became fluky. The big long swells did not trouble *Iota*, as with her boxy shape, hard chines and flat bottom, she did not roll like a deep-keeled yacht. Our progress was comfortable but slow.

While Simon and I had time to talk about our journey and what we were going to do in the future, we instead kept coming back to the eggs we were going to eat as soon as we arrived in Papeete. We had not recovered from the disappointment of finding those in Raroira were full of developing chicks.

'I'm going to have the first one scrambled with bacon,' I decided.

'I think I'll go for fried,' said Simon, 'or maybe poached. How do you say poached egg in French?'

Just as we sighted Mehetia, a high conical volcanic island to the east of Tahiti, a small French naval transport ship came into view. She altered course to come close and take photos of us. We dipped our flags.

When we made landfall on Tahiti we pressed the engine into service again – by now it was sounding as if it were on its last gasp – and powered our way around Point Venus and into the pass at Papeete, three days and four nights after leaving Motutunga. The Pilot Boat came out to meet us with Gui Gui, the immigration gendarme. As they towed us through the lagoon he spoke about the other yachts in port, then helped us drop our anchor and tie *Iota*'s stern up to the Quai Bir Hakeim. The comforting familiarity of Papetee was like coming home.

We wasted no time. At the café Vaima we ordered eggs – ridiculously expensive, but worth every centime. We both had omelettes.

la belle martinique

1965-1966

We arrived in Papeete just as Tahiti was again preparing for Le Fête. Two days of enthusiastic crowds and noise were enough for us so we sought refuge for the last few days of Simon's holiday in a peaceful, idyllic lagoon on the other side of the island. *Iota* looked tired, and rested after a job well done while we snorkelled on the reef and went for long walks. Coming down the mountain we could see her sleeping in the lagoon, cushioned by blue-green water and soothed by gently waving seaweed.

Simon returned to Sydney and reality. We had firmed up on our plans to ship *Iota* to the West Indies and I had a month to wait for the *Caledonien* to arrive. She was going to take *Iota* and me to Martinique where I would refit and await Simon's next holiday and a cruise of the Caribbean.

Life in Tahiti had not changed in the three years since I was there; days passed quickly with little accomplished, for much of the time was spent gossiping, visiting and receiving guests. Most evenings we gathered on one of the yachts to strum guitars and ukuleles and sing. Language was no barrier to communication.

I looked for, and found, members of the Tokoragi family who were in Tahiti – Les's two sisters, their husbands and his aunt and uncle. Tears came to their eyes when I played them Les's message – they were laughing and crying at the same time. I recorded a message from them to Les.

The waterfront in Papeete was busy. At the height of the season about 30 yachts of varying nationalities were tied up at the quay. They were yachts with personalities and came in all shapes, sizes and rigs, each strongly reflecting the different values, needs and characters of their owners. Trimarans were gaining in popularity; three years before they had been objects of curiosity, but now their construction and performance had improved and they were appreciated for their speed and stability.

One of the yachts invariably knew any newcomers, whose reputation preceded them; the cruising world was small and closely knit. We didn't necessarily like all of our fellow yachtsmen, but they were always interesting. Well known was Californian Ed Boden in his yacht *Kittiwake*, one of the several small Vertue class yachts chosen for single-handed sailing on long passages. They had come halfway around the world together. Ed's boat was built in England and he sailed her around the Mediterranean before crossing to the West Indies and through the Panama Canal. He was not in a hurry and took jobs as an engineer along the way to finance his journey. He was practical and had a firm principle: 'If there's anything aboard that I find I'm working for rather than it working for me – out it goes.'

From France came the 39-foot red steel boat *Joshua* sailed by the enigmatic Bernard Moitessier. Born in Vietnam, Bernard was well known in France for his books about his sailing exploits. The rumour was that he was going to return to Europe around Cape Horn.

During the month I had several neighbours. One was the well-known 72-foot racing yacht *Stormvogel*, built in South Africa for her Dutch owner. She arrived from Honolulu, and when we asked her crew what sort of journey they had experienced, the answer was 25 days, fifteen hours and 40 minutes. Her owner M. Bruynzeel made the Bruynzeel plywood of which *Iota* was constructed. He had not been on board for the trip, but was joining the crew for the voyage to Sydney for the Hobart Race. He asked me to a dinner party he was putting on for his crew. I couldn't help being surprised to find somebody in Tahiti who knew what he would be doing in 48 hours' time. One of her crew had sailed on the *Yankee* with Gordon, who had taught me to navigate, and yet another sailed on Chichester Harbour and knew my brother.

I met up with Anna, an English girl who had been a flight attendant in Australia. She had been learning Tahitian dances and become so proficient she was asked to join the troupe that danced each night at the Hotel Tahiti. She jumped at the opportunity and not only enjoyed it, but earned money too. She was a kindred spirit and accepted my invitation to stay on board *Iota* with me. We didn't spend much time together – Anna was out dancing most evenings and became a tour guide, escorting visitors to Moorea – but one evening we were together on *Iota*.

'Aren't you dancing tonight?' I asked her.

'No,' she replied, 'we're having a night off'.

'Seems like we're going to have to make our own dinner – we must be slipping – not up to our usual standard,' I said. 'Well there's a tin of spaghetti and meat balls. It's been a "last resort" for dinner for ages. I guess its time has come...'

I was just about to open it when there was a hail from the shore.

'Can we come aboard?' It was neighbours: engineer Bertrand and skipper Michel from the newly arrived French oceanographic research vessel, the *Coriolis*.

'We've brought food; and we're looking for company.'

I shouted back, 'You're very welcome!'

'Saved,' I said to Anna. 'You'll just have to wait for the spaghetti and meat balls!'

Coriolis was the creation of Jacques Ives Cousteau and named after the French mathematician who described the Coriolis force, the effect of the earth's rotation on ocean currents. A large motor yacht, she was fully equipped with sophisticated instruments. Her crew, six of them, were all oceanographers who doubled as skipper, navigators, deck hands and cook. They also had a little dog, Piccolo, on board. They became good friends and always included me if they were going snorkelling on the reef.

I had plenty of help to take down *Iota*'s masts and prepare her for shipping. The *Caledonien* came in to the wharf and soon afterwards Jean-Jacques and Pierre, my navigation instructors, came to see me. They had been quite anxious about leaving us in Taiohae and wanted to hear how we had fared. Invited for dinner I met up again with many of the other crew who had been on the journey to Nuku Hiva. Commandant Barral was still on board, but there was a new capitaine. Bosco Batty was all smiles; M. Ouseaux had given him a pet piglet in Santo.

Pierre helped me take *Iota* alongside for loading just before the *Caledonien* sailed for Panama. It was good to be back on board the familiar ship. For this trip she had her usual complement of about 50 first class and 60 tourist class passengers, but only a few steerage passengers. One of my table companions was Mademoiselle de Bressange. She was 'une dame d'un certain âge'. I gained the impression she had come on the voyage in anticipation of having an affair, but that it had not eventuated. She was doing the Marseilles to Sydney round trip so there was still time.

Most evenings one of the officers invited a few passengers – usually the same group – to 'prendre un cocktail' before dinner. Mademoiselle de Bressange was not happy when she learned the new passenger who came on board in Tahiti was included in le cocktail and she, who had been on the ship much longer, was not.

We had good weather all the way to Panama and started our nine-hour transit of the Canal just after lunch. It was fascinating to watch how big ships were handled through the locks with huge 'mules' humming loudly as they performed their task of towing the ship into the lock and holding her in the centre. This feat of engineering was opened in 1914 just a few days after the outbreak of World War I. The project was plagued by problems including diseases (particularly malaria and yellow fever) and catastrophic landslides. Over 27,000 workmen died during its construction.

At dinner Mademoiselle de Bressange was displeased. She had paid a great deal of money for her trip and expected to see the entire Canal in daylight. The locks were all well lit at night, but she could not see the scenery around the lakes. It was about 9 pm when we tied up to a wharf in Christobel and a party of us went ashore to sample the nightlife. The sleazy strip club was full of sailors of various nationalities – the audience was as interesting as the performers. As we walked back to the ship I wondered if it was wise to be wandering around in the dark even though there were at least a dozen of us. Happily we arrived back at the ship without incident.

First night in the Atlantic the pre-dinner drinks were chez le radio. I overheard an expression I had not come across before – 'con comme la lune' – and asked what if meant. Was it something to do with the moon? I gathered it was an impolite way of saying somebody was irrational – a silly bugger – and made a rude reference to the bottom of something or possibly someone! At dinner that evening Mademoiselle de Bressange continued to complain about not seeing the Canal in daylight.

'I went to the Commandant,' she said, 'and demanded to go back and do it again.'

'Really! That's ridiculous. Tu es con comme la lune.' Whoops, it slipped out.

She gasped, beat her fists on the table and stalked out of the dining room. All eyes were on her and then they switched to me. As soon as dinner was over I went up on the bridge. Jean-Jacques was on watch; he had heard there had been an incident.

'What did you say?' he asked.

'Mademoiselle de Bressange kept on about returning to the Canal so she could see it all in daylight.' I admitted what I'd told her and how she'd reacted. 'I didn't know it was that bad.'

'Mon dieu!' he exclaimed, and then he laughed. 'Bravo, Jenifere!'

A more compatible companion was Jenny, an Australian nurse who had worked for several years in New York. She also was disembarking in Martinique; we agreed it would be to our mutual advantage to keep together. We entered a dressing up competition and were given a partner, a list of objects to collect and an identity. My partner was the French Agent for Messageries Maritimes in Noumea en route to a new posting – a rather dignified man; he had to become a caveman and I, Diana, Goddess of the Chase. Jenny's partner was an elderly but spry gentleman who was to transform himself into a baby, and Jenny, his nurse. We had half an hour. I had a green tunic, laced my legs with dark marlin twine and went up to the upper deck – the dog deck. The only dog not locked in his cage was a miniature poodle so I grabbed him – he wasn't much of a hunting dog, but would have to do. He was so pleased to be the centre of attention. My partner excelled himself having unearthed a wig, a club and made a leopard skin loincloth – a yellow towel painted with black spots. We came second, and Jenny and her partner won – mainly because she made a production out of changing his nappy.

~

The *Caledonien* came into Fort-de-France early in the morning. The stevedores were waiting, came immediately aboard, picked *Iota* up and lowered her in the water over the side of the ship away from the wharf. I went down with her to put out fenders and unshackle the derrick. I heard my name called: I must go at once to clear customs and immigration. I tied *Iota* up to a ladder at the stern of the ship, climbed up and walked along the wharf to the gangway. A gendarme stopped me from going on board. Nobody was allowed on until the ship was cleared. I tried to tell him she wasn't cleared because of me. He didn't understand; he had been at the end of the gangway ever since the ship had arrived, was quite sure that nobody had disembarked and only the officials had gone on board. If I was the missing passenger, why was I on the wharf and not on the ship?

'I went over the other side with my boat,' I explained.

No doubt he thought something was wrong with my French or – more likely – me. Jenny tried to vouch for me to no avail so she went off to fetch the capitaine who managed, with difficulty, to persuade the gendarme to allow me back on board.

The customs agent, Guy, arranged to change *Iota* from a piece of cargo into a yacht. He introduced me to his brother Bertie, who used his powerboat to escort us to the Yacht Club. We left *Iota* on a mooring and sped out into the bay to say goodbye to the *Caledonien*. She bellowed her mournful siren and everybody waved. It was a sad moment.

Bertie was the proud owner of a small hotel, La Gallia, centrally located in the middle of Fort-de-France. It looked out over the green Savane, a park with a statue of Josephine, the eye-catching wife of Napoleon, who was born in Martinique.

Jenny and I shared a room on the top floor of La Gallia. Guy and Bertie were members of the yacht club and invited me to sail with them; they each had a Requin (Shark) – a fast, one design keelboat, ideal for trade wind sailing. There was a fleet of about ten of them and they were strongly competitive; we had some exciting races.

Le Yacht Club de la Martinique was much the same as any other yacht club except that rum punch accompanied the discussions after the race instead of beer. We quickly learned the difference between a 'petit punch' (neat rum) and a 'grand punch' (mixed with fruit juice), between the newer white rum and the older dark vieux rum. We listened to long arguments about the merits of the rums from the various distilleries on the island.

Reuni, the owner of a distillery, raced one of the Requins. He invited Jenny and me to see his property so Guy, Bertie and their wives drove us to the other side of the island to a dignified plantation house set in rolling green fields of sugar cane against a backdrop of mountains. It was furnished with French antiques – we could easily imagine we had moved into a past century.

We dined al fresco by the light of candles and a full moon with Reuni's mother, an elegant elderly lady, presiding. Waiters in livery served us. During dinner, we saw a moonbow, a ghostly, magic arc of white light in the sky; it heightened our perception that we were in an unreal world.

~

Iota's slipping could wait no longer; the weeks out of the water had rendered her antifouling useless and she had a growth of giant barnacles. Her hull needed work. Simon had ordered a marine petrol engine – certainly an improvement on our air-cooled diesel lawnmower engine – but it had spark plugs and my previous experience with those was unfavourable. However, with the reliable trade winds of the region it seemed unlikely we would often need to call on its services. The new toilet had already arrived from a chandler appropriately called Snugfit in Miami. Finding somebody capable of installing these items should not be too difficult. The chain plate bolts and keel bolts were on the list for checking and replacing if necessary. A new refrigerator was on its way from Japan and this was going to present a problem, not of installation, but of charging and battery capacity; worry about that later.

Up past the dry dock, past the main wharf, tucked into a dirty creek was the shipyard, Chez Grant. It catered mainly for the local trading boats, but an increasing number of charter yachts used the facilities; a few elegant hulls could be seen among their more earthy sisters on the slipway.

M. Grant was a round pink man with a retroussé nose – he was aptly named for, in French, his name sounded like 'Grunt'. His immediate response to every request was simply, 'Impossible'. Fortunately for his foreman Gabriel nothing was too much trouble; dark, wiry and with a cheerful, toothless smile, he had a rapport with the boats under his care and took pride in sorting out their problems and healing their wounds.

Iota soon established herself among the various other craft and looked comfortably at home among her companions. I started on the hull and quickly discovered that the idea of checking bolts was a good one; they all needed replacing. Only the best would do so I set about measuring and ordering monel metal at a vast price, from Snugfit. I wrote off and naively expected them to arrive on the next plane!

None of the shipping agents knew anything about the new refrigerator. Eventually it turned up, addressed in big capital letters to MS ASHFORD (my maiden name); they had been looking for a Motor Ship called Ashford.

There was a local trading boat on the slip next to *Iota* in need of time-consuming work. Her owner Geno was anxiously awaiting her return to service as he had a cargo of limes to take to Dominica; this was his living. Limes keep quite well, but not forever. His boat did not have an engine, but took advantage of the dependable trade winds that gave him a reach up the coast and across the gaps between the islands. It was a pleasant way to earn a living and he did quite well on it for he was the owner of a car, albeit not a very new one.

Eric and Susan Hiscock and their well-known *Wanderer III* made a quick appearance on the slip for a final coat of antifouling before leaving the West Indies and heading in the direction of Panama and the Pacific.

A 45-foot American yacht with a horrendous problem took their place – she had snubbed on her anchor and torn out her stem. M. Grant and Gabriel made a careful diagnosis of the gaping and expensive hole in her bow and discovered the damage was caused by poor construction, but how to tell the owners the repair would take time and be costly, especially when they didn't have a common language?

'Cherchez Mam'selle!' I was in demand as an interpreter and found myself in the middle of a protracted argument about yacht building techniques and prices. They reached an agreement mainly because my limited vocabulary of French boat building terms meant both sides had to think clearly and speak slowly so I could understand.

One morning I arrived at the yard to discover a new yacht had been hauled out. She sat up proudly in her cradle revealing the magnificent lines of her elegant hull – Hereschoff without a doubt. She was a truly beautiful craft and her presence dominated the yard. Her name was *Windward Star*; she had British registry. Her owner, a fresh-faced man in his thirties, was clucking nervously as M. Grant and Gabriel made their inspection. They all disappeared into the office to discuss their findings and I started work for the day on *Iota*'s less impressive hull.

'I wonder what she's doing here,' I mused. 'Why is her owner so worried? I wonder how long they've been together.'

It wasn't long before the familiar cry came again: 'Cherchez Mam'selle!' It was getting to be a nuisance and interrupting progress for the day.

M. Grant introduced me to M. Carter; we correctly shook hands. We discussed the work he wanted done – it was mostly routine – although, unusually, the yacht had a centreboard. It strained both my credibility and my vocabulary. M. Carter was concerned about the quality of work. He was American and seemed doubtful that anybody who couldn't speak English could possibly meet his exacting standards. What he was doing with a British yacht in a French port remained a mystery and he didn't offer to enlighten me.

~

Bertie told me all was in readiness for Mardi Gras, due to start at midday and continue until nightfall when it would abruptly stop. The festival was a mixture of Pagan and Christian – a time celebrating the end of the bad and the beginning of the new and the last opportunity for the populace to feast and celebrate before the austere time of Lent. Dressed in black and white they mourned the passing of the devil as he was paraded around the streets before being burned at sunset.

I went to the slip to find all the workers had taken a holiday. M. Carter was walking around his yacht looking disconsolate and unhappy.

'Where is everybody? Why is nobody working?' he asked.

'It's Mardi Gras,' I explained, 'and you can't possibly be in Martinique for Mardi Gras and not join in. I've a room overlooking the Savane – the best view in town. Why don't you come with me? It would be a shame to miss it.'

He took a bit of persuading, but eventually decided he could leave his precious yacht unattended for just a little while.

People were already gathering in town and we had to push through the good-natured crowd to reach La Gallia. I discovered my companion's name was Dan and his home was in California. I introduced him to Bertie who immediately prescribed 'un petit punch', to be followed by lunch of chilli crabs and a large carafe of his house wine. Dan relaxed visibly and I began to think he might discover what it was like to enjoy himself.

From the hotel we had a wonderful view over the park where the crowd was increasing. Everybody was dressed in black and white; some costumes were humorous, others were weird. In the centre of the square a funeral pyre had been built – a massive bonfire ready for the last moments of the cleansing ceremony.

A feeling of anticipation was in the air; there was a stir in the crowd and a cheer. The inspiration of the festival had arrived; the Devil, Vaval, King of the Carnival, was among us. He was a cheerful fellow, an effigy with a big smile and an even bigger red nose, and he filled the back of a truck. People linked arms and formed themselves into rows behind him, until solid black and white filled the square. The chant arising from the crowd continued for the rest of the afternoon, increasing in its urgency. It was hypnotic and could not be denied.

We joined a row of welcoming, cheerful faces. Linking arms we were swept along, pressed tightly into the crowd. We caught the mood and took up the throbbing creole chant: 'Vaval mô, Vaval mô, Vaval pa quitté nou – Carnival is dead, Carnival don't leave us'. Our senses were gradually numbed as our thoughts concentrated on the devil and the fate that was to befall him at sunset. We felt sad at his passing, but knew his demise would be the signal for our renewal.

Some costumes were humorous...

...others weird.

Vaval, King of the Carnival

The chant maintained its insistent rhythm; its primitive emotion was tense, triumphant.

As the evening sun cast its orange spell over the square the fervour mounted to an overwhelming crescendo. The time for the devil's departure was drawing ever closer. The last of the sun's rays penetrated the sky and, as darkness fell, so did the chant. An eerie silence replaced it as the devil was taken from his truck and placed on the pyre. As the flames mounted and engulfed him a wail arose from the crowd, a weird, haunting lament. There were tears in our eyes as we turned to each other, smiled and embraced.

'Now tell me your story,' I said. 'What are you doing with a British yacht in a French port?'

It was quite a simple story. The product of a well-to-do American family and a conventional education, Dan had married his childhood sweetheart and produced two children. He was an engineer and in charge of a project to build a tanker terminal off Antigua, and assemble pipelines, pumps and moorings for the ships. He had not been off American soil before and found the realisation that America was not the whole world quite puzzling. It was also liberating, exhilarating and intoxicating. He had started to question his values; and he had fallen in love, in love with a new way of life, with freedom and with a yacht. Her beautiful curves, her nobility and her promise of excitement had seduced him.

Forgetting about his job, his wife and small children, he bought the yacht and had come to Martinique to refit and make her ready for – what? He wasn't quite sure. It was a time of decision in his life; would his newfound freedom engulf him or would his conservative upbringing prevail?

'You'd better phone your wife and get her to join you,' I said. If they were going to survive together she needed to understand what had happened to him.

'She can't leave the children,' he declared.

'Yes she can. She'll find a way if she thinks it important enough,' I replied.

'She wouldn't come. She doesn't like boats.' Dan was looking for excuses. 'She wouldn't understand.'

'Don't discuss it with her,' I said, 'Just tell her to come. Maybe a cable's better – then there can't be any argument. "Need you, fly Martinique immediately" perhaps, or "Your presence desperately required" or "Get out here now!" She'll get the message.'

Two days later he greeted me at the shipyard with a smile.

'Joanie will be here next week.' He was pleased and gave me a brotherly kiss.

'Thanks,' he said.

~

Another attractive yacht came up on the slipway beside *Iota*. Her name was *Zigzag*. Attending to her needs was Percy, a tall, lanky white man with frizzy blonde hair.

'What a pretty boat,' I said. 'Where does she come from?'

Percy smiled, a big beam revealing his uneven teeth. He spoke with a West Indian lilt, 'Yes, she's luvly, in't she? She belong an American who live in Grenada. He got a café called Nutmeg – best in town. I work there when they're real busy, but mainly I look after this baby. She needs refastening so I'll be here a few weeks.'

Percy told me he was born in Jamaica and was a 'Red Leg', having had an English father and a black Jamaican mother. He was a philosopher. 'Nobody is ever happy,' he said. 'Those with brown skins want to be white, the white ones try to get brown; people with straight hair want it to be curly, and when it's curly they want it straight.'

He was garrulous and quickly made friends. He could not speak French, but enjoyed long conversations with Geno who spoke no English. Their communication didn't seem to need a common language.

The *Caledonien* came into Fort-de-France on her way back to France from Sydney, still under the command of Commandant Paul Barral. Simon had asked him to bring me a collection of useful items and he had readily agreed for he took an interest in *Iota*. He invited me on board to dine with Commandant Jean Garique of the French banana boat, *Pointe à Pitre*. Jean thought the party should continue so invited us all to dinner the following night on *his* ship.

Commandant Barral left early as the *Caledonien* was sailing; a cruise liner, the *Orcoma*, was waiting to take her place at the wharf. We watched the big ship come in behind the *Pointe à Pitre*. The pilot came on board saying the liner needed assistance; she had hit her propeller on a rock in Madeira and was going into the dry dock to change it for the spare one in the bottom of her forward hold. She had no lifting gear that could reach it so the *Pointe à Pitre*, please, should go alongside and pull it out. Jean consented and the pilot took the ship out into the harbour where he turned her around and came back to go alongside. As we approached, the pilot rang down to the engine room to go astern, but a frantic call came back to tell us the reverse gear was not working. A collision was inevitable. I stood by the rail, mesmerised, as the ships slowly came together for what seemed an eternity. There was an expensive crunch.

Jean shrugged his shoulders. 'Tant pis – it's only money, let's have another drink!'

He told us he was already in trouble. In a recent crossing of the Atlantic two expensive, high-powered racing cars were in the hold together with a large truck. In bad weather with huge seas the truck broke free and charged from side to side across the hold, swiping the cars as it went; it threatened to go through the side of the ship.

'C'était une salade des voitures!' he said.

~

The population of Martinique ranged from descendants of the original African slaves to mixed race Creoles such as Guy and Bertie, and the Becquis, the descendants of the original French settlers. I was introduced to a Becquis family who lived in a large house in Didier, an exclusive suburb in the hills above Fort-de-France. One daughter had married an American and gone to live in New York where she had two daughters. Her husband was considerably older than she was and she had difficulty adapting to life in the Big Apple. The marriage broke up and she returned to her parents in Martinique with her daughters. The older girl had sufficient French to be able to go to school, but the younger, aged about 11, could speak only English. They were looking for somebody to teach her at home, in English, and offered me the job.

I didn't really want the work but they offered me so much money that I agreed to do three afternoons a week as long as they provided transport to and from their house. Lily was a delight to teach; she was interested in her lessons and did her homework carefully. When I was shown to the schoolroom she greeted me enthusiastically. I taught all her subjects, not just the science and maths I knew, but also English, geography and history. Fortunately she had her textbooks so we followed them and learned together.

In history she was learning about early man, how he was a hunter-gatherer and lived in a cave. I told her he was smaller than we are today and that humans had evolved. She was curious about this so I expanded further and told her how horses originally had five toes; as they needed more speed to escape their predators they had run on three toes, then only one, with a huge toenail that had become a hoof. They also had evolved.

Next afternoon, instead of being shown to the schoolroom, I was ushered into the front parlour where eight senior members of the family were collected, all looking like thunderclouds. I gathered I had committed a terrible sin. The way the horse's hoof had developed had so excited Lily's imagination that she had told them all about it. They were believers in Biblical creation and were appalled to discover that Lily had not only been introduced to the concept of evolution, but that she found the idea logical and acceptable.

I was astounded to learn that people who did not accept evolution still existed; I had never met any before and thought they had been extinct for at least a century. My French was not adequate for a discussion on such a fundamental philosophy – there wasn't much point anyway. I was about to tell them what they could do with their job when I looked at Lily's face. She burst into tears and went around the room imploring them to let me stay. They had no choice but accede to her wishes, but asked me to refrain from raising the subject of evolution. It was difficult to avoid; Lily wanted to discuss why her family didn't accept it. We concentrated on English, maths and geography for another month, by which time her French had improved and she could go to school with her sister.

~

Chez Grant was not in a salubrious part of town and access to it by road was through a rough ghetto area. I didn't like walking through it by day and was particularly anxious to avoid it after dark.

One afternoon darkness crept up on me. I realised the choice was to walk through the ghetto or go by dinghy to the main wharf, scramble up a long ladder and hope the dinghy would come to no harm overnight. I was still trying to decide when Geno appeared in his rattling black car to check on his boat. He offered me a lift up town and I gladly accepted.

Geno explained he had arranged to meet a lady for a drink. He asked me to join them. I hesitated because I didn't want to be 'de trop', but it would be churlish to refuse. We stopped at a bar, Chez Henri, still in the less edifying part of town and ordered pastis from the rotund and jovial Henri. Henri's dog was equally rotund and jovial; he was also shaggy and large. Perched precariously on a tall stool by the bar, his ample bottom overlapped the seat. Henri served our drinks with a flourish and, with a similar flourish, presented one to the dog. The dog wagged his tail vigorously, wobbled and fell off the stool with a crash.

When a tall, slim Frenchwoman came to the table Geno introduced me to Emmy. Emmy had not long been in Martinique and was teaching physical education at the local high school. She was from the Pyréneés, with curly red hair and a prim, touch-me-not manner. She didn't seem to fit into Geno's world or Henri's Bar; I wondered why they were meeting.

When she heard I was staying at La Gallia Emmy's ears pricked up. She was looking for somebody to share her apartment. It was in Didier, therefore cooler, it would be cheaper than La Gallia and I could have the divan in the sitting room and come and go as I pleased. It would be good for her English and my French and my teaching job was in Didier. I listened with interest and promised to go and see.

As I climbed the bare stairs to the top floor of a block of eight units my footsteps echoed around the building. It was not well built, but it would certainly do for the next few weeks until *Iota* was back in the water. We struck a deal and I moved in the next day, pleased to have home comforts and a bit more space.

I quickly discovered I was sharing the apartment with Geno too. He came late each night, snuck into Emmy's room and left silently before dawn. They didn't realise the walls of the apartment were paper-thin or if they did didn't care – for their groans of rapture resounded through the building and continued for half the night, every night.

'What stamina!' I thought as I resolved to get *Iota* back into the water and habitable in the shortest possible time.

Geno's boat was ready first. He loaded the limes for Dominica and invited Emmy and me to partake of a pastis at Chez Henri on the eve of his departure. Jean, a chubby, smiling Chinese who tended the gardens at the airport, joined us. Emmy was 'désolé' at the thought of Geno's absence, but I was looking forward to a peaceful night.

It was not to be. Very soon I discovered I was now sharing the apartment with Jean as well as Emmy, and their ecstasy was no less disruptive to my sleep.

On the third night after Geno's departure I was taking the advantage of a lull in the lovers' activities and was sound asleep. It was well after midnight when I was awoken by a thunderous roar.

'Emmy! Emmy!' The bellow resounded in the stairwell, enough to waken the dead as well as the neighbours. 'Emmy! Emmy!'

'Oh, no,' I thought, '*Oh, no!*' Geno was back; what on earth was he doing in Martinique when he should have been in Dominica? He couldn't possibly be back – but he was – and Emmy was in bed with her Chinois and Geno knew. He must have spotted the car – or did somebody tell him?

'Emmy! Emmy! Tu es salope! Salope!' He knew anyway! The roar was almost a scream. By now he was hammering on the apartment door. He was a big man and I wondered how long the door would hold.

I pulled the bedclothes over my head, but couldn't pretend it wasn't happening. It occurred to me that one way out would be to install Jean in my bed so when Geno broke in he would think I was the object of Jean's attentions. Emmy beat me to it; I heard her shouting back through the closed door.

'Jean is sleeping with Jenifer. It has nothing to do with me. Go away! I don't want anything to do with you. You're bad for my reputation; what will the neighbours think of all this noise? And how dare you call me salope! Why aren't you in Dominica? No, I won't open the door. Allez-vous promener!'

There was a loud and angry exchange, but eventually Geno went away roaring like an angry bull, making it clear he was not convinced.

I eventually dropped off to sleep, hoping, when I woke up, I would find I had been dreaming. There was no doubt about it – Emmy's prim and proper manner hid a different reality.

There was no sign of Jean or any mention of the incident when Emmy and I met for breakfast. Maybe I had been dreaming. The thought of the Chinois hiding under the bed and the big angry Martiniquais beating on the door was suddenly funny. I could dine out for months on this story – but would anybody believe me?

~

I needed *Iota* back in the water as soon as possible. The keel bolts had still not arrived from Miami and I would have to do something positive about finding them. A phone call seemed to be the best way – after all Miami isn't far from the West Indies. The man on the other end of the line knew all about my bolts.

'We need your check because they're specially made,' he said. 'Didn't you get our letter?'

'Yes,' I replied. 'You wanted me to check if I wanted cup-headed stress bolts or hexagonal-headed threaded bolts. I answered cup-headed, please.'

'But you didn't send any money.'

'You didn't ask for any.'

'Yes, I did. I asked you for a check.'

Light was dawning. Americans don't know how to spell cheque! I hastily explained the misunderstanding and promised to cable the money right away.

The Banque National pour le Commerce et l'Industrie, the only bank in Fort-de-France, was a problem in my life. Apart from the concierge who cheerfully passed the time of day as he opened the door with a flourish and a bow, it had little to recommend it. My mail was sent there and I had an account into which Simon sent money each month. However, being 'étranger' – a foreigner – I was unable to persuade them to give me a chequebook. This meant every time I wanted money from the account I had to arrange a personal interview with M. Douage, the bank manager. We took an instant dislike to each other and he gave the impression he totally disapproved of me and of my spending any money at all.

'I have need of money, please. I wish to buy beer, croissants and paint for my boat.' I felt as if I had to account for every centime. I wondered about his reaction to cabling money to Miami.

'It is difficult. It is necessary to send the money to Paris, then to New York where it changes to another bank, then to Miami. It will take at least a week, probably longer.'

I would have to wait; there didn't seem to any way to speed things up. Five days passed and a cable came from Simon. Should he send money to Miami from Sydney? That meant going to the bank and cancelling the transfer I had already put in motion; I cabled back that all was under control.

Ten days passed – still no bolts. I rang Snugfit again. No money had arrived. Back to the bank I went. M. Douage thought it must be lost; he would send more.

'But you can't keep on sending my money into oblivion. You must find out where the first lot is.'

Grudgingly he agreed to cable Paris.

I cabled Simon, at great length, explained my predicament and asked him to send money after all. Two days later a parcel of bolts arrived at the airport.

In the meantime another complication had arisen at the bank. This month's cheque from Sydney, via London and Paris, had arrived, but the amount was identical to last month's. This was too big a coincidence for M. Douage; obviously it was a copy of last month's cheque. He would not pay it into my account until it had been verified and that would take at least a month. In the meantime I didn't have any money to pay for slipping the boat.

We had a heated exchange, which ended in a compromise. He would cable Paris rather than write. It was with real relief I closed the account before setting off on our cruise.

Eventually *Iota* had her new keel bolts, her new toilet and refrigerator, sparkling varnish, shining topsides and coat of antifouling. I anchored her among the other yachts in the harbour and moved on board. Jenny's return to Martinique coincided with the end of *Iota*'s refit and she was pleased to come and live on board and join in the social life of the cruising and charter yachts. Dan and Joan joined us in the harbour. Dan had managed to obtain the plans for his yacht, built in 1932, and was busy restoring her to the original layout.

Iota made friends with a yacht from South Africa. Her name was *Vega*, and on board were Rowena and David and their three-year-old son Richard. They were in Martinique to earn enough to buy *Vega* an engine. David worked as an engineer and Ro had a job in the local store selling duty-free perfume to tourists when the cruise ships were in harbour. They were a great source of useful information, which surprised me because their French was negligible.

One afternoon I ran into David in town. 'Come and have a drink,' he said. 'I've learned French and want to show off.'

We went into the bar in the Hotel Europe and, when the waiter came over, he held up two fingers as he carefully pronounced, 'Deux bières.'

The correct order arrived. 'See, it worked!' he boasted. 'It's all I know – it's all I need.'

David and Ro sailed *Vega* to Castries in St Lucia each month to buy provisions because they were cheaper and there was more choice. On one occasion Ro was busy selling perfume so they asked Jenny and me to go with David. We sailed through the night and anchored early in the morning off the town wharf to await clearance. A strong squall with heavy rain hit us. The holding was poor and *Vega* dragged helplessly towards the town garbage dump for she had no engine and there was insufficient room to sail out of trouble. The police rescued us just in time. They towed us to the wharf, but when I jumped ashore with our lines an immigration policeman tried to arrest me for illegal landing.

~

Jenny had a busy social life; she frequently went off on dates with the local residents and visiting sailors. Her selection of the men in her life, who were many and varied, usually left quite a lot to be desired, but she seemed to escape from her dalliances unscathed. I never worried when she arrived back on board in the small hours of the morning, or sometimes not until well into the next day.

One evening, when Jenny was taking more care than usual to

prepare to go ashore, I was concerned – we had heard rumours of riots and disturbances among the citizens of La Belle Martinique. I asked her who was causing her to take such trouble to look her best.

'He's called Raymond. He's an architect. Really nice,' Jenny replied. 'He's Martiniquais, but he speaks a bit of English.'

'Well, enjoy yourself,' I said, as she rowed ashore to the Yacht Club jetty. 'But do take care and come back early if there's any sign of trouble.'

'I won't be late anyway,' Jenny called back. 'He's nice, but not that nice.'

David came over after Jenny had gone.

'We're going over to Anse Mitan on the other side of the bay,' he said. 'I saw Bertie and he said the unrest is getting worse and it's best to move away from town. Do you want a hand to get *Iota*'s anchor up?'

'I'll have to wait for Jenny. I can't just sail away and abandon her. Surely it won't be that bad.'

The three charter yachts had already left and, as *Vega* sailed away into the dusk, the slight breeze scarcely filling her sails, I felt a sense of unease.

Just after midnight distant bangs woke me. Heavens – gunfire! I had heard it in films, but, unbelievably, this was the real thing. As I watched from the deck, a glow appeared in the sky and sirens started to wail. There was no sign of Jenny.

The gunfire became louder, the glow from the fires spread and buildings closer to town started to burn. I could see people, running and waving, silhouetted against the flames. It was time to go. Where was Jenny? The dinghy was ashore too.

I bent on a headsail, started the engine and went forward to retrieve the anchor. It was not an easy task on my own, but there wasn't any choice. As I shortened up on the chain I resolved that Simon was going to break tradition and buy me a present – an anchor winch. The wind came up and I sweated in vain to break the anchor out, urged on by the ever-closer gunfire.

As I went back to the cockpit to try to motor the anchor free a dinghy pulled out from the jetty. At last, here was Jenny, rowing as if her life depended on it. Maybe it did.

'Thank heavens you're still here!' she cried. 'That was frightening. Thanks for waiting.'

'Let's get going. You can tell me about it when we get moving.'

Together we hoisted the anchor aboard and stowed it. I set the main and jib and we sailed off into the night, leaving the rioters to their senseless destruction. As we went across the bay Jenny told me her story.

'We went to a restaurant near the airport,' she said. 'We were halfway through the main course when the owner warned us to go. My white skin and fair hair are a liability when the Martiniquais start rioting. He said the road back to town was blocked with fires and rioters and the only other road goes halfway round the island. I lay on the floor of the car under a rug. We were stopped and questioned three times and I held my breath. Raymond must have sounded convincing because they didn't search the car.'

'What are they rioting about?' I asked.

'It seems there's a man called Marney – a Martiniquais. He and two other men, also Martiniquais, defrauded the Government. They'd caught Marney and he'd accepted all the blame and spent two years in jail. When he came out, he'd asked the others for his share of the loot, but they'd laughed and said they'd spent it. So he shot them! Apparently he was wandering around in the ghetto area past the docks when a Martiniquais lady recognised him and told the police. Raymond couldn't explain why, but it started a race riot – black against white.'

'They must be more logical than that,' I said. 'He killed two of his own race.'

'Raymond said it always happens at this time of the year. It's the heat.' Jenny explained.

~

Fort-de-France was a popular port of call for charter yachts. *Flicka* was a converted 12-metre yacht, built to compete for the America's Cup in the 1950s. She offered exciting wet sailing and was the delight of her gregarious skipper, Jack. He loved his boat, but found a few of his guests intolerable. He told us the only way he survived one particularly obnoxious lot was to work out how much per hour, per minute, per second they were paying him for the weeklong charter.

The choice of those who preferred more stability was Mike and Annabel's *Spearhead*, a 45-foot trimaran. The couple were Australian, and Annabel's mother Dora was in Martinique visiting them. I enjoyed Dora's company; we hired a car and went exploring together. She was a widow and she told me she was going from Martinique to England; she had met an Englishman who wanted to marry her.

'I met him last year in Sydney. He lives in Cheshire in a big manor house,' she told me. 'It sounds wonderful – the kind of idyllic English country life most of us can only dream of. He seemed to be a kind and considerate man so I told him I'd go and visit for a while before I decided to say "yes".'

'Go for it,' I said. 'Why not, you've nothing to lose?'

Dora was staying with French couple Jacques and Simone who lived in an apartment not far from Emmy. Jacques was an engineer at M. Grant's shipyard, but I was warned he was accident-prone – working on a motorboat's engine he had dropped a spanner across the battery terminals causing an explosion. He was badly burned as were a Swiss cruising couple also on the boat at the time. I added the care of their cat to my daily tasks until they were out of hospital and back on board their yacht.

The officials who dealt with the yachts visiting Martinique were casual. Roget, an immigration gendarme, dropped by every week or so to find out which yachts had been visiting. He always brought a bottle of pastis to cheer our discussions on who had been coming and going, and with whom.

One frequent visitor was charter yacht *Westering*, a Tahiti ketch with owner, Mike, and his son Patrick aboard. Between charters they had little time to return to English Harbour in Antigua to pick up their next guests; they needed to sail through the night. Mike asked me to be an extra hand in return for my airfare back to Martinique. The first time I did this I had a problem with the Martinique immigration gendarme at the airport who wanted to know the whereabouts of my return ticket to Antigua. I told him that she was anchored in the harbour and that if he did not believe this he should ask Roget, who, it turned out, was his boss. This raised his curiosity – what was my relationship with Roget? And if I had a relationship with Roget I could have one with him. He said he would let me in if I would 'be his friend' and promise to ring him and make a date.

I asked Roget to give me a paper stating that I had a seagoing vessel in Fort-de-France and no need for an onward air ticket. When I flew into Martinique after my second trip to Antigua the same man was on duty. He wanted to know why I hadn't rung him. I showed him the paper signed by Roget and said if he let me in without condition I would refrain from telling Roget about his behaviour. It worked like a charm.

The charter yachts aimed to anchor together in Fort-de-France on Sundays. The bakery opposite the Cathedral made particularly delicious croissants so I rowed around the yachts first thing in the morning taking orders, then bought and delivered them. I invariably had a long, leisurely, sociable breakfast.

Simon mentioned that our friend Gordon was bringing the *New Endeavour* from the UK to Sydney for use as a sail training vessel. Built in 1919, she had been refitted and rigged as a three-masted topsail schooner. One morning a boat with an unusual silhouette appeared on the horizon heading for Fort-de-France.

I thought, 'One day a boat like that will appear and it will be *New Endeavour* with Gordon in command.'

It wasn't 'one day', but that particular day. As she came closer I could hear the resounding voice of the skipper instructing the crew – there was no doubt at all it was Gordon. The schooner stayed only for two days, but we had time for a happy reunion.

It was a particular joy when *Seawind* came into Martinique with good friends Mac and Muff. They had been nearly all the way around the world since we had met them in Tahiti and Bora Bora and were now on the last leg, heading for Panama and home to San Diego.

On their next cruise the couple were to visit the uninhabited Palmyra Island, a thousand miles from Honolulu. There they would encounter another couple, with an ill-founded yacht and no food. A heart-wrenching story would unfold – *Seawind* was too tempting – the pair murdered Mac and Muff and stole their boat. Back in Honolulu they were detained but not charged, as bodies were not to be found. Subsequently Muff's body was discovered and murder charges brought. I was to find the news of their deaths devastating – it was too awful to believe that such a delightful and competent couple who were always looking for ways to help their fellow yachtsmen should come to such a frightful end.

trade wind sailing in the lesser antilles

1966

Simon was flying to Martinique from Europe. From Madrid came a desperate cable saying the airlines were on strike, but that he would be in Martinique on Good Friday even if he had to charter a plane. The airport was deserted apart from a woman with a bright pink headscarf who was cleaning the café. She made my taxi driver and me a cup of coffee. As I drank it the jet roared in so I went to the window to watch the passengers disembark. I saw two stewards, five stewardesses – and Simon.

'Heavens!' I thought. 'He's chartered a 707! Typical!'

But no, he was the only passenger on the final leg of his journey from Puerto Rico.

'Just think of the service I could have had,' Simon said, 'but I went to sleep!'

There was an unusual southerly swell coming into Fort-de-France so we sailed across to Anse Mitan on the more sheltered side of the bay. Simon needed to find his sea legs before we set off. I was always surprised at how quickly he adapted to life aboard *Iota* – so different from going to the office each day – yet it was almost as if he had never been away. Several of the other yachts joined us and we sampled the many small restaurants offering the delicious Martinique mixture of Creole and French food. The seafood was a particular delight – rich soupe de poissons and spicy crab backs.

We made a plan for our cruise – south as far as Grenada, then retracing our steps to the north to Antigua before turning east. We were not sure how far we would go, but the Bahamas beckoned for a cruise next year so we needed to find somewhere hurricane safe and with facilities to slip the yacht. It had occurred to me that I could go back to the UK for a spell; it was eight years since I had seen my family.

When we left for St Lucia the trade winds were back to their usual regularity. We had a close reach across to Marigot Bay. From the big outer bay a narrow passage led into the inner harbour – the perfect hurricane hole. The shores of the bay were steep and wooded. Much of the land was subdivided and luxurious houses and a hotel were already in evidence. The tourists were coming!

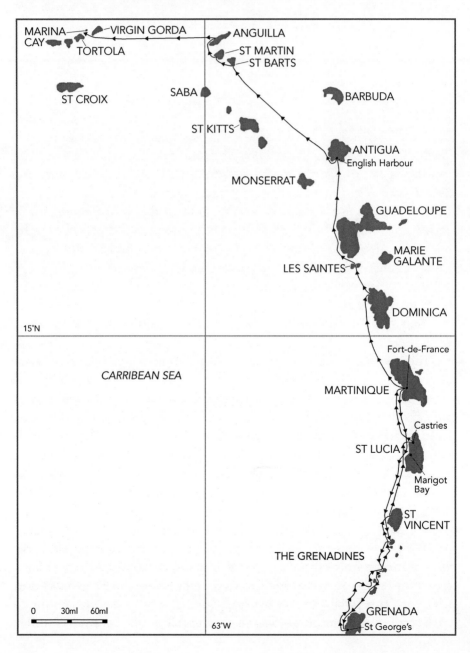

At the hotel we met up with the crews of other yachts anchored in the bay. The visitors' book asked what it was that we liked least about our yachts. Several comments were interesting, especially the one about a faultless yacht with a skipper who left much to be desired.

Iota had a glorious sail with a fresh 20-knot beam wind and a sunny day across to St Vincent until we were in the lee of the island. Then the wind came in strong gusts from varying directions. We sailed through a group of local fishing boats, all under sail, trying to harpoon dolphins; the sea was alive with them. A particularly strong gust distracted the fishermen and the dolphins escaped. The islanders also prized blackfish – toothed whales that once abounded in these waters. Although relatively small they were much bigger than the tiny boats that attacked them. Long and dangerous struggles ensued – the whales' frenzied escape efforts wrecked boats and drowned men.

A whaling boat off St Vincent

The anchorage in the bay off Kingston, the capital of St Vincent, was crowded and each time the tide changed confusion reigned. Some boats anchored fore and aft while others lay to a single anchor so they frequently swung on to each other. We went close inshore, taking advantage of *Iota*'s shallow draught, and managed to keep her out of trouble.

The Sugar Mill Inn, St Vincent

A leisurely walk along the beach took us to a picturesque village past old colonial houses in park-like grounds, full of memories of the days when slaves worked the plantations and their owners lived in luxury. The quaint Sugar Mill Inn was, as its name suggested, once a working mill. We enjoyed lunch looking out to the distant green islands of the Grenadines, set in a sparkling deep blue sea. This small group of islands stretches for about 40 miles between St Vincent and Grenada. Being comparatively low they do not block the trade winds nor gather the clouds that produce rain. Their dry, windy climate is ideal for sailing, but does not aid the farmer; fishing and boatbuilding are the main occupations of their inhabitants.

We left Kingston before the tide changed next morning as two other yachts had appeared and further entanglement seemed inevitable. Two hours of perfect sailing took us to Bequia. Its main settlement, Admiralty Bay, was full of activity. It was the centre for shipbuilding and repairs. Local boats were coming and going; shipwrights and sail makers were busy at their tasks.

Boatbuilding flourished in Admiralty Bay, Bequia.

A man walking along the street stopped to greet us. He was white with distinctive features – a sloping forehead and jutting jaw and eyebrows. The next man we passed looked like his twin; we soon realised that nearly all the population showed these characteristics. The original white settlers, as in other isolated places in the West Indies, had become inbred because they did not want to mix with black slaves. As a result later generations had seeing and hearing problems.

Not far from our anchorage was an idyllic beach. Clean, firm, white sand was well shaded by over-hanging trees and lapped by gently breaking waves. At one end there were fascinating caves to explore; at the other a stream of clear, fresh water ran into the sea. It was accessible only from the sea and we had it to ourselves. We spent a day in paradise, suspended in time.

We climbed over the hills along goat tracks to the windward side of the island and descended to a beach called Hope where a solitary boy was watching his cows. We could not induce him to speak so concluded he must have been deaf. A track through windblown scrub took us to the village of Friendship where the new hotel provided an indulgent lunch of succulent lobsters.

Our next island was Cannouan, a scrubby island with an abundance of cacti. A spired church of dark grey stone, gaunt and stark against the dry hills, was one of the oldest churches in the area – early 19th century. The headstones in the overgrown cemetery gave tantalising glimpses into the lives of the Scottish family who had lived there.

Two small boys were practicing their cricket. They told us they both were going to achieve fame and fortune playing cricket for the West Indies. We asked them their names; optimistic parents had called their eldest son Worrell and his little brother Garfield.

At Union Island the few inhabitants kept sheep and goats and struggled to grow pigeon peas and corn. Visitors came aboard, firstly a cheerful Mr Adams, who ran the guesthouse and most of everything else on the island. A young man who wished to sing to us followed him; he croaked his songs to the accompaniment of a broken three-stringed guitar and a tin of stones rattled by his grubby young brother. Another visitor was a jet-black bird called a grackle; he perched on the mizzen boom, head on one side, staring at us with his yellow beady eye and making noises similar to our previous guest.

It was only a short distance across from Union Island to Petite St Vincent, a small uninhabited island. Not long after we had anchored *Tamarin*, the small Top Hat class yacht we had met in St Lucia, joined us. On board were British couple Julian and Judy and their three-year-old son James. We compared sailing notes and heard about James' adventures and misadventures. He had wandered under a manchineel tree.

'We learned the hard way,' said Judy. 'The West Indians call it "the tree of eternal sleep" because if you go to sleep under it, you'll never wake up. The leaves provide good shade, but their sap is strongly acidic. If it touches your skin, it causes nasty weals.'

Judy pointed out the attractive trees on the shore and showed us the remains of the burns on James' leg. 'He's also been knocked over by a donkey, chased by a dog and fallen out of the dinghy. But he rarely complains.'

'Except yesterday,' said Julian, 'we were sailing along and he was playing with his toy boat down below. Suddenly he started howling – a dreadful catastrophe had befallen him! I asked him what the matter was. He sobbed, "I wanna go about". I had to laugh and that made matters worse – he was inconsolable.'

Hillsborough, on the island of Carriacou, was a port of entry for Grenada, but it was a wide-open bay. A local trading boat, rolling wildly, was its solitary occupant. We kept going, crossed the strait to Grenada and found a peaceful bay to anchor for the night. A welcome shower of rain washed our salt-encrusted decks.

St George's, the capital of Grenada, was a delightful town. It had an excellent harbour divided into three parts – for large commercial shipping, for local trading boats, and, the most picturesque, for yachts. This part included a yacht club and boat yard with slips. Fort St George, a formidable silhouette in the dusk, guarded the harbour. The hills around the town commanded spectacular views, but, frustratingly to would-be developers, the three best bits of real estate were occupied by the gaol, the lunatic asylum and the cemetery.

We hastened to the Nutmeg, the general meeting place and local café, where we found our friend Percy, crew of the sloop *Zigzag* that had been on the slip in Fort-de-France. Talkative as ever, he greeted us like long lost friends, introduced his boss, Carl, and offered to drive us around the island.

He took us along the south coast with its lovely, fjord-like inlets. It was rapidly changing, with hotels and exclusive retirement houses appearing among the lush vegetation. A wide variety of edible plants grew there: breadfruit and breadnut trees, ackee, soursops and sweetsops, calabash, all sorts of citrus, bananas, coconuts, nutmeg, cashews and cocoa. Percy knew where I could buy a West Indian cookery book so I could make local delicacies such as breadfruit chips, stuffed christopherines and blaff – fish marinated and boiled in a spicy broth.

Next day Percy's girlfriend Maree came with us, dressed in her Sunday best with a lacy stole and an abundance of bright jewellery.

Cannons at Fort St George overlook the capital of Grenada.

She was a plump, cheerful girl with a wide smile that turned into a giggle after half a glass of beer. Today's journey was to the east coast where big plantations of bananas, cocoa, coffee, nutmeg, cinnamon, cloves and tonka beans thrived in the rich soil.

As we returned to the harbour *Tamarin* was coming in. We had a happy reunion. James was still cheerful although he had tangled with a cactus while chasing a goat.

Hiring a car we went off together to Mount Horn. The road took us into the mountains through forest and past a still crater lake reflecting brilliant bushes of bougainvillea and oleander. We found an old sugar mill. Although the water wheel and grinding machinery were marked 'Glasgow 1872', they looked as though they could easily be persuaded to run again with a drop of two of oil.

Bananas had long since superseded sugar in this area. A steady stream of women and children came past carrying stalks of bananas on their heads to the packing shed. The stalks weighed from 40 to 50 kg and some carried two, walking with the graceful West Indian swing as if their load was only a feather.

James met a donkey foal and immediately they established a firm friendship. The donkey enjoyed being petted and poked and happily tolerated having his ears pulled. We had trouble separating them when it came time to leave.

The water wheel and grinding machinery were marked 'Glasgow 1872'.

James met a donkey foal.

Back in St George's the stevedores were having a party and invited us to join them. Everybody was dressed to kill. The men wore brightly coloured suits with beautifully pressed creases; they had white shirts, and ties that matched their suits. An exception was the gentleman in spotless white ducks and a red blazer; he looked extremely smart and knew it. The ladies were in lace and brocade and wore fanciful hats, feathered and flowered. The steel band struck up – about fifteen drums of various sizes played enthusiastically by boys in bright pyjama-like uniforms, who wriggled and twisted their hips. The party warmed up – it was time to do the limbo. As the bar was lowered the dancers' bodies became those of snakes twisting and wriggling closer and closer to the ground. As a last resort the ladies removed their hats.

Reluctantly we left Grenada and motored along the lee shore, close to the coast to admire the scenery. Villages clustered comfortably at the foot of steep hills descending sharply into the sea. Out of the lee the wind picked up to a brisk 20 to 25 knots and a short steep sea accompanied it. *Iota* romped through the water, but it started to rain; she was enjoying herself, but we weren't so we put into sheltered Tyrell Bay in Carriacou.

The next day brought more rain and a wind from the northeast. We had a rough beat to Bequia, but once there the sun came out. Carl had given us a chart to take to his friends who lived in a cave at the southern end of the island. We hired a jeep and drove along the rough coastal road to the narrow path that led to the Moonhole, the residence of Tom and Gladys Johnstone.

They had made their home in a majestic setting. Waves beat with a steady roar on the doorstep of a huge natural arch that spanned a platform of rock jutting out into the sea. Their furniture was minimal – rocks padded with cheerful cushions. We gained an impression of space and living with the sea; coral and shells decorated the walls. In an unexpected cave around a corner the water lapped almost to the foot of their bed – a perfect place to wake up. In spite of its simplicity there was an air of opulence and the Johnstones lived comfortably. Choosing one of many nooks in which to enjoy an evening drink was a delightful task.

Tom told us he had first become aware of Bequia when a freighter on which he was sailing put into St Vincent 30 years before. The beauty of the place remained in his memory so when it came time to retire from his business in Chicago he bought a block of land that included this promontory with its rock formation. Gladys said she thought at first they might be lonely, but no, their unique home brought them many visitors.

~

Flicka arrived. She was a great friend – her arrival in Martinique had always meant a party and a boisterous, late night. It turned out to be the last day aboard for Ron, one of her crew, and skipper Jack promised a night to remember. He called up *Spearhead*, found they were close by and free of charterers so Mike and Annabel were able to come. Also joining us was John Caldwell who, after several years chartering his well-known ketch, *Outward Bound*, bought nearby Palm Island where he was developing and subdividing. He had written several books about sailing around the world with his family – always entertaining because John adopted the principle that the truth should never be allowed to get in the way of a good story.

It was indeed a night to remember, but a rip-roaring sail across to St Vincent soon blew away a morning hangover. We should have reefed – the gusts were strong – but we held on to full sail to enjoy the speed, flying spray and frisky mood of the boat. We sailed right up to the head of Cumberland Bay before we found shelter close to the beach. We breathed again and ate a hearty lunch.

A man and two women came to the beach and planted candles in the sand in a long row with a short cross line in the middle. Another man joined them; he inspected the candles, vigorously ringing a bell at each one. To one side they marked out circles in the sand, divided each circle into segments and drew mysterious signs.

A crowd congregated, mostly women in blue and white dresses, and a few older men. They lined up along the beach and a tall man covered from head to foot in a brown cassock addressed them. They sang a hymn and intoned their prayers facing the sea. As we were directly in front of them, we had the impression that they were directing their reverent supplications to us. We went ashore for a couple of hours, climbing a path to the headland from where we could look down on the scene.

On our return the service was far from over; indeed it was just warming up. The singing and prayers had given way to a chant. The participants walked in procession around the candles, knelt before the circles and came into the water splashing and washing each other's feet. A few of the women began to cry out – long mournful wails – their hands clutched behind their heads and eyes rolling. One by one they seemed to go into a trance and they danced, rhythmically swaying their hips and shaking their arms and shoulders. As the wails of one woman began to die, another dancer would come forward and take up the chant.

At dusk they lit the candles. Gradually the activity died down; after about six hours of fervent communication with their higher being, the worshippers went home.

A crowd gathered on the beach to communicate with a higher being.

The wind stayed in the northeast, blowing strongly with rain squalls. We were reduced to reefed main and the No 2 jib shortly after leaving Cumberland Bay and battled with a 35-knot head wind and heavy rain all through the night heading for St Lucia. This was the most eastward island of the Windward group of islands. A final tack at dawn took us to the harbour of Castries. The hot showers and cold beer of the Reef Hotel were beckoning.

We were wary of the officials in St Lucia for their advice to visitors was, 'Don't be difficult because we're impossible'. Immigration came quickly out to clear us, but said Customs and Health were delayed. Simon told them that we were there to spend money and, if we were not cleared immediately, we would take our money and spend it in Martinique. The bluff worked. We lowered our yellow quarantine flag and moved over to the hotel.

The weather cleared for our crossing to Martinique. With the reef shaken out, the genoa set and the wind abaft the beam we lollopped across in long smooth seas. Suddenly, in the middle of the strait, a wave broke just ahead of us and a black shape appeared. At first I thought it was a rock, but a spurt of water came out of it with a hissing sound. I had to bear away sharply to avoid a collision with the whale, but we passed alarmingly close – I could smell its fishy breath. The giant lay on the surface for a few moments then dived off our stern, flicking up his tail, waving at us impertinently.

It took a while to catch up with the local gossip of Fort-de-France. Roget came on board, as usual with his bottle of pastis, and gave news of the other yachts. He warned us of a burglar in the anchorage; he stole only money, but his search left his victims' boats in chaos. Rowena and David had moved off their boat as their three-year-old Richard needed more room. Their flat was in the main street. Richard, who had been toilet trained from an early age, could take himself to the side of their boat and pee into the sea with no problem, but he had not yet learned to differentiate between staunchions of a boat and the rail on the veranda of their flat that overlooked the street below.

I went to the bank to see if there was any mail. The smiling doorman beamed when he saw me, greeting me like a long lost friend. His French was heavily accented so I had difficulty in understanding him.

He said that he was sure we must have had a bon voyage, or so I thought.

'Trés bon, superb, formidable,' I replied with an enthusiastic smile.

It turned out that he had said that M. Douage the Bank Manager had died of a heart attack! I felt my response was appropriate either way.

Simon wanted to see more of Martinique so we made an expedition through intensely cultivated and prosperous countryside to St Pierre and Grande Rivière. Although an open roadstead, St Pierre, on the coast directly beneath the gloomy slopes of Mt Pelée, had once been the principal town of Martinique. The volcano's eruption in 1902 destroyed the town. Pelée had threatened violence for several days, but the Governor had assured people they would come to no harm. No sooner had he retreated to Fort-de-France than the upper part of Mt. Pelée ripped open and a dense cloud shot out towards and over the town at a speed later calculated to be over 600 km per hour. The glowing hot cloud set light to everything combustible. From the population of over 30,000 there was only one survivor, a convicted murderer incarcerated in a dungeon; he was granted a reprieve. Although several ships were anchored off, only one escaped through the boiling sea, its rigging ablaze.

St Pierre had been rebuilt, but ruins survived and the museum displayed gruesome petrified human remains and heat contorted impedimenta of the day.

Grande Rivière, a picturesque fishing village on the northeast tip of Martinique, faced the wild winds and seas of the Atlantic. Whitewashed stone houses were gathered around a small black sand beach, the only landing place along the rocky coast. Fishing boats surfed in with their catch. Colourful and well cared for, their sharply pointed sterns were not ideal for their modern form of propulsion, the outboard motor. Their names were religious: *Espérence de la Vierge*, *Le Droit de Dieu* and *Voiles Apostolique*. The catch was mainly dorado, the brilliantly hued dolphin-fish that so sadly loses its glory on death. Women placed them, still dripping, on their heads and carried them away.

Fishing boats on the beach at Grande Rivière

A fine catch of dolphin fish

We left Fort-de-France at midnight and made our way out between a myriad of small fishing boats and even more fishing stakes. Dawn saw us off the northern tip of Martinique with a stiff breeze and choppy sea. We pulled down a reef and made a fast passage across the strait. A couple of squalls came and drenched us; the magnificent coastline of Dominica stood out clearly when the rain passed. Villages and rivers nestled amongst the lush vegetation of the steep green-clad mountains and valleys. We turned into Prince Rupert Bay, a wide bay offering little more shelter than a roadstead, and anchored off the town of Portsmouth. It appeared ramshackle from the offing and was even more so when we went ashore to clear.

The bay was named after Prince Rupert of the Rhine, a nephew of Charles I of England. When Oliver Cromwell took over Britain and executed the king, Rupert and his brother Maurice escaped to the Caribbean where they were privateers. They refreshed and refitted their ships in the bay.

A large tomb was dedicated to Lord Cathcart, a descendant of a long line of distinguished soldiers, who died of a 'bloody flux' on the passage out to an appointment in 1771 as commander-in-chief of the British forces in America. His tomb was resplendent in a coat of sickly bright yellow paint, applied in preparation for a recent visit from Queen Elizabeth.

The Indus River entered the sea at Portsmouth. We rowed up it in the dinghy, squeezing past two large derelict hulls at its entrance to find ourselves in a narrow, jungly stream twisting up the valley. On either side were mung trees with fantastic folded roots; vines hung from their branches. Dark and gloomy it was like a forest in a fairytale – imaginary grotesque faces squinted at us from the trees.

In Portsmouth we could hire a taxi; its driver's name was Joseph. We inquired at the local store and were told 'he's gone to come back'. This meant he was not here now but would not be long. He soon appeared to take us to explore the island.

Joseph introduced us to Mango, his pet mongoose, an attractive little animal with small rounded ears, short legs and a long tapering tail. Mango entertained us by playing with a ball and pretending to be dead. Mongooses were introduced into the Caribbean when the destructive cane rat threatened the sugarcane and a venomous viper called *fer-de-lance* threatened the slaves who harvested it. The rats climbed into the trees out of reach of the mongooses, but the snakes fared badly. The nimble mongoose avoids a snake's initial strike and dashes in to seize it by the back of the neck. However, having disposed of the snakes the mongooses turned to poultry, ground nesting birds and small mammals; they were an ecological disaster.

Much of the land was cultivated, the specialty crop being limes. The windward side of the island was more rugged and inaccessible. Here lived the last of the Caribs, about 200 of them, the only survivors of the fierce cannibal race that inhabited the islands before Europeans invaded. With pale skins, long straight black hair and high cheekbones they mostly ignored us but, when the car broke down, they gathered around, silent and curious.

Next day we had a dramatic view of Dominica as we sailed to Les Saintes. The mountain peaks were capped by dark thunderclouds and, through breaks, the sun streamed down, vividly lighting up a hill or valley. The sun reflected off the rain and there appeared a golden haze over the island touched here and there by the brilliance of a rainbow.

We wound our way into Les Saintes – French islands administered from Guadeloupe. The main village lay along the sweep of beach; the white houses with their neat red roofs sparkled. China blue and white painted boats were pulled up on the beach beside them. It was a chocolate box scene. We anchored amongst a flotilla of toy sailing boats each with a small naked boy swimming behind it.

The village was sleepy and relaxed with groups of people sitting outside their houses gossiping. They were fair-skinned and blond; each wore a straw hat with a wide brim. An affable and helpful gendarme entered us. We walked to a beach on the other side of the island accompanied by a puppy belonging to the local restaurant. His curiosity and joi de vivre were sheer delight. He found chickens, turkeys, cows, goats and sheep to chase or run away from, crabs to dig for on the beach and imaginary monsters behind the rocks to bark at. He was vastly amused when we swam in the sea and bounded in splashing us madly with his outsized front paws.

The well-preserved Fort Napoleon and its sister Fort Josephine commanded views over the village and beyond, to the channel where the battle of Les Saintes was fought between Rodney and de Grasse in 1782. Thirty-six ships of the British line fought 33 French ships in a spectacular victory for the British. The battle is famous for the tactic of 'breaking the line', in which the British ships passed though a gap in the French line, engaging them from leeward and throwing them into disorder.

Goats inhabited the fort; they chased each other around the

ramparts. Goats and sheep in the West Indies bear a strong resemblance to each other – it was, however, possible to distinguish between them, as goat tails go up and sheep tails go down.

We lunched in a tiny bar strewn with oddly assorted Victoriana: an ancient upright piano, a stuffed crocodile and boa constrictor. The room had dark flowered wallpaper and featured a painting in an elaborate gilt frame of a young man with a big moustache pushing a young lady dressed in white sprigged muslin on a swing in a sylvan glade. We conjectured about who had brought this odd assortment of objects to the West Indies – what was their history?

A six mile sail, which we dashed off in an hour with just a jib set, took us across to Guadeloupe itself. Deshayes, a tumbledown village with an outsize church and incongruous fluorescent street lights at the northern end of the island, made a good starting place for the crossing to Antigua, 47 miles reaching in open water to English Harbour.

We left as soon as we had enough light to negotiate a confusion of fish traps. It was important to arrive in daylight as English Harbour was notoriously difficult to find, its entrance hidden behind cliffs on a lee shore. Three successive huge seas hit us so we were relieved when the cliffs opened up and we could turn into sheltered water. I was certainly glad I had been there before, coming in on the charter yacht *Westering*. We anchored in a crowd of fluffy brown penguins just in front of the Admirals Inn.

Nelson's dockyard in English Harbour dates from 1725, as the base for a squadron of English ships whose main function was to patrol the West Indies and maintain British sea power. Being a hurricane-proof and well-hidden harbour it served the Admiral well. Many of the old buildings were intact and others had been carefully restored. Its romantic atmosphere was well captured in the Son et Lumière performance we viewed from a hill close to the Governor's Residence. It was a perfect, clear, starlit night, with only croaking tree frogs breaking the silence. Lights came on in the Residence and sounds of a minuet and revelry took us back to the days of Nelson. The noise of a fight from the dockyard interrupted the party. A shot rang out. Memorably, in the final scene the old buildings were floodlit as well as three large schooners lying off.

English Harbour was the centre for charter yachts. The chartering business had no rules or regulations and there was no tax to pay on the benefits. However it was not easy to become a successful charterer and the work was tiresome. Most of the guests came straight from their

New York desks; they demanded luxurious accommodation, gourmet food, unlimited drinks and a fast, comfortable, dry passage to the next port. A good reliable engine was essential for guests did not wish to spend their holiday time becalmed in the lee of an island and they had planes to catch. Guests paid well, but the season was short and the competition increasing.

Nelson's Dockyard, English Harbour, Antigua

Iota was the St Barts Yacht Club's first visitor.

St Barthelemy (St Barts) lies 70 miles downwind of Antigua. Once clear of Antigua's maze of outlying reefs we settled down to a comfortable night's sail. Our Walker log turned out to be useless as its spinner was fouled every five minutes by floating Sargassum seaweed; we had no way of telling how far we had gone. At midnight we dropped the main and just before dawn we picked up the light of the Gustavia. When it came time to take down the jib one of the hanks – at the top of course – had clipped itself on to the second forestay as well as its own. The sail defied our efforts to bring it under control. Eventually, by standing on the pulpit and prodding it with the boat hook made longer by lashing an oar to it, we subdued it. Confused seas added to our discomfort.

Gustavia had a new yacht club. We tied up to the club's jetty and the owner, Miles Reincke, his manager and his barman gave us a warm welcome. Miles said *Iota* was the first yacht to use the jetty – no doubt because the harbour was only half a fathom deep. Although it was early in the morning a policeman came out and nodded to us. This meant we were entered; there was no customs officer. Clearance was not required as the island was duty free and tax free. In 1784 the French gave the island to the Swedes in exchange for trading rights in Sweden and on condition that it remained a free port – the French smugglers, after all, had to have a base. The Swedes did not live there for long and in 1877 returned it to the French. Settlers arrived from Normandy. The women still wore starched and frilly white bonnets of old-time northern France and sat outside their houses, gossiping and making lace. The island remained a free port.

Old, thick-walled houses were built around the harbour. Shuttered to the street they opened onto secluded inner courtyards of perfect tranquility. Many were warehouses, but Miles had turned one into the yacht club, converting the upper storey into a superb flat for himself furnished with French antiques from the appropriate period. Below was a cosy bar bulging with stocks of rare and vintage wines, and rooms for guests. Miles turned dinner into an experience, dictating our choice so food and wine would enhance each other. In the evenings diverse and colourful characters patronised the club – black, white and brown, old and young, sophisticated and simple, resident and visitor, they conversed in a medley of languages; yet all were in harmony and appreciated the finer things of life.

Gustavia was still the centre of smuggling although the local inhabitants hotly disputed their part in the business. Law in the French islands prohibited the importation of non-French cattle but, being a free port, St Barts exempted itself. Cattle arrived from the English islands to be sold to a 'brother' and thus become French cattle. Usually the beasts stayed on board while the 'nationalisation' took place, but some were unloaded and fattened for a few months. A boat came in from St Nevis. She was beamy and completely open with a long boom twice the length of the boat and an equally big sail. She carried about 20 Brahman cattle and we watched while they were unloaded. With a rope around their horns and another under their belly attached to a halyard, each beast was pulled up by a team of men while others pushed from below or tugged at their tails. The animals were surprisingly docile and, in spite of their undignified landing, apparently unharmed.

'Nationalising' cattle at St Barts

St Barts, being low, is a dry island. The scenery, however, was soft and pretty with flamboyant trees in brilliant red bloom and many cedars, their flowers making a delicate white carpet. The island was unspoilt; tourism had not yet intruded into the peace of the countryside. We enjoyed our days there and could have spent longer, but the end of Simon's holiday was coming closer.

We had a lazy sail across to nearby St Martin, also known as Sint Maarten, owned half each by the French and the Dutch. The official language was (predictably?) English. Flying a Dutch courtesy flag we went into Philipsberg, the well-ordered main town of the Dutch half. It was a public holiday, but a willing taxi took us for a quick look at the main town of the French half, Marigot.

We visited Anguilla, named after an eel because of its low, long, twisting shape, anchoring amongst local boats in Road Bay. Ashore, swarms of people were reaping salt from a landlocked lagoon just behind the village. Knee deep in the lagoon and armed with shovels with holes they scooped up the salt crystals, allowed them to drain and emptied them into barges. Ashore the salt was shovelled into wooden boxes. Women and children carried the boxes on their heads to the salt heaps, while the men stood around and watched them. The heaps – sparkling white mounds around the edge of the lagoon – looked like huge snowdrifts. The salt was shovelled again, this time into barrels for weighing and loading onto a trading schooner. It was an inefficient process, but this seemed of little importance.

Salt making in Anguilla

Valley was the main town and the seat of government. At a small café we ordered drinks, which arrived with Larry, the café's owner, who joined us at the table. He had thin face with prominent bones, a milk chocolate skin and a mild manner. We were a captive audience.

He told us that Anguilla was administered from St Kitts, but that the Anguillans had been trying, unsuccessfully, to sever the union. The Prime Minister, an eccentric St Kittian, disliked Anguillans and resented spending any money on their infrastructure – as a result Anguilla lacked paved roads, industries, electricity, piped water, medical services and port facilities.

'We don't have telephones either,' Larry complained, waving his long fingers. 'A hurricane knocked over the poles so the government in St Kitts decided we no longer needed the telephone exchange and came and took it away.'

'There's only about 6000 of us, so we're too small to go it alone – we want to be a British colony, but nobody will listen to us. We're getting fed up with it.' His modest manner suddenly changed and his dark eyes glinted. 'Mark my words, there's trouble in the offing.'

A gentle overnight sail in kindly following seas took us to Virgin Gorda in the British Virgin Islands. It was a spectacular, rugged island. After clearing (for the twelfth time this cruise) we headed for the Baths at the southern end of the island. Another yacht was anchored off the beach. The possessions of her crew had been left on the sand while they explored the caves and a boy was rifling through them. When he saw us he took off, leaping from rock to rock like a mountain goat.

The Baths at Virgin Gorda

The Baths were colossal granite boulders and half-submerged rocks strewn across the beach as if a prehistoric giant child had scattered them haphazardly in play. They created grottoes, tunnels and arches. We squeezed into the caves through a narrow crack and found ourselves in an unreal world where shafts of light lit up tranquil pools full of brilliantly coloured fish. A fat grouper peered at us from between the rocks. We met up with the party from the other yacht and they rushed back to the beach to find out if they had lost anything. When we saw them again a few days later they said all was as they had left it; we must have disturbed the thief in time. They were grateful and bought us a drink.

In the evening we sailed across to Marina Cay to be greeted by Allan Batham and shown to a mooring in the safe, well-protected anchorage. We had been in contact with Allan and his wife Jean and had arranged to leave *Iota* in their care for a few months while I went back to the UK. The Bathams had sailed from the UK to the West Indies in their yacht *Aireymouse* and at Marina Cay found the island's lease was up for grabs, realised its potential and decided to stay.

They had developed the island to cater for guests accommodated in simple island-style bungalows, each with total privacy – many were Americans from New York. They also welcomed yachties and many

Marina Cay

charter yachts appreciated the opportunity to take their guests ashore for cocktails and dinner. Jean encouraged us all to become acquainted. At the pre-dinner cocktail party she expertly introduced us to each other, always leaving us with a common topic of conversation. She carefully arranged the seating at the dinner table so we had the opportunity to talk to somebody we would find interesting. Strong friendships were forged at Marina Cay and many of the guests returned, season after season. Simon had little time to enjoy the ambience; his holidays were over and work called.

As well as developing the cay as a tourist resort the Bathams were building houses on nearby Camanoe Island for sale to those who wanted to retire to paradise or, at least, visit it from time to time. There was a great deal of building material to be taken to the island. Supervising this was David, who spent most of his day in a Boston whaler with an outboard, plying between the airport on Beef Island, Marina Cay and Camanoe checking on deliveries. As he approached the jetty he would cut the engine at precisely the right moment, walk forward with the painter and step ashore. His timing was perfect.

At the slipway in Trellis Bay on Beef Island I arranged for *Iota* to be hauled out and given a coat of antifouling before I left her. David, who lived in a house just along from the slip, asked me to go to dinner with him at Marina Cay. I was staying at the resort while *Iota* was out of the water so accepted his invitation. He dressed for the occasion in smart long pants and a clean white shirt. As we approached the island's jetty he, as usual, cut the engine, picked up the painter – and stepped straight into the water. With the greatest difficulty I managed not to laugh.

'See you when you get back,' I said.

interlude in england

1966-1967

Iota secure, I flew back to Fort-de-France. In a week's time a ship I knew, the *Pointe à Pitre*, was leaving for Dieppe from where I could take a ferry across the Channel to England. Hoping her hapless commandant, Jean, would not be the victim of a third disaster, I booked a passage.

The week passed quickly. I had forgotten how many people I knew in Martinique and they all wanted to say 'hello again' and 'goodbye' over a week-long round of sailing, parties, eating and drinking. Emmy was pregnant, but did not reveal whether the father of her child was Geno or Jean. Perhaps she didn't know.

I went to the bank to check for mail. A letter from the bank itself informed me that money had been paid into my account – interesting – I no longer had an account. I went to see the new manager. The money, from Paris, was of the order Simon had sent me each month. I requested it in cash and then spent some of it cabling Simon to tell him to cancel any further transfers. He cabled back saying he had not sent any money for the last three months.

On the way down to the wharf to embark I checked again for mail at the bank. There was more money for me. I grabbed it and ran! If, one day, I were to return to the Banque National pour le Commerce et l'Industrie in Fort-de-France would there be a fortune waiting for me?

~

Life on board the *Pointe à Pitre* centred on the health of its cargo – bananas. Twice a day on the ten-day Atlantic crossing the first mate took their temperature: too high, they would ripen before we reached our destination and too low, they would spoil. Going into the hold between the crates of bananas was scary; what would happen if the crates moved with the rolling of the ship! 'Une salade de bananes' perhaps?

I had good weather and good company for the crossing and disembarked in Dieppe with a small bag of clothes – and a huge bunch of bananas. I caught a ferry across to Newhaven feeling out of place among the Continentals going on holiday in England and the returning Brits. They were all, every last one of them, wearing blue jeans.

My mother, brother Geoffrey, sister-in-law Carole and five-year-old nephew Alastair met me. In eight years so much had changed, yet so much remained the same.

My Mother made it quite clear that she was upset about my relationship with Simon – it made it difficult for her to discuss her daughter with her friends. She would like to be able to tell them I had married a successful good-looking businessman, lived in a big house and had 'nice' friends and clever children. It was to no avail; I enjoyed my life and was not about to change it so she could talk about me! Aunts and uncles were invited to renew their acquaintance with their wayward niece and tried hard not to show their disapproval. Uncle George was horrified when I served him beer from the refrigerator. Beer should be served warm; a desire for cold beer was the ultimate symptom of colonial degradation!

I visited my former school and sailing friends. Many of them, once with a wide range of interests, were now mothers with small children and totally occupied with their offspring. They reconfirmed my conviction that I did not want to be like them. The exception was my old sailing friend, Linda, who was leading a stimulating life in London; it was as if we had not been apart.

I rang Dora, with whom I had spent several enjoyable days exploring Martinique, to find out if she had decided to marry John. Yes, she had, but almost immediately she had run into dire domestic problems.

'I'm at my wits end.' She sounded desperate. 'No sooner had I moved into the house than John's son Douglas decided he wanted to get married and have the reception here. John doesn't approve of Douglas because he's a priest – John despises religious people; he thinks their religion is a crutch. And to make matters worse he's marrying a German girl! John was a prisoner of war in Germany and can't stand Germans. There was a frightful row. The cook walked out! It's a wonder I didn't too! So in a month's time I'll have a wedding, a house full of guests, a husband who will no doubt show his dislike of his son's in-laws and nobody to cook for them!'

'Dora,' I said, 'I'll come and cook for you. I'd enjoy staying in a nice house in the country and I can cook well enough.'

At the elegant manor house in Cheshire I cooked in an enormous kitchen with a central table and an Aga oven. A local woman helped me; she prepared the home-grown vegetables and did the washing-up. Although I walked many miles around the table, it was not hard work. I enjoyed long country walks with John and chatting with Dora about life in Martinique and Sydney. There was plenty of activity with people coming and going, and I stayed until the wedding was over.

~

Yachting Monthly magazine welcomed Simon's articles on our cruises, particularly because the long-time editor, Maurice Griffiths, was the designer of the Waterwitch. He was rather taken aback – the yacht he had designed for sailing on the shallow Norfolk Broads was cruising the high seas of the Pacific and Caribbean. He had not envisaged that her long straight keel and leeboards were ideal for achieving the maximum benefit from the shipper's cube. When I rang him he sounded pleased to have the opportunity to meet the 'crew' of his contributor and invited me to lunch in London.

I was intrigued to meet this leading figure in yachting circles – designer of 'different' yachts, editor and author. My first impression was of a well-trimmed beard, twinkling, penetrating eyes and old-fashioned courtesy. He greeted me correctly and took me to the chosen restaurant; it served tropical delicacies – he thought I might be missing avocados. He talked of his early sailing exploits on the east coast of England and of the small boats he owned and wrote about. His great desire was to make yachting more accessible to people 'on a small income'.

As I talked about *Iota* and her performance in conditions he had never imagined a Waterwitch would encounter, his eyes were focused far away; he was, at heart, a dreamer. Maurice was later to write in his book *Swatchways and Little Ships*:

> ...that the Waterwitch could also put up with any amount of rough weather offshore was proved over and over by some of the blue water voyages made by these yachts. Perhaps the most impressive were the cruises made by Iota, a Mark 11 version with leeboards.

Shortly after Christmas I went to the Boat Show at Earls Court. A popular social event as well as a trade display it provided an opportunity for yachties to catch up with each other and look forward to the coming sailing season.

My brother was there; I bumped into him on the second day strolling around the exhibits with yacht designer Uffa Fox and sail maker Bruce Banks, from whom I had ordered *Iota*'s new headsail. Geoffrey gave me a kiss and a hug and introduced me to his friends.

'This is my sister Jane,' he explained.

Uffa smiled as he shook hands, 'I've heard that one before.' His doubts were short-lived for Maurice Griffiths joined us and vouched for me as the crew of the Waterwitch, *Iota*.

There were several cruising yachts on display, floating on the pool – a magnet to the small and close-knit cruising community. Some of the yachties were living aboard the boat they were promoting. We all knew each other or of each other. The party was on. It was an ideal opportunity to buy the anchor winch Simon had promised me – I had plenty of advice – and I bought a radio direction finder, too.

~

Late one afternoon in London I was wandering up Shaftsbury Avenue towards Piccadilly Circus. I had an hour to spend before meeting up with Linda to see the latest musical. Shaftsbury Avenue – what a coincidence I thought. This is where Linda had come to have her fortune told, with great accuracy. The tragic accident that killed her mother, her sacrifice to look after her young brother, her return to her studies and the various men in her life – all had been revealed by the crystal ball. I looked across the road – what number had Linda said? I was sure it was number 33 – well, if so, it was that house over there.

I didn't make a decision to go up the steps; it was as if an unseen force was propelling me. As I climbed up to the door it opened.

'Come along, my dear, I've been expecting you. Why do you travel so much?' An elderly lady quizzed me over her glasses, took my arm and led me to her old-fashioned parlour. There was a clutter of knick-knacks around the room; the crystal ball was the centrepiece on the table.

'Sit yourself down,' she said. 'Yes, travel, you're always on the move. I see you driving something. It isn't a car. And I see tropical beaches, coconut palms and the sea breaking over the reef and washing onto the beach. Here you are with a man. You're dining together, on the lawn. There's a building, with Grecian pillars – elegant and imposing. And black waiters, all wearing white gloves. The moon is coming up as you sit there, a full moon, and it shines on the water between two rows of palm trees. The moon path is leading you across the water and you will follow it.'

~

The bleak January weather ensured I had no regrets about returning to the warmth of the West Indies. Six months in England was long enough!

I had bought some heavy, bulky gear for *Iota* – alkaline batteries, carpet, headsail, radio direction finder and anchor winch – so it was easier to return to the West Indies by sea. I booked a passage on a German ship, the *Hornstern*, sailing from Rotterdam to Puerto Rico. I took the overnight ferry from Tilbury to Rotterdam and dined with an army officer who owned a yacht on the Zeider Zee. He had just read one of Simon's *Yachting Monthly* articles, had been to the boat show and bought a Seafix radio direction finder like mine; with so many coincidences, we had plenty to talk about!

It was a depressing, dreary morning in Rotterdam; yellow streetlights reflected from evil-looking puddles in the gloom. The weather was bitterly cold and flurries of snow settled on the wharf and turned into slush. My taxi carried my luggage and me along the wharf to the gangway of the *Hornstern*. I noticed two large crates waiting to be loaded, both marked in big red letters 'Urgent – Handle with Care; Heavy; Sensitive Machinery'.

A steward showed me to my warm and comfortable cabin. My unpacking was interrupted by a massive bang that made the whole ship shudder. I went on deck to investigate – concerned wharfies were gathered on the after deck. One of the heavy crates of machinery had slipped out of its sling and fallen to the bottom of the empty hold; it was surprising it hadn't gone through the hull. We sailed without the 'urgent sensitive machinery'.

Navigation in the Channel depended heavily on radio beacons so I asked Kapitan if I could take my new radio direction finder to the bridge to see if it worked. He said I was welcome and he, personally, would be pleased to be my instructor. My little Seafix was not nearly as sophisticated as the RDF on the ship, but, with Kapitan's stern and expert tuition, I gained confidence I would be able to use it should the opportunity and need arise.

We had a calm, wintry trip down the Channel so there was a full complement of nine passengers for dinner on the first night. Then we ran into a gale; there was snow in the wind and the seas were rough. An unspoken competition developed between the four English and four German passengers to see who would be the last to succumb to seasickness; the Germans went down like ninepins, then the English until I was the only passenger left at the table. The steward tried to ensure that even I did not survive, by serving chocolatten soupen at breakfast after a particularly heavy night celebrating my birthday.

As we approached the volcanic islands of the Azores the crew prepared a waterproof floating mailbox. It contained cartons of cigarettes, bottles of vodka and brandy and all the postcards we had written. The local fishermen kept a watch for these mailboxes, knowing of their contents. In exchange for the gifts they put sought-after Azores stamps on the cards and posted them. We watched as the box drifted away in the distance, its flag fluttering merrily in the breeze, and hoped it would be found. We hoped in vain; our postcards never arrived.

One morning the bosun reported that we had used more water than expected. At breakfast time Kapitan requested that we not take long showers. In alarm one lady passenger asked him if we were going to run out.

'Nein,' said Kapitan. 'We vil have enough. I vil wash you.'

He meant to say 'watch'.

'What did you say?' I asked, raising my eyebrows.

'I said I vil watch you,' he replied.

'Oh, I thought you said *wash* – how disappointing.'

We suddenly found out that our humourless Kapitan was human after all – he smiled – and he grinned every time he saw me until we reached San Juan.

~

It was surprisingly easy to get from San Juan to St Thomas. The shipping agent booked me a seat on a plane and took me to the airport in his red sports car. They didn't charge me for my excess baggage.

In St Thomas it was a different story. I had difficulty finding a hotel, eventually ending up in the Grand, which was far from what its name implied, being next to a busy road and noisy. While a customs agent organised the paperwork I went looking for a boat to take my possessions and me across to Tortola and on to Marina Cay. The formalities on arrival in the British Virgins were, by contrast, minimal.

Nothing much had changed at Marina Cay – business was thriving and accommodation fully booked. Jean and Allan had decided to continue their voyage around the world that had been interrupted by the discovery of their island paradise. They were busily preparing their trustworthy yacht *Aireymouse* for the Pacific crossing.

The slip on Beef Island was available so *Iota* was hauled out. She had survived the six months on her own and needed only antifouling, her topsides painted and her brightwork varnished. I had won the battle against cockroaches – there were only corpses, thanks to large quantities of Harris's Roach Baits.

David had left and an English couple, Peter and Bobbie, now lived in the house up the hill from the slip. They were enterprising and good company. Although they had only been there for six months, Bobbie, a dress designer, had a shop in Road Town where she sold her colourful and distinctive clothes to tourists. She trained some local women to be seamstresses and her business was going from strength to strength. They owned a delightful dog called Ouaf. Peter had been reading a French version of John Lennon's *In his own write* and was amused to find 'Arfing round the bend' translated as 'Ouaffant au coin de la rue'. Ouaf often spent the day with me while Bobbie and Peter were at work. He was protective – growling and showing his teeth should anybody come near me. I felt safe in his company.

A low sand dune separated the airstrip on Beef Island from the slipway and Trellis Bay. One early morning while working on the boat I heard a small aeroplane coming in to land. There was a thud and then silence. I quickly climbed up the ratlines to look over the dune. The plane was in the middle of the runway, nose down with one wing up and the other crumpled on the ground. Peter came up quickly in his vehicle.

'Jump in,' he said, 'We'd better go and see if the pilot's okay. It's Len's lobster plane, the little amphibian. He goes out to Anegada to collect lobsters and sells them to the hotels.'

He drove quickly across the airstrip. The pilot was sitting in the open cabin door calmly pulling on his shoes and socks.

'Are you all right, Len?' we asked anxiously.

'I forgot to put my wheels down and landed on my floats,' he said ruefully. 'Yes, thanks, I'm okay.'

Inside the body of the plane live lobsters had escaped from their crates and were crawling down the cabin, an army of big, black, sinister monsters.

'You'd better get out of there,' Peter pointed at them in horror.

The pilot looked around. 'Oh my God!' he said, scrambling to his feet. 'Don't let them escape – they're worth a fortune!'

~

While *Iota* was on the slip I stayed at the recently reopened resort on a small island in the middle of Trellis Bay. It was convenient, but I soon discovered convenience was its only advantage. Fred and Isabel had taken over the lease, but they were confronted with every conceivable kind of trouble it was possible to have on a resort island in the Virgins. As soon as they had solved one problem, two or three more overtook them. Unlike Allan, his counterpart at Marina Cay, and although an erstwhile officer on the *Queen Mary*, Fred was not very practical. He had troubles with the outboard motors on which they depended to commute to the mainland, the generator had given up and, to make matters worse, the staff had left.

One evening I rowed over to the island as the sun went down. By candlelight it was difficult to see well enough to remove the paint I had splattered on me, but I realised there wasn't enough light for other people to see it either.

I went into the kitchen to offer Isabel a hand. She was grateful; as well as being cook, kitchen hand and waiter, one of her children was sick and demanding her attention.

'How many for dinner tonight,' I asked.

'Ed and Peggy are still here,' Isabel replied. 'And there's a strange young man who's sailing single-handed in a most unsuitable boat. Fred tells me there's another man coming on this evening's plane. He should be here soon. I've already fed the children so, with us, that makes seven. It's lucky there's no more because managing without the generator isn't easy. I don't know when it's going to be mended. Fred seems to have to spend so much time on the outboards!'

I had already met Ed and Peggy. A large, extroverted real estate salesman from somewhere in the middle of the United States, Ed had a loud voice and enjoyed using it to make sure we all knew he had a substantial house, a luxurious car and took expensive holidays. Peggy, who claimed to be a full-blooded American Indian, was the perfect foil. She changed her dress several times each day and ornamented herself with a variety of necklaces, bracelets and earrings.

Tony, a slim, sad-faced young man with drooping shoulders, fitted in well for he seemed to be just as incompetent as Fred. He had chartered a small yacht from a broker in Road Town. *Moonshine* looked better suited to racing around buoys in a sheltered bay than coping with trade winds in the Virgin Islands. He told us he was an experienced a sailor and owned a similar yacht back home in California, but he had sailed into Trellis Bay and promptly run aground. Deciding to take the anchor and dig it into the reef in order to pull the yacht back into deeper water, foolishly he walked across the coral without bothering to put on his shoes. Now sea urchin spines were painfully embedded in his feet.

I walked into the lounge to discover him lying, moaning on the couch while Peggy tried to dig them out with a rusty needle by the light of a candle. Ed was pouring generous drinks in order to, as he put it, 'dull the pain'.

We ate dinner by the light of a candle, Tony still moaning, Ed still pouring drinks and Peggy lamenting that there wasn't sufficient light for us to admire her evening attire. Fred despaired for he had at last managed to start one of the outboards and, in taking it for a test run around the bay, had lost the propeller – he had forgotten to tighten the nut. He had spent an unfruitful afternoon looking for it in a little rowing boat.

I felt rather than saw the appraising stare of the newly arrived guest at the other end of the table. His name was Richard and I learned he was an architect from New York with Hugh Hefner of *Playboy* fame as a client. He had Cary Grant good looks and a suave charm. Tomorrow, he told me, he was going to have dinner with the Chief Minister to open negotiations for land on which to build his client's new mansion; he begged me to join them. I had heard about the eccentric Laverty Stout and was intrigued. I spent the next evening fending off Stout's amorous advances; he took it for granted that any woman in any way associated with *Playboy* was of easy virtue.

~

With fresh antifouling and gleaming topsides *Iota* looked herself again when she went back into the water. I stayed for a few more days in Trellis Bay as it was closer to Road Town – the only place to buy stores for our next journey.

Another small yacht with two men on board came into the Bay and anchored close by. They introduced themselves as Bill and George – they were obviously brothers, fair and fortyish – so alike I thought they were twins. When they spoke they waved their long slender fingers and caught each other's gestures. They had chartered the yacht, *Pearl*, in Road Town and were disillusioned.

'Bitch of a boat – she won't sail to windward, rolls unbearably off the wind, has no headroom, is badly equipped and is insufferably uncomfortable,' said George.

'The galley has just one Primus burner that isn't gimballed and nowhere to put anything,' Bill continued her list of shortcomings. 'She isn't clean and she leaks too.'

'We like to go off for a week's sailing at this time of the year – just the two of us, away from our families – our wives get seasick – been doing it for years, but this is the first time we've come to the Virgins. It's disappointing because the wind is perfect,' George continued.

'How about going for a sail on *Iota* tomorrow,' I suggested. 'I'm looking to try out a new headsail. We could sail out to the Dog Islands and stop for a swim. They say the reef in the area is spectacular.'

They needed no persuading.

A 15-knot easterly trade wind gave us a comfortable fast reach to the spectacular Dog Islands standing out clearly in the deep blue sea. Enticing white beaches fringed the craggy green hills. We anchored off Great Dog and went snorkelling over the reef where schools of improbable fish swam in front of us, asking us to admire them. They wore every conceivable colour, boldly and successfully mixing shades that we would never dream of putting together.

Although my guests were alike in many ways, Bill was serene and sympathetic whereas George had a pragmatic, no-nonsense view of life. It was a surprise when I discovered Bill had a business manufacturing zippers (he called them closures) and George was a heart specialist.

'But don't tell anybody,' he said. 'I'm on holiday.'

There was no reason to return to Trellis Bay – nobody was expecting us.

'Let's keep going on to Virgin Gorda – looks as if there's an excellent anchorage in North Sound – the bay is surrounded by islands,' I suggested.

On the way we trolled a line with a feather lure and caught a fish we identified as bonita – dinner was assured! My guests cleaned the catch and we went ashore to light a fire on the beach and cook it – just a little butter and a squeeze of lemon – the fish so fresh it scarcely needed cooking. Salad and a bottle of wine completed a perfect evening meal.

We returned next day – another fast reach and exhilarating sailing. *Iota* behaved impeccably; my guests were impressed and lavish with their thanks.

I returned to Marina Cay and noticed a new yacht. She was a solid, beamy ketch and her hull gave the impression of strength rather than speed. Lazyjacks, ratlines and baggywrinkles cluttered her rigging. I wondered why she seemed familiar.

As I rowed up to the jetty in the dinghy a tall man stepped forward to take my painter.

'Jenifer Iota,' he said. 'You're the girl who was in Mau's Bar in Santo.'

I stepped ashore and he introduced himself. 'I'm Henk – I don't suppose you remember me. Last time we met I was on an island trading boat in Santo. I'd just found the sadly neglected *Dida* in Port Vila. I bought her and now I'm sailing her back to Holland.'

'I remember that night so well,' I said. 'Most of the officers from the Caledonien were there, and M. Ouseaux, the shipwright. And, yes, there was the crew of the island trading ship. You've come a long way since then – and so have I.'

'You're right,' he said. 'Let's go up to the bar and catch up.'

Henk and his girlfriend Rienna had sailed *Dida* to the east across the Pacific, no mean feat for a yacht not designed for long passages to windward. They had headed north looking for a favourable wind and sailed down the west coast of the States from Oregon and through the Panama Canal.

'We'll stay a few more months in the West Indies and then head home to Holland.'

Together we spent an entertaining evening revisiting the improbable stories and the eccentric characters in *Dida*'s history.

the bahamas – iota in her element

1967

I took the short flight from Tortola to St Thomas to meet Simon when he arrived from Europe. It was too late on the Saturday afternoon to return so we were faced with paying a hefty fee to Customs and Immigration for clearing us on a Sunday. The wind was blowing from the north, quite strongly with rain squalls – a typical 'norther' – and it made sense to stay for another day in Charlotte Amalie. By Monday the weather had cleared and the trade winds were back so we took a boat for our return to Tortola.

A comfortable hotel overlooking the busy harbour was our base. In the evenings a steel band entertained us. It was called Smarty Pans – they used traditional gin bottles and spoons to hit their pans, made from fuel drums – and played a variety of music from traditional steel band tunes to calypso and samba. It was an intoxicating melodious sound, numbing our senses with its insistent rhythm and toe tapping exuberance.

We spent a couple of days at Marina Cay and Trellis Bay, long enough for Simon to orientate himself and for us to say goodbye to our friends. Peter Island was our first anchorage, off a picturesque beach, and then we sailed to Crux Bay in St John. We had been warned that clearing through Customs and Immigration in the American Virgin Islands could be painful, especially for foreign yachts, but it was easier to clear in St John than in St Thomas. All the same they demanded passenger and crew lists, cargo manifests, deratisation certificate (I wouldn't have been aboard if we were sharing our yacht with rats) and a bill of health. It took time and patience, but we ended up with an impressive Certificate of Clearance.

We rushed to Culebra, an island just off the coast of Puerto Rico, trying to arrive before midday in order to enter. We succeeded, but the customs officer said he could not enter a foreign yacht.

'If I tell you my pay is counted according to the number of clearances I issue, then you certainly will understand how unhappy I am not to be able to enter you.'

Then he saw the barracuda we had caught along the way.

'It's too big – it's not safe to eat,' he said. 'You'll be sick if you eat one as large as that. You'll become violently ill and come out in a rash – it's called "scratching". Nobody dies from it, but some say death would be preferable. But if you want to go ashore and buy one you can eat, I wouldn't notice.'

We crossed to the other side of the big sound penetrating the middle of Culebra and anchored off a US Navy military base, apparently abandoned, but used for occasional shelling practice. It was a prohibited area for boats, although nobody took any notice except when the Navy was actually firing guns. A motor cruiser joined us. The owner, Jerry, recognised *Iota* from Simon's *Yachting Monthly* articles. He worked for the US *Yachting* magazine and wrote articles about his cruises, particularly in the Bahamas and Virgin Islands. We spent a pleasant evening with him and his wife.

We sailed slowly across to Puerto Rico, again faced with the irritation of entering on Sunday and having to pay a large fee. Entering and clearing procedures seemed to be governing our lives. Arriving just before sunset at an island opposite a town called Fajardo we tried to look inconspicuous. Nobody took any notice so we entered the next morning, again with ream upon ream of paperwork – but no fee.

Iota was given a berth in the well-equipped Isleta Marina next to a hospitable motor cruiser from New York. On board, friends of the gregarious owner of Trans Caribbean Airlines were being entertained. We spent two days making ourselves as prepared as possible for the next leg of our journey.

Ready to leave we had yet more clearance problems because of our lack of a radio. The officials thought it unsafe – no American yacht would ever be without one. Reluctantly they allowed us to go on condition we contacted them as soon as we arrived in the Caicos Islands, about 450 miles to the northwest.

With a 15-knot following wind, blue skies and easy seas we made good progress for two days. The first night we were off San Juan and the second saw us well out into the Mona Passage between Puerto Rico and the Dominican Republic. We sailed untroubled, despite the reputation of the Passage for strong currents and confused seas.

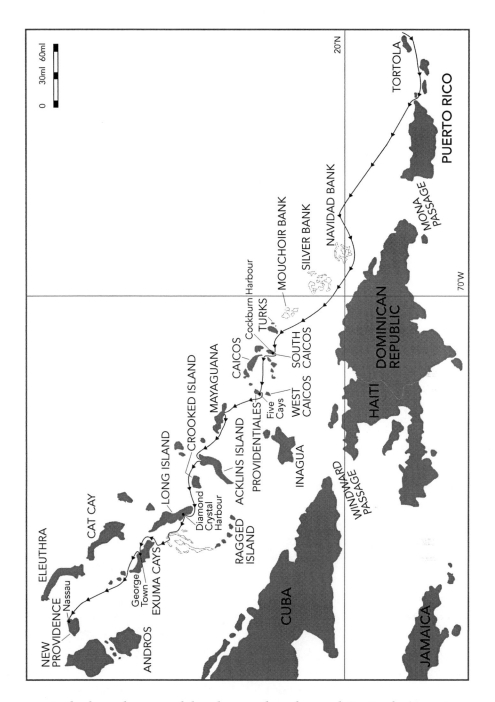

At dusk on the second day the weather changed. Instead of running before a southeast wind with the main, mizzen and genoa, we were on a close reach with a reefed main and the No 2 jib, the wind having swung into the north. The seas were short with vicious breaking crests. The

Dominican Republic and Haiti were to leeward of us. Foreigners were not welcome there; should we arrive there by mistake we would be locked in jail immediately.

We managed to hold a westerly course, but this took us further south than intended so we had to approach the Turks and Caicos through reefs and banks from the south instead of the clearer passage from the north. We avoided the Silver Banks, a chain of shallow reefs and low cays extending about 50 miles to the southwest of the Turks. The coastline of the Dominican Republic appeared and we looked for the lighthouse on Cape Viejo Frances. It lit up at nightfall and provided an invaluable fix.

When the wind came back into the southeast we piled on sail to arrive off the Turks Islands by nightfall. We had to negotiate a narrow passage between the Turks and Caicos. The chart showed flashing lights on the low scrubby islands Sand and Salt Cays to the south of the Turks. As the sun was setting Simon climbed the ratlines and sighted the beacons about five miles away; we were well placed to run between the two reefs in the dark. We waited for the beacons to light up. Nothing happened; just because there was a red flash on the chart didn't mean there would be a light. We were in a dangerous position in the channel between Turks Island and the Mouchoir Bank, with choppy seas and reefs all round.

The invaluable *Yachtsman's guide to the Bahamas* listed radio beacons on both the Turks and Caicos Islands. Intended for aircraft navigation they both transmitted strong reliable signals 24 hours a day. I pounced on Seafix. The beacons were ideally situated for us as they gave us bearings at right angles. We spent a worrying night trying to stay in one place, taking frequent bearings on the beacons, not liking to wonder what would have befallen us if they had not been working or if we had no Seafix. Never had dawn been awaited with more anxiety, or been so slow in arriving.

Eventually the sky lightened and a family of terns flew out to sea to go fishing. As the light increased Salt and Sand Cays reappeared. The wind came up from the southeast with the dawn so we had a broad reach across the Turks Passage and into Cockburn on South Caicos. We dropped our anchor on a sand patch opposite the Admiral's Inn with a feeling of accomplishment and relief. The commissioner, a Victorian-looking gentleman who wore close-fitting lace-up 'mosquito' boots and talked about 'important papers', quickly cleared us with the minimum of fuss. He would radio the coastguards at Fajardo to let them know we had arrived safely.

In Cockburn glistening white limestone houses and walls reflected the sun.

About 800 people lived in Cockburn, the main settlement of the Caicos Islands. A Loran station manned by fourteen US coastguards attracted highflying aircraft directly overhead, making vapour trails in the sky all day long. South Caicos was a popular refuelling place for small private planes and their pilots provided most of the hotel's business.

The first impression of Cockburn town was of glaring light – glistening white limestone houses and walls reflected the sun. There was a collection of brightly painted, higgledy-piggledy shacks and a few neglected salt heaps. In the packing plant women were cleaning big black lobsters. There was a clinic, but no doctor.

The Government Fishing Officer, Tim, a Canadian biologist, befriended us; he kindly let us use his house. He knew the Caicos Islands well as he travelled around them looking for lobsters. He filled us in on all the local activities and personalities – a rich collection of anecdotes for so small a community.

Tim told us that lobsters were abundant in the Caicos and were the main source of income for its inhabitants. Previously salt and sisal had been the principal exports. At one time the Caicos were famed for the quantity and quality of sponges growing in the shallow waters. They also exported conchs, both the dried meat, which formed a staple part of their diet, and the shells, used for making cameos. There was not much agriculture on the cays for there was little water and poor soil.

'They're called the islands of "salt, sand and sorrow". That just about sums them up,' Tim said. 'Despite that the people who live here are industrious and enterprising – it's surprising how they can wring a living – even prosperity – from a barren soil and the sea.'

His advice about the Caicos Bank was invaluable for it was shown on the chart only as vague dotted lines. This was an extensive submarine plateau about 60 miles across with an average depth of about a fathom. We intended to take advantage of *Iota*'s shallow draft and cross the Bank to Providentiales on the western side. Tim told us the water was shallower to the north.

He advised, 'When it's too shallow, turn south. If it's dark and deep, turn north.'

The north and west sides of the circular bank were delineated by a chain of low, thinly-wooded limestone islands; on the fringe of the south and east sides were small cays, rocks, shoals and reefs. The sailing directions warned that 'the bank is extremely dangerous being surrounded by reef and generously sprinkled with coral heads, rocks and sand banks'. The more poetic description in the *Guide* was that it 'resembled a necklace of islands, sparkling white in the sun'.

In the past the Caicos Islands were a favourite haunt of pirates, valued for their strategic place in the Atlantic and the many anchorages and hidden coves along the northern side. The notorious Blackbeard, Blondel, Delvin and 'Calico' Jack Rackham with his two lady pirates Anne Bonny and Mary Read, all used the Caicos Islands as a hideout and haven. They lay in wait for galleons bearing the tempting wealth of South American gold and silver to Europe via the Windward Passage between Cuba and Haiti. Their takings were plentiful and bloody.

It was windless when we left at dawn and remained so all day long. We had to motor all the way. It was very hot. Initially *Iota* had barely enough water beneath her – her shadow nearly joined her keel – but for the most part the going was easy in one to two fathoms, although we had to skirt around a few coral heads. *Iota* made a big wash and felt peculiar to steer. It was a weird sensation to be in pale green, shallow water, yet out of sight of land.

Eventually the cays on the other side came in sight, but it was difficult to know where we were because the land was low and featureless. The calm weather and heat haze gave strange visibility too; the cays appeared to be suspended in the sky and mushroom shaped due to their reflections.

The village of Five Cays on Providentiales had a church we could see from a distance. We anchored in less than a fathom of water and went ashore straight away, as there was a reception committee on the beach: Mr Hilton Rigby, the District Constable in his best cap, a few youths, a couple of women and hordes of children. They made speeches

Powering in shallow water across the Caicos Banks we took it in turns to con from the ratlines.

of welcome and told us they did not get many visitors so 'wanted to make the most of us'.

Mr Rigby offered to take us to West Caicos where there was an inland lagoon, home to spectacular roseate flamingos – he called them fillimingoes. He came on board early the next morning with a youth named Leroy Butterfield and a young nephew, Felix. He piloted us through coral heads out into deep blue water – from two fathoms to 2000 in a few metres – to an anchorage on the western side of West Caicos. As we went he told us about ships that had been wrecked around the islands; his stories ended when 'de ship altogether mash up on de reef'. We gathered the misfortunes of the mariners had provided a boost to the incomes of the residents of the cay – and wondered if they still did.

We scrambled ashore and walked through the remains of an old sisal plantation: a few crumbling buildings, an old steam engine and a railway track along a causeway through the middle of the lagoon. The fibrous leaves of the spiky sisal plant are used to make rope. In the dry limey soil the plant had an extended life span as it took longer for it to grow the flower stalk that ended its productivity.

The going was tough over jagged stones and through coarse grass, prickly scrub and cacti with sharp thorns. Mosquitoes rose by the thousand and attacked ferociously. My bare legs were black with them. Felix walked beside me and continually slapped me, leaving splodges of blood as he swatted. We saw fillimingoes in the distance – big birds with vivid pink plumage – but by the time we reached the other side of the lagoon they had flown away.

~

We were shown around the settlement of Five Cays. Mr Rigby's house was well made and furnished with ornate Victorian bric-a-brac. Leroy, on the other hand, lived in a poor shack made of rotting wood with an earth floor. The population was mainly older people, women and children; the men were away working as it was difficult to make a living on the island. Mr Rigby's daughter was in New York training to be a nurse. A teacher came once a week to the school. Conchs were the main source of income – the islanders dried the meat and took it to Haiti to swap for fruit and other foods. The whole village smelt of them as they were strung up to dry in the sun around the houses. There was a boat under construction, but where her wooden planks came from was a mystery.

Conch meat drying in the sun at Five Cays

To thank Mr Rigby we took Polaroid photographs of his many grandchildren. Dressed up for the occasion in their Sunday best the girls wore their hair pulled into plaits and tied with big bright bows.

Another of the attractions of Providenciales was a huge inland lagoon called Chalk Sound. Mr Rigby said it was 'a muss see'. We motored a couple of miles around the cay and anchored in a bay under Sapodilla Hill – it must have been all of 25 metres high. We took a picnic to the shore of the brilliant green lagoon, swam in the clear, warm water and ate our lunch on a little beach. A barracuda followed us as we rowed back to *Iota*. The oars dipping in and out of the water intrigued him – he almost touched one and then flashed away to a more circumspect distance. His big eyes and rows of sharp teeth gave him an evil appearance.

We decided to anchor overnight off Malcolm Roads on the west side of Providenciales to be clear of the reef and ready to leave before dawn for the trip to Mayaguana. To get there, Mr Rigby recommended a short cut through a gap in the reef that was 'not difficult to find'. We skirted around a large sandbank and weaved in and out of coral heads between the reef and the bank in shelving water. We could not retrace our path for, against the sun, we would not be able to see the coral heads. We had no choice but to keep going and hope the gap was 'not difficult to find'. A dubious opening in the reef appeared behind a patch of rock. Waves were breaking on it. Slowly we went through, expecting *Iota* to crunch on the rocks each time we dipped into a hollow. Mr Rigby's words, 'de ship altogether mash up on de reef', were ringing in our ears.

We sailed at midnight for Mayaguana in a warm, soft night, enjoying an easy and pleasant crossing and a full moon so bright we could almost see to read. When the sun rose the island was in sight. The main village, Abraham Bay, was reached through a pass in the reef the *Guide* described as 'intricate'. With a clear day, *Iota*'s shallow draught and the sun behind us it was easy compared to the previous day's scare. The bay was a wide expanse of shallow water. We edged as close to the settlement as we dared, but with just a foot of water under our keel we were still over half a mile from the fine, but not yet finished, jetty. The village was a further half a mile through a mangrove swamp.

The commissioner apologised for not coming out to enter us – the dinghy made him seasick! He was talkative and told us it was difficult for the few inhabitants to make a living on the island. They grew a few crops and went fishing. The most important feature of the island was the US Missile Tracking Station. Its officer-in-charge, Bud Boyvitch, came into town for his daily beer and took us in his jeep to show us around. The station was not in operation and Bud's job was to keep it in working order with the help of the islanders in case it might be needed. There was a six-kilometre runway, the longest in the world, built for bringing in Minutemen missiles. Planes could land a full complement of 10,000 men and their fuel and food requirements in 45 minutes. The base could accommodate 2000 air force personnel and had tanks to store a million gallons of rainwater; 50,000 watts of electricity could be generated. If anything should go wrong on the station, a siren would sound and a light go on in Bud's room to wake him up. The station was a communication centre – President Johnson's hot wire went through his room.

Bud cooked us dinner – Louisiana ham and eggs. The refrigerators were bulging with frozen food. He was like a fairy godmother to the local people; at a wave of his wand a jet plane would fly in anything required or take out sick people. When hurricane Donna wrecked the island in 1960 everyone was fed at the base for three weeks, even though it had suffered considerable damage. In appreciation most of the local residents had changed to Bud's Baptist religion.

We made our way eastwards, picking our way through the reef to an anchorage each night. At Pirates Wells, *Iota* rolled so we were pleased to leave. A fast and easy sail took us to a small, uninhabited island, French Cay, where we swam, fished and rambled. The wind failed and we motored the 20 miles across to Acklins on a smooth sea, although there was a long swell. Our new engine was proving to be another disappointment as it had to work hard to push the boat along and its spark plugs constantly demanded our attention. Just around the northwest point of Acklins was Atwood Harbour. Simon walked the five kilometres into the nearest settlement, Chesters, to see if he could buy petrol. He came back with some in the car of the obliging and kindly storekeeper, Frank Moss.

Frank told us the community subsisted mostly on agriculture and fishing. He also made money out cascarilla, a shrub native to the Bahamas – the quills of cork-like 'Sweet-wood Bark' were the source of an active ingredient used as a tonic or, in Italy, for making a liqueur. When burned the bark gave off a strong, aromatic, musk-like odour; it was often added in small portions to tobacco. There was also lignum vitae, an extremely hard wood. The inhabitants of the Bahamas were adept at exploiting the limited resources of their islands.

Next day a breeze came up from the northwest. According to the *Guide*, this heralded a blow from the north; it would be prudent to seek shelter. Portland Harbour on Crooked Island came with a recommendation that Columbus had found it 'greatly to his liking'. The other anchorages on the island were exposed to the west, but offered shelter from the north.

'I think we ought to go around to the west coast,' I suggested. 'We've got time.'

'But Columbus recommended Portland Harbour,' said Simon. 'It must be okay.'

'But it's open to the north,' I argued.

'It's behind the reef.' Simon could not be dissuaded from experiencing Columbus's favourite anchorage.

When we arrived Portland Harbour was calm and peaceful. We walked along the beach to Land Rail Point and bought tomatoes. Here was a well-established settlement with good roads, well-built houses and a school catering for older children from all over the islands up to the age of seventeen or eighteen.

Big black clouds were building up in the north; it looked like rain. A man was gathering seaweed in anticipation of the salt being washed out of it so he could use it as fertiliser. As we rowed back to the boat the northerly wind came in with a bang. It was a hard row through the swells now breaking over the reef. We laid out our heavy anchor and slid the weight down the chain.

After an uncomfortable night pitching wildly, we woke to a foul morning; it led into an unpleasant, rainy day. *Iota* was rolling and pitching so badly it was impossible to do anything. We could not get ashore nor could we escape out of the harbour because the overcast skies made it impossible to see the reefs. The respite from *Iota*'s violent motion at low tide was short lived. After a second anxious night the wind turned to the east and, sporadically, the sun came out.

It was an opportunity to escape. Simon pulled up the anchor and I put the engine into gear; it spluttered and failed. We had tense moments before I discovered Simon had not fully turned on the fuel tap. We only just avoided hitting the reef. I was furious with both Simon for being careless and Columbus for recommending the anchorage – and it showed.

Outside the seas were huge; we were glad to be running with them. Waves were breaking against the rocky coast in spurts of spray that reached higher than the hills behind. It continued boisterous and rough until we rounded the southern tip of Long Island; we then had a brisk reach along the coast to Diamond Crystal Harbour, the home of a salt company. Its small harbour was blissfully calm. We secured *Iota* to the jetty on one side and a tree on the other. Machines surrounded us – conveyor belts, tractors and dredges. There was a big office and a laboratory.

The salt company was American owned. After nearly four years they were just about to dispatch their first shipment. Salt water ran from the sea through canals into shallow fields, called pans, which were lined with marl. Wind and sun evaporated the water and left the salt to be raked up and stored in great white pyramids.

The manager was helpful and friendly; he arranged for fuel to be delivered – and water too. Bert, who supplied the fuel, offered to drive us around the island. He enjoyed showing us the features of his home and telling us about its interesting history. Being relatively fertile, Long Island was settled in 1790 by American Loyalists who grew cotton with the aid of their slaves. With the abolition of slavery the plantations were abandoned. Bert pointed out the ruins of a substantial plantation house now covered in bushes. Pineapples and sisal have since provided an income for the island.

Bert told us about pothole farming: crops grown in depressions and fertile holes in the limestone. We saw healthy bananas, pawpaws, mangos, pigeon peas, tomatoes, cabbage, onions and corn, all for the market in Nassau. The islanders also kept sheep, goats and pigs.

A road ran for the whole 100-kilometre length of the narrow island. It passed the main settlement, Clarence Town, noted for its two picturesque, impressive churches, St Paul's Anglican Church and St Peter's Roman Catholic Church. They stared at each other from twin hills on opposite sides of the town. Trained as an architect, Father Jerome was responsible for erecting both of them. His first attempt was St Paul's, but then he converted to Catholicism and constructed St Peter's in a similar style. It was better built than the Anglican Church – its walls were straighter and its towers did not lean.

~

The Exuma Cays, a chain of islands running from northwest to southeast, extend for about 90 miles. The *Guide* stated there are about 365 cays of varying sizes, Great Exuma being the largest. On the eastern side there is deep water, but the western side is shallow and studded with coral heads and reefs. Much of it is a Marine National Park, with a reputation as the finest and most colourful cruising grounds for small

The Catholic Church in Clarence Town was perched on a hill.

yachts anywhere in the world, and with an abundance of excellent anchorages. We had ten days to explore this paradise before we had to be in Nassau for Simon to catch his plane back to Sydney.

Setting off from Diamond Crystal Harbour at first light we headed for Hog Cay Cut at the southern end of the Exumas. It was 40 miles over a bank not more than two fathoms deep. We had a brisk wind behind us and piled on the sails. *Iota* sped through the shallow water in a series of headstrong lurches, again difficult and tiring to steer. One of us was always up the ratlines looking out for rocks and shoals and we changed places every hour. A lone porpoise joined us; he frolicked around then swam away to find his friends.

It was difficult to determine our exact position as the islands were low and featureless. The *Guide* warned us of strong tidal currents. The weed that frequently fouled our Walker log didn't help either! However the light tower on the Nuevitas Rocks, about halfway along the journey, gave us confidence.

We made excellent time, arriving in the early afternoon. With the sun behind us we picked our way through Hog Cay Cut among the sandbanks and reefs to find an anchorage. The pretty islands and the sea had the colours of jewels – the water around us was aquamarine and in the distance changed to emerald and turquoise; the shore was brilliant with jade and ruby foliage and pearl white beaches.

Next day we navigated carefully to Georgetown and dropped our anchor in Kidd Cove, named after the pirate who favoured the spot. We were able to buy fresh provisions, take advantage of the local laundry and enjoy a drink at the picturesque Two Turtles Inn.

Stocking Island was only a short distance across from Georgetown. The two yachts and a motor cruiser in the outer harbour were the first boats we had met other than local sloops. A clearly marked long, narrow and shallow passage led into the almost landlocked east lagoon. The chart showed it had a fathom of water at high tide, but when we went through the tide was low. An astonished man followed us in a dinghy, expecting us to run aground. *Iota* was gaining a reputation for being the kind of yacht that gets other yachts into trouble!

Slowly we made our way northwest, leaving early in the morning and stopping by mid-afternoon for a leisurely swim or a walk ashore. From the multitude of anchorages it was difficult to choose. We never tired of watching the changing colours of the water as the tide rose and fell. Some days we went outside into the ocean and on others we preferred the shallow water on the banks, picking our way by eye past sandbanks and reefs and playing the tides. We were astonished to have so much of this wonderful cruising to ourselves.

As we drew closer to Nassau there were signs of civilisation – spectacular holiday homes and beach resorts. We met other cruising yachts and powerboats.

We had an unfortunate encounter with one of them when needing to stop and change the plugs of our spluttering engine. Simon tossed the anchor over the side, not checking if it had dug in as we thought the job would take no time at all. A motor cruiser was anchored some distance away, but as the tide fell she moved into deeper water astern of us. She rather fancied herself for she was gleaming white and her crew wore smart uniforms.

In the meantime the wind came up. *Iota* was dragging, but we didn't notice as we were both bent over the engine. A hail from the cruiser alerted us, but our engine was still not working. We had to sail out of trouble. I pulled up the mainsail and Simon went forward to retrieve the anchor. Up it came, with the powerboat's anchor entangled with it. Trying not to look embarrassed, Simon nonchalantly shook them apart and we sailed away. Not a word was spoken.

We put the engine back together, but it was not healthy – reluctant to start, it spluttered when running and was inclined to overheat and smoke.

Our final journey was a fast 40-mile sail across the Yellow Banks to New Providence and the elegant city of Nassau.

Simon looks for a way through the reef.

homeward bound

1967

In Nassau we tied up at a smart marina among rows of sleek and polished yachts feeling like a poor relation. The service was unbelievable. Two people helped with our lines, another bought us a 'welcome' drink and yet another asked if we had any laundry – did we ever! Would we like to hire a car? Here's today's paper; just press the bell if we would like another drink – and if you would like to dine aboard, here's the menu.

It was the end of Simon's holiday – his plane left for Sydney in five days – why not end the cruise in style?

Iota's neighbour was a yacht in such immaculate condition I wondered if she ever went to sea. Shortly after dark the main hatch opened and a man came on deck. He was in his thirties with film star looks – too good to be true. He was studiedly casual and self-consciously elegant, the sort of man you read about, but never meet. He smiled at us, said hello and turned to pull a suitcase up on deck. It appeared to be an expensive suitcase. A grey-haired woman followed it, overdressed and with too much make-up.

She saw us and gushed, 'Well, all good things have to come to an end.'

The man helped her ashore. 'See you when I get back from the airport.'

We ordered dinner delivered to the boat and, as we sat in the cockpit, discussed what *Iota* and I would do when Simon returned to Sydney.

'I've booked you and *Iota* on the *Tahitien* from Panama to Sydney. She's due in Cristobel in a couple of weeks. But how are you going to get to Panama? There isn't any shipping from Nassau that will take a yacht. Cruise ships don't accept deck cargo. You're going to have to go across to Florida, to Fort Lauderdale, or maybe to Jacksonville. You'll have to find a crew to go with you – it's across the Gulfstream so the currents will be a problem, but you can go through the Everglades to Jacksonville.'

'The engine's about to give up and it's the Bermuda Triangle too.' I wasn't really looking forward to the crossing and arriving in a strange, crowded port – but there didn't seem to be any choice.

Simon read the paper looking for overseas news, but found only items of local interest. The headlines were: Britain's Biggest Boiler Bound for Bahamas.

'What's that about,' I asked.

'They're building a big new power station here; it must be something to do with that,' he replied.

Our neighbour returned from the airport. He was carrying another suitcase, equally as expensive as the last, and a different colour. He was escorting another overdressed grey-haired woman. They didn't acknowledge us at all.

'That's strange,' I said. 'It's one thing to entertain your aunt on board, but not all your aunts.'

'Wake up,' said Simon, laughing, 'He's a gigolo and those are his clients.'

'You mean he hires himself out?' I asked.

'Makes a fortune no doubt,' replied Simon.

'Maybe he'd like a trip to Fort Lauderdale,' I mused. Crossing the Gulfstream didn't seem so unattractive after all.

'What was that again about Britain's Biggest Boiler? Is it bigger than *Iota*? Where's it going to in the Bahamas? And where's the ship going on to?' I reached for the paper, but Simon had already grabbed it.

'That's an idea,' he said. 'If they're stopping to deliver a boiler they could pick up a yacht. Here – it says it's a P&O freighter on its maiden voyage with a state-of-the-art high-tech single-lift 60-ton crane. I'd better go and find the agent, first thing tomorrow.'

Simon came back all smiles. The agent had cabled the *Orcoma*. Yes, she could take the yacht, and yes, there was a cabin for me – the owner's cabin was free. The ship was going to Cristobel then through the Panama Canal and down the west coast of South America. She would be arriving at dawn in five days' time and would heave-to off the south coast of New Providence to unload the boiler onto barges.

'How much?' I asked.

'There wasn't much point in asking,' said Simon. 'Cheaper than a gigolo anyway.'

We could not trust our engine to take us around the island to where the ship would be off-loading; we needed the security of masts and sails. The problem was to find a well protected anchorage on the other side of New Providence, calm enough for us to lower the masts. We searched the chart for a likely looking bay, but it was all open, an exposed leeshore apart from what appeared to be a man-made harbour with canals leading to it. It was called Lyford Cay. We would have to go and look.

We walked into the city to hire a car. On the way we admired the intriguing blend of Victorian colonial architecture, wooden houses with big windows and balconies painted in bright colours, many churches challenging each other, and the picturesque pastel parliament buildings. We ordered a cold drink and sat in the café in the city's central park listening to a steel band improbably perched in a big tree with spreading branches. Two gangly boys were running and skipping up the path. When they came to the tree they stopped and wriggled their hips in time to the beat of the music, attracting the attention of the drummer who waved his drumsticks and laughed at them. Embarrassed, they went on their way, practising their bowling with the imaginary cricket ball that all small West Indian boys have in their pockets.

Back at the marina we asked about Lyford Cay.

'Yes, it would be ideal,' the receptionist told us. 'But you'll never get in. It's very, very exclusive. They have heavy security and no – but *no* – outsiders are allowed anywhere near the place.'

I pulled out our best clothes and ironed them. It helped a bit, but we didn't look very, very exclusive.

It was a pleasant drive across the island to Lyford Cay so all would not be lost if our mission was in vain. But what to do if we couldn't persuade them to let us stay there was a problem. It meant dropping our masts in Nassau and motoring around the island in the dark hoping our sick engine would last the distance. Better not to think about it.

We arrived at the main gates of Lyford Cay. Armed guards with dogs patrolled the securely fenced boundary. It was more like a prison than a resort. Simon asked one of the guards if he could speak to the secretary. There was a protracted discussion on the phone and eventually permission was granted – step one.

The guard jumped into his Mini Moke and escorted us to the secretary's office. We drove around the immaculate golf course and saw glimpses of huge mansions set well back in magnificent grounds. This was the playground of the Rockefellers and Vanderbilts; Princess Margaret and Tony honeymooned here and it was the setting for more than one James Bond film.

Simon went off to talk to the secretary while I waited and worried in the car. After an age he returned, his mission successful.

'What an unbelievable stroke of luck,' he said. 'The first thing I saw on the secretary's desk were some brochures from an Australian Trade Commission and I recognised a name on one of them – Philip Leery. He's a tall man with fiery red hair – unmistakable. He'd been in the secretary's office only last week. That did it. We were in! We spent the rest of the time discussing where we should tie up – he said we could use the caretaker's cottage. And we're not allowed to use money – no cash is permitted on the place. You book everything up and get sent a bill when you get home.'

As we drove back to *Iota* I asked Simon where he had met Philip Leery.

'Oh, I never have,' he said, 'but I once sat next to a man on an aeroplane who'd had an affair with his wife.'

We set off for Lyford Cay the next day.

Between spells of work, packing and stowing, we luxuriated. Next to the clubhouse was an enticing swimming pool. We swam and floated in it and sat beside it drinking long, exotic drinks. The carpeted changing rooms were full of hibiscus. An army of attendants polished mirrors and tidied up their clients' clothes. There was a sauna and a jacuzzi and a large motherly black woman who gave a fabulous massage.

Lyford Cay Golf Club and its Grecian pillars

On the last evening we dined at the golf club. It was a clear, gentle night and the tables were outside on the lawn. The food was superb, the service abundant. The black waiters all wore white gloves. I looked across at the clubhouse and realised the front of it had a row of pillars – Grecian pillars – elegant and imposing. A chill ran down my spine; I was suddenly back in Shaftsbury Avenue gazing into a crystal ball. And I knew what was going to happen next – the moon came up, a full moon. It shone on the water between two rows of palm trees and its path was leading me across the water. I knew I would follow it.

~

Our activities intrigued the students attending a diving school at the resort. In their high-powered speedboat, lately used in a James Bond film, they agreed to escort us out to the ship and bring Simon back ashore.

In a peaceful canal we prepared Iota *for shipping.*

We set off before dawn to rendezvous with the *Orcoma*. Two barges, lashed together, were there to meet her too. She came in and dropped her anchor just as the first rays of the sun were flickering in the sky. We could see 'Britain's Biggest Boiler' on the deck up forward and the new miraculous heavy lift was being brought into action to offload it onto the barges. It looked to be a very precarious operation.

'It's huge,' said Simon, 'Hope they don't drop it! *Iota*'s only a fraction of the size and weight of that.'

As the barges cleared the ship and started on their slow journey to the shore we took their place. We caught the swinging hook and fitted it onto our lifting gear. The speedboat came alongside and Simon stepped aboard; *Iota* and I were hoisted aboard the *Orcoma*.

The anchor was up and the ship underway before *Iota* was bedded down and secure. I watched and waved as the speedboat circled the ship and set off for Lyford Cay at full speed and in a flurry of foam.

An officer escorted me to the owner's cabin – so comfortable it seemed a shame I would be in it for just a couple of days.

I had never before been on such a new, high-tech ship, nor a British one either. The captain, chief engineer and first officer dined with the other officers, who changed into full uniform for dinner. Was it because they had a passenger? No, it was the custom of all British merchant ships.

As well as a new ship, the officers too were new; they were a remarkably young group, just out of school. Dinner conversation turned to Cristobel. Only two had been through the Panama Canal before and nobody had been ashore in Cristobel.

'I've only been there at night,' I said. 'We went to a strip club. The strippers were one thing, but the audience was just fascinating – an incredible mixture of extraordinary characters from just about every part of the world.'

This was an experience not to be missed – we would arrive in Cristobel tomorrow night and broaden our minds with a visit to the strip joint.

Eight young officers and I walked downtown to the nightclub. It was dark and sordid, furnished with bare tables and wooden benches, the atmosphere heavy with smoke from acrid cigars. An overweight swarthy man, his greasy hair slicked back, gazed mournfully into his empty glass and took no notice of the woman who was so enticingly revealing herself on the stage.

A group of noisy sailors of unknown European origin were embarrassed by the spectacle and cracked rude jokes. Two young men were holding hands and leering into each other's eyes – they didn't seem to be quite in the right place. Another man was paying full attention and making no secret of his arousal; he groaned enthusiastically as each item of clothing was discarded.

I wondered about the object of his admiration – a pretty blonde with a porcelain white skin and a tantalising figure, she had an artless air of innocence that belied her occupation. What was her story?

It was about two o'clock in the morning when we left – a large

'Britain's Biggest Boiler Bound for Bahamas'

Iota *was hoisted aboard in the boiler's place...and bedded down comfortably on the deck.*

enough group, we thought, to negotiate a dangerous downtown. The police thought otherwise. A van descended on us with a wail of sirens and bundled us back to the wharf.

The officers showed their identification to the guard on the wharf gate; he nodded and let them pass. He looked at me and said, 'What's that?'

'It's our supernumerary,' explained one of the officers.

The man looked doubtful, but said, 'Oh well, all right, but bring her back in the morning.'

I had achieved a new status in life.

The 60-ton lift was put in action again in the morning. *Iota* had to be taken across the deck of the ship and lowered into the water on the port side. It would have been a complicated task on an old-fashioned ship with conventional derricks; with this new, wondrous heavy-lift crane, it should have been easy. But they managed to hit *Iota*'s keel on the top of the hatch. A piece of wood flew off and landed on the deck.

I was fuming! The silly young twit on the crane was showing off and not paying attention. The bosun was sent for and he fastened the block on with a slather of waterproof caulking. *Iota* would leak for sure; I could only hope it would be controllable. I took her away from the side of the ship and tied her up at the head of the wharf as close to the guard on the gate as I could get.

The agent was a dark and dapper businessman, dressed in a black suit with a flashy tie. He was busy and had more important things to do than to worry about a female supernumerary with a leaking yacht. He said impatiently that it was out of the question I should live on board at the wharf and it was difficult to disagree with him.

'The Hotel Washington will have a room; it's the best hotel in town,' he said.

It was a massive pink building commanding a prime position on the waterfront. In its heyday it would have ranked with Galle Face, Raffles or the Oriental, but those days were long gone. Now the peeling paint, dirty windows and sparse furnishing gave off an atmosphere of gloom and dejection.

The receptionist was in keeping. She had a tired, discontented face and looked disapprovingly at me. Without speaking she produced an enormous key. Still silent, she led me along a maze of empty corridors to my allotted room.

The room was in proportion to the key. In the far corner was a small iron bedstead with a hard mattress; in the opposite, over there, was a cupboard. I gingerly looked inside, expecting something to jump out on me. Doors – unlocked and unlockable – led into rooms on either side and onto a veranda that merged into an overgrown lawn. Way above in the high ceiling was a fan, probably the original. It was turning lazily at one rpm and making no difference to the stifling heat. I didn't think I was going to enjoy my stay at the Hotel Washington.

The *Orcoma* left in the afternoon and, although my acquaintance with her had been brief, when she drew away from the wharf I felt my security going with her. I checked *Iota*; there was water in the bilge, but she wasn't going to sink immediately. I pumped her dry and left her, hoping she would still be there in the morning.

I was the only guest dining at the Hotel Washington, and probably the only guest. I retired very early and curled up on the hard bed, clutching my passport, my money and my camera. I slept fitfully, waking in alarm when the old wooden shutters creaked and groaned when the wind came up.

I checked on *Iota* first thing in the morning. The guard smiled at me as I went through the gates onto the wharf; it was a friendly smile and cheered me up. Having pumped the bilges dry again, I set off determinedly to find the agent for Messageries Maritime. The *Tahitien* must be due any day and how I was longing to see her again!

M. Bousac was apologetic. Messageries Maritimes were on strike. On strike! The *Tahitien* had not yet left Marseilles and was unlikely to do so for at least a week, possibly two, or maybe three! It was because of the officers; they wanted more pay.

How could they do it! The thought of a month in the Hotel Washington was too awful to contemplate. I wondered if Panama City would be any better – but I couldn't leave *Iota*.

There had to be another way, another ship among all those transiting the canal that could take me to Sydney – there just had to be.

'There's the *Mauritien*,' said M. Bousac after a long silence. He had been reading my thoughts. 'She got away just before the strike and is due here tomorrow. But she's going to Melbourne, not Sydney.'

He made a decision. 'I will cable the ship right away and see what is possible.'

I could have hugged him.

The reply came back within the hour. It was yes – they had deck space for *Iota* and a spare cabin for me. And they were stopping in Tahiti so I could off-load and wait for the *Tahitien* there.

The agent started to do some hasty paper work and I cabled Simon to tell him of my change in plans. A celebration was called for so I spent the afternoon buying a dress for the next part of the journey. There wasn't much choice and in desperation I settled on a prim dark grey number with long sleeves and a white collar buttoned high up to the neck.

The *Mauritien* was an elderly workhorse that should long ago have been put out to grass, but she was still pressed into service for the gain of her masters. From the moment I put my foot on the gangplank I could feel a sense of depression; she was not a happy ship.

The wharfies loaded *Iota* and I watched while the crew lashed her down, making sure they did not attach a line to an inappropriate fitting. I was five minutes late for lunch. The commandant and his capitaine were both seated at the table when I went into the dining room. I walked up and introduced myself. Neither men stood up, but they both shook hands, if a little reluctantly. When I went to sit at the empty seat on the commandant's left, he silently shook his head and pointed to a table in the corner.

I didn't miss any scintillating, witty conversation at the 'Captain's table'. The commandant was a weedy man with a dark, sallow, pock-marked skin and a large hooknose. His uniform looked as if he had slept in it. The capitaine was younger; his cropped fair hair stuck out from his head as if surprised by the chinless face below it and he had sad, watery blue eyes. Occasionally their gloomy silence was broken by low mutterings about the affairs of the ship. The third chair at their table, for the chief engineer, was unoccupied. I presumed he found his own company more exciting than that of his colleagues. I never met him.

I spent the afternoon ashore looking for anything written in English. I found plenty of copies of *Playboy*, but little else. I managed to acquire a pack of playing cards – I thought I might find an opportunity in the next few days to play solitaire!

We left at dusk for our transit through the Canal. The pilot boat came alongside and delivered two pilots, the senior one a loudly dressed, loudly spoken, gum chewing American with a baseball cap over his crew cut. He swaggered up to the bridge.

'Pleased to meet you, Captain,' he said loudly to the commandant who took an instant and obvious dislike to him.

The junior pilot was different. Tall and neatly dressed, he had more dignity and presence than his boss. He looked around the bridge and, seeing me, came across with a smile and an outstretched hand.

'Jenifer Iota,' he said, 'Remember me? In Papeete five years ago I was on the *Monsoon*. You came in just before we left.'

'Good heavens!' I said, my memory vaguely stirring, 'You're Frank, aren't you? Good heavens! What are you doing here? You've got a good memory, fancy remembering me after all this time.'

'I saw the yacht on deck, she's unmistakable,' he said with a grin.

The pilot listened to the crackle of his radio, frowned and relayed news that did nothing to appease the commandant's ill humour. Our transit was delayed – we would have to wait for several hours.

We tied up to a wall; the senior pilot retired to the pilot's cabin, the commandant to his. Frank and I climbed up to the small deck above the bridge and persuaded a steward to bring us chairs and coffee.

An apprentice pilot, Frank said he had another three months to go before he could take a ship through the canal on his own. He was looking forward to it, as his present boss was something of an embarrassment to him. Frank had sailed around the world since we last met and had news of many mutual acquaintances. We talked all night.

Just before dawn the senior pilot and commandant returned to the bridge. The pilot spoke into his radio and gave orders for the ship to get underway. He rang slow ahead on the engine room telegraph. Commandant exploded in fury. How dare this brash American usurp his authority!

The two men stood face-to-face, each shouting in his own language.

The rest of the transit was uneventful, but fascinating – with two pilots, one was free to explain the finer points of the operation of the canal and of life in Panama too. Frank spent all his spare time in the mountains where he studied the wildlife; I learned about boa constrictors, panthers and mountain lions.

They left us in Balboa and the *Mauritien* set off on the ten day crossing of the Pacific to Tahiti.

On the second day out the Radio Officer said a cable was coming through for me. It was long and in English. He was having trouble with its reception, but hoped to pick it up more clearly in the evening.

Le Radio was a studious-looking young man. He was wearing earphones and concentrating on his dials when I went to attend the arrival of the cable. Static came from the receiver. He waved at a chair and went back to his work. I sat quietly wondering what Simon could be wanting to tell me that was so lengthy. My thoughts were well away.

Suddenly Le Radio swung round, took off the earphones and said slowly without any expression on his face or in his voice, 'Si vous ne partez pas immédiatement, je vous violerez.' – If you don't go immediately I'll...

I jumped. Didn't that mean rape? I departed – toute de suite – wondering if that was what he really meant and at his use of the second person plural for such a potentially intimate relationship. So much for the prim dark grey dress!

The cable was on the table at breakfast. Simon said he had contacted Messageries Maritime in Sydney. They insisted I should stay in Cristobel and wait for the *Tahitien*. Too bad! I didn't tell the commandant – there wasn't much point.

The days across the Pacific passed slowly. I was glad of the playing cards, for I scarcely saw or spoke to any of the crew for the first few days. Commandant Bizarre, Capitaine Triste, a non-existent engineer and a sex maniac for a radio operator – they would have made ideal characters for a Somerset Maugham novel. Life gradually improved; the crew rigged up a canvas swimming pool on the after deck, introduced me to their library and invited me to their films. Perhaps they were human after all.

Two days before our arrival in Tahiti the commandant asked to see my passport so they could get the ship's paperwork in order. My French visa had expired many months ago! The commandant glared at me, his beady eyes glittering above his hawk beak nose. Not only was I guilty of not having been born in France, I had compounded the felony by not having a valid visa. They would have to take me on to Melbourne.

He looked further. My passport had no record of my entering or leaving Cristobel – they would no doubt put me in jail in Melbourne. Spending a further two weeks with him on the ship seemed to me a far worse punishment.

'No way,' I thought and went off to pack my bag.

I stood on deck as we berthed in Papeete, breathing the scented Tahitian air and enjoying the familiar, spectacular scenery. How good to be here again, even if only for a couple of days. It was Sunday so the wharf was deserted but for a Vespa coming along the quay towards the ship, groaning under the weight of its rider, a very large gendarme. It couldn't be – it had to be – he stopped at the gangway and looked up. It was! It was Gui Gui!

'Gui Gui!'

'Hello, darling!' he shouted. 'You're back again.'

'Gui Gui, I haven't got a visa.'

'Oh, you naughty girl!' he laughed.

Things were going to be all right.

He came up the gangway and disappeared into the commandant's cabin.

'They will off-load the yacht and you will come with me to the gendarmerie,' said Gui Gui sternly when he emerged some time later.

'Heavens,' I thought, 'we'll never both fit on the poor little Vespa.'

But we did – just. I perched on the remaining sliver of pillion seat and clung on for dear life with my arms around Gui Gui's ample girth as we bumped into town.

We only went as far as the Quai Bir Hakeim. Gui Gui took me to each yacht in turn and introduced me. We ended up on board *Porpoise* where I met Louise and her two young crew, Chris and Paul.

'I will tell the pilot to put your boat next to hers so you can live on board until the *Tahitien* arrives,' said Gui Gui, 'Now I will go and arrange it.'

'What about my visa?' I asked.

'Quelle idée! Le gendarmerie est fermé les dimanches,' he said – The police station is closed on Sundays.

~

It was easy to slip back into the improbabilities of Tahitian life. True to his word Gui Gui organised my visa and arranged for *Iota* to turn temporarily from a piece of cargo into a yacht tied up to the quay next to *Porpoise*.

Louise told me how she had become discontented with her conventional urban existence in Illinois; life was passing her by. Her lawyer husband consulted with a psychiatrist who said he could make her into a resigned housewife – for a price. She decided to take the money and buy a yacht instead. She had adapted readily to her newfound lifestyle and never looked back. Danish Chris and Norwegian Paul were enjoying the opportunity to see the world from a cruising yacht. They were both competent and easy to live with and uncomplainingly added the care of me to their list of duties.

Louise and I discovered we had a common love of riding. We set off before dawn to the stables, saddled up our mounts and climbed to the plateau to watch the sunrise. It was a rich experience.

Old friends reappeared: the Tokoragi family, Willie la Garde, the gendarme from Nukuhiva, Big Madeleine and No-pants Susie, and the Quinns girls. The camaraderie among the yachts was as strong as ever and most evenings we would congregate, swap sailing yarns, play guitars and sing. The crews of *Dauntless*, *Myonie*, *Vent de Suroit*, *Kyrenia* and many others made a diverse international gathering and again language was never a problem. I had an interesting offer to go and live alone on an uninhabited island 200 miles from Tahiti for a stunt to advertise a film. It was tempting, but not that tempting. Simon and Sydney were in my sights.

The *Tahitien* was three weeks late. Although I had met none of her crew, they had heard of *Iota* and were anxious to hear of our adventures. They loaded her carefully and I settled quickly into shipboard life again.

Most of the passengers were civil servants disembarking in Noumea. We arrived in the dark so the ship hove-to 50 miles from the coast to await daylight before entering the harbour. The sea was calm and the night balmy as the wind dropped with the ship's speed. The seductive black velvet sky with its sparkling stars was so exquisite nobody wanted to miss a moment of it. We danced all night on the open deck, swaying to the gentle roll of the ship and savouring the moments of time-stopped-still until the sky lightened and dawn brought reality again.

I teamed up with an unlikely trio. Garth, a Kiwi, was an aspiring television producer who had been in Europe to widen his experience. He had a quick sense of humour and a lively, imaginative mind. 'I've worked out how to behave in France,' he declared. 'When in doubt, shake hands.'

Des on the other hand was a stolid Victorian sheep farmer, Victorian not only geographically, but in his outlook. He had never met anything quite like the *Tahitien* before and was frequently stuck for words. Henri was the ship's doctor who struggled to maintain the dignity of his profession. He was young, carefree and totally devoted to the cause of enjoying his life to the full.

It was Henri who organised an expedition to climb a mountain in Noumea. The four of us, carrying our lunch, set off early on a local bus. We were in high spirits. We laughed and joked our way to the top through the thick forest. It had been raining and the path was slippery, but that added to the hilarity. We rested at the top for a while and admired the view. It was lunchtime. I proudly opened my bag and revealed that, instead of the regulation half-litre of the ship's rough red, I had persuaded the steward to give me a whole litre.

'What's so clever about that?' Garth and Henri burst out laughing, dug in their bags and each produced a whole litre too. We turned and looked at Des. He blushed, assumed his best sheepish look and produced a litre of wine as well. He was learning fast!

As we giggled and slid our way back down again it started to rain. We frequently fell over; once, all four of us landed in a heap on top of each other. We were covered in mud and arrived at the road, tattered, torn, bruised and bleeding, but still laughing. A local bus appeared as if by magic and took us back to the ship. The gangway was not for us – we were too dirty to be seen by passengers. The ship was loading copra so we sat on top of the bags and were hoisted on board in the sling. We slunk into the ship's hospital to clean up and bathe our wounds.

~

Sydney Harbour was looking its sparkling best as we sailed in. I suddenly realised it had been two and a half years since I had seen it. The pilot boat also brought the immigration and customs officials who, on hearing my suitcase was a yacht, radioed the press. There must have been a shortage of news for reporters were out in force when the ship docked. I ducked past them and ran as fast as I could down the wharf to where Simon was waiting. Gee, it was good to be home!

He came on board to help me off-load *Iota*. She had to be taken to the opposite side of the ship and lowered into the water. The wharfies hoisted us up and we were dangling over the open hold when a whistle blew.

'Smoko!' came the cry. 'We'll be back in half an hour.'

An article about me in the paper next day led to a television station, Channel 10, asking me if I would appear on a lunchtime magazine program, Girl Talk. I agreed to do it and made a date for the following week.

I had not been to a television studio before – this was going to be a new experience. I arrived in good time. A pretty girl greeted me and showed me into the waiting room. A door on the other side of the room said 'STARS'. I wondered what I would have to do to be eligible to go through it. Certainly, it was unlikely that I, on my first visit to the studio, would qualify.

The girl took me to the makeup room where she painstakingly applied powder, eye shadow, blusher and lipstick. I looked at myself in the mirror. The makeup, coupled with a professional hairdo, made me look rather good – a step on the way to becoming famous!

I returned to the waiting room and daydreamed about becoming a celebrity. I imagined myself on the receiving end of adulation and applause.

'Time to come to the studio,' I was woken from my reverie. A man opened the 'Door of the Stars' with a flourish and waved me through.

I was surprised and impressed. Just a little makeup was all I needed to qualify for this auspicious status of stardom. My ego swelled – maybe this was the beginning of a new brilliant career.

The illusion was short lived; the sign on the door had originally said 'STAIRS', but the 'I' had fallen off.

With three other guests on the half-hour program and commercial breaks I had little opportunity to speak. Channel 10 had several requests to hear more from me so they invited me back a week later with only one other guest, Colin Simpson, the well-known travel writer. We had an animated discussion about whether we were happier doing our laundry with our friends in the creek or pushing buttons on a washing machine. I opted for the creek and Colin for the washing machine.

We met again to continue the discussion at a dinner party hosted by Alex and Ann Dix.

~

Just before *Iota* and I arrived in Sydney, Alex had contacted Simon to tell him that Ann's father had died and that her mother wanted to spend several months staying near her son in Melbourne. Would we like to live in her house while she was away? Simon accepted the offer without hesitation, for the simple house in Newport overlooking Pittwater was ideal for us. He found a marina berth for *Iota* at the Royal Prince Alfred Yacht Club – just down the road.

Iota required yet another new engine – it would be our fourth. This time I was determined it would be a reliable water-cooled diesel. I calculated how much weight it would add to the boat and showed it was insignificant. Most ship's derricks could support 20 tonnes and, even with a new engine, *Iota* would still weigh less than five tonnes. Simon was convinced and decided on the impressive 15 hp Volvo Penta marine diesel. He toyed with the idea of shipping *Iota* to Noumea to have it installed there duty free and then cruise from there to the Solomon Islands, but was deterred from the idea when *Coriolis* arrived in Sydney and tied up at Circular Quay. Michel and Bertrand were still with her, but they had left their little dog Piccolo on a farm in Noumea. They invited us to lunch. Bertrand persuaded Simon that it would be safer to have the engine installed in Sydney.

While we were on board the press came to interview them. When we read the article in the paper the next day it bore little resemblance to what they had said. We laughed about it when we returned their hospitality at the Yacht Squadron and made up all sorts of improbable stories for them to tell next time.

Engineer Phil installed the engine. Although bigger, it fitted neatly. Simon's Scottish instincts were appeased when he found we already had a propeller of the right pitch and diameter – it had been used on engine number two, the hot and noisy air-cooled lawnmower diesel. The new engine was powerful enough for us to be able to fit an alternator to charge our batteries – we would have an engine that started when we asked it, ran quietly and smoothly without generating heat in the cabin and – at the same time, cooled our beer.

Geoffrey and Ruth Goodman were on their way home to Melbourne after nine months in the Barrier Reef on *Karloo*, the only other Waterwitch cruising the Pacific. Although there was a close resemblance between the two yachts, there were many differences. *Karloo* was a twin bilge keel sloop whereas *Iota* was a leeboard ketch. To Ruth and Geoffrey, headroom in the cabin was vitally important whereas we had to consider the shipper's cube. Their wind vane impressed me. Geoffrey said it saved many tiring hours of steering. He told me we should trim the sails so the steering was as light as possible and then a vane could manage well. If *Karloo* could have one, so could *Iota*. We visited Charlie who made all things for boats and told him what we wanted. He put his mind to the problem, went to look at other wind vanes – and came up with a device for *Iota* that worked like a charm. It was like having an extra hand aboard so we called it 'Charlie'.

Unlike previous times when preparing *Iota* for her next journey, I did not have a job that demanded my attention so there was time to catch up with my Sydney friends. The *Caledonien* was a regular visitor so we had an exchange of hospitality, going for dinner on board and then taking Commandant Barral and one or two of his officers to dinner at the Yacht Squadron. They were still chuckling about my brush with Mademoiselle de Bressange when I told her she was 'con comme la lune'!

Simon came to pick me up from the boat one evening accompanied by a familiar figure. It was Celestin Teretino 'Call me Les' Tokoragi – a delightful surprise! He now had a lucrative but hazardous job of diving for abalone off the south coast of New South Wales. We took him home and over dinner played the messages we had recorded from his family in Raroira and Tahiti. He was overjoyed and wept openly.

Simon was even busier at work, for the business was expanding and he was constantly employing new staff. The senior management had by now increased to ten. Quite often Simon would walk home from work some fifteen or more kilometers along the beach, but on days when the weather was unsuitable I would pick him up. We always had a drink in the boardroom before leaving so I met them all. My adopted role was to introduce their wives to each other. I also spent a morning a week horse riding – one of the drawbacks of my sailing life was that the other love of my life was being neglected.

The Solomon Islands and Papua New Guinea were in our sights for our next cruises. We made plans to ship *Iota* to Honiara in the Solomons. We would sail to Rabaul and then decide how we would spend Simon's holidays the year after.

It was much easier to find people with local knowledge of the area than it had been for Polynesia and the Caribbean. We came across district officers, medical staff, teachers and traders, all of whom had useful information. Equipped with a new engine, a wind vane and a basic knowledge of pidgin English, we were ready to embark on our next adventure.

rain and shine
in the solomon islands

1968

'She's not going to fit,' said Lyell Burrow, first officer of the *Tulagi*, the Burns Philp ship on which *Iota* and I were booked for a passage to Honiara in the Solomon Islands.

When she was berthed at Darling Harbour I had introduced myself and explained *Iota*'s needs. *Tulagi* was a small ship and I wondered if she had enough deck space for a 30-foot yacht. Lyell wanted to go and see for himself so I drove him to the other side of the Harbour. He took measurements and we went back to the *Tulagi* where he took more. Lyell shook his head.

I had to admit he was right. There was 30 feet of clear deck space just behind the bridge; *Iota* was 30 feet long at deck level, but her davits and pulpit added another four feet. This was a disaster – our cruise wasn't even going to start!

Companionways led down to the deck from the bridge on each side of the ship. I looked at the nearest one closely – if it wasn't there *Iota* would fit quite neatly – and I looked at Lyell.

'We can't dismantle the ship!' He understood perfectly what I was thinking.

'But it's only held on with a couple of bolts. And there's another companionway on the other side. You can manage with one, just for this trip,' I said, pleading.

Lyell hesitated. 'I'll have to think about it.'

'Thanks,' I said. 'That's really good of you. You don't know how relieved I am. I was really worried.'

He smiled. 'I only said I'd think about it.'

It took quite a while to load; with so little room to manoeuvre the derricks had to be lined up exactly. Lyell refused to be hurried. He placed the yacht neatly on the deck with inches to spare.

The *Tulagi* was a happy ship. The sailors were Malays, the stewards Chinese and all were cheerful and obliging. Captain 'Drunken' Duncan Barr left most of the running of the ship in Lyell's capable hands. Lyell came from Sariba, an island near Samari in Papua. His parents had a boat yard there and a slip and could take care of *Iota* if I wanted to leave her for a while. This was an interesting piece of information; I stowed it away in my mind for future use.

With little room to spare, Lyell placed Iota *neatly on the deck of the* Tulagi.

Tulagi's passenger accommodation was basic – five Spartan double cabins and two small bathrooms for ten passengers – eight women and two men. The bathroom for the women was embarrassingly inadequate so we deemed both bathrooms co-educational, on a first come, first served, basis. This did not worry Dave, a plantation manager returning to Bougainville after leave in Australia, but his cabin mate Wesley, a missionary, found the arrangement not to his liking. He protested, but his lone voice was decisively overruled. None of us ever coincided with him in the bathroom; we wondered if the situation so upset him that he had given up washing himself. Dave had us convulsed with laughter with his imitation of Wesley undressing under a dressing gown while the ship was rolling.

Three of the women passengers were visiting relatives who lived in the islands. Vera, my cabin mate, was to meet a new grandson – her son was in charge of the Solomon Islands police. Two sisters were heading for a third sister who lived in Gizo. They were born in the islands and looked on their visit as 'coming home'.

After four days we arrived at Norfolk Island to unload cargo. It was a hazardous process – with no harbour the ship had to anchor off and discharge her cargo into barges. The *Tulagi* was rolling so it was slow work – which suited us fine as it gave more time to explore ashore.

Captain Cook discovered Norfolk Island in 1774 and it was first settled as a convict colony in 1788. Some of the barracks and convict buildings survived, as did the jail and several bridges. At Bloody Bridge the body of a brutal overseer killed by the convicts had been walled up in the stones, but tell-tale blood seeped out through the still-wet mortar. Conditions for the prisoners were appalling: they were chained, lashed and kept in solitary confinement. For many, death was welcomed. We spent time in the cemetery reading headstones recording their gruesome fate. Some inscriptions listed the crimes committed, others were more poetic – 'He lied in vain and died in pain'.

The first convict settlement lasted until 1814 and the second for 30 years from 1825 until 1855. In 1856 Pitcairn Islanders, the descendants of the *Bounty* mutineers, were settled there. Many of the Norfolk Island inhabitants are direct descendants of Fletcher Christian and still have his surname. They spoke with an intriguing form of Elizabethan English.

We hired a car to admire the stunning coastline of this high island with its steep cliffs and attractive bays. Contented cows grazed on rich green pastures set among dark green Norfolk pines. It was so picturesque it was difficult to believe it was real – Mother Nature's artistic talent was on display. On the second day ashore Dave and I hired horses and rode along the cliff tops and into the forest, gaining an even greater appreciation of Norfolk's natural wonders.

We went on to Santo where I called on M. Ouseaux who had repaired the damage *Iota* had suffered on the *Caledonien*. He was pleased to see me again and hear our cruise had been successful. He had a new house and proudly took me up into the hills to a newly built Besser block home – such a contrast to his coconut shack on the beach. The linoleum had large, brightly coloured squares and the chromium and plastic chairs were lovingly arranged in two straight lines with their legs precisely on the corners of the squares, precisely in the middle of the room. I had an overwhelming urge to disorganise them. Requested to take a seat I sat in one of the middle chairs and managed to disrupt those on either side of it and kick the one opposite – but I felt guilty and carefully lined the legs up again, reflecting I had no right to inflict my taste on them.

~

Honiara had a thriving yacht club; it did not boast a lot of boats, but attracted many members as it was the meeting place for most of the European community. It was conveniently near the middle of the town and close to the wharf where the *Tulagi* was berthed. We arrived on Friday and *Iota* was not offloaded until Sunday so I had time to accept an offer of honorary membership and organise a mooring. The hospitable members included Dudley, who ran the Solomon Islands Postal Services, and his wife Thelma, who enthusiastically organised Honiara's social life. Jan and her boyfriend Ryan both worked for the government. Jan had just moved in with Ryan and was embarrassed that her own house was empty so she asked me if I would like to stay there. I accepted her kind offer.

Just before *Iota* was lowered into the water a package of frozen meat slipped out of a sling and fell into the water. Within five minutes the sea was turbulent with a frenzy of feeding sharks. We held on tightly as we took *Iota* to her mooring through the boiling water.

Iota's neighbour was a trading boat, *Coral Queen*. Her skipper, Harry Moss, made two of his crew available to help me raise *Iota*'s masts, move the lead, scrub her decks, wash her topsides and load water. In no time at all they changed her from deck cargo into a yacht ready for the sea. It was hot and humid so I was pleased to have the help.

I was soon to discover that the European residents of Honiara took their leisure time and pleasures seriously. They were delighted with a new face. I was invited to barbecues and dinners, to an art show organised by the dynamic Thelma and to the Police Club with Vera my former cabin mate. I moved into Jan's house on a hill behind the town and hired an elderly car that had to be cajoled into believing it had the will and the strength to climb the steep rise.

Next door to the Yacht Club on the waterfront was the Mendana Hotel, named after the Spanish explorer, Álvaro de Mendaña de Neira, who discovered the Solomon Islands in 1567. The proprietor of the hotel was a rotund gentleman, nicknamed Buddha, as he could usually be seen in a meditative posture in a throne-like chair overseeing his guests. He had a strict rule that after sunset all male visitors should wear either long trousers or long socks. Promptly at six his worried-looking henchman scurried around checking under the tables for any sign of a naked male leg.

The crew of a small aircraft who were making an aerial survey of the Solomon Islands were staying at the Mendana. They could only work for a few hours in the early morning before clouds covered the islands so they had plenty of leisure time. The pilot, 'No Worries' Russ, was a Kiwi who lived in Fiji. We met each day after his morning's work to make a decision – how should we amuse ourselves today? Should we fly, sail or drive?

Dramatic wartime wrecks were all along the coast of Guadalcanal.

It was an opportunity to make sure *Iota* was in good order so we started by sailing. Then we drove the old car along the coastal road in both directions. Along the shore we came across dramatic wartime wrecks. These were only a few of the dozens of ships sunk during the battles of Guadalcanal in 1942 and 1943. Prior to the war this stretch of water was known as Sealark Sound, but afterwards became Iron Bottom Sound.

Russ took me up in his plane to give me an idea of the interior of the island. Henderson Field, the airstrip, so bitterly fought over during the war, was being refurbished and the planes used the adjacent golf course instead. An apparently minor problem was that they shared it with golfers and cattle. We took off and flew around the island and over the top through cumulus clouds. Their formations over the mountains were magnificent pillared masses constantly forming and breaking up. The little plane bounced through them and occasionally the rugged grandeur of the mountains appeared through the gaps, alarmingly close.

'Don't worry,' said Russ, 'the highest mountain in the Solomons is 8,000 feet and we're at 10,000.'

Russ made a low pass over the golf course before landing to alert the golfers to chase away the cattle.

One afternoon we were sitting in Jan's house when it started to shake. Cups in the kitchen swung on their hooks and a picture fell off the wall. It was a weird, alarming sensation.

'It's only an earthquake,' Russ was reassuring. 'I've met them before in New Zealand – they happen quite often. Don't worry – this isn't a very strong one.'

Next morning when I went down to *Iota* another little yacht, *Omicron*, had joined her. She was only 20 feet long. Her owner, Dave, had sailed her from England. He asked if there had been an earthquake yesterday afternoon for, while at sea, the boat had started to shake and vibrate. He had noted the time – the exact time when the house on the hill had trembled. We were both surprised to discover an earthquake could be felt at sea.

~

The effectiveness of *Iota*'s antifouling had suffered because she had been out of the water for three weeks on the ship and I needed to give her bottom another coat before we set off on our cruise. The closest slipway was in Tulagi, 20 miles away across Iron Bottom Sound.

Harry Moss lent me Moses, his experienced first mate, to help me cross the strait. We had an easy sail, Moses enjoying a new experience. Russ, having completed his survey, was on his way back to Fiji. He flew low overhead and waggled his wings. I could hear him saying, 'Don't worry, you're on the right track.'

We tied up to a wharf near Tom Elkington's slipway. Tom had lived in the Solomon Islands for many years and was known as a 'before' – a 'before the war' resident. His venerable old trading boat, *Hawk*, had been built in New Zealand in 1881. She was 90 feet long, in excellent condition and had a well-disciplined crew. His wife Neysa invited me to dinner and told me it would be 'pot luck' because her woodstove was not working. Despite the substitute Primus having only one working burner (the cap of the other burner had gone missing) she cooked an excellent fish.

We talked about the various cruising boats that had visited them over the years.

'One in particular created the most sensational stir,' said Neysa. 'A big Tahitian fellow came into the harbour on a boat called *Dida*. He learned of the girls' boarding school run by a Methodist mission on an island in the middle of the harbour. The rule forbidding men on the island was a challenge and an irresistible lure. He anchored *Dida* close to the beach. After dark, when the moon came up, he sat on the bowsprit strumming his guitar and singing.'

Tom took up the story. 'His tactic worked like a charm. Marjorie, a teacher at the school, whose life was short on romance, fell for his charms. It was love at first sight and passion overwhelmed them. Marjorie left the school, much against the advice of her fellow teachers, and went off with him, never to be seen again.'

Iota on the slip in Tulagi

'Was that Eddie?' I queried. 'Sounds like him.'

'Why, yes,' said Neysa. 'Have you met him?'

'I met Eddie and Marjorie going to Noumea on a French ship a few years ago. He told me they met in Tulagi but didn't tell me how!'

I told them also how *Dida* and her various crew kept touching on my life – and how her stories had captured my imagination and made me dream I would go cruising around the romantic waterways of the world. I mentioned Jack who had sailed with Ellen and her husband from the West Indies to Tahiti; I told them about meeting Henk when celebrating *Iota*'s return to good health in Mau's Bar in Santo, learning he had bought *Dida*, then meeting up with him again in the British Virgin Islands. So many coincidences!

Tom escorted me back to *Iota*. As we went outside hermit crabs were scurrying around in their borrowed shells. One was different – I couldn't believe my eyes! A crab had taken up residence inside the missing burner cap of the Primus stove. Tom grabbed it. We then had to negotiate a plague of frogs – it almost impossible to walk down the hill without treading on one.

Two days later, slipping successfully accomplished, I sailed back to Honiara. The sky was heavily overcast with squalls of rain, so I was pleased to have Moses' company again. I was becoming accustomed to a climate of quick changes from torrential rain to brilliant sunshine.

Late one afternoon Thelma and Dudley drove me to the top of Mount Austen to admire the view. We drove through a shower of heavy rain. While turning on the muddy road the car slid sideways and became firmly bogged. We put branches under the wheels, pushed and pulled, but to no avail. The car was buried up to its axles. Thelma and I started to walk down the hill to find help while it was still daylight; Dudley stayed with the car. We were about halfway down when he drove up behind us – how he had managed to rescue the car on his own we never learned.

In Honiara the Queen's Birthday holiday continued for three days, the islanders enthusiastically embracing the celebrations. Flags flew, the police paraded and everybody partied with more enthusiasm than ever. I even dressed *Iota* overall for the occasion.

A few days later Simon arrived, landing on the golf course in a much-travelled Friendship. Thelma could not resist the opportunity to organise a party – to welcome Simon and say 'goodbye' to me.

On our way to Tulagi a thunderstorm passed to leeward of us – a dark, dense cloud with lightning falling out of it. We came in behind it

I dressed Iota *overall in honour of the Queen's birthday.*

A thunderstorm chased us into Tulagi

and tied up alongside *Hawk*. Tom came aboard and marked our charts, giving us the benefit of his wealth of experience of the islands. Neysa invited us to dinner again, this time with her wood stove and two Primus burners back in service.

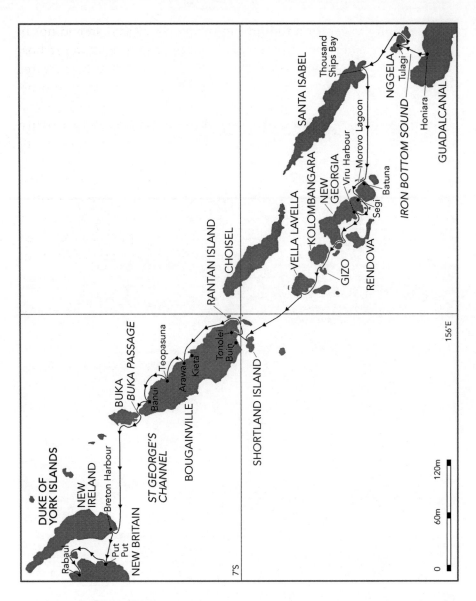

Tom and *Hawk* left early the next morning on a government charter to pick up schoolchildren starting the new school term in Honiara. We left soon after for Taroaniara on the other side of the bay to look up *Coral Queen*, Moses and his skipper Harry Moss. Harry was a mine of information about the islands.

After lunch we started up the six mile long, narrow Mboli Passage between the two parts of Nggela – Nggela Sule (big) to the west and Nggela Pine (small) to the east. It was like a river. We tied *Iota* to the remains of a wartime wharf in the middle of the passage and scrambled through thick vegetation to find the spring Harry said should not be missed. The clean fresh water gushing out of the rocks like a fire hose amazed us. We were reluctant to leave such a bountiful source of water. As the sun went down scores of birds yelled raucously at each other in the thick green jungle covering the steep-sided mountain. Noisy sulphur-crested cockatoos, brilliant red rosellas and smaller, brightly coloured birds went through their evening ritual of arguing about who was going to sleep where and with whom.

Slowly we went through the passage, stopping at a village where we bought a rope of shells – the local, old form of money. On the northern side of the island a stiff trade wind blew us along the coast to a sheltered, uninhabited bay. We explored along the beach and back into the dense jungle; every tree was hung with vines and orchids and the flowers were improbably bright.

Village girls return home bearing produce from their gardens.

Rain squalls bothered us again on our way to Santa Isabel, obscuring our objective and making navigation difficult. They cleared just in time for us to find the way into Thousand Ships Bay. A school of porpoises bounded up to escort us, leaping well clear of the water. Although we were going as fast as we could with a dark squall chasing us, they found us slow and dull and left after a while. We just made it to the first anchorage in the bay, before the squall hit.

Mendaña named Thousand Ships Bay on the southeast corner of Santa Isabel because it was large enough to hold a thousand ships and he thought this would impress those whom he hoped would fund his next expedition. In 1567 the 25-year-old nephew of the Governor of Peru had sailed in a southwesterly direction from Callao in Peru, unlike other Spanish navigators of the time who had taken more northwesterly routes. He had been searching for islands believed to exist 600 leagues from the Peruvian coast and rumoured to have been visited by the Incas, who found 'gold and silver, a throne made of copper, a multitude of black slaves and the skin of an animal like a horse'. He was disappointed not to find the riches he was seeking, but gave such an elaborate and glowing description of the islands, that he attracted funding for another expedition in 1595. He failed to find the Solomons again but discovered the Marquesas. The mapping of the Solomon Islands Mendaña had undertaken was inaccurate and two centuries were to elapse before another European, Louis de Bougainville, re-discovered the islands.

The geological survey team needed the services of this reluctant machine to search for nickel and copper near Thousand Ships Bay.

The two sisters on the *Tulagi* who were going to visit their other sister in Gizo told me about their nephew Jim, who was working with a geological survey team looking for nickel and copper near Thousand

Ships Bay. We climbed up the hill to find him. The path took us nearly vertically up a series of steps to a camp in a clearing. The team's huts were built, local-fashion, of plaited coconut leaves on a bare terrace sticky with red mud, for the ground had been cleared the because of the centipedes – big ones up to fifteen centimetres long, with a painful bite.

We met Jim, who introduced us to the rest of the team. There were nine of them, including two wives and two small children, the latter stained bright red with mud. Everybody's clothes were red and so were the dogs, Rufus and Rusty. Pleased to have visitors from the outside world they asked us to dinner. Afterwards, we slid down the track in the dark to the boat. We too were covered in mud so went for a swim fully clothed to wash it off before going aboard.

Invited back to breakfast we scrambled up the hill again in the morning. Jim told us we were just in time to witness the daily visit from Joe, their tame hornbill. The dining mess was a coconut-thatched shelter with the upper part of the walls left open. We heard him coming before we saw him, his wings making a whirring noise like an old-fashioned aeroplane. Joe was a big bird with a wingspan of nearly two metres, a huge beak and a long tail to balance it. He made a grand entrance, flying from one end of the mess to the other, swooping low over the dogs that leapt after him, barking and knocking over chairs. It was quite an act. During breakfast he sat on the back of Jim's chair and ate salami.

We left in reasonably good weather in the early afternoon to cross to New Georgia, just over 100 miles away, and made good progress until dark. With a strong wind astern and the genoa poled out we thought we were in for an easy night. It was not to be as the wind constantly changed both strength and direction; just as we managed to set the wind vane we would have to gybe or take in sail for a squall.

We were heading for the Marovo Lagoon, the world's largest saltwater lagoon. Long, narrow coral islands shelter it. We anchored at Batuna, a Seventh Day Adventist mission where Bob the missionary welcomed us and shared dinner on board with us. His wife was in Honiara having a baby and he was going to visit her the next day. He kindly invited us to use his house for showers and to do our laundry, even though he would not be home.

As he was going ashore next morning Simon slipped on the coral and gashed his ankle deeply, right to the bone. I wrapped it in a clean towel and he managed to keep it dry while getting back to the boat. I bandaged it and gave him penicillin as coral wounds notoriously go septic. We spent the next day quietly so he could keep his foot up and rest it. We had time to admire the scenery – the combination of dark green rainforest-covered islands, white strips of sandbars and beaches, the light blue shallows and the dark blue of the deeper sea was breathtaking! We were reminded of what Robert Louis Stevenson had written about the allure of the South Pacific:

> *It is not alone the forms of the mountains, the square cut cliffs, the pinnacled buttresses – the razor sharp edge against the heavens. It is not the greenness of the dales and hollows, nor yet the palms so ungainly yet so pleasing. It is not the perpetual songs of the birds. It is not the incredible generous, smoothness of the air, not the cleanness and lightness of the perfumes. It is not one nor yet all of them together; the spring of delight, I think, is mainly in the colours.*

This area was famous for woodcarving. Villagers came along in their canoes and offered us carvings of birds, fish, seahorses and porpoises, as well as totoishu – highly polished stylised human heads with a delicately patterned inlay of mother-of-pearl. They were fashioned from the local ebony – a beautiful hard black wood with lighter graining, rich brown kerosene wood and rosewood varying from a straw colour to gold and a deep red. Such fine artefacts were difficult to resist and remarkably good value so we bought many of them.

It was pouring with rain when a man came alongside in his outboard boat.

He introduced himself. 'I'm John Schenk. I live on the island just over there, Lilihina. Would you like to come across and get out of the rain?'

'That's very kind,' said Simon. 'Thank you.'

When the rain eased a little we motored across and tied up to his jetty. John, a retired sergeant major, was building a small hotel on the island. He told us how perfect the lagoon would be as a tourist resort and listed the many activities he would provide for his guests.

'There's potential for diving, snorkelling, kayaking, fishing and swimming. There's plenty of reef and it teems with tropical fish and lots of turtles. I've made a garden so I'll be able to provide them with local fresh food. They'll be able to interact with the local villagers, learn about their culture and buy carvings.'

He never ceased to talk and seemed lonely – he was alone on the island except for a couple of local workers. He hoped, when his hotel was established, there would be plenty of people for company. His garden was interesting, with nuts, pineapples, ginger, peppers, sweet potatoes, breadfruit and soursops. He was certainly hospitable and an excellent cook; for lunch he presented us with crayfish and a salad of watercress and onion.

We moved down the lagoon in fitful sunshine and showers. It was well buoyed and even in heavy rain we were able to find our way. The lagoon was dotted with islands, some tiny, others quite large, but only a few inhabited. We kept close to the coast of Vangunu, a high volcanic island with dense rainforest and a fringe of mangroves.

We were invited to Lilihina where the owner was developing a tourist resort.

At a narrow part of the lagoon near the airstrip at Segi was a Methodist mission with a large, elaborate church and a jetty in a state of disrepair. The wind was blowing onto the jetty and it swarmed with children so we opted to anchor on the other side of the lagoon in a well-sheltered bay. In the evening four completely silent Islanders in a canoe came up to look through our portholes. One of them, an elderly man, had big stretched holes in his ear lobes, which hung in loops. They had been chewing betel nut and had blank, expressionless faces.

The famous and successful Coastwatcher of World War II, Donald Kennedy, had his well-concealed headquarters at Segi. Eric Feldt, organiser of the Coastwatchers, described him as 'a determined man of middle age, with a strong personality'. He had a broad network of loyal villagers and was able to report Japanese aircraft and shipping and rescue airmen who had been shot down over the neighbouring area. He chose Segi because of the impenetrable jungle around it and the treacherous, uncharted reefs in the lagoon. Even our chart deteriorated into a few dotted lines and described the area as 'foul ground'. The Japanese were not prepared to risk their boats in these waters and never discovered him, although they were establishing a base in Viru Harbour only thirteen miles away.

It rained through the night and was still wet the next morning but, in spite of it, we continued through the lagoon. We persevered through the 'foul ground' and were soon battling a strong southerly wind that at least stirred up waves so we could see where the reef was breaking. We identified Heles Bar and crossed it in a froth of current and upset seas, then turned and ran more comfortably before the wind.

A heavy squall blotted out Viru Harbour. It was raining so hard we gasped for breath under the brim of our sou'westers. The squall passed, the wind died and then came again from the northeast against us, blowing the squall back again with even more rain. It was a frustrating day and we discovered a further disaster – one of the portholes was not firmly closed and rain had poured into the cabin, soaking our bunk.

Eventually we reached Viru Harbour, a sheltered inlet leading into densely wooded flat country. The passage twisted and turned around an attractive village. Opposite the village was an unsightly floating barge, the headquarters of a timber development company. We had an introduction so tied *Iota* alongside. As we wrung the water out of ourselves Simon laughed. 'This is meant to be the dry season!'

Clyde and Carol, the American manager and his wife, invited us to join them for drinks so we climbed up past the well-equipped workshops, offices and living quarters for the Filipino and Japanese workers to a luxuriously furnished, air-conditioned apartment. The barge had been built in Hong Kong and towed to the Solomon Islands by a Japanese ship. The company had timber interests in the Philippines and Malaysia. Simon discovered Clyde knew some of his friends in Malaysia so they enjoyed an interesting evening recalling their former lives.

The sound of ringing bells and chainsaws woke us in the morning. The sun was smiling down on us so we thanked our hosts for their hospitality and sailed to Rendova. The chart of Rendova Harbour, dated 1944, was not accurate, so we found our way in by eye.

The next day we lined up the beacons, crossed the Munda Bar into a well-protected lagoon and wound our way around islands and reefs. We entered the Diamond Narrows between New Georgia and Arundel Island and had a fast run through, the current rushing us along between the overhanging trees. Two women paddling their fully laden canoes kept up with us; they sang as they dipped their paddles into the water.

At the southern end of Kolombangara the chart, again dated 1944, showed Vovohe Cove. It indicated the shore with a dotted line and marked two beacons and four buoys. The depths it showed bore little resemblance to what our echo sounder was telling us. A caution on the chart read: 'It is reported that the beacons are overgrown and the buoys are missing' – at least that was right. It was difficult to realise that this tranquil anchorage had been the scene of such bitter and dramatic battles during the war. We had it to ourselves; bright butterflies visited us and we saw many equally colourful birds.

We enjoyed a spectacular sunset in Rendova.

Reluctantly we tore ourselves away and went on to Gizo, passing a small round island with pale green trees called Kennedy Island because JFK had been stranded on it during the war. Gizo was a dismal dirty town. The waterfront was lined with scruffy houses and behind them was a flat area of red mud they called a road. Neither of the stores had any fresh food. We went to the Gizo Club for a drink; dusty and ill kept

Approaching the Diamond Narrows

Tranquil Vovohe Cove had been the scene of bitter and dramatic battles during the war.

it was equally depressing with broken tables and chairs. The beach was littered with rubbish.

The redeeming feature was Eunice Palmer. We were able to bring her greetings from her son Jim, whom we had met in Thousand Ships Bay, and tell her I had met her sisters on the *Tulagi*. Eunice was born in the islands and had lived there all her life; her father arrived before the turn of the century, a pioneer indeed. Her husband, Ernie, was also born in the Solomons. He had run a trading boat, but was now organising a pearling business using black and gold-lipped oysters.

Eunice was full of information about the history and culture of the Solomon Islands. She told us about 'time before' when many of the Islanders had been headhunters and cannibals, particularly those on the eastern islands who were clannish and suspicious of outsiders. The inhabitants of the Solomons spoke over sixty different languages and dialects so groups had difficulty communicating before the introduction of pidgin English. On the same island the dialect spoken by coast dwellers was often different from that spoken by inland people. The Western Islanders were less warlike than those of the Eastern Islands.

'People don't consider themselves to be Solomon Islanders,' she said. 'They relate only to the island where they were born.'

When she heard we were traveling west Eunice asked us to take a parcel of books to her friends, Michael and Mona Georgetti at Mundi Mundi on Vella Lavella.

That night swarms of mosquitoes nearly ate us alive. Simon was particularly unhappy because he had suffered from malaria during the war. We had mosquito coils burning, sprayed every hour and slept under a net, yet still they managed to bite us. It was stifling hot. We moved across to another island for the second night and anchored off a Catholic mission. The children came down to the beach in the evening and sang to us.

We set off as soon as it was light enough and followed the outside of the reef, counting the gaps until we came to the one that took us into a hidden bay. We tied up to the jetty and wandered along a path lined with bougainvilleas and hibiscus to an attractive house set in a cheerful garden. Michael and Mona met us and introduced their three daughters and their friend Georges. They immediately invited us to dinner and Michael poured us a stiff ice-cold gin and tonic; he was obviously delighted to have new drinking companions. Mona, born on the shores of the Marovo lagoon, showed us around her garden where she grew all of their vegetables and introduced us to her chickens, ducks and turkeys. She was capable and industrious. Dinner was pigeon and turtle served with a host of home-grown vegetables and copious quantities of wine.

Georges, from a neighbouring island, visited every now and then, ostensibly to castrate the cats. He was originally from the New Hebrides where he had owned a trading schooner. He had a story to tell.

Mona and Michael Georgetti and their neighbour Georges

In 1933 he called at a remote outer island of the New Hebrides to see the government officer, the gendarme. It was pouring with rain and he arrived soaked to the skin at the house in the hills. The gendarme lent him dry clothes including the jacket of his uniform. Georges stayed for dinner and on his way back to his boat in the dark local villagers attacked him. They thought he was the gendarme. Georges' neck was broken and he was left for dead. The next thing he knew was hospital in Port Vila where, fortunately, after several months, he fully recovered. His three assailants were identified, captured and brought to Port Vila. Their crime was considered all the more serious because they had intended to attack an official, so they were sentenced to be executed by guillotine. Georges watched from his hospital window.

Georges described the scene. 'The man whose job it was to pick up the severed head and put it in a box with its body had hysterics because one of the heads bit him.'

It was the last time the guillotine was ever used.

~

It was 48 miles to our next port, just too far for us to make it comfortably in daylight so we planned to sail overnight, leaving late in the afternoon. However next morning one of Michael's daughters delivered a note: 'We are expecting you both for lunch – all prepared. Come whenever you're ready. We're into the gin. Georges is the cook.'

It was the end of our good intentions for, at five o'clock we were still getting over our lunch and preparing for dinner. We were in no condition to go to sea.

We managed to leave just before dark the next day in good weather, but it turned into a wild and stormy night. The sky was completely black – no moon or stars, but was lit almost continuously by lightning, a few flashes striking close to us – too close. It poured with rain. As we had plenty of time we hove-to and went below to wait for the flashes to go away. Dawn came reluctantly; the sky cleared and the wind freshened. We sailed into Shortland Island early in the morning, escorted by a school of porpoises.

The area was scattered with wrecked aeroplanes, overgrown landing strips and crumbling fortifications reminding us again that this area had witnessed the bitterest fighting of the war in the Pacific. On fleeing the islands the Japanese left behind everything from bodies to beer bottles.

Shortland Island was scattered with wrecked aeroplanes from the war.

There was a Japanese timber camp – Simon knew one of the owners in Sydney – but he had left the night before we arrived. We went to see the manager. The camp was poorly kept and dirty and had a reputation for being haunted by the devil – there had been several accidents including three deaths in the last few years. In one incident men were killed by the tree they were felling while having lunch in its shade.

Shortland Island was at the northern boundary of the Solomon Islands so we had to clear before entering New Guinea. Customs was on one small island and Immigration was at the Catholic mission on another small island opposite. The customs officer, a local islander, was carefully polite and meticulous but, oh, so, slow! Eventually, we motored across to the mission where Sister Frances stamped our passports. Father Joseph showed us around and apologised for not offering us a drink; they had not received their last order. He had been sending a telegram over the radio each day for the past two weeks saying, 'Man does not live by bread alone!' They advised us to enter New Guinea if possible at Buin, which had an airport but no anchorage, as the customs officer in Kieta was 'difficult'.

The fish were jumping so we trolled a line on the way to Bougainville and caught a small mackerel and a larger kingfish. We hooked a huge swordfish that stopped *Iota* dead in her tracks and almost managed to pull her backwards. Fortunately it broke away.

We went up the long inlet to Tonolei where there was another, much better run timber operation. Here we found Dick, the nephew of Thelma the energetic organiser of the community's social life in Honiara. He took Simon to Buin to the office of Malcolm the assistant district commissioner – ADC for short – who returned with them to enter us. *Iota* became the venue for a party with ten guests on board for drinks. Two newly arrived visiting directors had just seen a flying fish for the first time; their amazement was such they couldn't stop talking about it! We moved on to the Tonolei Club for dinner.

Simon was expecting a cable so we had to wait for the radio schedule before we left next morning; we were on our way at midday. Initially we made good progress, but, on rounding East Point, we turned north into a headwind. Rantan Island looked enticing – an ideal place to spend the night. Its soft, white beach was strewn with lovely and unusual shells and big, sculptured orchids in incredible colours were scattered in the thick forest. We had this Garden of Eden to ourselves. We sat in the cockpit with a glass of wine as the sun went down feeling contented; we had eaten well – freshly caught fish and home-grown vegetables, a gift from Tonolei. A calm, soft night with a slim crescent of moon followed a many-hued sunset; a myriad of stars twinkled above us. Cruising should always be like this.

At dawn a brisk cool wind was falling down from the mountains. After a few hours it fell away to be replaced by an equally brisk, but hot, southeaster. The weather was marvellously clear. We could see back into the mountains, several of which were the perfect cones of volcanos. The largest was active and could be identified by a plume of smoke by day and a red glow from its crater at night.

Nine hours after starting out, carefully avoiding Kieta, we arrived at Arawa Plantation. Scorched by the sun despite our efforts to keep it at bay we were grateful to accept the hospitality of the managers, Jan and Peter, who were looking after the thousand acres of cocoa bushes growing under coconuts palms while the owner was in Sydney. Dick had alerted them that we were in the area. They treated us to hot showers, cold drinks and a splendid dinner. Jan, a Dane, had been a professional plantation manager for many years, having worked with cocoa and coffee in the New Guinea Highlands and Brazil, rubber in Malaysia and coffee in Kenya.

He told us about the Panguna copper mine CRA were opening in the hills behind Kieta. Already 200 white miners had arrived in the district and the number would likely increase to 700. A new town would be needed, reached by nearly 40 kilometres of road up the steep mountain. The Bougainvilleans were resentful for they believed the minerals under the land were as much part of their heritage as the vegetation on it. They believed land could not be bought or sold, but only handed from one generation to the next. They took exception to the labour being brought in from other parts of New Guinea followed by the arrival of the workers' relations who lived in shanties on land belonging to Bougainvilleans. The inevitable environmental damage from the biggest open cut copper mine in the world was unimaginable and unthinkable.

'There's going to be trouble here,' Jan said. How right he was!

The feast of hospitality we received at Arawa was the beginning of a week of similar luxury as we sailed from one plantation to the next. On first sight it seemed the plantation owners and managers had an idyllic existence, but they also had their share of problems. At the beautifully kept, highly productive Arigua Plantation we accompanied the manager, Roy, as he went to talk to his labourers early one morning – a ceremony called 'lines'. He gave them their day's tasks and dealt with their problems. They were on a two-year contract and came from the mountains of New Guinea. Their skin was dark reddish-brown as distinct from the jet-black Bougainvilleans who called them 'Redskins' in a derogatory fashion. They were paid by the 'mark' – the collection of a stated amount of copra or cocoa or the clearing of a set area of weeds, so the manager did not have to constantly supervise their activities.

The managers led an isolated life and were very dependent on their two-way radios for communication; few roads existed and they mostly travelled by sea. Visitors were rare so they welcomed new faces and were generously hospitable. At Arigua we had showers, drinks and dinner – when a couple from a neighbouring plantation joined us – beds for the night and a houseboy to do our laundry.

As we made our way north we realised we were following the same path as the 'bone ship' that had been visiting the previous week. Japanese businessmen had chartered a local trading boat to look for relics of the war, seeking bones, boots, cooking pots and anything else that had belonged to their countrymen during the hostilities. They held ceremonies on the beach, burning aromatic lamps and bowing to honour their fallen comrades. The Islanders thought their behaviour strange and their appearance – baggy trousers, veiled hats and shoes with a separate compartment for their big toe – comical. They were still laughing when we arrived a week after them.

At Teopasuna we anchored close to the beach in front of the plantation house and met Malcolm and Heather. Their houseboy, newly arrived from the New Guinea Highlands, had never seen a boat with sails before and thought we were a 'sip belong tamburan' – a spirit ship bringing desirable manufactured products to members of a cargo cult who thought material wealth could be obtained through magic spells and religious rituals.

Mal and Heather's house was in a fabulous setting, close to the sandy, coconut fringed beach and surrounded by lawn dotted with bougainvillea and multi-coloured crotons. Talk extended well into the night.

My shipmate Dave from the *Tulagi* was managing the next BP plantation at Banui. Dave treated us like royalty, providing us with his guesthouse and a houseboy. For two days life was one long party with the neighbours coming by boat and on foot to meet us. Dave supervised the festivities from a comfortable chair, shouting in the direction of the kitchen, 'Cook, two pela beer 'e cum' or, when the cat jumped on the table, 'Cook, raus im pussy.'

Refreshed, we went on our way to the northern end of Bougainville and into the rushing currents of the narrow Buka Passage. We tied up to a jetty on Sohano Island at the western end of the passage and were welcomed by Des, the district commissioner and a keen yachtsman. This was the administrative centre of Bougainville, however Des told us the headquarters was moving to Kieta in order to be able to manage more effectively the expected trouble over the copper mine. Just in front of us on the jetty men were loading furniture onto a boat; Des asked for a dining table and chairs to be taken back to the house so he could entertain us to dinner!

At Madehas I rode an excellent horse between the coconut palms of a plantation.

Des and his wife Jeanne sailed with us to a small island called Madehas to meet its owner, Jock Lee. Here were more exquisite views over an extensive well-tended garden and across the water to mountainous islands. He had a tennis court and was pleased to have visitors who enjoyed playing. He was proud of his excellent horses and invited me to ride, escorting me around his cocoa bushes grown under coconut palms, where the grassy paths between were perfect for galloping.

Des advised us on the next part of our journey – we should go inside the reef to the northern end of Buka Island to Kessa Plantation where he would arrange for the owner to look after us. We would then be well placed for the 100-mile crossing to New Ireland.

He warned us, 'It may be a calm, sunny day on Buka, but in the channel – St Georges Channel – between Buka and New Ireland, more often than not there's a howling southerly and rough seas.'

Des was right. Although the weather was kind to start with the wind came in from the south and increased. We were heading west, close hauled – not *Iota*'s happiest point of sailing. In the afternoon a heavy squall heralded a foul night; the seas were building up and breaking. Occasionally *Iota* would fall with a crash into the trough of a wave and stop dead in her tracks. Waves came aboard with a terrifying roar, breaking over us with a sickening splash, drenching us and filling up the cockpit. Fortunately it drained quickly, but at times we felt as if we were in the sea rather than on it. We rolled a deep reef in the mainsail and set the No 2 jib. My main concern was that, with reduced sail, we would not be able to point high enough to make Cape St George at the southern end of New Ireland. I was so concerned I felt seasick for the first time in my life. At midnight I thought I sighted the lighthouse on the Cape – ahead and to leeward of us. I called Simon on deck; he confirmed it – and my seasickness vanished. She was going to make it! Well done, *Iota*!

A crowd gathered on the jetty at Madehas to wave goodbye.

We were due south of the Cape by 2.30 am and, at last, were able to bear away. In the morning the waves were over ten metres high, towering above us like the walls of a house. We were assaulted by fierce squalls with heavy rain blotting out the land. We were relieved to find shelter in Breton Harbour, a bay tucked in just behind the Cape and protected by an island.

This bay had been the setting of an improbable fraud in the late nineteenth century. The handsome, engaging, pious Charles-Marie Bonaventure du Breil, Marquis de Rays, fancied himself as King Charles I of Oceania. He had read of an idyllic land at the southern tip of New Ireland; it presented him with an opportunity to become wealthy as well as its king. Although he had never been there he advertised the charms of 'Nouvelle France' widely through Europe, seeking settlers. He described it as 'a Paradise with a climate similar to the French Riviera, with prodigiously fertile land and very friendly natives'. Several hundred gullible people responded, sold up all they had and gave their money to the Marquis to establish their new colony. In return he promised to bestow on them a title in their new land. He became rich and bought several large mansions where he entertained his mistresses.

In the 1880s those who survived the appalling conditions on the ships he chartered to take them to their new land were put ashore at Port Breton with three weeks' supply of food. They saw no sign of the rich, arable land they had been promised. Instead, the emigrants found a tangled jungle, poor soil, incessant rain and unfriendly, headhunting neighbours. Most died of malaria and starvation.

We sailed next day to Put Put, a pretty, well-protected bay on the east coast of New Britain, and then on to Duke of York Islands. We went first to the almost land-locked Mioka Harbour. In 1879 the famous American Samoan, Queen Emma, had arrived here with her lover, Tom Farrell, and established her planting and trading ventures. They were attracted to this group of islands for they had palm-shaded beaches, fertile coastland and plateaus, jungle-clad mountains and swift rivers. In those days this earthly paradise more closely resembled hell, for ferocious cannibals and diseases – malaria, dysentery and tropical ulcers – were waiting to strike. Not more than a dozen Europeans lived in New Guinea; they were missionaries and unscrupulous traders. Emma and Tom were involved in the rescue of some of the survivors of the Marquis de Rays scandal. In return, they gathered up the goods brought in to establish the colony.

At the time of their arrival in Mioka the Gazelle Peninsula on New Britain had a reputation for being the home of the most treacherous cannibals, but Emma knew it was fertile and that it offered opportunities. She hurried to acquire it before the Germans annexed it. Her brother-in-law Tom Parkinson braved the Islanders, taught them to plant coconuts and make copra and laid the foundation of Emma's great fortune. When the locals grew more accustomed to Europeans, their attempts at murder and cannibalism lessened. Queen Emma set up her court in the house of her dreams, Gunantambu, at Ralum near Kokopo. Her father, a much-married American, recognised eighteen children from his six wives. Many of them came with their families to New Guinea and were an important part of her enterprises. Emma sold her empire for a substantial sum just before World War I.

On the last day of the cruise we had a fine day with a free, fresh breeze. An exhilarating sail took us ever closer to the distinctive volcanoes surrounding Rabaul's magnificent harbour.

Distinctive volcanoes surround Rabaul's magnificent harbour.

papua new guinea – a country of contrasts

1968-1969

We sailed up Simpson Harbour to the town spread out along the waterfront and looked for a place to anchor. We headed for the few masts we could see, and as we approached, a man in an outboard dinghy came to meet us.

'Welcome,' he said, 'I'm Dick Stafford. You can anchor just astern of me – there's room – a yacht left this morning. They must have known you were coming.'

He came aboard, helped Simon with the anchor and told us about the facilities of the yacht club and the town.

'Give me a shout when you're ready to go ashore and I'll introduce you,' He climbed back into his dinghy.

Unlike the club at Honiara, Rabaul Aquatic Club had an Australian feel about it – the men collected around the bar and the women sat on the veranda talking about their children. However it provided the two most important things – hot showers and cold beer.

Simon had only two days before his plane left for Sydney. We talked about our options for next year's cruise.

'Remember Lyell Burrow on the *Tulagi*?' I asked, 'His parents run a shipyard on an island called Sariba near Samarai. I wonder if they could be useful.'

We made a plan. Simon would contact Lyell's parents and, if they were agreeable, we would sail *Iota* there over the Christmas holidays and leave her in their care while I had a few months back in Sydney. From there we would sail to Madang during Simon's annual holiday.

'Sounds good,' I approved.

We parted at the airport, hoping to be together again in four months time.

I set about all the jobs needing attention on *Iota*. I employed a boatboy, Orim, and set him to work cleaning bilges, scrubbing decks, collecting water and rubbing down the bright work ready for me to varnish. He took pride in the boat: 'Boat belong missus em e goodpela tomus.'

It took a while for us to learn to communicate with each other. One morning he was late. I said, 'I thought you weren't coming today.'

He explained, 'Me drinkim beer wantaim onetalk belong me, now me got sick belong head. Em e nogood tru.'

Boatboy Orim scrubs Iota's *deck.*

There are 820 languages in Papua New Guinea and many have fewer than 5000 speakers. My 'onetalk' is somebody who speaks my language – most likely a relative and certainly somebody who comes from the same part of the country. The pidgin language was certainly colourful. Orim carefully explained the subtleties of the word 'bagarapim' (to spoil). Something could be 'bagarap liklik', 'bagarap tru' or 'bagarap altogether pinis'. The development of pidgin English enabled wider communication, an essential step towards becoming a unified nation.

Life settled into a pleasant routine. I would collect Orim from the jetty at 8 am and he would work until noon. When I took him ashore I noticed a man was there to meet him. He was the pastor of the church that Orim attended, making sure that the church got its cut of Orim's earnings before he spent it all. I outwitted him by taking Orim to a different jetty – too far away from the yacht club for the pastor to be able to get there before he disappeared into town.

Cruising yachts came and went; for a one memorable week a record number of seven yachts was anchored in Rabaul Harbour. I was delighted when Ed Boden and his Vertue class *Kittiwake* sailed in. I had met him in Tahiti three years previously and he had news of many of the yachts in the Pacific at the time.

Most yachts were from Australia or New Zealand – *Nomad, Sheerwater, Aloha, Anglani, Rotorua* – staying for a week or two, but a couple had been there for a while so their owners could take a job and earn money for the next part of their travels.

Americans Dick and Abbie on *Meridian* had been in Rabaul for nearly a year. Dick ran the tyre and battery shop in town. He was outgoing and gregarious, the complete opposite to his wife. Abbie spent most of her days on the boat finding maintenance tasks to keep her occupied. She was a complex, reclusive character and rarely went ashore; Dick brought the shopping when he came back to the boat each evening.

Abbie was given to grumbling and found fault with the weather: 'It's either too damned hot or it's raining!' She complained about Dick spending time in the club before he came on board after work, but when I offered to take her to join him she declined.

'They drink too much and they're not interesting.' Abbie disapproved of and dismissed them all! Many of her grouches were outrageous but, in spite of them, she was good company.

Mauri Koa was a small sloop from New Zealand with a young couple, Robyn and Ian, aboard. They both had jobs ashore and were saving up for their journey home. We had a mutual fascination for volcanoes. Rabaul, situated within an active caldera and surrounded by volcanoes, is vulnerable to their eruptions. Frequently pumice floating on the water woke me as it clinked against *Iota*'s hull. It was sometimes so thick I thought I should be able to walk ashore. Pumice dust in the wind landed on my fresh varnish so I had to do it all again!

The volcano, Vulcan, had arisen on the eastern shore of the harbour during a major eruption in 1878. More catastrophic activity occurred in 1937 when Matupi and Vulcan exploded. Columns of smoke, steam and black mud reached a height of ten kilometres and caused widespread damage. The main road was buried under twelve metres of pumice and over 500 people were killed in their villages, bombarded by torrents of pumice and stones. It could well happen again – Rabaul's population lived under the constant threat of plumes of hot ash, and earthquakes.

One weekend Robyn, Ian and I sailed *Iota* around to the base of the volcano Matupi. We anchored in the bay and climbed up to the rim of the crater. Somebody had secured a rope so, with its aid, we slid about 25 metres down the steep sides. Inside was a belching inferno with steam hissing out of sinister cracks in the walls, sickly yellow crystalline sulphur deposits and a strong smell of rotten eggs. We gained an appreciation of the idea of hell – and why it was hot! We climbed out, thankful that the volcano had not chosen to erupt while we were in its crater.

Matupi – one of the active volcanos surrounding Rabaul's Simpson Harbour

Among the yachts was the bizarre *Kalasa*, owned by a Canadian, Harry. He was inspired by Joshua Slocum, the first person to circumnavigate the world single-handedly, and built *Kalasa* himself, creating a yacht strongly resembling Slocum's *Spray*. He thought *Spray* had not been strong enough so used much heavier timbers and more frames; as a result Kalasa drew eight feet and had only twenty centimetres of freeboard. He duplicated all the rigging, including the lazy jacks – she looked as if she was surmounted by an untidy spider's web. Her rudderpost was enormous; my arms were only just long enough to encircle it. When time came to leave Canada he did not have enough money to buy charts and anyhow did not know how to navigate – so what was the point of having them? He bought a tea towel with a map of the world on it and a friend gave him a set of pilot books for the Pacific Ocean. He intended to spend several years crossing to Australia from Vancouver, but arrived in Sydney after only six months. If he sighted land he could not be sure what land it was and the relevant pilot book was scarcely reassuring for it listed all the many hazards he might encounter. He invariably decided it was too dangerous and sailed on.

When he reached Sydney he sought a crew and met Adrienne, inexperienced, but keen to learn. She agreed to join him and lasted as far as Rabaul. On their way to the New Hebrides lightning blew off the top of their mast and the sails tumbled down to the deck; the headsail fell into the sea. They managed, with difficulty, to drag it on board. Adrienne headed for the galley; a cup of tea had become a necessity. As she was waiting for the water to boil, she heard stamping and shouting from the foredeck. She looked out through the hatch and saw Harry, naked, tearing out pages of a book, peeing on them and throwing them into the water accompanied by loud oaths.

'Harry, Harry,' she shouted. 'What are you doing?'

'It's alright,' he reassured her, 'it's not my best Bible.'

~

During the weekends I socialised with the people living ashore. We would go off into the countryside for a barbecue and a swim in a river. Everywhere we came across reminders of the war – tunnels into the hillsides, wrecked planes and old guns. One local man was fascinated by bullets and bombs and went looking for them so he could take them to pieces – he lost his leg! Rabaul had been virtually destroyed during the war and in the rebuilding was given wide streets and modern buildings.

The market had good-quality produce grown in the rich volcanic soils. Everything cost one shilling – for this you could buy three coconuts, two pawpaws and four avocados. It was not possible to buy one coconut, one avocado or one pawpaw because that involved giving change.

We went to the Kokopo Show, a crowded event where many of the New Guineans dressed in their colourful traditional costume. Their painted faces and bodies bedecked with feathers, flowers and shells were in startling contrast to the immaculate white naval uniform of the Governor, who came to officially open the proceedings. There were performances from troupes of singers and dancers as well as displays of produce.

Another reminder of the war

I spent several enjoyable and productive days with Shirley, a nurse at the Rabaul Hospital, and an able artist. Although she had the use of the family car, she could not drive and agreed to teach me to use oil paints in exchange for my driving us in her car to our painting venues.

Another woman at the yacht club boasted that her husband was 'Rabaul's leading lawyer'. It was no doubt true as he was Rabaul's only lawyer. Her airs and graces had not gained her any friends in the small community among either the Europeans or the New Guineans. She went to the store to buy a straw broom. When she came to pay for it the shopkeeper asked, 'Shall I wrap it, Madam, or will you ride it home?'

~

I wanted to see more of this part of New Guinea, particularly Manus Island in the Admiralty Group. The trading boat *Matarani* serviced these islands, but her schedule was 'flexible' – meaning she did not have a definite date of departure, and if she did, probably would not keep to it. This was island time. She eventually sailed with me on board to Kavieng, Manus and the Vitu Islands.

The *Matarani* could hardly be described as a luxury liner. She was 85 feet long, 21 feet wide, drew nine feet and had a crew of twelve. She was unspeakably dirty and riddled with cockroaches. My cabin was tiny – I shared it with mailbags and a collection of parcels. In it were a narrow two-tiered bunk that took up most of the width of the cabin and two small shelves. The mattress smelt musty, but the sheets were cleanish.

The skipper, Johnnie, and engineer, Philip, were Chinese–New Guinean and, having been to school in Australia, spoke good English. The alfresco 'dining room' was a table and benches at the stern and doubled as a lounge. It was prone to dousing with seaspray and had no protection from rain. I noticed many questionable smells on board apart from copra. The crew cooked over an open fire that smoked all day, competing with the strong twist tobacco they smoked constantly even while cooking.

The Matarani *was scarcely a luxury liner.*

It was preferable not to use the toilet after dark. When you put on the light the walls appeared to be painted a dark brown. It was an illusion. Armies of gigantic cockroaches scurried away to reveal the real colour – buff mottled with brown smudges. There was a shower, but no point in using it – I felt I would come out dirtier than when I went in.

We left for Kavieng with a full cargo and many passengers who were accommodated in a hold. They slept mostly on deck, all in a heap with some ducks. We went through Hanover Sound, winding through a scattering of pretty islands. Kavieng was a pleasant small town, shaded by casuarinas along its streets. On one street corner were two fanatical missionaries, a tall man with a patriarchal beard and a big coconut leaf hat and a smaller, pale, pimply youth. They told me they were trying to eradicate the use of the local language, for anything to do with the past culture of the island was demoniacal.

It was a 27-hour journey from Kavieng to Manus, the island made famous by the remarkable anthropologist Margaret Mead. She first studied the children of Manus Island in 1929 and returned in 1953 to study the dramatic changes that had occurred because of their exposure to the wider world during the war.

We arrived on Saturday, market day, and the town was thronged with people who had come to buy and sell. Some buildings and concrete foundations were reminders there had been a large United States Navy base on Manus during the war. A machine gun had been made into a memorial of those troubled times. In the small town were a church and a couple of Chinese stores – it did not take long to see the sights of Manus.

Our next call was in the Vitu Islands, a small group of volcanic islands off the north coast of New Britain. It rained on the way; it was a relief to arrive as it was virtually impossible to find a dry spot on the boat. They were lovely islands. Horseshoe-shaped Garove, the main one, was three sides of a huge sunken volcanic crater – a perfect anchorage. On the islands were four Burns Philp plantations and a privately owned one as well as the Catholic mission. The seven Europeans, all single men, were pleased to have a visitor. One of them took me up the hill on the back of his motorbike to look down on the big harbour. What a magnificent sight it was! I luxuriated – shower, dinner, bed, and breakfast ashore for the two days we were there.

We left loaded with copra and twelve labourers from the New Guinea highlands who had completed their two-year contract. Their baggage had been searched before they embarked and several items of plantation property were retrieved. They left with tears streaming down their faces – they had become attached to their plantation life. They spent the journey sheltering from pouring rain under the tarpaulin that covered the copra bags.

Johnnie and Philip had been hunting and returned with pigeons and a big fish so we had a feast to mark the end of my journey with them.

Matarani *in the attractive Vitu Islands*

I had booked *Iota* onto the slip on my return. She needed a coat of antifouling. Orim enlisted his friend Singon to help pull up the anchor as I had laid the heavy one, just to be sure, while I was away. Despite their combined efforts, it would not budge. I tried to motor it out in various directions, but still no success. It seemed as though we had not pulled up all the chain; the boys dived down to see what the problem was and reported the chain was wrapped around a pile lying on the harbour bottom.

We enlisted the help of two more boys who were used to diving. Firstly they managed to attach a line to the anchor, unshackle it and pull it on board. Then they freed the chain. As I pulled the chain on board I came to the part that had been wrapped around the pile. The links were as thin as a hairpin. The pile was sheathed with copper and electrolysis had set in, the iron anchor chain being the loser. It was amazing our efforts had not broken the chain, and certainly in another two or three days' time it would have parted. The exercise of pulling up the anchor took nearly three hours.

I stayed ashore with some friends whilst *Iota* was out of the water, for conditions at the slipway were not pleasant. The tide brought in water full of oil and rotting cabbage to ooze around the boat. It was intensely hot and the smell was unbelievable.

The night after *Iota* came off the slip I found to my horror that I had a rat on board. It ran across the cabin not far from my face. I leapt in a single bound from my bunk into the cockpit and spent the rest of the night sitting on the cross piece of the davits with my legs tucked up out of harm's way, regretting the mistake I had made of leaving a ladder lying against the yacht overnight. As soon as the shops were open I bought three traps; I arranged for Orim to stay on board and for me to return to my hospitable friends for the night.

Next morning I went to get a report on progress.

'You nogat findim rat, Orim?' I asked.

'Yes, Missus,' he replied, raising my hopes until I realised he meant, yes, he hadn't found the rat.

However he told me one of the traps had gone off and that a trail of blood led on deck. Together, we looked everywhere for the wounded rat, taking out all the sails and looking in lockers. We looked in vain. At lunchtime, Harry came rowing past.

'Your rat was on my boat this morning,' he said.

'How do you know it was my rat?' I asked.

'It was wet and had a broken leg,' he replied. 'It must have scrambled up my fenders.'

'What did you do with it?'

'I picked it up, put it in the dinghy and took it ashore.'

~

I returned late one afternoon to the yacht club after a day painting with Shirley in the country to discover a British naval supply ship had joined us. She was lying out in the middle of the harbour. A liberty boat came zooming in, dodging in and out of the yachts with her bow clear of the water; she slowed abruptly and went alongside the wharf. Her wake followed her and pounded on the shore. Club members had carefully placed some fill along the foreshore, and this was being washed away.

I walked along the yacht club jetty to find my dinghy; it was still afloat, but its two neighbours had caught under the jetty and were lying awash, swamped by the unexpected waves. I rowed past my neighbour's tossing yacht. Sally was indignant; she told me how the ship had arrived at lunchtime.

'There's two liberty boats – they're as bad as each other. At least ten knots through the anchorage – think they own the place!'

'Why haven't you complained?' I asked.

'Well, Dick was going to, but the child, you know, on the boat over there, the two-year-old, she fell over in the cockpit and gashed her head – badly – so they took her to hospital to get it stitched instead.'

I was appalled – not just at the plight of the child and the behaviour of the British Navy, but at the feebleness of my neighbours too.

'How long are they staying?' I enquired.

'Dunno.'

As I rowed over to *Iota*, the next liberty boat planed in. The dinghy pranced in the wash. On board, after I had changed and checked the anchor, I was still angry so I poured a stiff drink and went into the cockpit to relax and enjoy it.

Twenty minutes later in came the next boat. *Iota* tossed and plunged, some unseen gear crashed in the cabin – and so did my drink. Rum swilled in the scuppers. Outrage!

'This has gone too far! I'm not going to put up with it.' I vowed.

I leapt back into the dinghy and rowed over to the wharf, so incensed with injustice I gave little thought as to what I would do when I got there.

When I came alongside I realised the liberty boat was bigger than I had anticipated and high sided. When I stood up in the dinghy my chin was level with her gunwale. I heard the unmistakable sound of a bosun's pipe.

But it wasn't for me. I observed a row of stiff saluting backs welcoming a VIP on board from the shore. I waited until the ceremony was over, drew a deep breath and shouted as loudly as I could, 'Please may I speak to the driver?'

Somebody noticed me and produced a pimply-faced, naïve-looking youth for my consideration.

'You wanted me?'

'Are you the driver?' I asked.

'Well, yes, I suppose so.' He was uneasy.

'Do you realise you have washed away the yacht club wall, sunk at least two boats, half killed a child, and *spilt my rum*?' I shouted, warming to the task. 'You drive with absolutely no consideration for others. You should know that driving at 20 knots through an anchorage is not acceptable.'

There was silence and then he said, 'But I've got a schedule to keep.'

'You may have a schedule, but you've got no manners!' I think I said 'bloody manners'.

Impasse – I glared at him and he glared back at me, wondering what on earth had struck him. We had attracted the attention of several of the other sailors, who gathered around to see what would happen next. They looked surprised, bemused.

A different figure pushed to the front. He was tall and striking with piercing dark eyes, an immaculately trimmed beard, and a suit and tie improbable in Rabaul on any lesser figure. He was awesome. He was the VIP.

'Is there a problem?' he asked.

'Yes,' I said. 'You have washed away the yacht club wall, sunk at least two boats, half killed a child and *spilt my rum*. You have absolutely no consideration for others.'

His dark eyes glinted.

'Having a schedule is no excuse for bad manners,' I babbled on, 'and, for heaven's sake, there's no hurry – there isn't even a war on!'

Was that a suspicion of a disarming smile that softened his compelling eyes and hovered around his lips?

'We are not stowed for going to sea! Twenty knots through an anchorage is ...' My resolve faltered; my legs turned to jelly.

'You have my word; it will not happen again,' he said formally. The smile was under control.

'Thank you,' I said, with as much dignity as I could muster. I sat down in the dinghy, took up my oars and started to row weakly back to *Iota*. He watched thoughtfully as I pulled away. I lent on my oars and looked back at the liberty boat. Our eyes met. This time his smile escaped. He was irresistible; I had no choice but to smile back.

The liberty boat cast off and made her way slowly around the anchorage and back to her ship. I had definitely lost that encounter, but perhaps they had received the message – time would tell.

About twenty minutes later the next boat came heading shoreward. She seemed to be slower – yes, this was better, but she was coming through the yachts again instead of around them. Then, suddenly, I realised she was coming alongside. An arm shot out as she edged past and handed me – a bottle of rum!

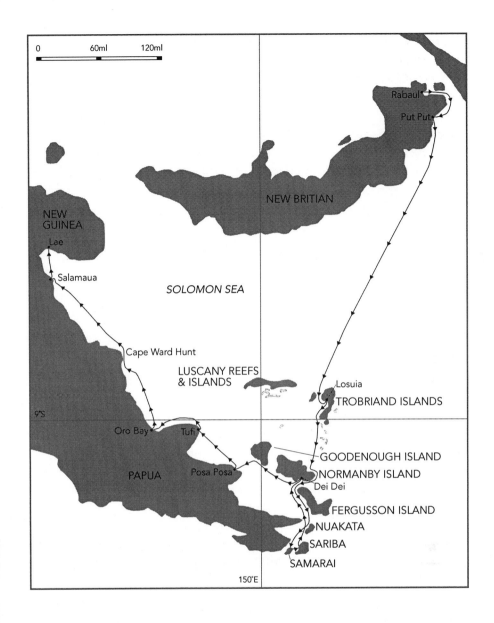

In the morning the ship had gone. She had crept away in the middle of the night without as much as a ripple.

~

As the end of the year came closer the season changed. It became even hotter and more humid. With no wind the weather felt equatorial; we were in the doldrums. It took its toll on the population and many people were sick, suffering from all kinds of infections, colds, tropical ulcers, malaria and gastric disorders.

Simon had heard back from Bunny and Grace Burrow – they would be delighted to look after *Iota*. Our plan to take her to Sariba over the Christmas holidays became a reality. I bought some stores ready for the trip. I thought we might be powering much of the way so I arranged for a supply of diesel fuel to be available for us in the Trobriands – and a carton of beer as well!

Time was short; we left Rabaul the day after Simon arrived, spent a night at Put Put and then went without stopping the 280 miles to the Trobriands. The sun beat down on us as we huddled in a small pool of shade under the mizzen awning. For three days and three nights we powered our way across the oily calm Solomon Sea, carefully protecting our skin from the burning rays. We soaked shirts in water and pinned handkerchiefs to our hats to shield our faces.

On the second afternoon a squall approached so we set some sail – it seemed strange to increase sail for a squall rather than reduce it – but the wind was fickle and short lived. It brought with it a big school of porpoises, hundreds of them jumping out of the water and going 'poof' in unison. We could hear them squeaking to each other.

The lighthouse on Cape Denis, the northern point of Kiriwina, should have been visible sixteen miles away, but no light appeared. When we judged ourselves to be about ten miles off the island we thought it prudent to stop and wait until dawn. Immediately, a breeze sprang up so we had to hoist our sails and heave to. Infuriatingly, it dropped again as the sun rose and we had to start the engine. We anchored off Losuia in time to accept an invitation to a Christmas Eve party aboard a neighbouring yacht.

Next morning we went to the village armed with jerry cans to find our supplies of diesel fuel. The ADC was expecting us and organised villagers to help us carry it back to the beach. They also gave us some yams. These are the staple diet of the Islanders and their cultivation forms an important part of their culture. In the centre of the village were their elaborately decorated yam houses where the annual crop was stored; their sleeping houses were packed closely together around them. The women, bare-breasted and decorated with necklaces and headdresses of beads, shells and feathers, were dressed in traditional grass skirts jutting out from their hips.

The Trobriand Islanders were famous for playing a unique and aggressive form of cricket. Missionaries introduced it to them as a substitute for the inter-group warfare that raged in the islands. Although it was still played with bat and ball, the teams averaged 60

Trobriand women wore grass skirts.

or more players. It was an excuse to sing and dance. When the teams came onto the field or when a player was declared out it was essential to put on a fine display – the display was more important than winning.

Boxing Day saw us on our way again, heading south. We were in tricky waters, noted on the chart as 'an area very shoal full of coral heads' – not where we wanted to be blundering around in the dark! We stopped for the night at a small island off the low, densely wooded coast of Kiriwina and set off early the next day for the high and steep Amphlett Islands. We had some wind and made good time, but, as the anchorage was deep and exposed and the wind holding, we kept on going to Fergusson Island.

We came into our chosen bay at dusk at the same time as a colony of hornbills came in to roost – at least a hundred of them. They clattered in, their wings whirring, then argued loudly with each other as to who was going to perch on which branch. Their squawks echoed around the bay until the sun was finally gone.

We wound between the reefs and through the narrow gap between Fergusson and Normandy Islands and then went a little way along the coast to a promising anchorage in an inlet between an island and the shore. Taking the advice of a local, we tied up to the jetty. Immediately people climbed on board and peered through the portholes. They were all sucking noisily on sugar cane. Then we spotted a notice informing us we were in a leper colony so beat a hasty retreat and anchored off instead.

The weather was breathlessly calm and hot as we made our way through the tricky Goschen Strait. It rained, firstly a series of squalls and then a solid downpour. Lack of visibility forced us to stop at the conveniently situated Nuakata Island. Happily the rain had eased by morning and we made a final dash to Samarai, the tiny 24-hectare island that once was the administrative centre of the area. Although the town was demolished during the war and the centre of government for the area had been moved to Milne Bay, it was still a major commercial centre for stores and banks. Many overseas ships used its facilities. Seventy years ago when the population of the surrounding islands was hostile its wharf was easily defended. For yachts the anchorage was bad, with little shelter and a strong current.

The harbour master was helpful and gave us a berth tucked inside the main wharf. The port captain also came aboard. He was harassed as he had lost his car, a Volkswagen. A ship had arrived from Europe and unloaded a dozen new Beetles to await transhipment to Port Moresby. They were lined up along the wharf and another ship arrived to reload them. The port captain parked behind the new vehicles and went on board the ship; he then had business on another vessel further along the wharf. When he returned the ship had gone and so had his car!

Simon booked himself on a plane to Port Moresby next day and I radioed Bunny and Grace to ask if they could send me, please, someone to help me find my way to their establishment on Sariba Island just opposite Samarai. Simon's launch to the airstrip in Milne Bay left just as the *Coralita* from Sariba was coming in. An hour later *Iota* was tied safely alongside the jetty and I was having morning tea with Bunny and Grace in their summerhouse.

Altogether they employed 50 or more people at the slipway. The place was a hive of industry, immaculately kept and well organised. Bunny and Grace had lived in Papua for about 40 years and were full of fascinating stories and information. Bunny spoke at least four of the local dialects.

Grace was bursting with news of Lyell – he had just passed his exams for his master's ticket and become engaged to Liz. She was thrilled, especially as she now had somebody who knew Lyell to listen to her news.

'I haven't met her yet, but he said he would bring her to meet us as soon as he could.' She was looking forward to the visit.

'You must be proud he's now a ship's master,' I said.

'Yes, but Bunny finds it difficult to accept his son is now more qualified to manage a ship than he is. He's always treated Lyell as if he was a novice. It will be quite amusing to see how they cope with his new status!'

I received wonderful hospitality; they gave me a room in their house and all my meals. I was totally spoiled. I stayed for a week making sure *Iota* was in a fit state to leave in their competent hands before I left for Sydney.

Sariba

It was a complicated and tiresome journey, firstly to Samarai and then a four-hour wet and rough trip to Milne Bay on an uncomfortable launch. Several of the passengers were seasick. The wharf at the top of the bay was deep in mud. We were piled into the back of a truck that took us to the airstrip in pouring rain. The strip had no shelter, however everybody and everything was wet anyway. We could hear the plane circling around in the clouds above us, but could not see it. After two hours of looking for a break in the clouds the pilot landed just before dark. Passengers coming in said there had been only ten minutes to spare before the plane would have had to return to Moresby. We had been four hours in the launch and three hours waiting for the plane with no shelter and nothing to eat or drink. The plane was an old DC3 with just benches along the sides. It was another rough trip.

I stayed overnight in Port Moresby and was expecting to leave at 11:30 the next morning, but the tanker drivers were on strike in Sydney and the plane was repeatedly delayed. We eventually took off exactly 24 hours late, had to land in Townsville to refuel and stop again in Brisbane. I felt as if I had been travelling for weeks.

~

I returned to Sariba early in May. The flight was less frustrating than my journey back to Sydney, but five minutes after I landed at the airstrip in Milne Bay down came the rain and it rained for the next week. Lyell and his fiancée Liz were at the airstrip. Having been introduced to the family, Liz was on her way back to Melbourne to prepare for the wedding. Lyell had taken her to Milne Bay in the *Coralita* so I returned with him and caught up with the Sariba news, the main item being that Bunny was in Sydney seeking a cure for his chronic bronchitis. Lyell was running the business in his absence.

I had three weeks to prepare *Iota* for her next trip, but could do nothing for the first week because of the rain – 28 centimetres fell in five days; Sariba caught the edge of Esta, a late cyclone, with wind up to 90 knots. *Iota* was tied up to the jetty and I was sleeping ashore when the blow came. I headed off down the jetty to check her lines and make sure fenders were in place, but realised there was no way I would reach the end without getting blown into the sea.

Samarai was without radio contact for three days and, on Sariba, several trees had fallen, one of them cutting the power lines. When radio contact was eventually re-established we learned the islands in the direct path of the cyclone had suffered extensive damage.

The wet weather acted as a trigger for flying ants to swarm; a few days later they were everywhere and in everything. A light on the jetty near *Iota* attracted them. They came to die – *Iota*'s cover sagged under the weight of their smelly bodies.

Life at Sariba involved a disciplined routine. Meal times were strictly observed. Particularly important was morning tea in the Summer House, when Grace held court. It was an opportunity to learn about the social issues and attitudes of the people who lived on the island. Grace considered them to be part of her family and they came to seek her help and advice. Bunny and Grace were revered and respected by their staff; Lyell was less tolerant – I heard him shouting one morning, 'You want independence yet you can't even keep your toilets clean!'

A new Danish engineer, Lief, arrived but he was having a struggle to cope with unfamiliar conditions. His skin was winter white and covered in pink blodges from mosquito bites. He turned up for work on the first day in a boiler suit over a shirt and a pair of socks and wondered why he was hot. I met him wandering along the beach still in long trousers and carrying a rolled umbrella 'in case there were wild dogs about'.

The days passed quickly as I cleaned, oiled and varnished. Lyell put *Iota* up on the slip and the boys gave her a coat of antifouling while I took the opportunity to go to Samarai to buy provisions for the journey.

Simon arrived on time. He came into Milne Bay on the battered old DC3 complaining that the co-pilot kept coming back into the cabin to stare at the wings through binoculars; definitely unnerving.

He recovered over a delightful dinner with Lyell and Grace who had just learned that Bunny's health had improved and he was on his way home. The next day was Saturday, always a busy day. It was payday and the workers liked to go to Samarai to join the crowds and spend their hard-earned cash. Grace went shopping too and came back with a present for me – a packet of Honey Blonde hair colour – because I complained that my dark roots were showing.

A dawn start enabled us to catch the last of the tide through the China Straits. As we came through the wind freshened and took us to Nuakata where we had stopped overnight on the way south to Sariba. We had found it an attractive island and thought to explore it further.

We had an enchanting anchorage to ourselves. Sundown was heralded by a crescendo of noise. Quarrelling black cockatoos dominated the orchestra. Croaking frogs, chattering crickets and the arguing flying foxes accompanied them. Intermittently, yelping dogs provided the higher notes and the percussion came from a strange unidentified bird making guttural thumping noises. When the blood-red sun finally gave up the day the total silence was broken by a man singing a weird, resonant song in the distance.

In the morning we walked across to the northern side of the island, an old man from the village guiding us to the track. He leapt ahead up a steep watercourse, jumping from rock to rock while we slipped and struggled along behind, trying to keep up. Rather than admit defeat, we told him we could now find the way and sent him back to the village with a cigarette. The path plunged into the jungle. It was humid and breathless under the trees and we dripped with perspiration. On the narrow ridge on top of the mountain a delicious wind cooled us.

The village on the north coast of the island boasted a mission and a government first-aid post. We met the 'doctor-boy' who said he mainly dispensed chloroquine, penicillin and bandages. His English was excellent – the Papuans spoke English rather than New Guinea pidgin. He could speak Motu, the language of the region, but had difficulty with the local dialect. He showed us the track around the island back to *Iota*. In a village along the way we swapped a Polaroid photograph for two drinking nuts and a pawpaw. We met a man trying to shoot flying foxes with a catapult on the end of a long stick.

~

Mountains surrounded Sewa Bay, a big inlet about eight kilometres long and five wide with a narrow entrance. As we came into the bay a boy came out to us in his canoe. He politely introduced himself, 'I'm Alexis. Mr Wilkinson has sent me to say that you are welcome at his house.'

He came aboard, took the tiller and steered us through the reef. We tied up at a jetty and met Jack Wilkinson, his Papuan–Malay wife and two of their five daughters, both very striking girls. Jack ran a lucrative trade store and had a copra and cocoa plantation. He was worried about an infestation of Pantorhytes beetles, large weevils that attack the cocoa pods. Many chemical sprays had been tried without success. Jack had five labourers picking them off, one by one, from the bushes.

'The only way is to control them is to hit each one over the head with a hammer,' he said.

In the morning we moved away from the jetty as two trading boats came in, the *Govelin* to unload stores and the *Peter Ikori* to load copra and cocoa. Jack's workers and the crews of the boats cheerfully carried bags and cartons up and down the wharf, shouting to each other and laughing. We gained the impression they did a minimum of work with a maximum of noise.

We had an eventful day sailing along the coast of Normanby Island heading for the hot springs at Dei Dei. There was a good breeze. A crowd of locals waved to us madly from a small island off the coast; there were people running along the beach frantically trying to attract our attention, swinging their shirts and flashing mirrors at us.

'I wonder what the trouble is?' I asked. 'An accident – some kind of an emergency?'

'I suppose we'd better find out,' said Simon, reluctantly. 'We'll gybe around and go a bit closer.'

They came paddling out in their canoes to meet us; they were standing up, waving and shouting. Then we realised they were yelling, 'Wan tabbac! Wan tabbac! Tabbac!'

We freed our sails and moved away from them; they chased us for a while, yelling angrily, but the breeze was brisk and we easily outstripped them.

We were just getting over our indignation when there was a bang and *Iota* gave a series of lurches. She had hit a submerged log. She was not leaking – all was well – but the day had not finished with us. The wind dropped. While waiting to see if it would come back we admired a pretty white beach. Suddenly we were stuck on a reef. Fortunately *Iota* had not been going fast. Simon took an anchor out in the dinghy and five minutes of hard pulling saw her free again.

He was philosophical. 'Just because a reef isn't marked on the chart doesn't mean it isn't there!'

Not wanting any more misadventures we waited for a local boat to overtake us and followed it up the tortuous passage to the Methodist mission at Salamo. Four young men from the mission came aboard; two were from the UK Volunteer Service Overseas and two from the equivalent Australian organisation, Australian Volunteers Abroad. They were indignant. Not being of a religious calling, they found the mission principles hard to take. No alcohol was allowed and they should not expect the Papuans to do menial tasks – so they had to cook, wash up, clean and launder for themselves. They wondered why they had volunteered.

They told us there had recently been a series of strong earthquakes and that the hot springs at Dei Dei had become hotter. The government had been prepared to evacuate the area, a difficult operation as the population was scattered in isolated groups. The activity settled down, but they were on the alert for trouble later in the year as the increased earthquake activity seemed to coincide with the time of the highest tides.

'How can we find the springs?' Simon asked.

One of the boys pointed to the other side of the bay. 'Watch for puffs of steam and feel the temperature of the water. There's a river coming into the bay from the springs – the water in it is hot.'

Sure enough, as we sailed over to the other side of the bay in the morning, we saw steam rising from the bushes. In spite of the instability of the area a group of soldiers was widening the road and building three bridges, two of them over steaming hot rivers and the third over a cold one. The sergeant sent two of his men to escort us – it wasn't a good idea for us to go wandering around on our own – there were traps for the unwary. In places the crust was thin and we might fall through into boiling mud or a superheated geyser.

We crossed a hot river on a primitive log bridge and then climbed a hill. The flora changed dramatically; it was dominated by a species of eucalypt that thrived in the hot steam and the smell. We came to a spectacular treeless region with boiling rock pools and mineral deposits in bright colours. Foul-smelling, thick, bubbling mud went 'ploop' and fountains of hot water spurted out of the ground with a 'whoosh'.

~

Along the rugged coast of Ferguson Island we kept close inshore, then crossed the strait to Goodenough Island, a conical volcanic mound, to enter a bay on the southern side. A man showed us where there was a shallow patch close to the shore to anchor. A crowd of village children gathered on the beach and stared at us, watching every move we made. Simon squeezed some limes and they yelled 'Ah!' each time he threw a skin overboard. The higher he threw the skins, the louder the 'Ahs' – he and the children were as bad as each other!

A fresh wind the next day took us across the bumpy Ward Hunt Strait. With main, genoa and mizzen set, we bowled across to Posa Posa. The intricate harbour, full of mangrove-clad islands, appeared to be quite unrelated to the chart. We had it in delightful isolation.

We set off again at dawn and had trouble finding a way out through the maze of identical islands. At one stage I thought it would be our lot in life to be there forever. Eventually we rounded a corner and found a gap. It was a long, hot, windless day powering through mostly uncharted, muddy water. We picked up the lighthouse on a reef about ten miles from Tufi and, soon after, saw white leading beacons in the hills. We lined them up carefully; they took us uncomfortably close to a reef.

Cape Nelson, of which Tufi was a part, was different from the rest of the coast. It featured deep fjords formed from the lava flows of dormant volcanoes Mounts Victory and Trafalgar, 1500-metre sombre monsters hovering in the background. Flanked by sheer, forested slopes with waterfalls, we went up to the end where the river came out of the mangroves and anchored off a small settlement.

The villagers were preparing a feast in honour of a man who had died two months previously. One of the relatives told us they abstain from eating his favourite foods during this period and then invite the neighbours from all around to an event that goes on for a week. They were busy preparing their costumes and collecting food for two hundred guests.

Also living in Tufi was Hugh, who ran the store and a small guesthouse. He once was stationed there as a patrol officer and liked it so much he decided to stay. He had built himself a delightful house – all from local materials. A swimming pool was set in a garden of scented flowers. He invited the other European residents of Tufi to join us for dinner – the ADC, the patrol officer, the schoolteacher and the nurse with their families. We sat on the terrace looking up the fjord as the sun set behind the mountains. It was a lively party with interesting, kindly folks who lived in very beautiful surroundings.

Just after breakfast the next day Simon developed malaria. His hands and feet were white and numb as he shivered in the blazing sun wrapped in blankets. Chloroquine tablets ensured that he recovered by the evening so we were able to continue to Oro Bay.

On this leg of the journey we noticed the engine was overheating and starting to make unhappy noises. It seemed to be a problem in the gearbox. A gentle breeze came up so we drifted into Oro Bay and hoped, optimistically, that after a night's rest it would feel better. Simon noted the nearby government hospital was inappropriately situated on Cemetery Point.

The wind was fickle, but we had just enough the next day to ghost to a little bay near Cape Ward Hunt. Mount Lamington brooded in the distance with a wisp of smoke coming out of its top. It had erupted explosively in 1951 killing about 3000 people. The administration had not taken the warning signs seriously and refused repeated requests for evacuation from the DC. The damage extended over a radius of at least 20 kilometres.

We made another dawn start on yet another windless day. After half an hour the engine stopped with a clatter and left us becalmed and stranded, embarrassingly close to Red Rocky Point. We took turns in the dinghy to tow *Iota* out of trouble, around the craggy cliffs.

A day later and still no wind – it was obvious, if Simon were to be back at work at the appointed time, that we would have to put into Lae, about 120 miles away, rather than continue as we had intended to Madang. The course change could only take place in our minds.

Our sails hung limply in the breathless air; time passed slowly and progress remained elusive. A school of small black pilot whales came jumping past us, 'poofing' in unison as if scorning our plight.

On the afternoon of the third day a cloud appeared on the horizon, and a dark squall held the promise of wind at long, long last. It came closer and we wondered how much sail we dared to hold. When it arrived, it hit with a flurry of soaking rain. *Iota* leapt into action, glad to be on the move again. My turn first – I left Simon at the tiller and celebrated with a much-needed bath. I assembled buckets, soap and shampoo and indulged in an orgy of cleanliness as the sails filled and the yacht romped through the water. I remembered the packet of Honey Blonde hair colour Grace had given me as an improbable parting gift. Why not? I applied it to my hair, but before I could rinse it out the rain stopped. I had to use seawater for the job. My hair turned bright canary yellow. Simon laughed unsympathetically at my predicament.

Fortunately, a few more brief squalls came our way. We made the most of them – at one time we were sizzling along in a 30 to 40 knot wind and pouring rain with all sail set, on a pitch-black night punctuated by blinding flashes of light and crashing thunder.

After four days and three nights we reached Salamaua, a well-ordered, attractive village, just 20 miles from Lae.

Lae, at the head of the bay, was not a good anchorage as it was unprotected from the east, the direction from which bad weather would most likely arrive. The yacht club was tucked up an inlet that was not big enough to accommodate *Iota*. The club offered us a mooring, but Simon had a mistrust of strange moorings, so laid the big CQR on a steeply shelving mud bank. We went ashore at the Hotel Cecil's jetty.

Because of its lack of a safe anchorage Lae saw few cruising yachts; we came to the notice of the local press and a reporter appeared to capture our story.

'Gee, the sun's played havoc with your hair,' he said as he left.

A visit to the hairdresser became a necessity.

'The sun's bleached the red out of your hair,' diagnosed the Chinese hairdresser, 'We'll put it back in and then darken it.'

Five hours later, despite all her efforts to dampen down the conflagration, I had become a fire-engine redhead. Simon's attitude to this radical change in my image was typically phlegmatic, but I noticed some incredulous (and rather suggestive) stares from the members of the yacht club.

~

Simon departed and, back at work, addressed himself to the problem of getting *Iota* back to Sydney. He discovered the *Slott*, on charter to the Carlandar New Guinea Line, Sydney-bound and due to berth in Lae in six to eight weeks. Perfect – it would give me time to see a bit more of this part of New Guinea.

I went to Bulolo in a semi-articulated truck – an excellent way to travel, perched high up so I could see well, and less dusty than a car. Jock the driver had been doing the trip for eighteen years so I was in safe hands. We crossed the wide, muddy Markham River on a low bridge that needed rebuilding; it could take only a limited load so the trucks were a quarter loaded – scarcely economic. On the other side the road ran beside the river; it was often flooded in the wet season. We then climbed. The road was spectacular with many steep, sharp corners. We came across a truck that had skidded into the ditch and stopped to pull it out. Jock's semi shook like an angry caterpillar as it pulled – its back writhed up and down.

Four hours after starting out we arrived in Bulolo, a former gold-mining town. The company that worked the gold had set up a new plywood factory using hundreds of acres of virgin klinki pine – an ideal wood for the purpose. Happily, they were replanting trees so the industry would be sustainable – if they grew fast enough. The couple I stayed with were all kindness; Barbara showed me around the town and Nick took me to the factory. A fascinating mill rotated the logs and peeled them into veneers. These were dried, trimmed, glued and pressed. The hot press was new – an awesome, complicated machine.

The next day I went to Wau with the sister from the local hospital. At her postnatal clinic I sat and watched while the babies were weighed on a spring balance under a mango tree. They all looked healthy, but malaria was a problem; those whose mothers had insufficient milk were handicapped. The sister said she only handed out powdered milk for supplementary feeds in cases of real emergency because of the risk of gastroenteritis – nothing was ever sterilised.

~

There was one other yacht anchored off Lae, a very famous one. *Sirius* was the first Australian yacht to complete a circumnavigation of the world. Her binnacle was proudly displayed in the entrance hall of the Royal Sydney Yacht Squadron. Laurie Crowley owned her, and his son Dennis lovingly tended her. Laurie ran the local airline and offered a spare seat on a plane if it was going somewhere I would find interesting, and Dennis promised to keep an eye on *Iota* while I was away.

I went to stay with my friends in Rabaul and spent a week catching up with their news. It was a good time to be there, for the yacht club was in party mood. Four yachts were leaving – including Ian and Robyn on Maori Koa – so the members were making sure they were sent on their way with happy memories. We picnicked, barbecued and made merry for the whole weekend. Abbie wanted to visit the New Guinea Highlands. She told me Goroka was about to hold a major event, a sing-sing. Held only every five years it was a rare and tempting opportunity – we booked a flight and five night's accommodation at the Bird of Paradise Hotel that had views over the surrounding mountains.

The sing-sing was indeed spectacular; people from over 100 tribes had travelled many miles to show off their traditional costumes and dances and their tribal customs and rituals. They had vividly painted faces and bodies; the designs were intricate and must have taken hours to achieve. Their headdresses and necklaces featured feathers, beads, shells and animal teeth. Some had many layers to their costumes, others little covering for their bodies except carefully applied grey mud that made them look like ghosts. The men looked warlike and ferocious and carried spears to emphasise the effect.

A leaf dancer

The men looked ferocious.

Back in Lae attention was focused on space ship Apollo 11 carrying the lunar module in which Neil Armstrong and Buzz Aldrin were about to make the first manned landing on the moon. I watched the amazing event on a television set in the crowded bar of the Hotel Cecil.

Dennis came one morning to tell me that Laurie had a free seat on a plane to Finschhafen. Would I like to take it? Would I ever! A government investigator had chartered the plane so he could enquire into a shipwreck. *Blanche*, a new government trawler, had run onto a rocky headland. There had been no casualties, but the boat broke up and disappeared. The New Guinean skipper apparently had made an expensive mistake.

Rain in Finschhafen meant we could not land; we'd need to wait in Lae.

'Come back in two hour's time and we'll try again,' said Laurie. 'I'll radio the friends I've arranged to look after you to tell them you'll be later than expected. They'll meet the plane and put you up. Their names are Peter and Helen. He's the government officer who organises the copra co-ops. They're quite young – you'll like them and they'll enjoy having you!'

I thought it would be pleasant to pass the two hours in the nearby Botanical Gardens. I was wandering around admiring the colourful creepers and tropical trees when I realised I was being followed. A man was stalking me. I thought if I ran he would run too and no doubt overtake me. So I turned around and walked back along the path towards him. He tried to grab me, but I swung my heavy camera and hit him hard over the head. To my surprise, he said, 'Me savvy missus,' and ran away. It was scary; I learned a lesson and the camera was never quite the same again.

At the club Peter and Helen introduced me to many of the Europeans who lived in Finschhafen. Most worked for the government, but one was the manager of a big cattle ranch close by. He invited me to spend a day on this beautifully kept Brahmin stud with its 1500 elegant, purebred cream-coloured cattle with lop ears, humps and very cute calves. They lent me a horse – a lovely grey – so I thoroughly enjoyed my day. It was the sort of life I could easily take.

~

Just before I departed from Lae the inevitable happened – weather from the east, at night, of course. It came in with a bang and it stirred the bay into froth. Metre-high waves were breaking onto the beach too close to *Iota*'s stern. We were on a dead lee shore. I thought about letting out more chain, but there wasn't any room so I went below and tried hopefully, and fatalistically, to sleep.

Bang it came! Thump! Bang! The noise had to be investigated. I went on deck and found we were entangled with a large iron mooring buoy; it threatened to come through the hull. As *Iota* pitched and strained in the seas, she had straightened her chain and fallen back. It was an appalling night; cold rain beat into my face along with the salt spray and *Iota* was rolling uncomfortably.

What to do? I reached for the torch and looked around – the other spare mooring buoy, closer to the shore, showed through the rain in its beam. If I took a line from the buoy we were tangling with, through the loop on the other buoy and back to the yacht and then pulled?

It was worth a go – I had to do something. I found two long lines, one to attach the dinghy to the yacht and the other to operate on the buoys. I lowered myself into the plunging dinghy and managed, with difficulty, to tie a bowline onto the loop of the buoy under the stern. Then I set off to the other buoy; it was only just out of the breaking waves. It was eerie out there on a lee shore in pouring rain, with a gale force wind and big waves. I didn't feel very safe! Eventually I found the second buoy and put the line through its ring. Now I had to just get back to *Iota*. I pulled on the other line and slowly made my way back to her relative security. She was still banging into the buoy.

'I'll soon fix it!' I said to her. 'Just hang on!' I pulled on the rope; the thumping continued. I pulled more, and more. Still the buoy under the stern crashed into her hull. I put the torch on the further buoy – it was a lot closer and coming ever closer as I shortened the rope. Instead of pulling the close buoy away from the boat, I was going to end up entangled with two buoys. In spite of all that effort I had only made the problem worse!

Surely it can't be dragging; moorings don't drag – though this was a New Guinea mooring, so maybe it could. Anything could happen on a night like tonight; I began to think there was no further point in trying to be rational.

The second buoy was only a boat's length away before it fixed the problem.

~

The *Slott*, a small freighter of Norwegian registration, had been in Singapore before her new charter to the Carlandar New Guinea shipping company. She was running late so missed her allotted berth and had to anchor off for a couple of days to wait for space at the wharf. Eventually she squeezed in behind a BP ship, the *Braeside*. She was almost empty and well out of the water so her crew were taking the opportunity to paint her boot top a bright grass green.

I went on board to ensure she had enough deck space to accommodate *Iota* and meet her Norwegian captain, Rolf. He welcomed me with a cheerful smile. He had a happy, easygoing attitude to his charmed life. Nothing was too much trouble and no problem was too difficult to solve. No, there wasn't enough room on deck, but they could put *Iota* on top of the hatch; she would be loaded last thing. She would have to be turned sideways – not easy – but they would manage; it would be a problem to find something to tie her down to, but they would think of something and manage that too. There wasn't any proper accommodation for me, however I could use an indentation in the funnel they called the 'hospital'.

'It's a bit hot, so nobody gets sick,' said Rolf. 'But you're welcome to sleep with me if you like.'

He looked knowingly at my bright red hair.

Iota was ready to be loaded, her masts down and lashed on deck. Dennis volunteered *Sirius* for the job of towing her to the wharf. It was windy with an irregular swell. The towrope was too short and when *Iota* took off in the swells a couple of times she threatened to surf aboard *Sirius*'s stern.

Arriving at the wharf was difficult; we had trouble picking up the line from the ship. Eventually I managed to secure *Iota* between the bow of the *Slott* and the stern of the *Braeside*. It was not very comfortable, but at least it was safe – until the *Braeside* decided to go. One of her officers fortunately noticed us before they set their propellers in motion. *Iota* had to get out of the way and all I could do was take her alongside the *Slott* further aft. With no line to the other ship, I would have to use fenders. The green boot topping paint was still wet; in no time at all I was covered with it. It toned in well with my hair.

Simon had loaded *Iota*'s lifting gear onto the *Slott* in Sydney. They lowered it down from the deck high above us and I shackled it on to the chain plates. Then there was a long, long wait.

They loaded her after midnight. The sideways turn was successfully accomplished and *Iota*'s keel touched down on the hatch.

'We're sailing now,' said Rolf. 'Do you want to come up to the bridge while we're leaving?'

He noticed my questioning look; *Iota* had not been lashed down nor had the derricks been stowed.

'We'll fix it in the morning.' He gave a broad, dismissive sweep with his hand.

'I think I'd better get cleaned up. Is there a shower I can use? Do you have turps and a rag, please?' I asked.

'Shower?' Rolf looked surprised at the request. 'Hadn't thought of that. Yes, you do look as if you need a shower. You'll have to use mine, you're very welcome.'

He showed me to his cabin and shouted to a passing Chinese sailor in an unknown language. There was a polite knock on the cabin door and I was handed a giant-sized container of turps and large piece of rough sacking. It took quite a while to remove the paint.

I turned out the light in Rolf's cabin before I opened the door to go out on deck. It was very dark; the ship was blacked out and the night sky overcast. I had taken only two steps along the deck when something attacked my legs; I just managed to stifle a scream. It was a booby bird – a gannet – taking refuge on the deck of the ship. I had walked straight into it. We both got an awful fright.

I waited for a while to recover my composure and for my eyes to adjust to the dark and then set off for the hospital, down a companionway and across the deck. The thickly greased cables from the unstowed derricks were draped over the companionway. I walked straight into those too. I cursed loudly and then fell over an unseen something on the deck. Red hair or not, I was going to have to get this ship a bit sorted out in the morning and at least establish a hazard-free route from the bathroom to my 'cabin'.

The sailors started to stow the derricks at dawn and ended my short, hot night's sleep. I went up on the bridge where Rolf showed me the chart and the route he planned.

'We'll be off the Trobriands tonight and go through this passage in the reef here.' He pointed with his finger. 'We usually go through this gap over here, but we're late, and this will save nearly a day.'

'The lighthouse wasn't working when we came through at Christmas time,' I said.

'They must have fixed it by now, surely,' said Rolf.

But they hadn't and even Rolf thought it too dangerous to tackle the narrow passage at night without a light. We remained three days late.

We had strong headwinds as we sailed south parallel to the Australian coast. The *Slott*'s aging and ailing engines groaned with the strain and our speed dropped to eight knots. Being yet another day behind schedule didn't perturb Rolf.

'We're always late, we keep island time.' he said. 'They're used to it – they've even come to expect it!'

The ship's engineer, Sven, was also Norwegian – a jolly round man with a fair skin that suffered from the sun; first officer Hans was a Swede – an older man, gentle and kindly. The four of us spent many companionable hours on the deck sheltered from the wind by a wooden lattice up which climbed an artificial ivy plant. Rolf used to inspect it every morning to see if it had produced any flowers.

'Nothing again today,' he would sigh. 'Must be the wrong season.'

Just before our arrival in Sydney I dismantled the plastic frangipani lei I was given when leaving Lae. I stitched the flowers onto the ivy plant, behind the leaves.

Rolf was delighted. 'I told you the fertiliser I gave it last week would work,' he said ingenuously.

He asked where we would be heading on our next trip.

'Probably to Indonesia and then to Singapore and Bangkok.'

'Would you like our charts?' Rolf offered, 'We're on charter on this route for the next three years so by the time we have to go back to Singapore they'll be out of date and we'll have to buy new ones.'

'You're very kind – are you sure you won't need them?'

'Quite sure,' said Rolf. The charts appeared in *Iota*'s cockpit next morning.

We were five days late when we finally berthed in Darling Harbour. Simon came to the ship, but couldn't stay. He had arranged a tow for the engineless *Iota* and asked Neil's wife Joan to collect me.

I introduced Rolf to Joan and he proudly showed her the flowers on his ivy plant.

'Lovely, aren't they?' he said. 'I gave them some fertiliser and they responded so well. Anyway, they won't be unloading the yacht until this afternoon so you've got time for lunch.'

What a lunch it was! The wine flowed freely and it was followed by copious quantities of aquavite so by the time *Iota* was off-loaded, I was beyond worrying about the sideways turn in reverse. Fortunately, all went well and Max came in his launch as *Iota* landed in the water and took her away to the marina.

~

Simon found a lovely house at Whale Beach. It was Sydney living at its best. *Iota* was on a mooring close by at Sydney Yacht Squadron's new premises in Careel Bay. There was a big room under the house so we were able to unload everything moveable and paint, varnish, oil or repair in comfort. Simon crossed the road to the beach for a run each morning before work.

I caught up with my friends and bought Simon some new clothes – shopping was not something he did for himself – and went back to my weekly riding session. Our only problem was the return of Simon's malaria on several occasions. He needed an addition to his medical staff so chose Tony who had experience in tropical medicine. Tony eventually found a drug that fixed the problem.

Engineer Phil took *Iota*'s broken-down engine away to his workshop and discovered the gearbox had totally seized. He was mystified as to why this had happened. He replaced the gearbox and reinstalled the engine. He was ready to take *Iota* for a test run.

'Okay,' he said, 'put it in forward gear and we'll see what happens.'

To go forwards I had always pushed the gear lever to the left, but Phil's alert eye noticed that the lever, where it was attached to the engine, moved backwards.

'No, forwards,' he said.

'But that is forwards, we're going forwards,' I replied. 'That's what I always do.'

He scratched his head and after some deep thought said, 'I think we'd better have a look at the propeller.'

'It's one we already had – we used it on a previous engine,' I said.

'It's precisely the right diameter and pitch, but it rotates the wrong way!' he observed when *Iota* was slipped again.

We had done nearly a thousand hours in reverse! No wonder the gearbox had objected. It had never occurred to me that propellers could be left or right-handed. I yet again cursed the air-cooled lawnmower engine!

~

We applied for an Indonesian sailing permit as soon as we decided this would be our next cruising ground. Six months later there was no sign of it; the Indonesians had a notorious reputation for reluctance to issue permits. Simon contacted the British Consul in Java and told him of our problem. Just as we were thinking we would have to abandon the cruise for the year the Consul performed a miracle and the permit arrived.

Now we could confidently prepare for our departure. We loaded all of *Iota*'s gear back on board and stowed away provisions. We changed the colour of her topsides to a pale grey as the black paint made her too hot. It seemed a wise move in tropical temperatures, for our comfort and *Iota*'s health as well. She was looking smart – paint and varnish gleaming. She was ready to go. After a final slipping we would sail to Sydney Harbour in preparation for loading her onto the *Browind* that would take her to Dili in East Timor.

I had been putting off having my booster vaccinations because I always reacted badly to typhoid injections. It could wait no longer. The morning *Iota* was going on the slip my fever was in full swing. I felt wretched so I rang the boatshed owner to ask him to take *Iota* off the mooring without me. I would be down later with the key to open her up.

'Don't worry,' he said, 'she's already up on the slip. Her hatch was open.'

Fever notwithstanding, I rushed to the boat shed. The hasp on the hatch was broken – a thief had been at work. All our navigation gear was gone, including the main compass, handbearing compass and echo sounder. Fortunately, he had not found the sextant and chronometer. We had a week in which to replace everything. It was a worry because it would have been so easy to overlook some vital piece of equipment that had been stolen. The echo sounder came in two pieces – a transducer attached to the hull and the instrument inside the cabin. They had to match so once we had taken *Iota* into Sydney up she went on the slip again to fit the new transducer.

What promised to be a calm, well-organised departure turned into a frantic, anxious rush, but we made it! Just!

to the spice islands in the footsteps of wallace and darwin

1970

Iota travelled to Dili in East Timor with 40 horses and 200 sheep as companions on the deck of the *Browind*. She just fitted onto a semitrailer bound for Singapore. The animal carers took all the spare accommodation – there was no room for me – so I flew to Dili with an overnight stop in Darwin. As I waited for my luggage at the airport I saw a familiar figure. It was Hans, the first officer of the *Slott*.

'Good heavens!' I said. 'Fancy seeing you! What are you doing here?'

'I've come to join a ship. The first officer got sick and I'm his replacement. And what about you – where's *Iota*?'

'She's on a ship heading for Dili. There wasn't any room for me – the ship is full of sheep. I'm stopping overnight and going on to Dili tomorrow.' I replied.

'That's my good fortune anyway; let's have dinner together this evening – I've got a story to tell you.'

As we dined he related the next episode in the saga of the *Slott*.

After dropping us off in Sydney they went on to Melbourne to pick up a cargo to take back to New Guinea; it included explosives. They were making their way north again and were off Jervis Bay when a fire broke out in the engine room. They controlled the fire sufficiently to be able to limp into Sydney Harbour. It was a Sunday so their efforts to contact the Sydney agent for the shipping line were in vain. They anchored off Rose Bay. A Maritime Services launch went to investigate this unexpected intruder and discovered the scruffy-looking ship had not only been on fire but carried a load of explosives as well.

Although the ship did not explode, the Carlandar New Guinea Line did. They withdrew from their charter and banished the ship back to Singapore – immediately!

'We'd given you all our charts of the South China Sea!' said Hans. 'And we didn't remember until we actually needed them!'

'Oh dear – they're on board *Iota*. How did you manage?' I felt responsible for their predicament.

'We put in here, Darwin, to buy some new ones. Both Rolf and I had been to Darwin before so we managed to find our way without a chart. Rolf is still with the Slott somewhere around the coast of Africa.'

I had the impression Hans was happy he wasn't still on board. Next day I flew the short distance from Darwin to Bacau in East Timor. It took three trips by an ancient Dove plane to transfer everyone from Bacau to Dili, a 20-minute trip over the rugged coastline.

I had been booked into a non-existent hotel in Dili, but was gathered up and taken to the Miramar, a basic beachfront hotel near the town. It advertised 'private bathrooms, fans and bells'. It was the centre of Dili's social life and the main meeting place – it suited me well.

The town was full of young Portuguese soldiers doing their military service – about two thousand of them. They seemed to outnumber the Timorese.

We were using escudos and centavos with their improbable coinage and notes. Sixty plus 30 centavos was one escudo, but nobody ever had any change anyway, including the post office, which gave change in stamps. One couple who bought a bar of chocolate were given the change in bubblegum.

Smelling like a farmyard the *Browind* arrived – unbelievably a day early. I looked out over the lagoon one morning and saw her coming in through the reef with *Iota* dangling over her side. I rushed to the wharf. The pilot boat with its complement of officials was just about to leave. I took a flying leap into the boat as she was pulling away from the jetty. It took them by surprise. They were not pleased – I couldn't go anywhere near the ship until she cleared.

The *Browind* stopped and, as the launch approached they lowered *Iota* the rest of the way into the water with one of their crew on board. The captain was waving vigorously; his voice came over a loudhailer demanding we take the yacht away from the side of the ship. The officials had no choice other than to put me aboard. Thank goodness the engine started immediately. The sailor undid the shackle and I motored away accompanied by cheers from the bridge. I anchored opposite the Miramar behind the reef. Subsequently the officials were obliging – a helpless demeanour was a sure way to get their co-operation.

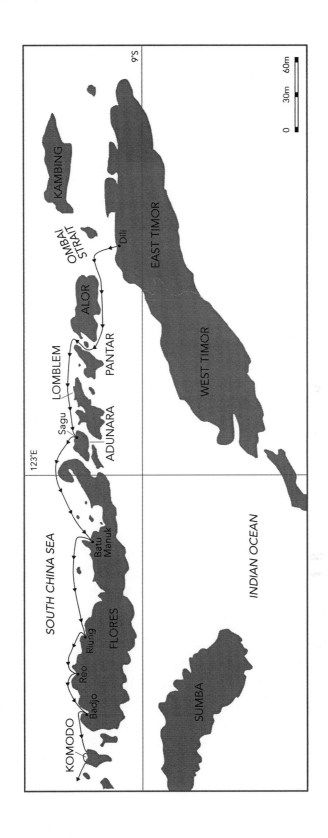

Another visiting yacht, the New Zealand schooner *Red McGregor*, was in trouble, having arrived with two of its crew missing. When in Darwin two men had approached the skipper, wanting to go to Timor to look for their stolen catamaran and to be put ashore on the south coast. The skipper had agreed, but by mistake the two men had found themselves in Indonesian West Timor. With no visa for that country they had been detained briefly, then had to make their way across mountainous country with few roads or tracks to Dili. In the meantime *Red McGregor* had arrived in Dili with a crew list stating six people had left Darwin. Not surprisingly, this had made the officials suspicious; now the other four were in detention too.

The men who had stolen the catamaran had run her onto rocks on the south coast of East Timor and wrecked her. They had made their way to Dili and were living in the Beach House, a basic shelter populated by hippies trying to get visas to go to Indonesia. The thieves' prospects were bleak because they had no money and no way of earning any. They were Norwegian so it occurred to me they might try to stow away on the Swedish *Browind*.

The captain of the *Browind* invited me to lunch on board. His name was Stefan and he was Polish. We found ourselves conversing in French. I warned him that he should expect stowaways when he went on his way, and subsequently learned I was right.

Three of the Beach House residents helped me to step *Iota*'s masts. They suggested a trip up into the hills so we hired a Land Rover, complete with driver. The road twisted along the coast to begin with, past beaches with crowds of fishing boats drawn up. Turning inland we climbed, with the horn constantly blaring. We negotiated washaways remaining from last year's wet season and crossed wide valleys each with a stream – a trickle of water now in the dry season, but a wide, raging torrent in the wet. Rice grew here and buffaloes were browsing in the straw. Further up, we came to coffee plantations. Picking was in progress – diminutive Timor ponies carried big sacks of beans back to the village.

Emera was a small town dominated by a Catholic church that perched on a hill and looked down on the daily activities of its congregation. We were there on a Saturday – market day and cockfights. The market was busy, but the produce was of poor quality and there was little variety. In the dry season it was a struggle for anything to grow. Tobacco and betel nuts were plentiful however; many of the villagers had red mouths and black teeth.

We watched the cockfights. A crowd gathered around betting on the two contestants while spurs were bound to their legs – razor-sharp five-centimetre blades. The white cock in the first match ran away and promptly had his neck wrung. The second fight was a whirl of feathers for a couple of seconds; the loser dropped stone dead and the victor was snatched up by its owner who did a victory dance, swinging the cock by its legs around his head.

Back in Dili I met up with an American couple, Miller and Libby, who were waiting for a trimaran, *Cygnus*, to arrive from Darwin. She was to take them on the adventure of a lifetime to Surabaya. Simon and *Cygnus* arrived on the same day and we all had dinner together at the Miramar. *Cygnus*'s crew included English skipper Dave, Alan from Wales and John, an Aussie. Dave and Miller were radio astronomers – the boat was named after a star of particular interest to them.

We set off from Dili with a promising morning wind, but it came to nothing. Our plan was to go through to the north of the islands to take advantage of the many anchorages and better shelter. The *Pilot Book* warned us of the constant strong south-flowing current – the result of warm water from the shallow South China Sea to the north of the islands making its way into the deep cold Indian Ocean to the south. As we approached the Ombai Strait – the gap between Alor and Kambing Islands – it became apparent we were making no progress. Swept to the west into a series of confused tidal rips we battled on for a couple of hours with the engine flat out, but with no help from the wind. The seas were menacing – although stirred up only by the current. Rippling overfalls sounded like wind, only to disappoint us. Steep and irregular waves came from all directions and often climbed aboard; their white tops shot up in bursts like strange cauliflowers.

Turning into calmer water we kept close to the south coast of Alor through the night. We saw no settlements along the shore, but high in the hills lights shone all night. By mid-morning next day we were in tide-rips again at the other end of the island.

We anchored in a shallow patch of sand dubiously defended by a reef against the heavy swells, laying out three anchors – two from the bow and a stern anchor to keep bows to the swells. Briefly we went ashore for a respite from *Iota*'s pitching and to stretch our legs. The land was barren and dry. The inhabitants of a couple of huts behind the beach – two men, two women and three boys – stared at us and ran away.

It was an uneasy night as *Iota* swung dizzily in the currents and jerked on her chains. The constant roar of swells breaking on the beach and the occasional succession of big seas thundering on the reef scared us half to death. Fortunately they did not break near us, but we scarcely slept.

We disentangled our anchors in the dark and set off to battle the Pantar Strait. Initially the seas were large and chaotic, but dawn found us in smoother water and making progress. A school of porpoises woke themselves up and came over to encourage us. With a strong current against us we advanced painfully slowly until the first whisper of wind came in from the south. We hoisted every sail we had. As the wind increased, *Iota* began to make headway.

We entered the narrow part of the strait with the wind now a boisterous 20 knots, all sails straining and the engine at full revs. We burst out the other side in a froth of white water and with a sensation of achievement and relief. As we passed through we saw an isolated village – a collection of huts and a church clinging to the dry, steep hills clad with coarse grass and stunted trees.

The night was calm, the sea now smooth – at least we were comfortable while we waited for the wind. Next day a light wind took us along the coast of Lomblen, past an active volcano with a plume of smoke rising from its top and streaming white flows of lava running down its sides. The rim of the crater was bright yellow with sulphur. Huts were clustered at its foot, their owners making use of the fertile volcanic soil, but under constant threat. Out to sea, praus with their coloured sails slid along as if on an invisible tramway.

We came into Sagu Bay in Adunara late in the afternoon and anchored amongst an assortment of local craft. Our immediate neighbour was a big, beamy boat with a long bowsprit and a white cock that crowed all day and all night. Half a dozen men came out from the village, welcomed us and chatted for a while. Simon was pleased to find he could communicate quite well; his ability to speak Indonesian made an immense difference to our enjoyment of the cruise.

They asked Simon if I, nonya, could speak Indonesian too. I recited the conversation I had learned by heart from Lesson 1 in my phrase book.

'Selamat pagi, pak. Bagaimana kabarnya.' ('Good morning, father. How are you?')

'Baik baik saja.' ('Very well.')

'Dan bagaimana Tristan and Halimah?' ('And how are Tristan and Halimah?')

'Tristan baik baik saja, tepati Halimah sedang sakit.' ('Tristan is well, but Halimah is sick.')

'Ah, sayang sekali! Sakit keras dia?' ('Oh what a shame! Is she very sick?')

'Tidak, dia hanya tidak enak baden.' ('No, she is just not feeling well.') My performance never failed to reduce them to tears of laughter.

We walked to the village less than a kilometre away, gathering an ever-increasing crowd until, in the village, we were surrounded by swarms of people jostling for a better look. The local policeman inspected our papers and asked us what they said. He escorted us around the village, chasing the children away from our path.

They were good-looking people with fine features and a graceful bearing. I tried to take photos, but, as I raised the camera, the children ran in front and blocked the view. At each click there was a deafening shout. Simon had trouble with the children for they had never seen human legs with hairs on them before; they wanted to stroke them.

Many houses were on stilts, built over the water at high tide. It solved the sewage problem, but made access difficult. We visited the crumbling Rajah's palace – a depressing building with rotting wooden floors, rusted corrugated roof and cracked walls – but it made a home for three families.

The evening was visiting time on *Iota* and, although many people were obviously itching to come and look, we limited them to six at a time. When we said we wanted to be alone our visitors politely left.

In the morning the policeman met us on the beach with two horses for us to ride to the village. Simon declined, but I decided to try. The horse objected to me. He flattened his ears, rolled his pale eyes and snorted. He was only little so two men held him down and hoisted me aboard. It was difficult to keep my legs tucked up so they didn't tangle with his, but I made it to the village without falling off.

The cock lay fast asleep.

Our visit was an excuse for the villagers to go sailing.

The praus were packed with brightly dressed girls and men beating drums and gongs.

The schoolmaster managed to keep his class in school so I found it easier to take photos. I snapped two girls, each with a cock fast asleep in a basket on her head, spinning kapok onto a bobbin as she walked. Cocks were pets – small boys invariably had one tucked under an arm. The cocks seemed resigned to this role in life and to being carried around all day.

Our visit was a major event in their lives so the afternoon was declared a holiday; they would go sailing. The bay swarmed with boats. Small boys whizzed along in precarious dugout canoes with triangular handkerchiefs of sail; their bigger brothers sailed canoes with outriggers. The praus, colourful and noisy, were crowded with brightly dressed girls and men beating drums and gongs.

These larger boats were expertly handled – fortunately – because a competition developed to see which of them could come the closest to us. They tacked a little way ahead just before the shallow water and came yelling past us with inches to spare. That night the people lit fires around the bay, and the hillsides were alight with flickering flames.

We left early next day, rounded the tip of Flores late in the afternoon and looked for an anchorage. We saw a prau in a small bay, anchored in fifteen fathoms on coral – not for us. However they waved to us and invited us to tie *Iota* alongside. She wasn't the quietest neighbour, having a complement of nearly forty people, including many squalling children. They swarmed onto *Iota*, but we managed to lure them off again by taking Polaroid pictures of them – on their own boat.

She had solid wooden frames and her hull was made from heavy planks fastened with nails and caulked with bark. Her sails were supported by a thick mast and a heavy gaff and boom. Her bowsprit was almost as long as her hull. We could see through the deck planks over the hold to their cargo of cement. The low, flimsy bamboo deckhouse where they slept curled up on mats obviously leaked. Forward was the galley, a hut containing an open fire that gave off acrid smoke, and aft was a box with a hole in it – the toilet.

The evening was a little quieter and the children stopped crying, but just as we were preparing for bed they decided they were going, despite the lack of wind. We had to put to sea for the night.

'Probably for the best,' Simon observed. 'They might have been pirates and we could have woken up with our throats cut. We must have been mad to have trusted them.'

We had intended to put into Maumere Bay the next day, but a 20-knot southerly with a choppy sea made it a beat to windward.

Rather than fight it we resolved to use it; good wind was too precious to waste. We fell off along the coast and a fast reach for a few hours put some miles behind us.

Tanjung Batu Manuk was a spectacular rocky headland. The *Pilot Book* claimed you could anchor in a bay on its eastern side, but the small-scale chart was not helpful. Investigation revealed an unexpectedly good anchorage with outlying reefs to keep out the swells. It was a stark scene – the white beach was backed by steep, bare, rocky red hills.

Iota *at anchor off the spectacular rocky headland Tanjung Batu Manuk.*

We spent the hour of sundown marvelling at the complete quietness of the place. Unlike New Guinea where a crescendo of noise filled the evenings, here there was an eerie silence. The only sound was the lapping of small waves on the beach. In the morning a solitary monkey prowled along the shore, emphasising the loneliness of the place.

After a leisurely morning we sailed along the coast of Flores. It had a geometric look – conical volcanic hills with V-shaped valleys. We passed another active volcano with a plume of steam. The shores were uninhabited; most of the population lived up in the hills. We found another silent and isolated anchorage in Sopu Bay.

The way into Riung was complicated, but this time we had a detailed chart and it was low tide so we could easily see the reefs. We passed a small island with a crowded settlement of colourful houses. Men came out in a canoe and showed us where to anchor.

'This is the place ships,' they said. 'The praus go over there.'

Canoes surrounded us and a curious figure appeared in the throng. He had red shorts, a red shirt and an odd red hat. He was the police boy and was to escort us ashore to see the commandant.

We hastily gathered together papers and went ashore followed by an armada of canoes. Soon a swarm of children accompanied us. We were taken to a house on stilts, wading through the mud and up a shaky plank that creaked under our weight. People crowded into the house until it creaked and swayed. I thought it would collapse.

The villagers crowded into the flimsy house.

The police contingent – two in uniform with rifles, and the commandant – had an escort of boys almost as numerous as our own. They went through the barrage of usual questions and had a problem because Simon was born in Cairo and they didn't know where Cairo was.

'Negara President Nasser,' said Simon – 'The land of President Nasser.' They nodded and their faces lit up with understanding.

I went off to photograph buffaloes that were wallowing in the mud. They took one look at me, climbed to their feet and stampeded around the village, bellowing, heads down with their massive curved horns sticking up. A tethered cow tolerated my approach and the children led her into the sun so I could take my pictures.

It was a long hot run to Linggeh next day and I arrived feeling exhausted and irritated, too, by the swell coming in. The holding was poor so we had to put down two anchors.

The town of Reo was only a few miles away up the river. We walked to town hoping to be able to buy diesel fuel. It was hot and tiring along a rough path, up and down. We were ferried across the river in an unstable canoe.

A customs officer took charge of our papers and showed us to the big Catholic mission. They sent a boy with us to look for fuel. It was quite a big town, with Chinese stores flanking the wide, dusty and hot main street. We went from place to place, but no fuel was forthcoming. Feeling despondent we went back to the mission. Simon set off again, this time with the pastor, a cheerful and determined young man who was firmly resolved to find some for us.

I stayed at the mission, inexplicably aching. I asked for water, so they boiled some for me and, seeing it was too hot to drink, another boy fetched a glass of grey-coloured water, fishing out two flies and a cockroach with his fingers.

I was saved when Simon returned in triumph. He and the pastor had finally extracted about twenty litres of fuel from a reluctant Chinese woman and bought four large bottles of beer as well – hot, but *oh* so drinkable! Simon said the pastor was magnificent and had refused to give up. We repaid his kindness with Polaroid photographs, which he received with awe and profuse thanks, then with the customs officer escorted us back to the boat. Later, when Simon took them ashore, they parted in tears saying how good it was of us to have called on them.

That night I realised I was sick. My temperature was 102° and I woke in the middle of the night in sheets saturated with sweat. In the morning I felt better and my temperature was sub-normal so we pressed on – it was only a short hop to Badjo. The pattern was to continue for the next week – aching limbs, aching head, loss of appetite and energy and a high afternoon fever. I was also bad tempered.

Badjo was a picturesque tangle of houses over the water, each with its boat tied up. It was swarming with people. We went past to a bay about a mile away where there was a welcome patch of sand to anchor on, and peace. We had just put up our awning when the police arrived, complete with guns. They told us to move to the village and go to see the commandant. Simon argued, but they were inflexible. We took down the awning and moved. They said we should anchor just off the village, but it was in ten fathoms over reef and rock. Simon let the anchor go and we backed up to see if it would hold. It didn't and *Iota* easily dragged it. It snagged and let go again. Simon pulled it up and it appeared with a lump of coral wedged in the flukes. My fever got the better of me. I pointed to the echo sounder and the coral, turned on the nearest policeman, pulled his gun away from his ear and shouted, 'You silly bloody fool!'

Badjo was a picturesque tangle of houses over the water.

They went into a huddle, saying, 'Nonya marah!' – 'Mrs is red – furious!' They stared at the echo sounder. We went back to our patch of sand and Simon walked with them to the village to try to make peace. Apparently the echo sounder had done the trick – they called it radar – but my temperature was back to 102°!

It was a rough crossing to Komodo; tide-rips and whirlpools were whipped up by the current. We put into the first bay, which appeared to be well protected although encumbered with coral. Simon ventured ashore, but it was not easy to land and the hills were covered with prickly plants making it difficult to walk around, let alone creep up on one of the famous Komodo dragons. He came back covered in mud.

We moved around to a bay on the other side of the island where the crew of a prau were mending their boat. They had seen a small dragon that morning. We hoped we might be lucky enough to find one, but my fever soared to an alarming 103°. We reluctantly abandoned the dragons and went on to Bima where there was a doctor. I was disappointed – I had been looking forward to making the acquaintance of the world's largest living reptile.

We sailed in through the narrow entrance to the big bay at Bima at sundown. Praus were anchored around the jetty. They directed us to a gap between them, but there wasn't much room.

Simon investigated ashore in the morning. The officials were helpful, organising laundry, bread, fuel supplies and the doctor. The town teemed with people, bicycles and little horses pulling carts. We climbed into a cart and the horse trotted off, weaving along the road, in and out of the throng. He kept to a steady trot regardless of who was in the way. The driver announced our presence by putting the end of his whip in the wheel spokes, making a rattling noise. The town sprawled with closely packed tumbledown houses and the dusty, crumbly road was lined with bundles of little red onions put out in the sun to dry. There were chickens, dogs, goats and the distinctive Bima smell.

There was little room to anchor between the praus in Bima.

The doctor was having his siesta. We waited for an hour with his other patients staring curiously at us. Eventually an Indian orderly appeared armed with a thermometer. He went around putting the thermometer into the mouths of the assembled patients, but without washing it in between. Sitting next to me was an elderly, dishevelled gentleman who had been chewing betel nut; red slobber dribbled down his chin. When my turn came, I firmly closed my mouth.

Dr Hassan looked like Peter Sellers in a mad movie and wore a mask. When Simon explained about my 'sakit panas', he waved his stethoscope around and, feeling my clammy skin, said, 'Ah'.

He offered to give me an injection of tetracycline, but when we looked at the row of veterinarian-type metal hypodermics, each with a fly perched on its needle, we opted for a course of antibiotic capsules. The consultation was free, but we paid for the antibiotics and bundles of other unidentifiable pills.

The activity around the harbour in the morning was chaotic. Praus under sail were manoeuvring into and out of the jetty to load. They did not have the luxury of an engine. One was loading horses – more than thirty of them – and their hay for the journey was piled on top of the cabin. The prau had little freeboard and the horses' noses were not far off the water when she sailed in the evening, looking like a floating haystack.

Horses were loaded onto a prau and their hay for the journey was piled on top of the cabin.

Simon's holiday time was running short so we had to set off for Bali. Sailing along the chain of islands was hard work as the wind kept shifting strength and direction. We seemed to be constantly changing and trimming sails. The wind was mostly light in the lee of the islands, but an occasional unexpected blast would come down a valley. In the straits between the islands, we expected a fresh wind and rough sea. We sailed through the first night across the Alas Strait making good speed. Simon bore the brunt of the work, my watches getting shorter and shorter as my fever returned. In the afternoon of the second day we closed the coast of Lombok, but it offered no anchorage. The mountains ran precipitously down to the coast and obviously continued to run steeply downwards under the sea.

Praus anchored in Bima

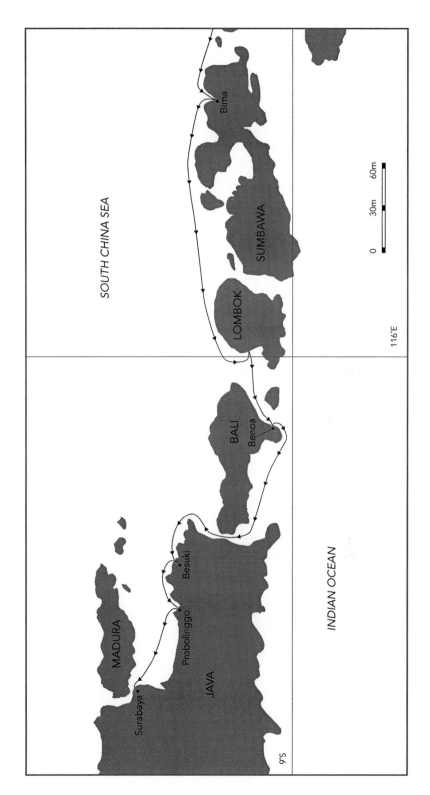

In the evening I suddenly felt better – the antibiotics were working. I cooked a respectable meal and stood a four-hour watch while Simon grabbed some much needed rest. We spent the second night at sea, but next day were relieved to find an excellent anchorage in a peaceful and attractive bay called Temborbor. A volcano dominated the scene.

A river flowed into the bay and houses were scattered along the shore. We saw motionless fishermen wearing conical hats standing up to their waists in water, fishing with long poles. They resembled herons and I suspected they had one leg tucked up.

We took our laundry ashore, washed, and wallowed happily in a dam of dubiously clean but cold water, watched by a small crowd who politely kept their distance. I went for a walk around the bay escorted by succeeding families. With great pride they presented their houses, their horses and cows, boats and fishing nets, bicycles and cooking pots for me to admire.

Quite late in the evening the village chief came out and asked us to go ashore to meet the police. After our experience at Bajo we resolved to stand our ground, so we laughed, gave him a cigarette and said 'No'. Simon firmly refused to go ashore.

Eventually they came out to us, the police handing us their rifles so they could climb on board over davits from their double outrigger canoes. A crowd came on board – police, commandant, head of the village, head of the district and their aides. We chatted for a while – they were jovial, enjoying themselves and it seemed as if they would stay all night. They asked why we had come there.

'To wash and to sleep,' said Simon. 'Washing we have managed, but sleep, not yet.'

The commandant was looking a little seasick so the party took the hint. They climbed back into their canoes and we handed them their rifles.

Ampenan, the main port of Lombok, was completely open. A swell was breaking on the shore. Outriggers rowed by four men were working hard to load copra and coffee onto the praus anchored off. Many bags met with disaster. Seeing their problems we remained on board – going ashore would have meant the inevitable officials anyway.

In the evening outrigger canoes set off for their night's fishing, each with a pressure lamp to attract fish. We set off for Benoa at 2 am picking our way out of the anchorage using a searchlight to avoid the anchored praus. It was impossible to distinguish the lighthouse from the streetlights around it. By dawn we had made good progress and were well out into the Lombok Strait.

We picked up a strong southerly current and, although we were not going fast through the water, we were making twelve knots. The enormous blind swells were spooky, as if some supernatural force was creating them. It was hazy and the Bali coastline was low and featureless so when the Bali Beach Hotel loomed in sight, sticking up like a sore thumb, I marked it on the chart. It was then possible to fix our position. It was essential to find out what the current was doing to us for if we were swept past the entrance to Benoa Harbour out into the Indian Ocean, it would have been difficult, if not impossible, to make our way back against the current.

We picked up the buoys and leads that guided us through the reef extending several miles from the coast. The swells gradually abated and we wound our way up into the harbour, having made – with the aid of current – our fastest passage ever.

~

Bali was different from the other islands we had visited. Suddenly we found ourselves in greener and more lush surroundings – we had crossed the Wallace Line. The Line was identified by British naturalist and explorer Alfred Wallace who noticed differences between the animals of Lombok, which resembled those of New Guinea and Australia, and those on Bali, which were clearly related to those in Asia. Wallace, a meticulous observer, noticed small variations in apparently closely related species of animals, particularly butterflies and birds, and theorised that they came about as the animals changed to adapt to their environment. He developed a theory of 'evolution through natural selection' and sent a memoir about it to Charles Darwin. Darwin had similar views, but had been hesitant to make them public because he thought they would be extremely controversial. Their joint paper was presented at a meeting of the Linnean Society in London in July 1858.

The anchorage at Benoa was plain and ugly in strong contrast with the rest of the island. The stone pier with its fuel tanks and tumbledown sheds was reached from the shore along a potholed causeway flanked by shallow pools; here salt of dubious cleanliness was being made. A strong tide in the harbour made rowing ashore in the dinghy hard work and, at low tide, the steep, slippery steps were perilous.

The sheds usually housed large numbers of personnel – the harbour master and officers for customs, immigration, police and health – but the only person there when we arrived was the immigration officer. As he entered us he explained it was the beginning of a three-day holiday, the Balinese New Year – one day to prepare, one day to celebrate and another to recover. We accepted his offer to take us to the main town, Den Pasar, to see what was going on. People were everywhere; streamers fluttered from arched bamboo poles to decorate the streets. The traffic was complete confusion, with people, bicycles, pony carts, jeeps, cars and motorbikes all dangerously weaving and intertwining, hooting, honking and ringing bells.

The local public transport was a bemo, a three-wheeled van carrying six – and often many more – people. We took one to the Bali Beach Hotel at Sanur. Welcomed as a landmark at sea, we found its ten stories out of place in Bali. Of the many guests we were the most appreciative as we sat on the terrace drinking icy cold beer and eating delicious Indonesian food. It had been a while since we had encountered such luxury.

'How about we have a night ashore?' asked Simon, reading my thoughts.

'What a good idea!' I replied.

We wandered along the beach and came to the Hotel Tanjung Sari. Yes, a beachfront bungalow was free and it would suit us fine. This elegant hotel was built on the site of a temple and retained much of its mysterious atmosphere. It had a tranquil garden and a gallery of antique Balinese artefacts. Our bungalow was cool and comfortable, exquisitely decorated; the welcome drink of arak, rum and orange was memorable, the food delectable and the service attentive and charming. We savoured every moment of our stay.

We came back to the harbour after our indulgent night ashore to find our friends on *Cygnus* had arrived. They had been lucky enough to see a Komodo dragon.

We rented a Honda motorbike and explored the island during the five days remaining before Simon had to head off to Europe for three weeks. He was to return to Bali and we then would sail *Iota* to Surabaya and, from there, ship her to Singapore.

The Honda was a painful and precarious way of getting around. Simon wasn't used to changing gear, and starting off was a real problem; I clung tightly to him in order not to be jolted off the back. Each traffic island had a shrine on which were placed offerings to keep travellers safe – we appreciated them! The roads were rutted so we were soon jarred and sore. We stopped frequently to explore on foot this fairyland world of spirits, gods, temples, shrines, mysterious rituals and its rich culture of art, theatre, music and dancing.

Hinduism had become intricately woven into the ancient beliefs of the Balinese. These people were concerned with the never-ending battle between good and evil – everything they did was devoted to encouraging the good spirits and placating the bad. They believed good spirits came out of the volcanoes and that bad spirits lived in the sea, hence they preferred to live inland with their backs to the sea. The people who lived around the coast of Bali were mainly Buganese Muslims.

The villages consisted of several family compounds enclosed by a high stone wall. The gateway into the village was narrow and immediately facing it was a curved wall. This was to confuse the evil spirits and make it hard for them to enter, as they have difficulty turning corners. In the middle of the village was the temple and the market, often shaded by a sacred banyan tree.

Between the villages all possible land was used to grow rice; the terracing extended like a gigantic auditorium in all directions. The sculpting of the hills and the intricate and sophisticated irrigation system had been developed over centuries. The Balinese were the most successful rice producers in Indonesia, planting and harvesting rice throughout the year, so all stages of development could be seen at any time. Buffalo or bullocks ploughed the paddies, which were then flooded. Planting was done by hand and, as the rice grew, the plants were allowed to dry out. Strips of white cloth fluttered over the grain to scare away the birds. The ripe grain stalks were cut, gathered into bundles and threshed by pounding with long bamboo poles. Offerings to the good spirits on the many little shrines in the paddies helped to ensure a good crop.

Except for harvesting, mainly men worked in the rice fields, with women attending to the marketing and preparation of food. Children worked hard from quite an early age, fetching water and wood, tending the cows and ducks. The ducks were quite delightful and never failed to make us smile. They marched in single file to the fields in the morning, a leading duck close to the white flag dangling from the end of the long bamboo pole held by the boy behind them. When they reached the chosen area the boy planted the flag in the ground and the ducks fed around it until evening; then the regimented line reformed and returned to the village. Ducks and buffalo were at home in the paddies, always looking contented.

The arts of Bali were an integral part of everyday life. Everybody was involved and everybody was creative, unlike in our culture where a few professionals practise the arts and a small minority appreciates them. We met woodcarvers, stonemasons and painters. Others worked with metals or fabric. The women made attractive offerings to take to the temple and wove intricate baskets and mats from palm or banana leaves.

The gamelan music was hypnotic. The instruments were mainly percussion – all manner of gongs, xylophones, cymbals, drums – and flutes. At times the music was gentle, pure and bell-like, inducing a meditative state, but, with a sudden change in tempo and dynamics, the music became insistent and almost violent, building up an inexorable tension.

Balinese dances usually told a story about the clash between good and evil and were influenced by the Hindu Ramayana. We went to see as many as we could to admire the control the dancers had of every muscle in their body, their eyes, facial expressions and fingertips. Their costumes were exquisite.

We saw the Barong – a mythical animal, part lion and part dragon – the enemy of evil. His role was to drive away Rangda, the Goddess of Darkness and Evil who appeared as a monkey. The Barong would be taken to a village should the priest decree it needed cleansing. Two men inhabited his body and he danced and jigged around. He appeared to have a sense of humour.

The Legong, a graceful dance for girls before the age of puberty, demanded classical and precise movements. It was amazing that children so young could remember the complex movements. Their youth gave the dance a feeing of purity. They often performed it in a trance.

The Ketchak, the monkey dance, was exciting. It was not accompanied by the gamelan but by a crowd of men – at least 80 of them, closely packed around the dancers. Their sweating brown backs, fluttering arms and vibrating fingers glistened in the flickering lamplight. They made fierce, eerie, hissing sounds; they moaned, shrieked, cried, bellowed and chattered 'ketchak, ketchak', like monkeys. The story was also from the Ramayana – Good King Rama seeks the help of a band of apes to rescue his wife from the evil King Rhawana.

Cockfighting was a favourite pastime of the men. The cocks were pampered and frequently taken out of their wicker cages to be admired by their owners who spent hours discussing their merits. The fights took place in the forecourt of the temple and, although the actual combat itself was usually quickly over, the betting beforehand was noisy and frantically excited. Cock fighting was well organised with strict rules.

The barong meets a monkey.

The performers of the legong dance were often in a trance.

We heard of a major festival soon to take place at Mengui, the second temple of Bali. This large temple was surrounded by a moat. It was a typical Balinese temple, having three separate concentric areas.

The outer court provided various shelters for preparing offerings as well as a cockfighting arena and a kul-kul tower, which contained a big drum, beaten in various rhythms to call the village council, sound an alarm or relay news. On this festival day the court was full of stalls selling refreshments and drinks, toys for the children, cloth and a host of other items. It was buzzing with activity, gaiety and good humour. Delicious spicy aromas wafted from the stalls and intermittent roars came from the cockfighting arena as the cocks sparred.

The second court was reached through an impressive raised gateway with carved portals. This court was for dance performances and the gamelan band. Another massive and equally elaborate gateway guarded the shrines in the inner court. On top of the largest shrine, which was decorated with snakes and mythical animals, were three empty chairs. These were for the three principal manifestations of the Hindu god – Brahma representing fire, Sewa, water and Vishnu, earth. The priest was in the inner court, an old man dressed in white. He communed with the spirits, sitting cross-legged, ringing a bell, lighting incense and making offerings of wine while muttering incantations and performing rituals. The temple guardians wore white sarongs and black and white checked shirts to keep the evil spirits at bay.

A stately procession of women bearing offerings at the Mengui temple festival

The purpose of the temple festival was to persuade the good spirits to enter the temple. They were attracted to the good things in life – food, cockfights, music, dancing and fine clothes. During the afternoon a long procession of women came single file into the temple. It was an impressive sight, hundreds of them, each with an offering on her head, moving with grace and elegance. They looked exquisite in colourful sarongs of hand-woven cloth frequently with gold or silver thread. The sarong was bound in place with metres of tightly wrapped cloth called 'stacking'; over the top was a badju, a long-sleeved waisted blouse. The offerings were the most painstaking arrangements of all manner of food – brilliant pink cakes, moulded rice, chicken and every kind of fruit. Some were in silver bowls, others in ornate baskets. They were fixed into a frame, up to a metre high. The women carried them carefully up the steps and down the other side into the inner court and placed them in front of the shrines. They sprinkled them with holy water, took flowers in their fingertips and flung them to the ground in front of the shrine. The gamelan played its haunting music and incense pervaded the air.

~

The bright spot of Benoa was Muhammad, who appointed himself as our boatboy. He was a great help and very able. He came each morning with fruit and vegetables, took our laundry to his mother and fetched water. He scrubbed the decks, cleaned the topsides and bilges and slept in the cockpit if we were away overnight.

After Simon left for Europe I joined forces with the crew of *Cygnus*. The six of us hired a jeep so we could explore further afield in the middle and north of the island. Leaving Muhammad in charge of the two yachts, we elected John as our driver and set off early one morning packed in like sardines, our bags strapped on the back. We had difficulty accommodating Miller's preposterously large hat.

The Sangeh Monkey Forest, a sacred forest of huge trees, was inhabited by two troops of grey monkeys. We had bought peanuts along the way – a mistake because the monkeys quickly detected them. At least a dozen of them crowded into the jeep and made a very thorough search before we had a chance to get out. Libby had her packet whipped out of her hand and Dave lost his from his shirt pocket – and the pocket as well! We fought our way out of the vehicle and left them swinging from the roof by their tails. They cajoled, begged and threatened for peanuts. One big male grabbed my skirt and bared his teeth. They climbed onto our shoulders and ran around doing gymnastics to attract attention.

In the middle of the forest was a cool, mossy temple where the other troop lived. They were better behaved. A delightfully polite young monkey sat on my knee taking the nuts carefully and alternately with his hands and feet. He knew immediately when the bag was empty and shuffled off, belching and scratching his behind.

We stopped frequently. A cockfight, a barong cleansing a village, roadside stalls selling all sorts of delicacies, several temples, a dance rehearsal – all attracted out attention so that darkness was falling as we climbed up to Bedugul in the mountains. The temperature fell dramatically and, at nightfall, we needed jerseys. The local hotel

– losmen – was basic but well situated on the shore of the crater lake. Having a shower took courage for the water was nearly freezing and the bathroom not the most inviting. We ate dinner wrapped in blankets.

Next morning was market day. We admired showy orchids and enormous cabbages and sampled carrots – so young and crisp we ate them raw – and a divine type of passionfruit.

Alan and Dave watched while the monkeys inspected our jeep.

'I won't get out until you give me a peanut.'

The road to the north coast was steep. We had magnificent views, but the town of Singaraja on the coast, formerly the main town when the Dutch were in charge, was hot, dusty, dirty and unattractive. We stopped only for fuel.

The striking temple at Sangist was made out of rich pink-hued sandstone and its terraces were elaborately and intricately decorated with carved mythical figures. The impact of beautifully balanced archways and an inner court full of frangipanis and feathery trees with delicate, white scented blossoms was ethereal, overpowering.

Turning inland again we began the steep climb to Kintamani where we planned to stay for the night. The jeep began to splutter and became sicker and sicker until it finally refused to go any further. We came to a halt in the middle of a small village and were immediately surrounded by curious, but not very helpful, villagers.

We were despondently thinking we would have to spend the night there when John discovered a broken gasket in the fuel pump and mended it using a piece of cardboard, a band-aid and a pair of nail scissors. He had brought tools from the boat, anticipating such a circumstance. We were even more admiring than the villagers and drove off to their cheers.

We climbed on through rainforest and coffee trees and suddenly came out into the open. The sun was setting over the crater lake in front of us and, beyond, the tops of Bali's three big volcanos floated on the evening mist.

The losmen at Kintamani was comfortable and we had it to ourselves. It even had a cistern in the toilet, although it didn't actually work. Mine Host was welcoming and, in no time at all, had the beds made, drinks poured and dinner served. We passed a companionable, contented evening in front of a blazing log fire.

We set off in the early morning mist to climb Mount Batur. As we walked down the steep side of the crater to the lake the clouds rolled away and the day started to warm up. Firstly we were taken across the lake to Trunjan, an isolated village on the far shore of the lake. The people who lived there were descended from the early Balinese and had an animistic religion. They were surly, quite different in their attitude to us from the Balinese we knew. Their main claim to tourist fame was that they did not burn or bury their dead, but left the bodies in an open coffin to rot or to be eaten by rats and birds.

Two of Mount Batur's three craters were dormant, but regularly, every half-hour, the lower one erupted with a loud roar and a blast of hot ashes and rocks. We climbed the middle one, a hard, hot walk. We followed a lava flow, climbing and scrambling up the sharp rocks and through thick volcanic ash. It was almost impossible to get a foothold and each footstep gained was an achievement. We slid most of the way down and, exhausted, were happy to climb onto horses to take us back up the escarpment to the road.

Mount Batur's lower crater erupted every half hour.

Back in the Benoa Harbour Muhammad had done a great job and our yachts were in good order. He offered to take me to a play in the village not far from his home on the other side of the harbour. It started at midnight so we rowed across on the evening tide and I had dinner with his family.

About 10 pm we went off to catch the 'bus', designed to carry about 25 passengers but crammed with at least 60 of us. The driver, unable to see where he was going, was directed by shouts. The bus broke down so we pushed it for the last stretch.

A great throng of people – two or three thousand – waited for the play to begin. I seemed to be the only tourist and Muhammad's friends were curious about me.

At midnight the gamelan players, dressed smartly in red and white, took their place and played an overture. For the first hour of the play my interest was captured – it had a complicated, improbable plot and the costumes were elaborate and colourful. The audience was spellbound and roared with laughter at times but, as it was in Balinese, I missed out on much of the meaning. About 3 am a truck took us home and I slept on Muhammad's brother's veranda until the tide changed in the morning and I could go back on board.

Muhammad appointed himself as our boatboy.

Simon returned from Europe and we bid farewell to a tearful Muhammad. We wrote him a reference recommending him to yachts that came into Benoa in the future.

The *Pilot Book* was very specific about the tides and currents in the narrow Bali Strait between Bali and Java. We would be in the transition period between the two monsoons and have a half moon. We could expect to have four and a half hours of north-going stream to help us just after dawn. There was no anchorage along the south coast of Bali so we would have to leave late in the afternoon, sail through the night and heave-to while we waited for dawn. Unbelievably, the lighthouse lit up – not flashing the signal indicated on the chart – but at least in the right place and flashing. It was a great help; we were able to keep a fix on it.

At dawn the current behaved precisely as predicted and started to flow northward. We shot through the strait at an ever-increasing speed with a determined southerly wind to help us. We saw the ferry plying between Bali and Java – an elderly, rusty lady that clattered, shook and belched out clouds of oily black smoke in her efforts to stem the current.

The seas were confused, but the wind held strong and steady and we had an exhilarating sail until we started to round the northeast corner of Java. At sundown we were off a string of small islands and reefs that protected a bay. The *Pilot Book* described it as offering 'shelter for small native craft with local knowledge'. Several praus were anchored in the bay, but we had only a small-scale chart so picked our way in by eye. We held our breath and blessed *Iota*'s shallow draught as the coral passed just beneath our keel.

The banks, reefs and fish traps encumbering the approaches to Surabaya made night sailing hazardous so we stopped for two more nights on the way. At Besuki we had our sundowner watching the crews of colourful koleks preparing them for the night's fishing. The koleks lay in their dozens on the glistening beach appearing as ants, their high curved outriggers becoming a confusion of insect legs. Behind the rice paddies a distant volcano puffed clouds of white steam.

At Probolinggo we clung off the end of the breakwater and our evening entertainment was watching the koleks manoeuvring in and out of the harbour. Their curved masts supported striped sails in yellow, orange and deep red-brown. Their hulls were elaborately painted in a rainbow of bright colours. At night their hurricane lamps looked like rows of streetlights out at sea.

We carefully followed the buoys and beacons into the Surabaya Strait. They were clearly shown on the chart and described in detail in the *Pilot Book*. We came to two wooden structures called Castor and Pollux Beacons, both with their lights flashing. The *Pilot Book* said they marked a channel dredged to two and a half fathoms. A man in a canoe was fishing between them. As we came closer I suddenly realised the man was not sitting in his canoe but standing beside it. We lost confidence in the channel markers and turned north to join the other boats heading for Surabaya.

The commercial part of the port of Surabaya was full of ships of all shapes and sizes, nearly all in poor condition. We anchored off Poras, formerly a yacht club but now a nightclub. There was little room. On the harbour wall rested the sad wreck of a trimaran, stripped to a bare shell. Her crew had caught hepatitis and one of them had died.

Koleks set off for their night's fishing.

Striped sails complemented hulls of bright rainbow colours.

Surabaya was not a pleasant place; the heat and noise were overwhelming. It was intensely humid with barely any wind. It didn't cool off at night and we woke up, if we slept at all, sweating and stifled. Nothing worked efficiently, communication being particularly bad. The roads were in a dire state of repair, most of the railways had long since collapsed, lighthouses didn't work and the wharves were tumbledown. The telephones were hopeless and it was only by bribery and luck that you could phone Djakarta. Local air services used wartime DC3s and navigation aids were primitive.

The traffic was congested. Bemos and betjaks – bicycles with a seat for two passengers on the front – together with bullock carts and broken-down trucks caused frequent stoppages to the traffic.

Our main complaint was of the noise. A nearby ship charged its batteries all night and another, in for repairs, broadcast the radio at full blast over a loudspeaker all day. The nightclub's amplified band started up at 6 pm, playing until midnight or later. At times the clamours of the port overlapped. Although the power supply failed every other day, we didn't even have that respite because the nightclub added the clatter of a generator. It was as if the port tried to drown out the smells of the sewers with noise.

Not that there were any sewers! Every morning we witnessed a procession of labourers going to the wharf, who frequently ducked over the wall to relieve themselves. They were away from the view of their land-based colleagues, but not from those of us on the water. Our breakfast was often in the company of a row of bare, defecating bums.

Cygnus arrived shortly after us. I was pleased to see them because Simon was about to leave to go back to work in Australia. They greeted us enthusiastically – they had made a great discovery.

'We now know why we couldn't work out why the praus don't capsize,' Miller told us.

'Why couldn't you?' we asked.

'Because they do! We saw one to windward of us. It was hit by a gust of wind and heeled over, heeled over some more, and a bit more. Then it capsized,' he said. 'Its cargo came floating out of its hold and other praus came rushing in to collect it.'

'Nobody seemed to worry about the people in the water,' added Libby.

We called on the British Consul to thank him. He had been instrumental in ensuring we had an Indonesian sailing permit. He was generously hospitable and we went several times to the Consulate – a beautiful old Dutch residence surrounded by a peaceful garden. The hot showers were particularly welcome and food and drink were abundant. We were invited to a formal Sunday morning reception and were served a rijsttafel, a Dutch-Indonesian banquet. The guests welcomed our new faces – a change from the ones they had met so many times before.

The manager of the brewery and his wife invited us to Tretas, a resort in the hills where they had a weekend house. It was about 50 kilometres from Surabaya and high enough to be pleasantly cool. It was formerly a Dutch stronghold guarded by notices saying, 'No Chinese, No Dogs'. It was a delightful day spent alternately wetting ourselves inside with beer and outside in the pool.

On the way back to the harbour we came to a halt in a queue of traffic. The level crossing gates were closed. After a while a man on a bicycle came to sell us satay, cooked on a brazier of glowing charcoal on the back of his bike. Eventually the gates opened and we went on our way. No train had used the line for many, many years, but the satay man bribed the level crossing keeper to close the gates with the promise of half of his profits.

One of the few remaining members of the yacht club, Mr Sasmita, together with his wife, took us to the market. They were experts on spices and explained the uses of the many powders, fruits, seeds, pods, roots and barks on display. I bought material for a badju, the waisted Indonesian blouse worn with a sarong. The dressmaker could not believe how broad I was across the shoulders – she took the measurement three times. The Sasmitas invited me to their home and dressed me in Indonesian costumes from different districts. Their neighbours bought clothes for me to try too.

We also met Mr Tiano, a jolly, rotund young man who repaired ships. He introduced us to his mother-in-law, Mrs Ong, an English woman who had lived in Indonesia for many decades. She had a collection of unlikely stories and an abundance of energy. They took us to the several restaurants in the town – small, unpretentious establishments that offered the most delectable food. Dish after dish appeared at the table: braised pigeon, frogs' legs, smoked crabs, duck liver, whole fish cooked in tamarind sauce and many more, produced in the tiniest and most primitive of kitchens. At the night market we had a competition to see who could buy the cheapest backscratcher. In spite of our best bargaining Mrs Ong beat us by several rupiahs and had an ear pick thrown in as well.

I was invited to try on Indonesian costumes from different districts.

Mr Tiano organised a boatboy for me. His name was Nadus and he was invaluable, helping to ready *Iota* for shipping and keeping watch when we were ashore.

~

Simon, back in Sydney, wasted no time in arranging for *Iota* and me to be shipped to Singapore. I spent the next few days preparing her for the trip.

The *Hoegh Dene* arrived in the main port of Surabaya – 12,000 tons of sparkling, clean, Norwegian ship. I went to see the first officer, whose name was Olé; he said he had plenty of deck space and could load *Iota* any time. First I had to have the paperwork completed and this turned out to be a nightmare.

I spent the whole of the next day trying to collect the necessary pieces of paper, gaining the impression that everybody was out to make it as difficult as possible. The harbour master accused me of not reporting to him on arrival; no, they had not lost the registration certificate – the reason they couldn't find it was because we had not presented it to them when we arrived. It turned out we had seen a pilot in an adjoining office and they eventually discovered their copy of the certificate in the harbour master's desk drawer. About two hours later, I was handed two lines of typewriting – a permit to sail.

The health authority wanted a deratisation certificate and told me the port was infected with cholera – 300 cases last week. While we were discussing this Miller and Libby came in. Miller was in a bad way; he was suffering from vomiting and diarrhoea and was becoming dangerously dehydrated. I could think only of cholera but, fortunately, an injection fixed his problem.

At the immigration department they had difficulty in accepting a female captain; in Indonesia women hardly exist, let alone run ships or sign papers! Worse was to come with the chief of export customs. I went to his office with the agent; he did not look up as we went in and ignored my 'good afternoon'. I put out my hand and said, 'Good afternoon' again. This time he grunted. I took my hand away because I thought he might bite it. The agent must have sensed we were not going have a harmonious relationship for he said a few rapid words in Indonesian and rushed me out saying, firmly, that *he* would finish the papers.

I waited until the next afternoon and was preparing to go and load *Iota* on the *Hoegh Dene*, papers be damned. However the agent brought me a bill for a 'custom's fee' along with a customs officer dressed in an immaculate white uniform to accompany me to the ship. At last the formalities were complete, the bribes paid and I was free to go.

Alan came over from *Cygnus* to give me a hand. The customs officer objected so I told him he would have to pull up the anchor himself, as obviously, being a woman, I couldn't. I'm sure he was glad he had changed his mind, for when the anchor came up it was covered in evil-looking, smelly, sticky black mud – or worse! It was a while before we made it presentable enough to come on board.

We went alongside the ship and shackled onto their derrick. The crew lifted *Iota* level with their gunwale. It was safer not to be on board the yacht while they were manoeuvring her out of the water so I told my companions to go aboard the ship. Alan jumped off but the customs officer refused. Two Norwegian officers saw my dilemma and came to my rescue. They ordered him off – they were bigger than he was so he had no choice.

Iota was bedded down carefully and Olé whisked Alan and me off for a cold beer. I went to the British Consulate to have a farewell drink and collect my mail and was chauffeured back to the wharf in her Britannic Majesty's car complete with a flag. I remained safely on board until we sailed. About a dozen friends came to see me off; happily, Miller had recovered sufficiently to join us.

Olé introduced me to his captain, Martin, and the chief engineer, Bengt. They had not had a passenger on the ship before and welcomed the novel experience. They were a compatible team, the only discord being over the lutefisk, a traditional Norwegian delicacy of fish, usually cod, beaten and soaked for several days in a caustic lye solution. When it was cooked it turned into an unattractive soapy substance. Martin loved it, but to Olé it was repulsive.

'Not lutefisk again!' he would complain. 'It's not edible by normal people. It looks and tastes like a chunk of phlegm.'

I had a problem with the ship's Chinese laundry. The steward, who spoke little English, whisked my clothes away as soon as I had taken them off. They came back sparkling clean but also starched, including my underwear. I tried to explain I didn't want my clothes – particularly my bras – stiffened, but to no avail. I tried washing them myself and hanging them to dry in the bathroom, but the steward plucked them from the rail and took them away.

Martin invited me for a pre-dinner drink in his cabin and asked if all on the ship was to my liking.

'Everything's perfect,' I said, 'except for just one thing. I can't explain to the steward that I don't want my clothes starched, particularly my underwear. My bras stand up without me in them.'

He nearly died laughing and, to my embarrassment, told our dining companions of my predicament.

Our first call was at Panarukan where we stopped briefly to load tobacco. We sailed around Madura through the night passing through swarms of fishing koleks. We announced our presence with powerful searchlights and a siren constantly sounding a warning. A sailor watched from the bows and he rang a bell – once for a boat to port, twice for a boat to starboard, and three times for a boat dead ahead. The bell rang constantly, but its purpose was not clear because at 19 knots we had no hope of changing course to avoid them.

The *Hoegh Dene*, a welcome and important ship, was delivering foreign aid in the form of bulgur wheat. The agent in each port went out of his way to entertain her captain who invited me to accompany him on his excursions. Semarang was a busy port on the north coast of Central Java, and from there the agent provided a car and driver to take us to the historic inland town of Jogjakarta. We visited the ancient Buddhist temple at Borobodur, built in a circle around the top of a steep hill. The sandstone terraces were carved with scenes depicting episodes in the life of Buddha. Much of it had been restored, particularly the upper terraces where rows of Buddhas sat cross-legged in cages under a large cupola.

Our route took us through the Sunda Strait on our way up the west coast of Sumatra. Martin caught my enthusiasm for a closer look at the place where the volcano Krakatau exploded with tremendous force in 1883, killing 36,000 people – most in the 40-metre high tsunami generated by the eruption. The explosion had been heard as far away as Perth. We passed close to Anak Krakatau (son of Krakatau), an active volcano growing about fifteen metres a year out of the caldera of the former Krakatau. Brown and barren, no life had yet taken hold on its shores; its crater was a veritable inferno. The chart warned of submarine volcanic eruptions in the area.

A giant-sized Buddha statue near Borobudur

The west coast of Sumatra was attractive, with a high mountain range covered in jungle close to the coast, the home of the endangered Sumatran tiger. Martin and Olé looked down from the bridge as the ship glided passed idyllic islands off the coast.

Martin said, 'I've always wanted to spend some time on an island like that. In your boat, you could stop as long as you liked, but I have to keep going.'

'Maybe we could swap for a while,' I suggested. 'We could cast you off with your favourite music and writing – Grieg and Ibsen perhaps?'

'And as much lutefisk as you can eat.' Olé joined the conversation.

'You'd be monarch of all you survey; of your right there'd be none to dispute,' I continued. 'Then I could take over your role as ship's master. I've always wanted to be the master of a ship like this.'

'The problem about being a ship's captain is that you first have to go through the pain of being a first officer,' said Olé.

~

The wharf at Padang, a flimsy wooden structure, was tucked away behind an island and it took two pilots and a tugboat over an hour to berth us. They had to be careful not to hit the fragile quay because the slightest blow would have caused it to collapse.

The ship was to load several hundred tonnes of cassia and rubber, the rubber bound into bales. One of them slipped out of the sling and went bouncing along the wharf like a gigantic ball. It was a difficult cargo as it had to be stowed with sheets of plastic and talcum powder between the layers to prevent them from sticking, otherwise the rubber would vulcanise itself in the hold into a solid mass – an embarrassment at offloading.

The loading needed plenty of labour, but it was the beginning of Ramadan when a public holiday was to be followed by a day of fasting. The stevedore said he could bribe his gangs into working if they were given more cigarettes. The ship carried a large quantity of cigarettes and reckoned on about fifty cartons per port. In Padang the officials came with a long list of varying numbers of cartons for each member of the police, navy, customs and immigration. When they refused to give me a shore pass – my Indonesian visa was cancelled in Surabaya and I was not signed on to the ship's crew – Martin refused to part with any cigarettes until I had one. It was produced immediately.

Again the agent provided a tour for the captain and his passenger. We took the road to the mountains, passing through several villages. In one of them we watched a monkey at work picking nuts from the coconut palms. He was a big, silky-haired fellow with a flagrant red behind. He was taken to a tree and told to go up it. Instead, he sat down, grumbled and scratched himself. He climbed halfway up and slid down again. He wanted a drink of water – he scooped it up from the stream in his hands. Next time he made it to the top of the tree and leapt into the crown. He contemplated for a while and then pulled and twisted the nuts and threw them to the ground with a swish and a crash, aiming at his handler. He rested for a while and then came sliding down again. He had another grumble, another scratch and another drink.

The road climbed steeply up the escarpment. We were surrounded by misty clouds veiling the thick jungle and the many waterfalls. Higher still, the cloud lay below us and the sky cleared. The scenery was magnificent, with rice terraces stretching into the distance. We overtook an antique steam train with a long funnel, scarcely visible for steam and smoke; its carriages were bulging with people, produce and animals.

Our guide took us to the weekend house of the chief of the Indonesian navy, beside a crater lake, Lake Singkakak. He was anxious we should be impressed by the ornate residence and its furnishings in bright plastic and chromium plate. Martin had to write his appreciation at great length in the guestbook.

Surrounded by majestic mountains Lake Singkarak was beautiful. Found only in this lake was a species of small fish, Ikan Belibis, and while we had a refreshing swim and enjoyed the tranquillity of the place our hosts caught some and fried them for our lunch. We ate the whole fish including its head and bones.

We continued on to Bukittinggi, climbing up to 930 metres. Martin's guidebook described Bukittinggi as 'a busy market town halfway between the heavens and the rice paddies, with spectacular views of both'. The Dutch built it as an outpost called Fort de Cock in 1825. It was a pleasant town with a cool climate, and noted for its 26-metre tall clock tower, the Jam Gadang.

After three days, despite the wharf labourers stopping for prayers or not appearing at all, we had the rubber aboard. We sailed back through the Sunda Strait and directly to Singapore. The mates were busy down in the hold driving the forklift to finish stowing the rubber. Olé wore a worried look as the deep storage tanks were about to be waxed ready to receive a latex cargo. Bengt went on a keep-fit campaign and was absent from the dining table, busy clocking up 20 kilometres a day on the bicycle machine by the bridge. Martin talked about the delights of Singapore's nightlife.

As we approached the equator the weather took on a doldrum feeling; the sea became steely still and murky. Many low islands appeared, gloomy in the haze. The big metropolis took shape and we came into the Singapore Roads with row upon row of ships of all shapes and sizes and of every nationality.

We anchored amongst the host of ships, no longer standing out as big and smart for there were many bigger and newer ships. We were quickly cleared and the officials provided me with two pieces of paper – all that *Iota* needed to turn from a piece of cargo into an ocean-going yacht. The papers I had had so much trouble in obtaining in Surabaya were of no interest to anybody.

The agent said *Iota* should be discharged immediately. We were fifteen miles from the yacht club on the other side of Keppel Harbour – reportedly full of strong tidal currents and much congested. It was also getting dark.

'I don't really want to do that,' I thought as I went to change into boat clothes.

Martin didn't think it was a good idea either. He discovered the ship was going to bunker the next day at the fuelling dock only a mile away from the club and managed to persuade the agent to leave the unloading until we were there. I breathed again, changed back into my dress and enjoyed my farewell dinner.

Offloading the next day was no problem. The yacht club provided a guide; I motored the short distance and moored *Iota* fore and aft to buoys allotted to her. The *Hoegh Dene* stayed for another two days and nights so I joined Martin in his exploration of Singapore's nightlife, which ranged from a sophisticated nightclub to a parade of transvestites in the famous Buggis Street. Then she was on her way again and I returned to reality and the task of making *Iota* a more suitable companion for the other yachts that were her neighbours.

singapore – an island state on the move

1970-1971

Singapore was in the grip of change at the beginning of several decades of economic and social development. All over the island blocks of concrete flats were appearing – vertically stacked matchboxes each with a flag of washing pushed out of the window to dry on a bamboo pole. The high-rise apartments were replacing the traditional kampongs, and department stores were taking the place of the picturesque, if ramshackle, shophouses in the city. New roads and industrial estates were springing up and a new airport was planned. There was a spurt of office building activity. In Orchard Road there seemed to be another modern hotel every time I went to town, each grander and more luxurious than its rivals.

The Republic of Singapore Yacht Club had become a victim of the expansion. As the Royal Singapore Yacht Club, it had had a convenient and well-appointed clubhouse adjacent to the main harbour. When the land around the harbour was reclaimed for new wharves the club was no longer on the waterfront, and found itself an inconvenient distance inland. It had to move. The site chosen was several kilometres to the west at Kuala Pandan, the mouth of the Pandan River, an area of mangrove swamp downstream from a Malay kampong. At times it had a dubious smell. The swinging area was insufficient so the yachts had to be pinned fore and aft. It was silting up quite quickly too and even *Iota* had trouble going in and out at low tide. I was told, 'You don't go aground – the water just gets too thick to go through!'

The club would to have to move again as a new bridge would soon prevent boats with masts from entering the river. Land reclamation was in full swing. Red dust settled on the yachts, stirred up by a procession of trucks carrying fill. The hills of Singapore were being lowered and the sea filled in.

The yacht club had good facilities: a jetty, swimming pool, showers and excellent catering. I found it was easier and cheaper to eat at the yacht club than to take a taxi into town to buy food. The club watchman, a spectacular elderly gentleman with a flowing grey beard and long white robes, spent much of the time kneeling on his prayer mat, bowing to Mecca and chanting like a muezzin.

Mr Ong ran the boatyard facilities, but he didn't have a cradle big enough for *Iota*. I was recommended a shipyard in Kallang Basin run by Ho Ah Lam. We had to go through the congested Keppel Harbour with its strong tides to reach the yard on the other side of Singapore town. I had plenty of willing and able helpers to accompany me. Yacht club member, Peter, was a harbour pilot who specialised in taking tankers through the shallow Singapore Strait; Americans Chuck and Pam were fitting out the trimaran, *Niki*, that they intended to sail around the world; and at the last moment Jan joined us – he was the Norwegian skipper of a ship that serviced the oil rigs. He was also the one who had kept Simon and me awake in Surabaya by charging his batteries all night. The falling tide was with us through Keppel Harbour and three hours later we were at our destination.

Kallang Basin was crowded with boats.

The water in Kallang Basin was a disgusting black with oil floating on it. The yard was hot, smelly, airless and crowded with boats of every imaginable kind – freighters, junks and sampans, motor cruisers and a few yachts. The noise was incessant: on one side was a steelworks and on the other an amusement park and nightclub. The tide was too low to slip *Iota* when we arrived, but when I returned next day she was out of the water and two men were scrubbing her bottom.

Ten days later *Iota* was back at the yacht club with new portholes, new toilet cocks, a reinforced samson post, a straightened anchor shaft, freshly painted topsides and a coat of antifouling. The engine had been serviced – this was the first time we had finished a cruise with an engine that was not a cause of concern. In spite of being hot and dirty, the yard was efficient.

~

Christmas was coming. I sent a card to the friends I had made in Martinique – Dan and Joan. I was working on the boat one morning when I was called to the phone. What a delightful surprise! It was Dan.

'We're here too,' he said. 'We're staying for two years – I'm building an oil terminal in West Java. We had a year in Korea and got here only last week. Joanie and the children are here too. We've found a house in Bukit Timur, not far from the racecourse.'

I soon found myself having dinner with them, exchanging stories about what we had been doing since we had last met five years ago. Joan and I explored Singapore together while Dan was away through the week. The children were at school and Joan's amah looked after the house so, like many ex-patriot wives, she had time to spare. We wandered around the city streets where there was always something unusual or interesting to see. Shops selling similar items were grouped together: there was a row of shops selling shoes; others sold baskets, kitchenware or fabric. All the coffin makers were together in one street and so were the piles clinics. Many of the shopkeepers came to their customers, pushing trishaws heavily laden with every conceivable type of merchandise from brushes, candles and masks to vegetables and cooked food such as fried bananas, pancakes and satay. We had our fortunes told and watched a snake charmer.

My social life kept me busy. Miller and Libby looked me up as they came through Singapore on their way back to America and, a few days later, *Cygnus* arrived with Dave and Allen on board. Stefan, the captain of the *Browind*, came to the yacht club to find me and took me back to his ship for dinner on board. Before leaving Dili, he told me, he had ordered the ship's crew to search for stowaways. They had found the two Norwegians hiding in a lifeboat. He had thought their chances of survival were slim if they stayed in Timor so had kept them on board, put them to work for their keep and taken them back to Sweden.

Several people at the yacht club wanted to learn to navigate so I offered to teach them. I had a class of seven: Chuck and Pam, Geoff and Charles, the two officers who looked after the British army's pretty yacht *Adventure*, Pat and Gene who were restoring the junk *Sam Hok*,

Singapore's picturesque shophouses

Plying their trade on the Singapore River

Hawkers with their wares of masks and brooms and brushes

and the Vice-Commodore of the club, Wong Eng Sang. Many islands surround Singapore so there is no clear horizon; it is also on the equator – not the ideal place to learn navigation. At least my students could learn the theory, practise using the tables and work out their position using approximate figures.

I started by finding out how much trigonometry they knew. All were familiar with sines, cosines and tangents so I introduced the idea of triangles with sides that were the arcs of circles. Again they had no problem with this concept. Encouraged, I introduced spheres, the spherical earth and planets spinning around the sun. These immediately presented Eng Sang with a problem. I explored a little further and found out, yes, he believed the earth was round, but that it was a disc, a tiddlywink rather than an orange. Singapore (on the equator) was at the edge of the disc and we should avoid going too far or we might fall off. My best efforts and those of my pupils failed to convince him otherwise. The others were a success – they all learned how to take a sight with a sextant and use the almanac and tables to work out their position.

The yacht club organised races at the weekend – there were classes for 505s, GP14s and a handicap class for larger keelboats. I teamed up in a GP14 with Dorothy who was an enthusiastic, capable dinghy sailor. It was an opportunity to visit the two other clubs that had GPs and sail on different waters.

The 'Round the Island' race was an annual event. It started on the western side of the causeway at two o'clock in the morning and finished, usually about twelve hours later, on the eastern side. I sailed with David and Ditas in a Folkboat – ideal for the conditions, being easy to handle and capable of making the most of the light airs. It was a windless start, but the tide took us down to the end of the Johore Strait and we were off Jurong at dawn when a breeze came up. The most difficult part was going through Kallang Harbour against the strong tide. The traffic of tugs, bumboats, lighters and ships of all sizes, all on different and unpredictable courses, was frightening. The presence of so many yachts under sail must have been a nightmare for them too. The crowds of ships at anchor in the Singapore Roads also presented a problem. Further along the coast it was all too easy to find ourselves on the wrong side of one of the many long fish traps, with no way out at the other end!

~

Don was a big bear of a man, hairy and hugable. He shambled along on oversized, turned-out feet and an untidy handlebar moustache dominated his face. His wife Jerrie was a complete opposite – she was small and neat. Her overdone clipped English accent and her elaborately coiffured hair contrasted with his American drawl and his unkempt mop.

Once a pilot with Air Vietnam, based in Saigon, he had wisely invested in a yacht. When the Vietnamese government invented a retrospective tax to help recoup the costs of the war and decided that Don owed them many thousands of dollars, he took the option of pulling up his anchor and sailing away. He came to Singapore.

The yacht, *Binasue*, was a 40-foot Choi Lee built in Hong Kong. She was not an ideal cruising yacht, being flighty and tender, but she was in keeping with Don's ambition to belie his comfortable looks and be dandy and dashing. He told exaggerated stories of her speed and extolled the virtues of her accommodation, the main one being an oversized double bunk in the forward cabin. He hinted this was the scene of exciting athletic feats.

'He likes it every night,' said Jerrie, with a smirk and a knowing wink.

They invited me to go with them to Malacca for a long weekend – leave on Friday, sail through the night, spend Saturday and Sunday ashore and sail back to Singapore through Sunday night. It sounded like a pleasant enough way to pass the time.

'Earl's coming too,' Don said. 'He's an experienced sailor and he'll make up the party.'

Earl turned out to be an American serviceman on leave. Although he spoke at length of his heroic sailing adventures, it soon became apparent most of them had turned out that way because of his incompetence.

Although the yacht had a perfectly satisfactory engine, and such wind as there was, was a head wind, Don's pride did not permit him to use the motor to wriggle out of the confined anchorage and the narrow Yacht Club channel. He raised the main and a light, full-cut genoa, cast off the moorings and shouted a confusion of commands. Chaos reigned for the next ten minutes as we bounced off two moored yachts and came to a halt on a soft mud bank at the side of the channel. I noticed Jerrie stayed below while this was happening.

Reluctantly Don started the engine and backed off the bank. As we motored out of the channel he looked around anxiously to see if anyone was watching our humiliation.

The wind increased in the afternoon and came around to head us as we sailed past Jurong and out into the Malacca Straits. As the yacht heeled way over, Don's eyes lit up. Jerrie took photos of him from her position in the doghouse as he posed at the wheel. His jaunty yachting cap and hairy brown torso were being recorded for posterity.

We fell off a slightly bigger wave and there was a series of crashes from below.

'Lockers must have come open. They always do,' said Jerrie without surprise.

I went to check and found all the lockers on the windward side of the cabin had flung open their doors and discharged their contents onto the cabin sole. I thought about picking it all up – but what was the point, it would only fall out again.

'Why don't you put catches on?' I asked.

'Well,' Jerrie explained, 'you see, it's like this. Don does all the work on deck – that's men's work. I don't go on deck because my hair gets blown around. But I do all the work below, that's women's work. Problem is, I don't use a screwdriver, that's men's work. So anything needing a screwdriver below deck doesn't get done.'

Rather than add to this explanation Don decided we should tack, so tack we did, hauling the flimsy genoa around the rigging. As the sails filled on the other side and the yacht dipped her lee rail into water, there was another crash from below. Not to be outdone the port lockers had dispensed with their contents too.

We were sailing as close to the wind as the full-cut genoa would allow – which wasn't very close. As the sun dropped to the horizon the wind increased further and as *Binasue* went through the waves the full foot of the sail filled with water. This was not good for either the sail or the progress of the yacht, but Don didn't appear to notice.

Eventually Earl suggested we make the change while we still had enough daylight to see what we were doing. Don wouldn't hear of it.

Jerrie retreated to the galley from her position in the doghouse and set about preparing food. She was an excellent cook and we were hungry. Her shout that dinner was about to be served and Don's decision to change the headsail came simultaneously. He won, of course.

By now it was dark, pitch dark. Don unearthed the new sail from the forepeak and Earl went forward with him to help. I stayed at the wheel; changing headsails was obviously men's work. They dropped the genoa – into the sea. Fumbling in the dark, they eventually managed to control it.

While they were transferring the halliard to the other sail it escaped and ran up to the top of the mast without taking the new sail with it. There was no spare halliard and even Don thought it overdoing the heroics to climb to the top of the mast to retrieve it. We would have to sail through the night under main alone.

We ate our cold dinner in silence. Don took the first watch. The crew retired below and left him to do battle with the unbalanced yacht.

I went on deck at midnight and found Earl at the wheel. There was still a little wind, but the sea had flattened. The mainsail was hauled in although the wind was abeam.

'Where are we?' I asked. 'What's the course? Any lights?'

'Course? Lights?' Earl sounded as if he had never heard of the words.

'I suppose we have a chart?' I tried to keep sarcasm out of my voice.

'I think there might be one,' he replied innocently.

I stared into the black night towards the coast; I couldn't detect even the loom of a light.

'We should be able to see the lighthouses on the coast quite clearly,' I said to myself. We had to be miles out to sea. I went below and found the chart.

'I think we ought to close the shore and find out where we are,' I said to Earl. Would the yacht tack without her headsail? Maybe it would be better to wear around rather than be stuck in irons. She was so far off the wind it wouldn't make much difference.

'I'm tired. I'm going below.' Earl abruptly abandoned the wheel and disappeared down the hatch.

I gybed and headed for the shore, close-hauled on the other tack.

The boat laboured without her headsail and had lee helm; it took a lot of concentration to keep her on course and moving through the water.

Two hours later I detected the loom of a lighthouse. I went below to look for the handbearing compass. It was not apparent. Don and Jerrie were asleep, crammed into the single berth in the after cabin. I shook Don awake.

'Where do you keep the handbearing compass?' I asked.

'Don't need one of them,' he said. 'I manage with the main compass. It's good enough.'

Did he have the same attitude when flying?

There was more shipping closer inshore and I had to keep a constant watch and take evasive action a couple of times. The wind dropped and the boat became even more difficult to handle. I stuck it out for another hour and then went below to rouse Don.

'Your watch,' I shouted at him, but there was no response. 'I can't manage anymore. It needs a man.'

That worked; he went up on deck.

Earl was asleep in the saloon so the only free bunk was the nuptial couch in the forward cabin, the scene of the nightly coupling. The bunk was wide at the top, but it tapered rapidly and extended under the foredeck, which came down close to the mattress well above my knees. I struggled to insert myself into it and was still trying to work out how they managed their gymnastics when I fell asleep.

The wind returned with the dawn; it came from the south and pushed us into Malacca at lunchtime. It was Don who suggested it would be prudent to use the engine to take us up the narrow channel; he must have learned something. We tied up to a wharf.

Don and Earl disappeared ashore, Don to find a small boy to go up the mast to retrieve the halliard and Earl, it turned out, in search of catches for the locker doors. Jerrie and I sorted out and stowed the chaos in the cabin. Earl spent the rest of the afternoon fitting the catches. He worked carefully and neatly; Jerrie and I were fulsome in our praise, but Don looked scornfully on this awful spectacle of a man doing work unsuited to the macho image.

We found a nearby restaurant for dinner and retired early to be ready to explore the antiquities of Malacca next day.

~

Enggow loved me dearly. He was always waiting on the jetty when I came ashore and he greeted me with a smile and a joyful wagging tail.

When I was in the yacht club he sat by my chair, his devoted brown eyes looking up at me hoping this might be one of the rare occasions when my heart softened and I bought him an ice cream in a cone.

His enjoyment of an ice-cream cone was absolute. He carefully licked the cream with his long pink tongue, his eyes half-closed in rapture. When it came time to eat the cone, he would nibble with his front teeth and savour every crumb.

A big red dog, he belonged to the Chinese caterers at the club. Although he loved me and had a reasonable rapport with his owners, he disliked people with dark skins and had been known to bite.

The clubhouse, as befitted Singapore's equatorial climate, was open to allow any breezes to waft through and cool us. One evening I was sipping a beer and talking to friends. Enggow had given up on the ice cream and was asleep by my chair. It was the usual gathering – Pam was at my table and we were discussing dress patterns while her husband Chuck was comparing notes about boat fittings with Pat and Gene. Other yacht club members were sitting at a couple of other tables. Ah Song was officiating behind the bar tonight and his brother, Kai Meng, was cooking.

Two strangers were leaning against the bar – a scruffy pair, dark skinned and rather sinister. Pirates looked like this; they didn't seem to belong in the yacht club surrounds. They finished their drinks, put down their glasses and left. Instead of walking straight out of the club they detoured and came around close by my chair. Enggow leapt out of his dreams to my defence; I caught his tail and pulled. The men walked quickly out of the clubhouse.

Ten minutes later they were back armed with wooden clubs and they came straight for Pam and me; we fended off blows.

Enggow, wisely, disappeared into the darkness. Gene and Chuck, who had not witnessed his bad manners, woke from their surprise and came to our rescue; they grappled with our assailants – fists flew. Pat phoned for the police.

The scuffle was short-lived; Gene's large bulk and Chuck's training in such matters were too much for the aggrieved pirates.

When the fight stopped we took stock of the situation. It seemed I had been too late in restraining Enggow; his teeth had nipped the Lascan leg and its enraged owner was hell bent on revenge. Pam, a nurse, inspected the offended leg – it was not a serious wound – but Gene had lost a contact lens.

We looked at the polished aggregate floor of the yacht club; the chances of finding a contact lens on it were negligible, especially with the inadequate lighting. We might find it if we felt around with our hands.

It was a job for everyone including Ah Song and the pirates. We all sank to our knees and started groping.

The policemen's eyes nearly popped out of their heads.

'Is there trouble here?' they asked as they came into the clubhouse and saw the improbable sight of a dozen or so people crawling around the yacht club floor.

'Somebody got bitten by a dog,' said Chuck as if this explained our strange behaviour.

'Must be rabies,' diagnosed one of the police, taking a step back, 'You'd better all go to the hospital.'

We were sitting all in one group now; the police and the pirates had left and Enggow was back by my chair with an innocent – or was it smug – look on his face.

Suddenly Gene said, 'I've found my lens!'

'Where?' we asked in disbelief.

'In my eye! It's under my upper eyelid. It was displaced and I didn't notice.'

~

Four of us went on the trip to Taman Negara, the national park in the middle of Malaysia about 600 kilometres north of Singapore. We travelled by second-class steam train from Singapore – there was no first-class on Mondays. It was comfortable as we had the whole carriage to ourselves. The train stopped at every station and many other places that were not stations. At some of these wood was loaded to fuel the boiler.

The journey was a welcome opportunity for us to learn more about each other. I knew Dave, skipper of *Cygnus*, as we had met and travelled together in Indonesia. He was a quiet, absent-minded astronomer who often seemed to be living not just on another planet, but in another galaxy. Joy, wife of harbour pilot Peter, also lived in another world for she was psychic and often had conversations with those who had passed on. She frequently amazed us by exactly describing people we knew whom she could not possibly have met. Ruth, Joy's friend, was Australian, a nurse at a Singapore hospital. She had travelled widely and spent much of her time and all of her money playing golf.

We arrived in Jerantut at dusk and had difficulty finding the caretaker of the rest house where we had planned to spend the night. Fortunately, we did find the district officer and he kindly sent out one of his numerous servants to wake him up for us.

The most interesting thing about Jerantut was the birds – eastern swallows, migrants from China. They came in their thousands to roost in the evening like a cloud of black snow flakes, squabbling noisily and settling for the night on the telephone wires hanging over the street. Eventually they all faced the same way, at precisely the same distance apart.

The next day we had to find our way to Tembeling, a small kampong on the river where we were to meet the boat to take us into the national park. We eventually squashed onto a bus that bulged with people and their market produce. The road climbed from rubber plantations into wilder country.

Embarking on our journey up the river to Teman Negara.

Tembeling was the scruffiest place I had ever visited. The houses were a collection of squalid, tumbledown shacks made of rotting wood and rusty corrugated iron, perched high on the river bank. Between them and the river was the sordid accumulation of their year's rubbish, waiting for the annual flood to clear it away. The people were dirty and the grubby children snivelled. The reason for their apparent poverty was not obvious for the soil was fertile and there was plenty of water.

A three-hour trip in a canoe-shaped boat with a powerful outboard took us to the park headquarters at Kuala Tehan, on the junction of the Tembeling and Tehan Rivers. The facilities were good; we had a large bungalow to ourselves with hot water. The food and service were excellent.

The park features jungle that has been undisturbed for 130 million years so it contains specialised and outsized plants and animals. It is home to over 10,000 plant species including the world's largest flower, the strange *Rafflesia*, which grows up to 90 centimetres across. We didn't see one, but our guidebook told us it was a parasitic plant with no roots of its own and, to attract pollinating insects, it produced a strong smell of rotting meat. Among the 350 animal species in the park are one of the world's biggest moths, the Atlas moth, with a 25 centimetre wingspan, and a 55 centimetre stick insect. There are also cicadas, katydids, grasshoppers and crickets responsible for the cacophony of jungle sound. In the dense vegetation the large animals – tigers, rhinoceros and elephants – are rarely seen.

Mohammed knew the river well.

Our first day's expedition took us to a waterfall up the Tehan River, our outboard motor having a hard time of it fighting against the current. Our three boatboys knew the river well. When the river became shallow we got out and pushed. The water was cool and clear, shaded by the jungle.

We cooled off in the waterfall amid hundreds of butterflies; we counted at least fifteen types. There were also swarms of industrious ants and brightly coloured toadstools. We drifted back down the river on the current. Without the noise of the engine to disturb them, we saw a bright green lizard sunning itself on a rock and many more birds, mostly with bright plumage and making a variety of shrieks and cries. French birdwatchers told us they had already identified more than 90 species during their five-day stay.

We would have a good view over the jungle from the hill behind the park headquarters if we cared to climb. It was hot and humid so we proceeded slowly and sat on top looking out over the dark green, dense jungle as far as the eye could see in all directions. Higher hills stood out in the background. We saw hornbills, a black monkey with a long tail and a two and a half metre monitor lizard with large scaly plates along his sides.

Leeches were giving us serious trouble. They were able to detect us by smell and vibration from a long way away and stood on their heads waving their bodies around, ready to pounce. They quickly looped towards us and climbed onto our boots and up our legs. We stopped frequently to de-leech ourselves. Dave was particularly in strife because he had not heeded advice to equip himself with close-fitting jungle boots.

The leeches did not trouble our guides. We observed more closely and saw them looping over their bare feet in order to reach us. We never discovered what made us so attractive and our guides so unattractive to these blood-sucking creatures.

Back in the bungalow we discovered huge leeches bursting with blood attached to our feet and around our waists at the top of our jeans. When we pulled the creatures off we continued to bleed because leeches inject an anticoagulant as they suck. It was fortunate, or maybe well planned, that there were red quarry tiles on the floor.

Dave said sardonically, 'They prove the Creator has a sense of humour.'

It was Ruth who discovered that leeches dislike soap. We swabbed our legs with shampoo, rubbed soap on our boots and sprayed our jeans with insect repellent. Triumph! It worked perfectly and from then on, none of us, except Dave, had a leech. They climbed onto our boots, started on their upward journey of exploration and then looped back down again.

It was an overnight expedition to the High Hide. Our boatboys took us eight kilometres up the Tembeling River, wider than the Tehan River and with several rapids. The current was stronger and the engine was at full throttle. Mohammed on the bow gave hand signals to the boy at the stern, indicating which way to turn. The battle between the boat and the river was fierce.

Along the way we caught some fish. We were not very good at it, but the boys cast with great accuracy and provided our lunch, lighting a fire and cooking their catch. We had a swim and then set off along the track. The boatboys carried all our needs: bedding, food and our personal rucksacks. We stopped, looked and listened – there was always something to be inspected: a butterfly, toadstool, an exotic creeper or a fearsome insect.

A giant tree fell to its death not far from us, but so dense was the jungle we could not see it fall. We heard, however, a series of groans and creaks and then a roar and more cracks as it destroyed with its weight other plants in its path. The awesome hush in the jungle after the crash was gradually broken as the birds and insects started their chatter again.

The hide perched in the treetops, looking out over a small clearing in the middle of which was a salt lick to attract the animals – a stage waiting for the actors to arrive. Our guides made up our beds, fetched water and then left us. We climbed up the long ladder and settled in the hide in the gathering dusk.

The jungle was gloomy even in the daytime, but as the sun went down and cast longer shadows it became eerie. The foliage took on weird shapes and we imagined monsters peering at us. The noise of the various insects reached a crescendo as darkness fell. It was an alien, ghostly environment. With the light almost gone, deer barked from the left and right.

We took it in turns to keep watch. About two in the morning Joy spotted a deer. Scarcely daring to breathe, we peered out to see six of them grazing in the moonlight.

Our guides escorted us back to the headquarters. We expected a hard day, but the track was mostly easy. We crossed a sizeable river that cooled and refreshed us and negotiated several fallen tree trunks. Dave lagged behind and missed the track. We waited for him, but when he did not appear, retraced our steps to look for him, calling as we went. His answer came from far off to the left. It made us doubly cautious for a while; it would have been so easy to become irretrievably lost.

We came across a clearing with a group of basic shelters – just four sticks holding up a thatched roof about a metre from the ground. It was home to a group of the aboriginal people of Malaysia, the Orang Asli. About 150 of them, fully nomadic, lived in the Park. Later we met several of these small, curly-haired people, who had thick lips and slanted eyes. They gave us a blowpipe demonstration and could hit a bird from a considerable distance.

~

Just before I went off to Taman Negara, an 85-foot yacht came in to the Singapore Yacht Club from Hong Kong where she was built. *Intrepid Dragon* had a conventional yacht hull, but a junk rig. On board were her owner, Jack, and his wife, Maureen. They lived in luxury with air conditioning, radar and a paid crew – two Filipinos.

They asked me if I would join them for a trip to Sarawak, Bali and Christmas Island for they needed a navigator. I had told them I would be away for two weeks and expected them to have departed by the time I returned, but they had waited for me. I had intuitive doubts about going with them, but Maureen came over and implored me to join them – she was worried as Jack did not know how to navigate. It was hard to say 'no'.

We had an uneventful trip to Sarawak; there was no wind so we motored all the way. The last part of the journey was up the winding river. We met a large ship that had its bridge on the bows so the crew could see around the bends.

I learned more about Jack. He had an electronics business and had employed Maureen as a designer. She was good at her work and continued to do it after they were married. Their relationship was not a happy one. Although Maureen did her best to please, Jack was constantly criticising her; he had a cruel streak and the atmosphere was usually tense. He liked to play Scrabble and was remarkably good at it; he had to win. As I learned more of the two-letter words he frequently used I sometimes was able to beat him – but it wasn't worth it.

Kuching was fascinating. We anchored just beyond the town in front of the new gold-domed mosque where the muezzin called the faithful to prayer at dawn and dusk. On the other side of the river was the attractive, beautifully kept palace of the Rajahs Brooke. The historic town was pleasant, well laid out and comparatively clean. The narrow main street behind the waterfront was a picture of colourful, well-preserved Chinese shophouses and fascinating roofscapes.

We anchored in front of the new gold-domed mosque.

The main street of Kuching

When the three Rajahs Brooke ruled Sarawak – known as the golden age – the various tribes who lived up the jungle rivers in longhouses constantly fought each other. They were enthusiastic headhunters. The longhouses still existed, but headhunters had taken their last victims at the end of World War II when quite a few Japanese were added to their collections.

Jack was in radio contact with Bruce who worked at the American consulate; they were looking forward to meeting. Bruce offered to take us to visit a longhouse about 60 kilometres from Kuching. He owned a large American car – the sort that goes all the way down the road without moving. Being low to the ground the car was not suitable for the few and rough roads, but Bruce was determined to impress so off we set. As we approached the longhouse along a wet, unmade road the car slid into a ditch and became bogged. People appeared as if by magic and helped to pull the vehicle out.

The car slid off the road and became bogged.

The longhouse was built on stilts along the riverbank, mainly from wood, with plaited coconut frond walls. At least a hundred families lived there, each allotted a room at the back. In front of their rooms was a covered gallery, and in front again, an open area used for drying rice and peppers.

On the way home Bruce stopped so I could take a photograph and I noticed oil running out of the car. A stone had pierced the oil sump – we could drive no further. The local missionary rescued us. He drove to the neighbouring leper colony where there was a telephone and arranged for a truck to come out and take us back to town.

Rice and peppers drying on the galleries

For the next part of our journey there was a little wind so Jack decided we could sail. It was the first time the sails had been used. As the crew hoisted them on their bamboo spas, dust fell onto the deck. There were borers in the bamboo!

We stopped at a tiny, uninhabited island on the southwestern tip of Kalimantan where the fishermen smoked their catch. They invited us to try some; it was so delicious – succulent with an irresistible flavour – that we had difficulty in restraining ourselves from eating all they had. We thanked them with malaria medication.

The wind deserted us so we were powering through the Java Sea at night. Jack checked the radar and was concerned because there was a blip coming towards us, moving at considerable speed, so fast it could not possibly have been a boat.

'It's just a radar blip,' I said. 'Nothing to worry about.'

He was not convinced; it was pirates coming to attack us in a speedboat. He went below to fetch his gun, loaded it and walked around the deck waiting for a pirate to appear so he could shoot him. The attack never eventuated.

We met the same huge blind swells in the Bali Strait as we experienced in *Iota*. By this time I had had enough of the *Intrepid Dragon* and was looking for an excuse to leave them and make my way back to Singapore.

At Kuta Beach Maureen bought a shirt for Jack as a present, but he was displeased – she had not bargained adequately and had paid too much for it.

'Anyway, how dare you spend my money without asking me!' Jack shouted at her. Maureen cringed; she had only been trying to please him. I asked them if they would kindly refrain from arguing in front of me. Jack replied that he would do what he f...ing well liked on his own f...ing boat and I could f... off.

I said yes, I would – willingly.

Saying goodbye to Maureen I asked if she would like to come with me.

'Yes I would, but I haven't got any money. Although I went on working after we married Jack never paid me. He gives me enough to buy food, but that's all.'

'But Maureen,' I said. 'That's slavery – you shouldn't put up with it.'

'I don't have a choice.' She was close to tears.

The immigration police were not bothered by my changed status and there was a seat for me on a plane leaving for Singapore the next morning.

I booked into a hotel on Kuta Beach, went for a swim in the surf and sat on the beach strumming my ukulele, singing the only song I knew. A small boy came and sat at my feet and gradually more and more children gathered around. I felt like the Pied Piper – I taught them the song and we sang it together in English.

*I'll be a dandy and I'll be a rover,
You'll know who I am by the song that I sing.
I'll feast at your table, I'll sleep in your clover;
Who knows what tomorrow will bring.*

*I can't be contented with yesterday's glory,
I can't live on promises Winter and Spring;
Today is the moment and this is my story,
I'll laugh and I'll cry and I'll sing.*

*Today while the blossom still clings to the vine
I'll taste your strawberries, I'll drink your sweet wine;
A million tomorrows may all pass away
Ere I forget all the joy that is mine today.*

~

In Singapore I found the noise of heavy trucks coupled with the red dust made the yacht club mooring intolerable. One of the GP14 owners we raced against was a member of the RAF Changi Sailing Club; they welcomed cruising yachts and he would be pleased to introduce me. He presented me with a pass to enable me to come and go into the club. I sailed around there with some friends and anchored *Iota* off the beach – the only yacht there. It was a considerable improvement and a relief to be in clean water and clean air.

The members, mostly RAF personnel, were hospitable and sociable. There was a variety of dinghies racing in handicap races and I was invited to sail in a GP, a Lark and a 505. I reciprocated by gathering up a few members in the late afternoon and we sailed *Iota* around Pulau Ubin, an island conveniently situated in the Johore Strait a few miles down from the yacht club; it made a pleasant evening excursion.

I had a visitor – Tony, Simon's colleague, the tropical medicine specialist he had employed to cure his malaria. He persuaded the club boatman to bring him out to *Iota*. His visit was a particular surprise because security at the yacht club was meant to be tight and it should have been impossible for him to enter without a member's pass.

'How did you get in?' I asked.

'I came in a taxi,' he replied. 'The man on the gate just waved me through. He didn't even try to stop me.'

As we were eating lunch in the clubhouse the commodore came over and said I was a security risk being a woman on my own, and would have to leave. Strict security was extremely important for the club; they didn't want drug dealers and gun-runners using the facilities. I introduced my companion. Tony told him how he had managed to enter without a pass and suggested that my presence was indeed a minor problem compared to the unrestricted access he had experienced from the road! The commodore was embarrassed; he would look into this security lapse and thought it would be all right if I stayed for a few more days.

Oggie, an aircraft maintenance engineer, helped me take *Iota* back to the main harbour of Singapore for slipping before Simon and I left on our cruise to Bangkok. We had an eventful journey. Just after we set off a squall with blinding rain hit us. Rather than try to pick our way through the fish traps, we anchored. While getting the anchor up the cap came off the winch and oil spilled on the deck, making it dangerously slippery. Then the engine stopped – we were out of fuel. I changed to the other tank, but the engine had to be primed. Oggie knew about aircraft engines, but not marine diesels. I bled the air from the system and managed to start it again. We arrived off Kallang Basin only to find the river was closed by a dredge with buoys all round and notices saying, 'Keep out'. Fortunately, a police boat saw our predicament and escorted us through a gap.

It rained almost continuously while *Iota* was on the slip, stopping just long enough for her to have a coat of antifouling. Back at Kuala Pandan things had temporarily improved, for the rain had made the road impassable and the trucks were forced to stop for a few days. When they started up again the red dust was kept at bay because the road was damp. I caught up with my friends who had the latest news. *Binasue*, with Don and Jerrie on board, was on her way to Bali. A freighter had rammed and nearly sunk a 70-foot ketch off Horsburgh Light and *Intrepid Dragon* had lost a mast at the Cocos Keeling Islands; maybe the borers were responsible.

Horse racing in Singapore was a well-supported and popular pastime. There was a splendid racecourse and a training school for apprentice jockeys. I was introduced to Dick who ran their course. He was between two lots of apprentices; twelve had graduated, but their replacements had not yet arrived so he had racehorses requiring their daily exercise. This was invitation enough for me and, early each morning for a week, I sat on a magnificent black horse while he galloped around the track. It was an exhilarating experience.

singapore to bangkok – memories, monkeys and monks

1971

Our next cruise was going to take us up the west coasts of Malaya and Thailand to Bangkok. The time had come to load provisions and prepare for Simon's arrival. I organised duty-free stores and the paperwork for our clearance. The forms had to be signed by the ship's captain, so I assumed this title and Simon became my first officer.

Fortunately, I booked a hotel for the night Simon arrived in Singapore and equally fortunately, I told him which one – for I missed him at the airport. The chaos of reconstruction was such that I waited in the wrong arrival hall. I felt slightly foolish as I made my way, on my own, in pouring rain, back to town.

We spent the next day organising the bank and mail and finalising our departure papers. I had arranged a farewell party at the yacht club. Ah Song recommended a 'steamboat', the delicious Chinese version of a fondue, as the best way to cater for the thirty or so friends I had invited.

It was a lively and enjoyable party so it took an effort to arouse ourselves next morning. We had a long way to go before nightfall and needed as much daylight as possible. In the first glimmer of light, with the aid of Chuck and Pam, we disentangled our lines and motored out of the channel.

Keppel Harbour was already buzzing with activity. We had to dodge ferries, junks, barges, lighters and a couple bigger ships but it was not quite such an ordeal as previous times as the current was not as strong, even though it was against us. Still, it was a relief when we emerged unscathed into the Singapore Roads.

As usual the Roads were crowded with ships of every conceivable size, shape, condition and nationality. Many of them were anchored, but others moved unpredictably. We quickly learned to look for the black ball in the rigging denoting that a ship was anchored, and to be wary of the others.

Singapore was the fourth biggest port in the world and all the ships approaching from the north and west converged on Horsburgh Light at the southern tip of Malaya. They continued along a narrow channel for 34 miles to the Singapore Roads. It was vital we were out of the shipping lane before dark – I told Simon about the ketch that had been rammed and nearly sunk by a freighter.

The weather was not kind; thunder and lightning punctuated the steady rain. One heavy squall reduced visibility and gave us some anxious moments. The seas were lumpy and confused. As we came closer to Horsburgh Light the shipping seemed to converge on us. A few freighters overtook us, uncomfortably close. A ship whose modern bulbous bow and flared stern gave her an air of self-importance swaggered past all the old lady tankers and ponderous containerships in a flurry of wake.

We rounded the lighthouse with an hour to spare before the drab wet day gave way to pitch black night. The commercial shipping was now joined by fishing vessels. These had bright lights that alternately flashed and eclipsed as they rolled so we seemed to be surrounded by lighthouses. We had one scare: a near miss with an unlit fishing boat suddenly appearing from out of a wave beside us.

We anchored off Pulau Tulai.

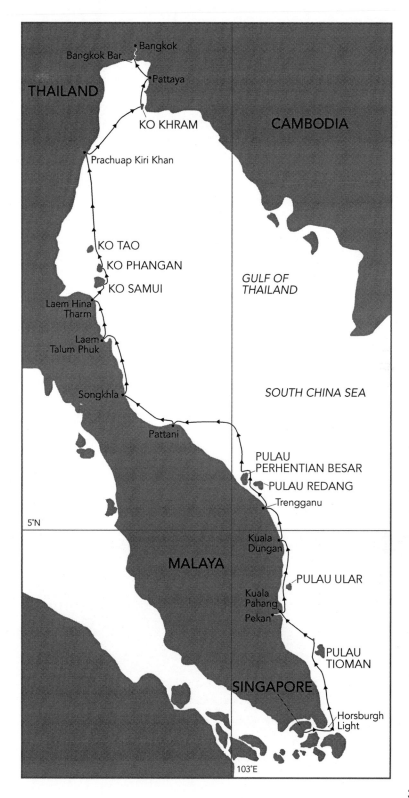

Conditions improved through the night and at dawn a fresh southerly built into a brave wind that blew away the rain and took us to Pulau Tioman. As we came into the anchorage we saw a motor cruiser rolling to her anchor like a demented soul so we kept going for another ten miles to Pulau Tulai, a smaller uninhabited island. Here we found a deep calm bay with a white sand beach and shady trees. It provided a welcome opportunity to relax after the hustle and bustle of our departure from Singapore and the hectic night at sea. We spent the day ashore, sitting in the shade or in the water, picnicking and collecting shells. Eventually a fishing boat came in and interrupted our solitude, staying long enough to ice down their catch and swap a fish for a packet of cigarettes.

We left in the dark. The wind came with the dawn and we had ideal conditions for our windvane, Charlie, to do the steering. We didn't touch the tiller all day and made a fast passage, 35 miles in six hours, to Kuala Pahang.

Several fishing boats were entering the river and one of them kindly came over to show us the way across the bar. The rolling swell across it was trying its best to break. We followed closely and anchored off a fishing village of flimsy wooden houses on stilts. Fish laid out in the sun to dry gave off a pungent smell.

The fishing village of Kuala Pahang

The fishing fleet woke us before dawn with a roar of diesel engines as it went out after the day's catch. We pulled up our anchor shortly afterwards, but headed in the other direction, up the Pahang River to the town, Pekan, where the Sultan of Pahang held his court. Simon had spent the last few months of the war in Pekan as Officer Commanding Pahang District. Now, 26 years later, he was revisiting it.

We anchored off the jetty by the main street, left the dinghy on the pavement and walked past the market towards the police station and Simon's erstwhile office. The flags were out, those of Malaya and the State of Pahang.

'How did they know I was coming?' wondered Simon.

The chief of police occupied the office that used to be Simon's.

'You're sitting at my desk,' Simon told him, 'and you still have the same pictures on the wall.'

The policeman smiled. There was to be an official parade later in the morning, for the King of Malaya was visiting Pekan. We should make our way to the town square where the ceremony would take place. The flags were in his honour – not Simon's.

The army brought out three large guns for the salute and lined up in dress uniform. The spectators wore their colourful national costume, a sarong of silk interwoven with glittering gold or silver thread and ornate high-peaked headdresses. The assembly rose and bowed when the chief minister arrived and took his place at the front.

'I remember him,' whispered Simon. 'I wonder if he remembers me?'

Wailing sirens announced the arrival of the sultan and his wife in a yellow Rolls Royce. They were dressed in purple silk. Men holding big yellow parasols with tassels on them escorted them to the gilt dais. Sirens sounded again and the first gun of the salute boomed out announcing the arrival of the king and the queen, both dressed in pink; his majesty wore his many medals. The troops presented arms, the guns boomed on, more flags were unfurled and the king inspected the troops. Everybody stood up and recited Moslem prayers before taking their leave of royalty with more bows and hand kissing.

As the sirens faded into the distance the chief minister came over to talk to us. Yes, he did remember Simon – and how good to see him back for a visit! He introduced us to the Controller of the Sultan's Household, Captain Ali, a delightful gentleman who spoke excellent English. He lived in the house where Simon had once lived, a dignified wooden residence with large rooms. He took us there and introduced us to his wife. She also spoke good English – they both had travelled widely.

Arrival of the guard of honour

The king greets his subjects.

Simon lived here as military commander in the Pahang District of Malaya at the end of the war.

The Sultan of Pahang's new Istana

Simon discussed the changes that had taken place since the end of the war. 'You can get here by road now. When I was here there was no road along the east coast of Malaya and I pedalled a bicycle up and down the fifty miles of coastline, mostly along the beaches.'

'We have television and this house now has bathrooms with running water and flush toilets.' Mrs. Ali asked Simon if he would like to have a look around – for old time's sake. As Simon inspected the house he exclaimed when he saw furniture that he remembered.

'Does the Sultan still play tennis?' he asked. 'We used to play quite often.'

'Yes, he does,' said Captain Ali, 'but he now has a new court – it's floodlit; the old one had to make way for the new bigger Istana. Would you like to have a look at the Istana? I will arrange it.'

It looked like an elaborate hotel and had cost 55 million rupiahs to build. There were two stories, topped by gold domes. Downstairs were a banqueting hall and a ballroom where last night 250 people had feasted and danced. Upstairs – we took our shoes off to go upstairs – were the guest rooms, one of which was reserved for Tun Razak, the Prime Minister. They were luxuriously appointed and opened on to private verandas. A new wing had recently been added where the Sultan had his personal suite. It was indeed lavish; the bedroom was furnished with an unbelievably large bed.

In a separate part of the Istana was the throne room, elaborately and richly furnished with deep-pile carpet, chairs upholstered in velvet and two canopied gilt carved thrones. It was used only once each year for a three-hour ceremony.

We had a quick look at the sultan's stables, the golf club and the tennis court. Captain Ali introduced us to the sultan, still dressed in his purple sarong. He claimed to have remembered Simon and invited him to play tennis just as he had done 26 years before.

On our way back to the court, down came the rain; the sultan sent a message to say that, instead of tennis, would we like to go to a royal banquet the following week? We had to decline for lack of time, but went to the golf club and had dinner before going back on board.

We wound our way down the river again next morning before the tide had risen. Thanks to vigorous waving from people along the banks we managed to avoid the many islands and sandbanks. We went straight out to sea from Kuala Pahang and along the long sandy coastline where the Charlie was again pressed into service.

The east coast of Malaya was not well provided with anchorages. The towns along the coast were mainly at the mouth of a river, blocked by a constantly shifting sand or mud bar. Some of the islands off the coast provided shelter and we chose Pulau Ular – Snake Island – to break our journey to Kuala Dungan. Arriving late in the afternoon we negotiated an unexpected reef and had difficulty finding enough room to anchor between the dark jagged rocks. It was not a good anchorage – *Iota* bounced around all night – so we left with no regrets early in the morning.

We approached the bar at Kuala Dungan with trepidation as the tide was low and still running out. Lying off were two large barges. Our shout roused a watchman on one of them – he appeared from his hut, rubbing his sleepy eyes. He waved cheerfully and indicated we should keep to the northern bank.

We kept close to the headland in shallow water. The waves were steep and *Iota* was behaving badly – she was headstrong and it took all our strength to keep her straight. After what seemed an interminable battle with her we were in relatively calm water inside and could breathe again.

This was a port of entry so we presented ourselves with our papers to a customs officer.

'How long are you staying?' he asked. 'Have you any guns? Do you have passports?'

That was all – there was no paperwork.

In the seemingly disorganised market fresh fruit and vegetables were abundant and of great variety. As well as the more usual papayas, pineapples, oranges, pomelos, limes and, of course, bananas, there were mangosteens, a sweet soft fruit hidden under a thick, dark red skin and rambutans, like a lychee covered with a furry red coat. Durians were in season; although a favourite of the Malays, the smell of its pungently offensive skin deters most Europeans from trying it. The vegetables – cabbages, cauliflowers, aubergine, cucumbers, tomatoes and carrots – were of excellent quality.

Turtle eggs, misshapen leathery packages, were a seasonal delicacy. The beach just north of Dungan was a famous breeding ground for turtles, the females coming ashore at night to dig holes in the sand and deposit many hundreds of eggs. They covered them and left them to incubate. The hatched babies ran the gauntlet of hungry birds on their scramble into the sea.

We hired a car and drove to Bukit Besi – Iron Hill – where one of Simon's friends had profited from an interest in a mine. The road passed through jungle and swampland. A party of monkeys crossed the road in front of us; we watched them leap into the trees and swing from branch to branch, chattering noisily to each other. We passed men clearing the land to plant oil palms; it looked like a hot job, struggling with fires and smouldering tree trunks in the blazing sun. In many places oil palms were replacing the traditional rubber.

Bukit Besi was now a desolate place as the ore had been worked out and the mine recently closed. Machinery was idle and men sat around with nothing to do. Trains and trucks were lined up, but there was no sign of movement. The railway control officer was still in his uniform; he had seen off a train about two weeks ago, otherwise he sat in his office hoping another one would come or go – a forlorn hope.

When we left Dungan the bar was quiet and had plenty of water over it. The wind deserted us so we had to power and steer all day. Our destination Pulau Kapas was a truly delightful island, again uninhabited, with lovely beaches. In the jungle behind the coconut palms lived screeching, brightly plumed parrots. We slept in the cockpit under the stars and it even became cool enough for us to need blankets; for me it was the first time for many months.

Kuala Dungan

A big roll of black clouds with ragged edges chased us into Trengganu. We could see the sand bar quite clearly. We lined up the leading beacons, but as they took us right over the bar we ignored them, came in by eye and anchored in front of the customs house.

Four customs officers and their boss were in the office. They were reading newspapers when we went in, the boss at a raised desk while the others were seated at lower desks. It became clear that they didn't have enough to do. No ships visited Trengganu in the monsoon season, between November and April. In the other season two ships per month came from Taiwan to load logs, a small junk came each week from Thailand and an occasional prau called in from Singapore. We were a bonus to be fully exploited!

They produced every conceivable form for us to fill in and decided to seal our alcohol and cigarettes. This took a long time because they had to make lengthy calculations to determine how much two people should smoke and drink in two days. It had to look right on the form!

It was a busy harbour. Tugs towed rafts of logs out to a ship lying off; local junks with woven rattan deckhouses dodged each other and many ferries. The town was uninspiring, with its old tumbledown wooden and corrugated iron houses. Many were built on stilts over the water with a boat drawn up and fish drying on racks outside. The sewers were open. A high population of flies and – no doubt – rats flourished in the unsavoury streets.

Tumbledown wooden and corrugated iron houses lined the waterfront in Trengganu.

Down a back street we came across a fascinating shop run by an elderly Chinese gentleman dressed in pyjamas and attended by several sons and sons-in-law. They sold Malay silver and bronze ware, locally woven silk and ceremonial hats. Batik was made in a nearby workshop, just a corrugated iron roof over a muddy floor. Two men were working, the cloth laid out in front of them on tables. Behind them were big vats of hot black wax heated with coconut husks, tubs of dye and steaming hot water. They dipped a metal pattern into the wax and laid it on the cloth. Then the cloth was dyed, the dye taking only to the unwaxed part of cloth. They washed the wax out in hot water, allowed the cloth to dry and repeated the process with another colour.

The muezzin woke us just before dawn; a host of fishing boats with noisy engines thumped past us. We hastened to retrieve our anchor, follow them across the bar and turn north again.

There was no harbour between the Malay border and the first anchorage in Thailand, 73 miles away. This was too far for us to cover in one day so we had to sail through the night. The border had a reputation for being infested with pirates so we had thought about buying a gun – I had asked a British army officer at the Singapore Yacht Club what he thought. He said it was pointless to have a gun unless we were prepared to fire the first shot. We thought better of it.

We kept well out to sea and had it to ourselves – no fishing boats, and, happily, no pirates. First light revealed Thai fishing boats with a distinctly different shape from the open Malay boats and their exaggeratedly high bows and sterns. The bigger Thai boats had their cabins aft and a derrick forward; from a distance they looked like old-fashioned steam engines.

We closed the coast and anchored in shallow water behind casuarina trees on a sand spit called Hlaem Ta Chi. Next day the wind was reluctant to help us so we had to motor for 20 miles to reach Songkhla, a port of entry, and a modern town with good-looking buildings. A new breakwater and a dredged channel led into a big brackish lake behind the town. We threaded our way in between a confusion of fish traps.

Flying a yellow quarantine flag we anchored opposite the police station. A smiling policeman noticed us and waved. Simon rowed ashore to meet him. His name was Sergeant Major Roengchai Petswan and, happily, he could speak Malay. He told us to see immigration in the morning, but in the meantime if we took our laundry to the police station he would arrange for a girl to do it for us. He gave us cups of sweet tea and rice cakes and promised to keep an eye on *Iota* while we were ashore.

Entering was a lengthy process. It took most of the morning to fill in six copies of each of the many forms – written in Thai. The officers had difficulty translating it into English and did not have any carbon paper. We must have signed our names a hundred times, but nobody thought of looking at our boat. They could not understand why I was the captain and Simon the crew.

We explored the town in a trishaw, looking into a school – where solemn children in clean blue and white uniforms were being taught by saffron robed monks – and one of the many wats, or Buddhist temples. These had high steep roofs with orange tiles and elaborate carving on the eaves and windows. A hotel on the beach gave us an excellent lunch. We noted the beer had changed from Singapore Tiger to Bangkok Lion.

The waterfront was packed with colourful boats, floating in a sea of fish and cuttlefish bones. We stepped gingerly over still-snapping rays and slimy messes of cuttlefish and squid. Women cleaned the fish, throwing the guts into the water. The smell was overpowering so we retreated to the crowded market.

The Songkhla waterfront was packed with colourful boats floating in a sea of fish and cuttlefish bones.

The obliging Sergeant Major Petswan lent us a car and driver to take us to a big town, Hat Yai, about 25 kilometres inland from Songkhla. He said it was best known for its massage parlours and nightclubs. We drove through rice paddies and plantations of rubber trees and betel nut palms to the town that had developed when the rail link between Bangkok and Singapore was built. There was a surprising number of hotels to accommodate the hoards of visitors who came from across the border from Malaya, no doubt to sample the massage parlours and nightlife. We were there when school came out and hundreds of neatly uniformed children disrupted the traffic.

We stayed in Songkhla for two days and then sailed overnight to a wide shallow bay, Hlaem Talum Phuk. During the night the wind came in from the southeast and enabled us to put Charlie to work again. We anchored in the middle of the bay in sticky mud among fishing stakes.

Another delightful overnight sail with a full moon and Charlie steering took us to Ko Samui, a coconut island with rugged granite hills. Unlike the mainland where the anchorages were shallow, muddy and fringed with mangroves, the islands had relatively clear water and clean beaches. Three boys in a canoe greeted us.

Ashore, behind the beach with its coconut palm fringe, was an area of rice paddies and gardens. We followed along a path and came to a village. The villagers were hospitable, inviting us into their wooden houses and bringing out their treasures for us to admire. We wished we could speak Thai – our only way of communicating was by signs and drawings.

They showed us where we could draw water from a well to do our laundry and carefully watched what we did. One of the older ladies peered down my dress to see if I wore a bra. Most of the women wore sarongs and blouses in the Malay fashion, but the men wore baggy black trousers, hitched up at the waist with the crutch somewhere near their knees.

Thai dogs were emaciated, mangy creatures, tolerated only as scavengers; they had to look after themselves. They howled rather than barked and, at dawn and dusk, set up a chorus of yelping. In Ko Samui a big black dog living with a family was an exception. He behaved in a way we expected from 'man's best friend' and delighted in eating coconut.

Next morning we were woken by the noise of a buffalo pulling a cart full of coconuts. The cart had solid wooden wheels – slices of tree trunks that were not quite round – so the cart swayed drunkenly as its wheels squealed in protest. The buffalo's harness was a simple yoke

The buffalo stood quietly while the boys unloaded his cart.

and the beast was guided by a rope through his nose. His long curved horns belied a placid nature and he stood quietly while the boys loaded the coconuts into canoes.

It was a boisterous sail across to the next island, Ko Phangan, a few miles further north, where we anchored off the village. Again we were greeted politely. Villagers took us to the school where the neat and well-ordered children were learning arithmetic with Arabic numerals. They stared at us with solemn faces and stood in regimented lines to have their Polaroid photos taken.

Again we communicated by drawing pictures. My sketch of a monkey resulted in enthusiastic pointing towards the hills so we went on a monkey hunt. Half the village started out with us, but numbers gradually dwindled as we left the coconut groves and began to scramble up the steep granite rock face. We were beginning to wonder if monkeys were worth the effort when we came across a waterfall with a clear pool at its base. Although no monkeys were to be seen, the refreshing swim compensated for the effort.

Back on the beach a frisky young buffalo cow was pulling a cart with a load of copra. Unlike her sedate relative of the previous day at Ko Samui, she resented being photographed and lowered her head, pointing her threatening horns towards me as she frolicked past.

We had intended to stop at Ko Tau, but the wind was boisterous and the only bay offering shelter was inhospitable – steep-to with a rocky shoreline. We took advantage of the favourable wind to sail on through the night to Prachuap Kiri Khan. Charlie managed to control the boat again in spite of lumpy seas on the beam. At nightfall the wind freshened to 25 knots so we changed to the No 1 jib and pulled a reef down in the main. Even so, *Iota* was sailing fast.

When the dawn came to show us the morning scenery we saw many identical horn-shaped and conical islands and hills sticking up out of a low-lying plain. It was hazy so distances were difficult to judge. We had trouble in identifying our position, particularly as we had travelled further through the night than we had thought possible. We had nearly sailed past Prachuap Kiri Khan before we realised where we were.

Fish laid out to dry at Prachuap Kiri Khan

Small boys tried to board us before we are had anchored – Simon chased them away. From the town came the noise of trains and the usual howling of dogs. TV aerials topped the rows of tumbledown houses. We went ashore, landing on a disgusting beach of slimy mud scattered with fish entrails. Dogs, bald with running sores, were scavenging. We tried picking our way along an unmade road among fish and squid drying in the sun, but soon gave up in disgust.

Tired, we to bed early only to be rudely awakened by a boat coming alongside. It was the harbour master's officials. They asked 'Where from?', 'Where going?', 'Why?' and 'Any cigarettes?' They received equally short answers.

We moved to the other side of the town where it was cleaner and the houses were more salubrious. A tribe of monkeys lived at the bottom of a nearby hill with a pagoda perched on its top. I bought them some peanuts and immediately had monkeys climbing all over me. The big king monkey chased the others firmly away. He sat serenely and politely eating his fill before he allowed the others the few remaining nuts.

The main street was full of shops, each selling everything. It was a Thai custom to placate evil spirits by fastening flowers to the bows of a ship so we bought *Iota* a bunch of artificial carnations tied in a red scarf.

Our next anchorage was behind a headland we had mistaken for an island. Again the water off the coast was shallow and, although we anchored in only one fathom, we seemed to be miles from the shore. In the morning the tide was out and we were nearly aground. A solitary monk came to look at us. He had an old saffron robe, a shaven head, a toothless grin and a shaggy dog. He waved and said, 'Okay.'

The desolate, muddy beach was riddled with crab holes. If we stood still, the occupants emerged – bizarre black creatures with big scarlet claws. There were also many mudfish, a type of lungfish with huge bulbous eyes. They crawled out of the mud onto sticks and stones to breathe air. Pickled mudfish was an esteemed Thai delicacy, noted for its strong smell and particular taste, but alive they certainly did not look appetising.

Out to sea a procession of fishing boats passed all day long and when we came to leave at night on the high tide their lights ringed the bay. A zephyr of wind enabled us to pick our way out between them under sail. We ghosted silently past, giving the fishermen a fright when *Iota*'s sails suddenly loomed up in the light of their lanterns. 'Wah-ah-ah,' they wailed – it was an eerie sound. The other boats took up the cry and the bay soon echoed with the news of a foreign, phantom ship in their midst.

We had a calm, clear night and by daybreak were more than halfway across the Gulf of Thailand. By midday we reached Ko Khram, an uninhabited and uncultivated island covered in low scrub. The long white beach was strewn with thin white bubble shells. We enjoyed a lazy day of pleasant solitude.

We motored the fifteen miles to Pattaya, a popular holiday resort. What a contrast! The bay was full of boats – fishing boats, ferries, tourist boats, water skiers, paragliders and small sailing boats. A big schooner was about to take some tourists for a sail.

Pattaya had many hotels and restaurants – Italian, French and Mexican – but only the roadside stalls provided Thai food. Tourist information catered mostly for the German majority among the visitors who were taking advantage of cheap charter flights and package tours.

The attractions advertised were swimming in the sea or the pool, elephant and pony rides, fishing, waterskiing and parasailing.

We lunched ashore in one of the hotels. A gibbon living up a tree beside the path to the hotel had become an expert at stealing sunglasses from visitors. He would leap out of his tree, snatch the glasses and dash out of reach, chattering with mirth. A notice reassured guests that his spoils would be retrieved and given back to their owners at 6 pm.

The expert sunglasses thief

Pattaya was an engaging place, but not restful. By day the water was swarming with activity and at night a cacophony of pop songs from the many nightclubs trying to out-blast each other kept us awake.

In a flat calm we motored to Ko Sichang where a large wat on the hill presided over the village. We viewed, heard and smelt the scene from the boat. People swarmed on and off the ferries that came and went with loud insistent blasts of their hooters. As darkness fell the fishing fleet returned and the bay became a confusion of moving lights. After they had unloaded at the jetty the boats anchored off. We spent most of the night on deck fending them off in the rain. We left early; it was a dismal morning with little wind and a heavily overcast sky.

Bangkok's wharves were about sixteen miles upstream from the mouth of the Chao Phraya River. The river approach was by a narrow dredged channel about five miles long, across the bar. A pilot vessel with a flashing light marked the entrance to the channel and a series of numbered buoys and transits led into the river. Navigation was difficult in the drizzle and almost impossible in the downpours. The low, featureless land was not visible from the sea. Irregular waves of dirty brown water were trying to break in the shallows.

A ship loomed out of the gloomy rain; we thought she was a pilot ship, but as the rain cleared briefly we saw she was a freighter waiting for the tide. The black and white chequered pilot ship was beyond her. The rain closed in again.

Two junks were sailing along behind us. We waited for them to overtake and tucked ourselves in behind them, hoping they knew the way. They were sailing surprisingly fast considering their heavy loads of stones. They had tattered sails and a tangle of spas and sheets.

After crossing the bar we anchored for the night at the mouth of the river opposite Samut Pakan, a customs and immigration station. Waterbuses with huge outboards kicked up an irritating slop and deafened us all night. Their drivers knew only two speeds – flat out and stop. Next morning a boarding officer joined us for the tedious journey up the river to Bangkok. He reclined on cushions in the shade of the mizzen awning as we struggled against the current in the heat of the day, inching our way up the river, sometimes hardly making way on the bends.

We tucked ourselves in behind two junks, hoping they knew the way across the Bangkok Bar.

Because of the amount of traffic, crossing the river to avoid the stronger currents was fraught with danger. Freighters, warships, junks, long strings of lighters, ferries, tugs and outboards – all moving much faster than us stirred the muddy river into a chop. We had plenty of time to observe life along the banks where houses clung, each with a jetty and a boat.

Eventually we came to the main wharf area where some surprisingly large ships were alongside the docks and more were tied to piles in midstream. The traffic and noise were frightening and we were suffering from the intense heat.

It was a relief when a customs launch met us and took us in tow. In it was Mr Surin the shipping agent whom Simon had arranged to organise shipping *Iota* back to Sydney. It was difficult to find somewhere safe to tie *Iota* up, but he eventually obtained permission for us to lie alongside the police boats in a klong, a canal, next to the wharf. Although not ideal the conditions were bearable. We were out of the big waves and confusion of the main river, and secure from thieves for we had a day and night police and customs guard. It was unspeakably dirty.

I went off with Mr Surin who had difficulty in accepting me as the ship's captain, to sign in with the customs while Simon packed up his things and cleared loose gear from the decks.

Completely overcome by heat and exhaustion we retreated to the Oriental Hotel, where the luxuries were so numerous and so welcome we couldn't decide what to indulge in first. As we quenched our thirst with iced drinks and showered in hot water we scarcely gave a thought to *Iota*. Even Somerset Maughan and Joseph Conrad could not have appreciated as much as we did the luxury of this famous old hotel, with its teak furniture and canopied beds.

~

We had been given an introduction to Chitr, the Thai agent for an Italian airline. He was a small man even for a Thai, with a captivating personality. He turned out to be the kindest, most hospitable and helpful of contacts we had ever met. He came to dinner with us at the Oriental and arranged to meet us the next day to make sure we could find everything and everybody we needed. We dined among palms and exotic flowers on the balcony overlooking the busy scene on the river. The rain cleared to reveal a breathtaking sunset.

True to his word Chitr organised for our mail to be delivered, booked Simon a flight to Switzerland in two days' time, and introduced us to a co-operative bank. We even had time to have a memorable lunch of braised duck and ginger. He insisted I should stay at his house after Simon had left.

We also had a contact at the Thai Ministry of Defence. We were received with bows and salutes and found Group Captain Chindra Raminda welcoming and helpful. Importantly, he was a sailor – he organised the king's dinghy races. He was looking forward to visiting *Iota*. He promised to write personally to the customs office to make sure we had no problems when we came to shipping out the yacht. The large maps of Thailand on the walls of his office made us realise what a difficult task the defence of Thailand was, for it shared long, vulnerable boundaries with many countries, some of whom were not very friendly.

After Simon left I had only two days to prepare *Iota* for shipping on a Dutch ship, the *Straat Tauranga*. Mr Surin provided two hands to help me, but neither could speak English. We started early in the morning by moving the lead and then we lowered the masts. It was hard work in the blazing sun and high humidity. I had to do much of it myself as I was unable to explain to the boys what to do and a mistake would likely end in disaster.

Group Captain Chindra visited me. The police, who until then had paid little attention to *Iota* or me, were impressed and overawed by such an important visitor. Suddenly they accorded me wonderfully attentive service; they rushed to carry my bags, put a pole in the water so I didn't fall in whilst walking the plank onto the jetty, and brought me iced water to drink. Despite our lack of a common language they invited me to have lunch with them at the wharfies' canteen. I walked around looking at what everybody was eating and when I saw something I recognised I pointed to it. The wharf workers were abuzz with curiosity – it was unusual for the police to take a lady to lunch.

I accepted Chitr's offer to stay at his house. He had given me his address written in Thai so the taxi driver, with instructions from my attentive policemen, managed to deliver me safely to his house at Sam Sen on the other side of Bangkok. The traffic was unbelievable – not only heavily congested but also totally undisciplined. Horns sounded constantly; the blasts were particularly furious if somebody dared to put a foot onto a pedestrian crossing. Drivers specialised in cutting in – the ruder and more blatant their actions, the louder and more vigorously the offenders hooted, shook their fists and swore at their victims. They frequently ignored traffic lights and drove on the wrong side of the road when it was free; when the lights changed nobody could move. Add level crossings, potholes, broken-down cars, intense heat and humidity – I was in need of resuscitation when I arrived at Chitr's comfortable house.

Chitr prescribed a hot bath and cold beer. His housekeeper, Tip, spoke a little English so we were able to communicate. She fussed over me like a mother.

Over a delicious Thai curry Chitr told me his story. His father had been the Thai ambassador to Italy and he had married an Italian so Chitr was half-Italian. He had been brought up in Italy and, although his English was excellent, he could not then speak Thai. It had taken him three years after his return to Bangkok to become proficient. He married a Thai girl from a similar aristocratic family to his own. Thai tradition demanded he should move into the house of his father-in-law's family, but he compromised by building a house in his father-in-law's grounds. Several years and two children later he divorced his wife who moved next door, back to her family. Chitr had to stay put as he owned the house, but not the land on which was built. Around the house he built a high wall with a gate so the children could move freely between their parents, who never met.

Next day I had to visit various shipping offices to sign forms. Then *Straat Tauranga* came alongside and I went on board to meet her officers. We arranged to load *Iota* on the morrow. The only deck space big enough to accommodate her was forward, but here there was only a five-ton lift. The first officer opted for the top of No 1 hatch, hoping to organise his later cargo so the hold would not have to be opened until Sydney.

One of the police boys helped me with the loading. The klong was choked with floating weed with long tough tendrils waiting to entangle themselves around our propeller. As we were about to leave the klong and enter the river a dredge came around the corner to go alongside the wharf. She was obviously going to block the exit. I couldn't turn because the lowered masts limited the range of the tiller, dared not reverse because of the weed, and the current was taking us on. We missed by inches.

The *Straat Tauranga* was discharging into lighters at least six deep. We attached ourselves to one and waited in the blazing sun. The wash from passing traffic was a problem and we had constantly to fend off, a dangerous process. One particularly big wave crunched *Iota* against her solid neighbour. I hardly dared to look, but happily only the spreader of our lifting gear was shattered; *Iota* herself was intact. We were lucky.

I was worried that *Iota* would be sandwiched between two lighters. We gradually came closer to the ship after each lighter had received her fill and disentangled herself from the crowd. At last, four hours later, we were the centre of attention.

Despite the broken spreader loading was smooth and easy and *Iota* settled onto a comfortable bed of sawdust bags. The first officer led me away for a welcome beer and lunch in air-conditioned luxury.

He told a salutary story of rescuing an English hippy from an upturned canoe on their way through Indonesia. The young man had been trying to cross from Sumbawa to Flores in the small native vessel when it was caught by the current, overturned and swept out to sea. When the *Straat Tauranga* picked him up he had been in the water for fifteen hours.

~

With *Iota* safely on her way back to Sydney I could embark on seeing the sights of Bangkok. It was the weekend so Chitr had time to take me to the Royal Palace, the residence of a former king. It was a magnificent complex of temples and halls used for ceremonial occasions. Particularly impressive were the shrines, elaborately decorated with brightly coloured porcelain. Their pinnacles soared into the sky.

We went through a doorway guarded by happy-looking giants to the Temple of the Emerald Buddha. A notice on the door forbade 'microskirts and slippers', but in order to go into the Temple we had to remove our shoes anyway. We left them among a jumble of assorted footwear and went inside. Here the congregation sat cross-legged on the floor and monks led the chanting.

Incense was burning and offerings of flowers decorated the altar. The main shrine rose nearly to the roof and towards the top was set the metre-high Buddha, cross-legged and meditating, carved out of solid emerald. This was a particularly holy place because the temple was built around Buddha's remains – in this case a bone from his arm. Judging by the number of Buddhist temples that claim to possess these relics, the Buddha must have had many more than four limbs.

Chitr organised my sightseeing, beginning with a visit to the floating market. I made an early start, taking a taxi to the jetty in town where I embarked in a boat equipped with a powerful outboard. We travelled along the river in a turbulent froth of water stirred up by the river traffic. The banks were lined with lighters sometimes five and six deep. We turned into a klong in which the current was running strongly. In the narrow canal there was scarcely enough room for boats to pass each other. We went through a residential area with houses on stilts fronting onto the klong. Children dived from their verandas into the murky water. Then we came to the floating market, full of sellers with their produce. It was a colourful scene – the people wore cheerful clothes and hid from the sun under bright umbrellas. There was much good-natured bargaining but, because of the crowds, patience was a necessity for both buyers and sellers.

Happy giants guard the entrance to the temple.

Bangkok's floating market

I then went to Ayutthaya, about 80 kilometres from Bangkok and the capital of Thailand from the 14th to the 18th centuries. It had been a powerful and prosperous kingdom in due course weakened by rifts among the royal princes. The Burmese had taken advantage of this and had overrun the city in 1767 destroying many of its splendours. A few wats remained, including the one I visited. It was a monastery – a school for novice monks. They were learning to manage with no material possessions except two pieces of saffron cloth and a begging bowl; they were not to eat after 11 am and were to have their heads shaved each month. Some were not doing so well; we saw monks eating and smoking late in the afternoon and several saffron-robed, long-haired youths were walking down the street holding hands and clutching transistor radios to their ears.

The Buddhist nuns had white robes and shaven heads. They were friendly and made a production of posing for photographs with toothless smiles. On the way back to Bangkok we stopped at the Summer Palace of the former King Chulalongkorn who had employed Anna Leonowens as governess for his many children. At the turn of the century when Europeans were becoming intrigued by the exotic east the Thais 'discovered' Europe. They considered it desirable to acquire European knowledge and tastes. White Italian marble statues of voluptuously naked women graced the garden at the palace.

On this tour I met Marsha, an American lass, who, like me, wanted to visit Chiangmai. We agreed to travel together and met again back in Bangkok to make arrangements. The overnight train had a clean and comfortable first class air-conditioned sleeper. In the restaurant car the menu was in Thai so we adopted the strategy I had used on the wharf – wander around, look at what the other passengers were eating and point to something recognisable. In the morning we woke to a rural scene with a backdrop of mountains, the countryside becoming more wooded as we slowly climbed.

On arrival in Chiangmai hordes of people immediately surrounded us, all trying to persuade us to let them take us to their hotel, organise our tours or drive us in a taxi. When Marsha saw a bus marked 'Rincombe Hotel' she said, 'Come on. Someone told me it's okay.' We climbed aboard, escaping from the touts.

We cooled off in the pool and studied our collection of pamphlets, all advertising similar tours. A couple of phone calls later and we had a minibus, a guide and a driver to ourselves for as long as we wanted them.

We stopped to photograph a boy and his buffalo.

Chiangmai was a long-established walled city far less congested and much cooler than Bangkok. There was a remarkable range of handcrafted goods to tempt us – all well made and excellent value. We watched skilful girls weaving silk and cotton on hand looms to create tantalising fabrics in brilliant jewel colours. We came across a village specialising in lacquer-ware and another producing handmade silver bowls. The pottery industry had broken away from the traditional Celadon glazes and new colours and designs were being produced for articles such as dinner services and ashtrays. We saw intricately carved teak furniture. Yet another village specialised in making rice paper umbrellas, an industry in which the whole family participated. The women soaked and pounded the rice fibres into sheets and dried them in the sun; the men made the ingenious frames whilst even the tiniest children painted the finished articles, deftly and surely creating decorations of flowers and dragons.

It was the wet season in Chiangmai and the countryside was bright green with young rice plants. One road was flooded and two large elephants were kept busy pulling vehicles out of deep potholes. Women and children were fishing in flooded canals using a square net dangling from a pole. The fish appeared in the canals as soon as they were full of water, but how they survived the dry season was a mystery to me.

One day's expedition was into the mountains. A good road took us as far as the present King's summer palace – a modest house set in pleasant gardens. It was cool and secluded. Nearby was Wat Suthep, an attractive temple reached by climbing up 300 steep steps flanked by stone serpents, whose ornate heads greeted us with surprised expressions as we began our climb. From the top were magnificent views across paddy fields to Chiangmai nestling in the valley. The river snaked off to the sea, followed closely by the railway line. From the other side we looked out onto the rugged jungly mountains, home to the many Thai hill tribes.

We visited two of the more accessible groups, the Meos and the Karens. The Meos were a fascinating people with a distinctive and well-developed culture. We went into the house of one family – a wooden shack with mud floor and thatched roof. An open fire smoked in the corner and only one room was divided off – a sleeping place for the men. When we first met the family we thought the grandparents were looking after the children, but then realised the stunted growth and wizened appearance of the parents were the result of many years of smoking opium. The father smoked a pipe to show us how it was done and the children gathered around awaiting their turn.

These people had high foreheads, slant eyes, hawkish noses and coarse black hair. Their clothes were made from hand-woven black cloth worn with many necklaces of heavy silver. They showed us an elaborate wooden rice mill and a spiky wind instrument that emitted moaning sounds.

Buddhist monks in the village were trying to convert the animist Meos to Buddhism before Chairman Mao took the opportunity to convert them to communism. As they walked past us one of the monks tried out his English saying, 'Okay – shake hands.' I offered him my hand, but he fled in horror, clutching his saffron robes, for serious monks are not allowed to touch women.

The Karens were more used to receiving tourist visitors. Crowds of children gathered around us asking for money. They were all smoking pipes and were dressed in roughly woven red and white tunics. One child was playing with a half-dead baby rat; when it expired he threw it away and licked his fingers. They were an inscrutable, truculent people.

~

Meo people

From an early age, the Karens smoked pipes.

Teak was prized for durability; its value and desirability had led to severe over-cutting in tropical forests, those in northern Thailand being no exception. These large deciduous trees once extended over large areas of Thailand, but now existed only in the mountains. Their cutting had been restricted. Attempts were being made to grow plantations of the trees, but little had been achieved, probably because nobody wanted to wait the 80 to 100 years for them to grow to maturity.

Elephants were dragging logs out of the river and stacking them ready to be made into large rafts to be floated down the river for milling in Bangkok. Five elephants were working, each with a mahout sitting on its neck, guiding the elephant with shouts and his feet behind the animal's ears. Fully grown and used to their tasks, the elephants worked with great intelligence and precision, cooperating with each other as they knelt down to get their trunks or tusks under the log and lift it precariously onto the pile. Frequently a log toppled over the other side of the heap and they would patiently go round and lift it back up.

One of the elephants had a calf, about five years old and not yet weaned. Enthusiastically he joined the others, trying to do his best to help, although while nobody was looking he went up to the pile and pushed a log off the top. The elephants knelt down so we could climb onto their backs; they took us, swaying, down to the river to fetch another log.

Elephants stacking teak logs

We left Chiangmai reluctantly and flew back to the crowds and heat of Bangkok. Marsha left the next day for Penang and Kuala Lumpur, but I spent a few more days in the comfort of Chitr's house.

Chitr's aunt had died while I was in Chiangmai; she had been the oldest and most senior member of an aristocratic and wealthy family. Her body was at the temple, where her family and friends assembled each night. Each day the women were busy preparing food and offerings of flowers. It was a continuing social occasion at which the family of the deceased did their utmost to impress. The assemblies took place nightly in the first week, then would do so with less regularity until a hundred days had passed, when the final cremation would be a lavish ceremony indeed.

Chitr told me of two more impressive wats I should visit. Wat Po was a beautiful tranquil place, home of the Reclining Buddha, a colossal statue about fifteen metres long, so large it was difficult to see it as a whole. The impressive Golden Buddha was at Wat Traimit. Made of solid gold he was about three metres high and weighed over five tonnes.

Such statues were in various poses and styles. When Buddha meditated he sat cross-legged with his hand turned up to receive enlightenment; if standing with one or two hands raised he was calming either the sea or his squabbling relations. He also walked or reclined into Nirvana and, in the latter case, always grew to a gigantic size. A few images showed an emaciated Buddha with protruding ribs – Buddha was fasting. All Buddhas had long ears, a sign of longevity. Ayutthaya Buddhas had flames on their heads, but Sukhothai Buddhas didn't and were usually made of bronze. Chinese Buddhas were fat and happy and Cambodian Buddhas had European features.

Buddhist philosophy teaches that suffering is a necessary part of man's lot in life and is caused by striving after earthly goods and succumbing to earthly desires. If these were rejected in this or in a succeeding life you would receive enlightenment, enter into Nirvana and be relieved of having to live again. The taking of life was forbidden, but it was not hard to find a way around the problem – 'I didn't kill the fish, I just pulled it out of the water and it died,' or 'I only held the gun – the bullet killed him.'

~

The girl in the shop where I bought a length of Thai silk had recommended a beauty parlour down one of the less salubrious streets of Bangkok, the area of bars and massage houses. It was called 'Charming Moon'. Nobody could speak English, but they understood that I wanted a facial, pedicure, manicure, body massage and a haircut. It was very good value; they quoted 500 baht and we agreed on 400 baht.

First came the facial, a communal affair, with ladies stretched out on couches while the operators applied and smoothed in a variety of creams. One woman had a white mudpack on her face and neck; she looked like a ghost. Upstairs I was stretched out on another couch and basted with oil. Every muscle was painstakingly and carefully massaged. Then we hit a snag; I had to be steamed in a box, but being so much broader and taller than the average Thai woman, I didn't fit. It was all the more difficult because I was so oily that when the girl pushed one bit of me in, another bit would slither out somewhere else. She eventually imprisoned my head firmly in the hole in top of the box and pushed me in with the door. Every five minutes I was anointed with a milky solution designed to bleach my skin to desirable whiteness.

I was washed, dried, powdered and taken downstairs again for a simultaneous manicure, pedicure and haircut. Three girls were pampering me, all at the same time. Other clients were undergoing similar treatment. They appeared to be the madams of nearby establishments and girls were parading before them in their bikinis or less while their merits and charms were discussed. I much regretted not being able to understand their comments.

Chitr took me to a farewell lunch – my favourite duck with ginger. He told me Thailand had made remarkable strides in the last ten years, but much remained to be done. In the early 1950s the World Bank had refused to lend money until Thailand showed signs of wiser spending, suggesting that inefficiency, corruption and a lust for power had created problems in all areas – agriculture, irrigation, industry, education, health and communications. Teacher training had improved and now every child went to school, rice farming was more efficient, but while I was there questions were being asked about a new dam that had not materialised despite the allocated money being spent!

Thais appeared to be resigned to corruption and inefficiency being a way of life. When a former prime minister died it was revealed that much of his wealth had accumulated because he had organised the passage of large quantities of opium through Bangkok from Laos and Burma. The populace seemed to think these were normal perks of office. The incumbent head of the country was criticised for his failure to deal with the increasing lawlessness in Thailand, but in sharp contrast the Royal family were held in high esteem, and were greatly loved and admired.

I stopped in Singapore for a few days on my way back to Sydney. It seemed cool, organised and efficient after the hot, humid congestion of Bangkok. Chitr was right when he said, 'We could do with Lee Kuan Yu here.'

iota returns to the south seas – tonga and fiji

1972

Tongans have a rapport with the sea and a natural ability as seamen. Their government was taking advantage of this to boost its economy and had formed a shipping company with two ships, the *Tauloto* and the *Nuivaki*. *Iota* and I were booked to sail on the *Tauloto* from Sydney to Nuku'alofa.

There were many delays to her departure. The certificates for *Tauloto*'s derricks could not be found so the wharfies would not work. By the time they had finished testing them it was raining. It was also raining when *Iota* was loaded – we were alongside just after dawn, but had to wait until the afternoon before we were hoisted on board.

Eventually we got away and I stood on the deck of the ship as we sailed down the harbour. A young Tongan sailor sidled up to me. With meticulous politeness he told me his name was Langi and asked me if I would be his girlfriend for the voyage. I thanked him and explained I already had a boyfriend who would not appreciate my having another one. He was disappointed, said he understood and walked sadly away.

The crew, apart from the captain and chief engineer, were mostly Tongan. The radio operator was a gentle, softly spoken Pakistani and the one of the engineers was a fiery redheaded Dane with a Tongan wife. They were a happy and cheerful bunch.

Captain Jim Stott and Chief Engineer Syd Sandilands had both returned from retirement to help establish the Tongan shipping company. Jim's wife had recently died so he was glad to have the distraction of going back to sea. He was a kindly man with a kinky sense of humour, and given to composing rhymes. He struck precisely the right note with the Tongans, being firm, but he also understood their idiosyncrasies so they liked and respected him. He left as much of the running of the ship as he could to his first mate to allow him to gain experience.

Syd was a typical ship's engineer – a large, grey-haired man with a strong Scottish accent – and was the perfect foil for Jim's whimsical humour. We gathered each evening in Jim's cabin to drink gin before dinner; it was a time of joviality and laughter.

The weather was kind all the way to Suva and for much of the journey five albatrosses accompanied us. During the three busy days following our arrival I explored the facilities for yachts. The Tradewinds Hotel catered for visiting cruising boats. About 20 minutes from town, it was a well-protected hurricane hole with good facilities. Some of the yachts were familiar – Bernard Moitessier was there with his red steel *Joshua*. Since I had last met him in Tahiti he had competed in a nonstop single-handed race around the world; he had been winning when he decided he didn't want fame and fortune and stunned the world by abandoning the race and returning to Tahiti. His book describing his experience, *The Long Way*, had been published the previous year.

I recognised the large sloop *Windrift*, whose owners, Jerry and his attractive blonde wife Sharon, Simon and I had met in New Zealand where their boat was being built. They were from the British Virgin Islands. *Windrift* impressed Jim because she was equipped with radar. He failed to notice Sharon who was sunbathing on the deck beneath it. This omission prompted a poem.

> *Sing a song for Jimmy Stott*
> *A sitting in his chair.*
> *What's the thing that I can see*
> *On that ship o'er there?*
> *A radar set bethinks me.*
> *Great Stott you're getting old!*
> *On the deck below the radar*
> *A girl with hair of gold.*

The Royal Suva Yacht Club was conveniently close to town, but the yachts were anchored a long way from it. I tried in vain to buy a Fijian courtesy flag, but was more successful in tracking down 'No Worries' Russ, the aerial survey pilot who had taken me joy-riding in the clouds over Guadalcanal. We met for a drink and recalled our millionaire lifestyle of trying to decide whether to fly, sail or go for drive.

We had a pilot from Suva to Lautoka and back again to Suva, so he was on board for two days and became part of the family. His name was John, the son of an erstwhile bishop of Suva. He knew every nook and cranny of the islands and was an expert chart marker.

I spent the afternoon in Lautoka wandering around town with my admirer Langi, who was buying presents for his family. Peter, the hospitable agent, took Jim, Syd, John and me to visit the five clubs of Lautoka. It was well after midnight before we had sampled them all. Syd complained of a sore head in the morning.

Back in Suva we dropped off the pilot and collected two new passengers, New Zealanders Dennis and Jean, who ran the YMCA hostel in Suva. They were good company and full of interesting anecdotes about life with the Fijians. They contributed to the cocktail hour hilarity in the captain's cabin.

The ship developed an electrical problem affecting the air conditioning. It was Sunday so it was not repaired, as Tongans were not allowed to work on a Sunday. That night we crossed the Date Line so next day it was Sunday again. It took a day to work on the problem so we were uncomfortably hot for the three days. I wondered what would have happened if all the ship's electrics had failed.

It was dark when we arrived in Pago Pago; it was a clear night with a full moon. The fantastic harbour was indeed a beautiful sight, but the light of day took away the romance. It turned the lights of the Korean fishing fleet into rusty, rundown, swayback ships and revealed the anomalies of the American impact on the island – including fully armed police and traffic jams.

A cable car crossed the harbour to the top of the mountain. Although it was unnerving as the car swayed in the strong wind, the awesome view was worth the ride. The powerful TV transmitter sited on the mountain had six channels intended for educational purposes, but the material broadcast seemed to have little relevance to the needs of the people.

Jean, Dennis and I spent the afternoon on a bus that took us around the harbour, past the tuna factory and further around the coast to the east. It was a pretty coastline with small offshore islands, but the hills were so steep that little that could be cultivated.

Syd's wife Mary joined us in Pago Pago. She was an American and we were curious to know how they had met. They smiled; it had happened during the war. Syd had been in the British army and Mary in the American navy. On a train Syd had lured Mary into the connection between two carriages and kissed her. She had responded by hugging him – so enthusiastically she broke his rib. Then followed the embarrassment of having to admit how he had become unfit for duty. Nobody had believed him, but it was the beginning of a happy marriage.

Syd and Jim had a wager. They were betting on how long it would be before one of the Tongan sailors propositioned me. Jim thought one of them would try before we arrived in Fiji, but Syd was of the opinion it would not be until after. The prize was a bottle of expensive brandy. They asked me coyly if any of the sailors had approached me. When I told them, yes, it was while we were sailing down Sydney Harbour, they nearly died laughing.

'She didn't even get to the Heads!' said Jim.

The Tauloto *in Pago Pago*

A pilot boarded the ship off Apia in Western Samoa to take us into the harbour with their new tug. Although quite large, the harbour was encumbered with reef and there was not much room for a ship the size of the *Tauloto* to turn; the tug's assistance would be welcome. She had a bright green hull and yellow and red funnel and looked like a tug in a children's storybook; Jim named her *Little Toot*. We saw her in the distance and, although the pilot radioed to her, she did not approach. Eventually – after we had turned – with much shouting and arm waving she was persuaded to take an interest in us. We came into the wharf, the sailors secured our lines and the pilot went ashore to move a Japanese training ship further down the wharf to make room so the *Tauloto*'s afterhold could be unloaded. Tommy the agent came on board and we had a cup of coffee. Syd came up to the bridge having shut down his engines. Black smoke coming from the side of the ship caught his attention. He peered over the side – *Little Toot* was still engaged with the ship and pushing her heart out although we had been tied up for at least half an hour.

The *Tauloto* was late and Tommy was relieved and pleased to see us for we were carrying essential cargo. The other Tongan ship, the *Niuvaki*, was anchored in the harbour waiting to be loaded with timber to take to the States so the crews celebrated their meeting. Jim was again inspired to verse.

> *The Tauloto came into Apia;*
> *'Good heavens,' said Tommy, 'you're here.*
> *I must remonstrate*
> *You were running quite late*
> *For you come bringing cargo and cheer.'*
>
> *The Tauloto came into Apia;*
> *'Thank goodness,' said Tommy, 'you're here.*
> *A crisis averted*
> *With effort concerted*
> *We had almost run out of beer.'*
>
> *The Tauloto came into Apia;*
> *Niuvaki was already here.*
> *Opportunity seizing,*
> *The meeting was pleasing;*
> *That all enjoyed it was clear.*
>
> *The Tauloto came into Apia;*
> *Little Toot gave a shove at the rear.*
> *But after an hour*
> *We'd all had a shower;*
> *She had only pushed over the pier.*

Tommy showed us around the island that was well endowed with immense churches – we gained the impression they all were trying to outshine each other. He took us to see the new parliament house – a modern version of the traditional Samoan meeting house, to Robert Louis Stevenson's residence where the head of state now lived and to the famous Aggie's Hotel where he introduced us to the legendary figure of Aggie Grey herself. Now aged 75 Aggie possessed all the charm and energy that made her so much more than an innkeeper. Daughter of the son of a well-to-do British merchant in Fiji and the daughter of a Samoan chief, Aggie well understood the two very different cultures; over the years she had contributed to much of the modern history of the islands.

The Japanese training ship was smart and full of electronic gear. They were experimenting with direct control from Japan; why they were training officers to run a ship designed to manage without them was a mystery to us. At 6 am the entire crew came onto the wharf in full white uniform, including hats, to exercise. After 50 fast press-ups they went jogging with hats still in place. The Tongan crew looked on with amazement – and so did we.

Offloading Iota *in Nuku'alofa*

On the way to Nuku'alofa we stopped briefly in the Vavau Group to offload a bulldozer needed to help build the new airstrip. When we arrived in Nuku'alofa the launch taking our lines tied them in knots so it took a while to secure the ship alongside the wharf. Clearance was also a lengthy process; the immigration police and customs were not going to be hurried. The crew were waiting impatiently to go ashore and the welcoming crowd was straining to come on board. At last the all clear was given and a mad rush ensued, the two-way traffic of heavy Tongans on the gangway causing it to sag and groan.

Captain Hills-Willis, known as Captain Hillbilly, was responsible for the Tongan merchant fleet. Hillbilly was a small rotund man, completely bald and given to sweeping statements announced firmly in colourful language. He greeted me with, 'That bloody yacht – never had so many letters in my whole life. Can't stand people who write letters they expect me to answer!'

Margie, his wife, was in many ways similar and they shouted each other down.

It was all bluff, for after a couple of Jim's gins they gave me the royal treatment. They had arranged between them what was going to happen to *Iota* and me. *Iota* was allotted an iron buoy in the main harbour almost as big as her and I was to stay with Margie in her house next to the Dateline Hotel.

Before Hillbilly went off to New Zealand on the afternoon of our arrival he introduced me to a helpful man in the marine department on the wharf. He telephoned customs for me; they said they would worry about the yacht on Monday and on the Monday they said they would come on Wednesday. They never did appear.

The *Tauloto* sailed again for Sydney. I went to say goodbye and thank them for a fun trip. Mary had lost the key to the cabin and nobody could find a spare. She and Syd were in despair, but Jim was chortling.

Mary lost the cabin key,
She knew not when it went.
Syd came home, said 'Goodness me!'
And climbed in through the vent.

After a couple of days I had organised help to raise *Iota*'s masts. I took her into a small, walled boat harbour sheltered from the seas. The rigging went smoothly and by the end of the day we had water on board and had moved the lead. The boat harbour was much more snug than lying to the buoy outside and it saved a long row in choppy water so I stayed there. I put out anchors fore and aft to hold *Iota* off the wall and moved on board.

I was introduced to the yacht club and made an honorary member. It had a pleasant enough bar and friendly members, but it had only three boats. This was partly explained by the Tongan law that makes any occupation involving commerce or pleasure illegal on a Sunday. They all worked on Saturday morning, so the boat owner would have only Saturday afternoon for sailing.

On Sundays nothing happened at all except for the continuous succession of church services of all the many denominations vying for Tongan souls. The strict Sunday observance posed problems – if the Saturday plane service from Apia could not land because the grass strip was wet, parliament had to be hastily summoned to allow it to land on a Sunday. Taxis stopped abruptly at midnight on Saturday and there was no way of persuading them to continue to your destination. Contracts signed on Sunday were void. Gardening, fishing and any kind of work or sport were against the law – but neither could you be arrested on a Sunday.

The SDA church, which celebrates the Sabbath on a Saturday, had difficulty raising a congregation because their adherents could not find jobs; their church forbade working on Saturday. However they found a neat way around the problem, deeming that Sundays were really Saturdays; the Date Line swings around Tonga so it has the same date as Fiji and New Zealand, but it is one day later than Samoa.

I was joined in the harbour by a single-handed Canadian yacht, a Vertue class called *Bonaventure de Lys*. John Struchinsky who sailed her had been at sea for several weeks and had become land shy. Approaching land was altogether too dangerous and if he overcame that problem, he would have to face up to people. I took him to the yacht club where he felt at home and quickly overcame his shyness.

We explored Tonga together. I hired a car and had to buy a Tongan driving licence – a useful source of revenue for the government. Tonga Tapu, the principal island, is flat – the highest point being about 30 metres – and not large, so it did not take long to explore. It was possible to cover all the usable roads in a day, even though a speed of over 30 kilometres per hour was either forbidden in town or impossible out of it. The volcanic soil was fertile, but an increased population was putting greater demands on it and there was a danger of it being depleted.

The climate was surprisingly cool, and after dark and sometimes even during the day I needed a sweater.

Nuku'alofa, the capital, was a shabby town. The main street was bordered by scruffy shops invariably out of stock of the particular item you needed. With patience and perseverance you could find most things, but it took time. The market, however, was good, especially on Saturday when there was a wide range of vegetables. On the waterfront was the king's white-painted wooden palace with a red dome roof, surrounded by Norfolk Island pines. Next door was a mansion, the home of the leader of the Mormon Church.

The villages in the countryside were neat and clean, houses varying from the traditional 'grass hut' through wood and corrugated iron to imposing brick structures. Often a heap of bricks denoted a thrifty Tongan who had worked in New Zealand and invested in bricks, which could not be shared by his numerous relations. If he had returned with money they would have begged or stolen it away from him. Someday he would earn more, enough to complete his house – if he didn't lose interest beforehand.

Each village had several churches. Methodism was the official religion of Tonga and favoured by the Royal family. Some groups had broken away from the original church and at least three forms of Methodism were represented. There were also expensive Mormon churches in nearly every village, each built in brick with a basketball court behind.

The windward side of the island was the most interesting. There was a fifteen-kilometre stretch of volcanic rock etched into platforms and caves, riddled with blowholes that exploded with a roar and a rush of spray. It was cold and wet watching the pounding seas and I was glad to be seeing it from the land rather than the sea; a boat would stand no chance.

John was fascinated by a place where centuries ago rocks had been intricately arranged in relation to the paths of the stars and planets. The early Polynesian mariners were keen observers of the heavens and skilful navigators. Their bold voyages in canoes across the Pacific were not haphazard and it was not only by chance they arrived at their destinations. Polynesian navigators employed a whole range of techniques including the flight of birds, the winds and the weather as well as the motion of specific stars and planets.

The Haamongaa Maui also intrigued us. It was an archway consisting of three limestone slabs about five metres high and six long, thought to have been built at the beginning of the 13th century as the gateway to the royal compound of King Tui Tonga Tuit Tui. There have been various theories put forward that the structure was more than just an archway – it has astronomical significance and a resemblance to Stonehenge – but none has been proven.

John decided to sail on to Fiji before he became a landlubber. He tangled with Tongan officialdom and even after four hours of going from office to office still did not have all his clearance papers. He went to the hospital to get a health clearance only to find everybody was at a football match.

Iota was leaking quite badly – the newly painted, bright red slip in the corner of the harbour seemed to be the only answer. Slipping was easy, but it took a long time with a dozen helpers inching the cradle out of the water with a hand windlass. Although I could see from the inside where the water came in, from the outside it was not apparent. The local carpenter wanted to patch on the inside so I lost faith in him, but together we recaulked, glued and screwed and eventually all was well.

The slip had the disadvantage of being outside the only public bar in Nuku'alofa. Having been pestered by drunks all day I was dubious about spending the night on board alone. Margie offered me a bed and Hillbilly recommended one of his workers to spend the night on board. Margie spent the evening complaining about her relationship – or lack of it – with Hillbilly. Hillbilly had moved into the house he provided for his Tongan mistress, who had produced his child. He now wanted Margie to adopt the child! He was outrageous and she was bitter. I wondered why she stayed with him.

When I went to check on the boat first thing in the morning the 'guard' had gone and so had most of Simon's shirts, the radio, a camera, ten bottles of rum and some cigarettes. Fortunately I had asked him to sign the visitors' book so the police went straight to his village and found him passed out from drinking overproof rum. They recovered Simon's shirts, the camera and the radio and took the offender to the police station.

A large Tongan policeman came to the boat harbour to deliver me a subpoena. He insisted on bringing it aboard rather than my going ashore to collect it from him so I pushed the dinghy over to the wall for him. He immediately capsized it and both he and the subpoena were soaked.

I dutifully went to court to attend the hearing and give evidence if required. A thin, creepy Indian lawyer with long spidery fingers approached me. He told me he was engaged to represent the defendant. He asked me if I would be merciful and forgive the crime, just as Jesus Christ had forgiven sinners. He tugged on a gold chain around my neck thinking a cross would be dangling from it, but it was a shark's tooth. I told him it was not up to me for the police were the prosecutors. He crossed himself and said something about Jesus overturning the tables in the temple. The proceedings were all in Tongan, but I gathered the young man pleaded guilty and received the punishment of four months in jail.

~

The King celebrated his birthday with a public holiday and a parade. Margie lent me a hat and gloves and we were shown, with ceremony, to our seats. Everybody who was anybody was there and the rest sat on the other side of the park. At the appointed moment the British Consul drove up in a rather worn out car and an even older grey morning suit and topper. The guns fired a 21-gun salute, the troops presented arms and up drove a big black car – an old Chevie, but very dignified. The King was an enormous man and wore a pale brown uniform, dark brown gloves and sunglasses. The parade was inspected – the Royal Guard smart in red and white uniforms, the Tongan Defence Force in green battledress and the cadets in grey shorts, white shirts and barefooted. All marched together and individually, the only disaster being when three dignified members of the Guard at the head of the column failed to hear an order to halt and marched on. It was as if the head of a caterpillar was taking off, leaving its body behind. The crowd roared.

The King made a speech about Japanese swords; it was scheduled to last for ten minutes but went on for 40. A dozen soldiers showed off their skills with a jeep; they drove it on, disassembled it, carried it across an imaginary bridge and put it together again, all with great speed and efficiency. The soldiers marched off leaving only the driver; to his horror, the jeep wouldn't start! The crowd roared again!

The Tongan king was omnipotent, nobody having sufficient rank or power to thwart him. He was well educated and had lived most of his life outside his kingdom. He specialised in thinking up odd and expensive ideas for his subjects. He decreed that Tongans needed abacuses; thousands of them were sitting in the government store. His most recent escapade was to build a concrete island on Minerva Reef and plant a Tongan flag on it, thus enlarging his kingdom. Convicts, including three murderers, were the construction crew. There they indulged in their profession, resulting in four more murders.

The King arrived for his birthday ceremony...

...and inspected his troops.

The jeep wouldn't start and had to be pushed.

The British Consul gave a cocktail party in honour of the New Zealand Trade Commission. About 200 people eagerly accepted their invitations – it was a break in the quiet of Tongan life. They all knew each other; I was the only stranger. Royalty was represented by the Crown Prince, a large young man addicted to riding his motorbike during the night and playing snooker, as well as the King's eldest daughter, Princess Pululeva, whom my friend June had taught when she was at school in Auckland. Her dress was striking, her traditional ta'ovala – a wide woven pandanus belt – being cleverly incorporated without appearing to enlarge her substantial hips.

An English woman, Angela, came over to talk to me, telling me she sailed enthusiastically when she was back home. I asked her where home was and she told me Chichester Harbour. My ears pricked – that was where my brother sailed; she knew him well. While her husband Ken was busy building Tonga's new airstrip she spent her time painting. She invited me to join her so we spent several days together, visiting outlying villages and watching the everyday lives of the inhabitants as we sat in the shade endeavouring to capture the scene.

One village was host to a colony of flying foxes.

In one village where we went to paint was a colony of flying foxes, several hundred of them, all hanging upside down by their back legs from the trees. They were sacred, which was just as well for them for they were not congenial neighbours – they ate all the fruit in the village and smelt. At night they made a lot of noise, quarrelling and squabbling. They had a metre wingspan, the wing being a membrane stretched between their front and back legs. Their flight was characteristically slow and spooky.

The Tongans were agriculturalists, mostly producing subsistence crops, but growing sufficient to export copra, bananas and vegetables.

There were biscuit and desiccated coconut factories, but otherwise no industry. They regarded tourism as an unfortunate necessity, but were hoping to make money eventually from their ships. In order to do this they needed to be much more efficient. The *Tauloto* brought in about a thousand tonnes of general cargo, but her back-loading was only a few hundred tonnes of copra, the price of which had recently fallen.

Most of the people were relatively poor, with the definite exception of the King and Chiefs and their relations. Large families were the rule and attempts to promote family planning had not met with much success. It used to be the law that each boy on reaching the age of sixteen was given three or four hectares of land to farm. However there was not enough land for this to continue, with the resulting formidable problem of a large proportion of the population with nothing to do except sit around all day and stare. The Tongans seemed to live entirely in the present and were oblivious to threats to their future. They were able to work in New Zealand for six months periods, but of course the taste for the goods that money can buy led to further discontent.

Although they frequently indulged in raucous laughter over trivialities, the Tongans were rather sombre and had a preoccupation with death. They all rushed to the radio when, each evening, preceded by a hymn, the deaths of the previous day were announced in a hushed voice. Funerals were elaborate and well attended, often accompanied by a brass band. The mourners all wore black and the belt – taʻovala – chosen for the occasion was longer than usual and old and scruffy like a ragged doormat. People wore mourning for many months. They buried the dead in cemeteries that took up much of the precious land and carefully tended the graves, covering them with a mound of sand and decorating them with flowers and empty beer bottles.

One day the arrival of a cruise ship shattered the peace and quiet. She had a Greek crew and carried nearly two thousand Australian tourists. There were people everywhere; taxis, bicycles and horses charged up and down the waterfront. A local handcraft market was set up in the town and there was a roaring trade in woven mats, trays, hats, carvings and shells. Tongan baskets were famous; beautiful ones that took weeks to make were available at little cost. The tourists bought, toured, feasted and rushed around for eight hours. Then they left us in peace and Tonga some thousands of dollars better off – painful but profitable!

Shortly before Simon arrived the *Tauloto* reappeared and stayed over the weekend. Sid's wife Mary was on board again and Jim was his usual hospitable self. We waded through a prolonged deluge to the Dateline Hotel for dinner and the Saturday night entertainment of Tongan dancing. After the show the dancing became a 'free for all' and a succession of somewhat inebriated Tongans kept Mary and me on our feet. At 11.30 we ordered a taxi. By midnight it had not appeared and then it was Sunday. As it was still pouring with rain the manager took us home. Jim was typically poetic: 'When the music diminishes, the taxi finishes.'

The rain stopped in time for the grass to dry out for Simon's arrival. He came on the first plane to land after nearly a week. We went about the process of clearing and spent a frustrating day trying to acquire all the necessary papers. On the third attempt we found a customs officer who stated we could not visit the other islands because a previous yacht had taken in marijuana. We managed to talk him out of that. He told us we had to have an agricultural inspection in order to obtain a rhinoceros beetle clearance; this mouse-sized shiny black beetle with a formidable horn on its head was sure death to coconut trees. It took two attempts, each involving a five-kilometre trek to the hospital, to obtain the required health clearance. We ducked out of paying duty on our stolen rum and received a sheaf of papers. Now we could go. It was all formality; nobody read what we wrote on the forms.

Before setting off we asked for a forecast at the weather office. The forecaster told us Tonga was under the influence of a convergence, a meeting of the two systems that caused cloudy, unsettled weather. However, a high-pressure system was approaching and he noted sagely that good weather follows bad and vice versa.

We loaded our duty-free stores and listened to the radio; our departure made headlines in the local news. It was time to go. Noumuka was an inconvenient 60 miles away. Nuku'alofa was on the southern side of a big reef-infested bay that needed daylight for safe navigation. We would have to anchor off a small island off the outer reef so we could leave at night and make Noumuka the next day. The weather was promising, the sky partly overcast but clearing and the wind in the southeast. We anchored comfortably on a sand patch about fourteen miles from Nuku'alofa and set the alarm for 2 am.

We woke to find a starless night and the wind in the north; it was cold and the waves were beginning to come around the reef. We stayed put. Dawn brought an unpleasant grey morning and a low barometer. It seemed prudent to return to a safer haven.

We went back inside the big harbour, but were reluctant to go back to the paperwork and officials of Nuku'alofa. We found shelter instead off an island called Fafa. An extensive reef surrounded it and there was a sandy patch for us to anchor on. Through the day the wind increased and there were scuds of rain, but the sea could not get to us.

We were both awake at about 2:30 am and it was raining heavily. We congratulated ourselves on not going to sea. Then, suddenly, the boat heeled over to a terrific gust of wind; we waited for the lurch and snatch when the boat pulled up on her chain. It didn't happen.

We rushed on deck. We were dragging – fast. We could scarcely stand for the wind and rain. We subsequently compared notes with another yacht whose anemometer recorded its maximum reading of 80 knots continuously for three hours. We started the engine and tried to raise the anchor, but realised that, even if we managed, we would not have the power to return to the island against the wind. We let go all 30 fathoms of chain in the desperate hope the anchor would snag on something before *Iota* hit one of the reefs that were waiting downwind to grab her. A quick look at the chart showed fifteen to eighteen fathoms in the harbour and no way at all of avoiding the reefs.

Simon stayed at the tiller with the engine going full throttle and powered into the wind while I went below and put on my warm clothes and a life jacket. I pulled out the life raft and collected a survival kit – flares, passports, money, water. I relieved Simon while he dressed and we had a can of beer. Eventually the rain eased and we could see the lights of Nuku'alofa and a flashing beacon on the nearest reef – all too clearly. I took a fix on them every five minutes and read the echo sounder – a constant fifteen fathoms. We were not moving. We thought the wind was easing and, just before dawn, the barograph took a tentative upward smile.

Dawn did not break; the black night slowly merged into a dull grey morning. Fafa appeared about half a mile away and waves were breaking on the reef all too close behind us. By 7 am we could see enough to think about recovering ourselves.

The 30 fathoms of chain and 30-pound CQR were almost immovable. Simon struggled away, but the chain slipped off the gypsy, ran out with a frightening roar and stopped with a shattering jerk. He started all over again, link by link, but this time I secured the chain as he pulled it in so we could not lose it all again.

Over an hour later the anchor broke out and we powered back to Fafa against the still strong but not vicious wind. This time we laid out our 'portable mooring', the 60-pound CQR. Three fishermen who had

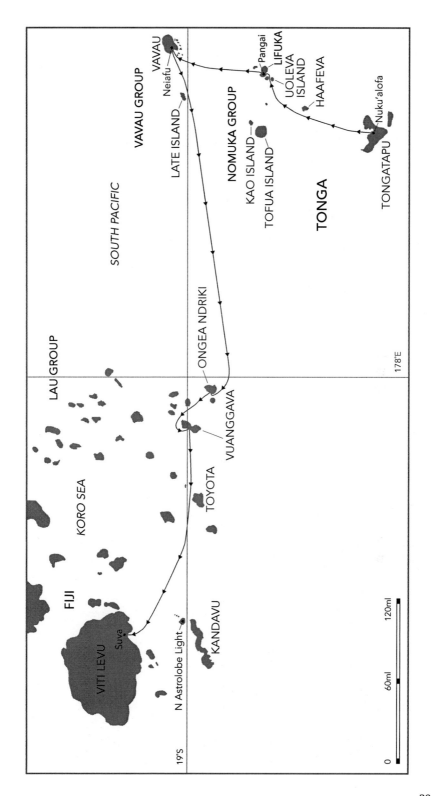

spent the night on Fafa, their boat securely on the beach and tied to a palm tree, passed us on their way back to Nuku'alofa. They tossed two fat fish onto *Iota*. We breakfasted on them, stowed the life raft and flares, bandaged Simon's torn fingers and wondered why anybody ever went to sea.

The wind slowly changed from north into the west and then to the south. The storm abated enough for us to go ashore – we staggered up the beach like a couple of drunks, unaccustomed to land that was not rolling. It was a pleasant island.

When the wind turned into the southeast we set off again, late in the afternoon. Outside the harbour the sea was confused and we sailed with a reefed main and No 1 jib, hoping to keep our speed to about three knots so as to be off Noumuka at dawn. Lights came up behind us that appeared to belong to a large yacht. For no reason at all, I said, 'I bet that's *Stormvogel*.'

Dawn showed us the high volcanic islands of Tafua and Kao and, as the sun rose higher, the low island of Noumuka became clear. In the distance we saw the large yacht putting into a bay on Noumuka, but we continued towards the Haafava, a few miles further north; it had an anchorage with a wide sandy bay that several sailing friends had recommended to us. We sailed in through a maze of reefs; it required careful navigation so I had the hand-bearing compass constantly in hand.

During the night a boat came into the bay and turned a searchlight on us. We wondered who would sail among the reefs in the dark – it had to be a local boat. Dawn revealed she was the government boat *Fangailifuka*. One of the crew came over to tell us Dr Bill Tufui was ashore and expecting us. Simon had met Bill – he was medical officer for the Haapai Group and had attended a course in Sydney organised by Simon's firm.

He was not, as we had expected, on a routine medical round, but on a fund-raising mission for the Red Cross. He had with him an eight-piece brass band, a loudspeaker, a family-planning sign, a dentist, a Peace Corps nurse for the baby clinic, an American Mormon missionary, two Red Cross workers and two American tourists.

We did our laundry with water from the dispensary tank accompanied by brass brand practice. During the morning boats from all the neighbouring islands came for the 'show', bringing donations of copra for the Red Cross.

The show eventually started three hours late. The band sat under a mango tree and the villagers gathered around. The Methodist minister, dressed in a black suit and bowtie, opened proceedings with a prayer and sat sombrely looking askance at the ensuing capers. The band struck up. Bill started the dancing and made Simon join in. I persuaded the captain of the *Fangailifuka* to dance with me. His bright red pullover was too small for him and ended up many inches above the bulge that was his waist; the sleeves stopped above his elbows.

The Red Cross workers found the village roll. As people came up with gifts, they crossed them off the list and announced their name and the amount of their donation over the loudspeaker. Some gave a little money, others a woven mat. It was a form of blackmail, each family feeling ashamed when another gave more. Bill had boundless enthusiasm; he danced and conducted the band with gusto. As the total approached $50 he cajoled the last few cents from the village. They finished up with a grand total of $54.72 and about twenty mats.

Dr Bill Tufui's boundless enthusiasm for Red Cross fundraising

A feast was to have followed, but as it was so late the party from the boat took their food away in plaited coconut baskets to eat on the way to Noumuka. We were left to the mercy of the Methodist minister to whom, unfortunately, Simon had taken a dislike. He took us to his house by the church and we sat on the floor to eat our 'feast'. The house was none too clean and swarmed with flies. We were given chicken that obviously had led an energetic life devoted to slimming, a pig's head spilling its brains and a leathery octopus cooked in taro leaves – none of which titillated the appetite. The Minister's wife appeared, as fat as he was thin, and presented us with a woven tray designed, she said, to carry whisky glasses. It was an appropriate gift from the church.

After a decent interval we escaped. With the minister we went back to the boat in procession to discover that somebody had stolen our dinghy painter. The minister said obviously the culprit must have been the one of crew of the *Fangailifuka*.

As Simon rowed him out to see *Iota*, the minister emphasised that the present of taro and yams he was giving us was indeed a gift – no money required – but if we happened to find a polo neck sweater suitable for a man of God…

'It shouldn't be "Beware of Greeks bearing gifts", but "Beware of Tongans bearing gifts",' Simon complained when he returned from taking him ashore.

We had a brisk wind, dead to windward to our next island, Voleva. The sea was calm and *Iota* made good speed. She went well to windward unless the sea was rough – then, with her boxy shape and hard chine, she struggled.

A long white beach lured us ashore and we met temporary inhabitants who were collecting copra. They took us to their hut and gave us coconuts to drink. They were preparing their main meal of the day and opened the earth oven. We sampled their meal of various baked roots and fish cooked in coconut milk. It was delicious and we appreciated their hospitality. We gave them cigarettes, which greatly pleased them.

We went on to the main town of the Haapi Group, Pangai on the island of Lifuka. The approach was studded with reefs and there was a complicated array of beacons. We waited for a local boat to catch us up; it was an open boat, powered by a Seagull outboard and full of people hiding from the sun under black umbrellas. One of them offered to pilot us in so he came on board and wove us in and out of the coral heads. As soon as we anchored two policemen and a customs officer boarded us. They were out to be difficult – our pilot must have come from Australia, our clearance from Nuku'alofa did not mention Haapi and we could not visit the islands to the north because of a rumour that treasure was buried there.

Pangai had Burns Philp and Morris Hedstrom stores, many churches and the government resthouse. Bill Tufui and his wife Ofa lived in a house opposite the hospital, and with Bill away again, Ofa showed us around the island. She borrowed a neighbour's utility and put two armchairs in the back. Simon and I sat in regal style while she drove us first to one end of the island and then to the other. It was low tide and people were wading out onto the reef looking for shellfish and octopi. Between the islands was a steady stream of people carrying bags of copra, picking their way across the exposed reef. Many were on horseback.

Mr Ila Prescott also lived in Pangai. Captain Hillbilly had given us an introduction to him so he was expecting us. He was a seasoned raconteur and gave a splendid account of the story of the sinking of the *Port au Prince* in the waters of Haapi. She was a British privateer said to have had a cargo gained by illicit raiding in the Spanish Main. On arrival in Tonga she had been boarded by hordes of Tongans who had looted and destroyed her by fire. They had killed all of her crew except for Will Mariner, then a boy of fifteen. He had written about his enforced stay giving the first detailed account of the ways of the 'Friendly Islanders'.

At low tide horses carried copra between the islands.

Ila told us that the people of Pangai and many others had searched, without success, for the treasure, which was reputedly lying in the wreck of the ship. Treasure fever was still running high, but as the wreck was on the windward side of the island it was difficult for divers to find it. There was another rumour that a New Zealand yachtsman had already found some of the gold and had reburied it on another island.

The next day was a Sunday and, as usual, all was quiet except for the sound of church bells and singing. We walked to the windward side of the island, less than a kilometre away, through gardens and cemeteries. One contained a bronze statue made in New Zealand of Shirley Baker, an early missionary and later the first Tongan Prime Minister. It looked strangely out of place amongst the palm trees and tropical gardens.

Much against the wishes of the difficult customs officer, but with the concurrence of the chief of police (on condition we did not ask for any help to raise our anchor) we left on the Sunday afternoon and picked our way for a few miles along the reef to anchor off the northern end of Lifuka. We left early the next day and sailed close-hauled to Vavau. We sighted the island before dark and at nightfall the lighthouse lit up. We hove-to off it for the rest of the night. In the morning the wind failed so we powered into Vavau in huge blind swells coming from the east.

Port of Refuge, Vavau

The islands in the Vavau Group were different from the other Tongan Islands, being higher and flat topped. The sea had eroded the soft volcanic rock at the base of the sheer cliffs so the islands resembled mushrooms. There were many caves.

We made our way to the main town, Neiafu. It looked as if it had seen better days. We found three other yachts there and were joined by two more, one of them being the yacht that had overtaken us in the dark as we were leaving Nuku'alofa. She was indeed *Stormvogel*; my psychic guess had been spot on. She was on charter to an Indian millionaire and his wife. They invited us on board for a drink and told us their dinghy had been washed overboard in the storm that had caused us to drag. Amazingly, a week later when visiting another island many miles away it was returned to them, having been washed ashore there. They felt a real attachment to their dinghy after that.

Pat Matheson, the wiry, sunburnt widow of an American doctor who had spent most of his life in Tonga, was one of the three Europeans who resided in Vavau. The others were Catholic priests. Pat came on board to invite us to dinner. She told us a great deal about Tonga and the Tongan way of life. She liked it so much that she intended to spend the rest of her days there, keeping a home for her daughter and two adopted daughters, all of whom were being educated in the States. She had particularly vivid memories of the hurricane that had swept through the islands in 1961, causing real devastation and partly accounting for the poor appearance of the town.

At anchor off Neiafu

Vavau was expecting new wealth from the hotel due to open in a few months' time. There was a hive of activity, but the new building seemed to be a long way from completion. The new airstrip to serve it appeared even further from being usable, a jumble of fallen trees marking its length.

Ofa Tufui had given us a letter of introduction to her brother-in-law Saia and we spent a delightful day looking for him. We engaged a Mini Moke with a helpful driver who entered into the hunt with enthusiasm. We found Saia's village quite easily and plunged off the road into the backblocks interviewing most of his relations. After several wild goose chases that took us to thickly wooded countryside and overgrown but productive gardens, we eventually found Saia working in his son's garden. He was an older and less boisterous edition of his brother Bill and welcomed us with a wide, happy smile.

He showed us around the garden. There were several acres of bananas, coconuts, pawpaws, yams, cassava, two types of taro, sugar cane, pineapples and mangoes. There was also Tonga kava – low bushes with twisted branches, the bark of which is used to make the narcotic drink better known in Fiji. There were also tutu trees, a variety of mulberry used to make tapa cloth. We arranged to meet Saia in two day's time in Neiafu market.

Locals at Neiafu market

The Saturday market was a major social occasion, thronged with people buying and selling their produce and exchanging gossip. We met Saia; he brought two big baskets of vegetables from his garden and a live hen for us. We declined the hen, a docile and rather thin, elderly creature and she appeared grateful. We went with him to the Vavau Club, an old building with a fine view of the harbour. The barman supplied us with all the local news and gossip. He told us there were only fourteen members of the club as the others had failed to pay their dues. He related the life history of each one of them.

We left Neiafu in the afternoon and sailed a few miles to Port Maurelle, anchoring close to an uninhabited beach in a deep bay ringed with coconut trees. On Sunday morning we could hear the church bells from the village in the next bay and later some youths riding horses came along the beach, shouting and whistling to attract our attention. We ignored them, assuming they either wanted to look at the boat or ask for cigarettes, or both. When one yelled out, 'I've got a present for you', we knew we were right.

In the evening a boatload of women and boys came into the bay and methodically turned over the copra lying on the beach to dry. We wondered at all this work going on – it was Sunday – and concluded, again correctly, that it was going to rain. It waited until the morning, but then came from the northwest with squalls. We moved to a more discreet distance from the shore and waited for the southeaster to return before setting sail for Suva, 300 miles to the west.

It was still a bit overcast when we left, but the forecast was favourable and the barometer high. We cleared the volcanic island of Late early in the afternoon, closely inspected by five curious gannets as we sailed past. They made several attempts to land on our masts, but eventually flew off to glide low over the water in their search for food.

Charlie steered through the night until dawn when the wind failed. Instead of the weather clearing, as we had hoped, it was becoming increasingly overcast and it was difficult to take sights through the gaps in the clouds. In the afternoon the wind freshened and we could sail again. The wind and sea built up and we reduced sail until, by 9 pm, we were experiencing a boisterous 35-knot wind and rain. We hove-to and waited until morning.

The grey dawn did not present an agreeable sight. The seas were breaking, the sky was completely covered and the wind was strong enough to howl in the rigging. We sailed on, worried about not being able to fix our position, for we were approaching the eastern Lau

Group, a string of islands surrounded by reefs on which many a boat had met its end. We were aiming for a gap at the southern end of the chain. The charts warned of strong and unpredictable currents so we were not happy using dead reckoning to find it.

We sailed on, sextant and chronometer to hand all day, hoping for a glimpse of the sky. In the early afternoon a watery sun appeared vaguely for a few seconds. The boat was rolling heavily and the horizon more often than not was obscured by waves. However, I managed to run the sun briefly along the horizon before they both disappeared – the sun for the last time that day. The sight gave us a line slightly south of our course and for the moment we were at a safe distance from the reefs.

Rain came with the wind that was now over 40 knots; it was too much for Charlie to manage. *Iota* rose valiantly to each wave, trying, as usual, to keep her decks dry. Although the moon was full there was no glimpse of it. Turbulent waves assaulted us, the wind howled and the rain beat on us almost horizontally. We were cold and wet so we hove-to again and retreated to the cabin where we were comparatively comfortable.

The nearest island in the Lau Group was Ongea, about 20 miles northwest of us if our dubious sight was credible. At 4 am we freed the main, pulled out the No 1 jib and rushed northeast in a froth, the log clocking off over 15 miles in the next two hours. We kept a careful watch; while we were on top of a wave we both thought we could see a blacker patch ahead in the black night. Dawn was a long time arriving for we had travelled nearly 300 miles to the west, but when light eventually came into the sky it showed us there was indeed an island about five miles away. Other islands appeared in the distance and we were able to identify Ongea. Soon we could see the breakers on the reef.

There was a wreck of an old trading boat on the reef – an ominous reminder to the unwary. We came to the end of the reef and turned into the lee, the mountainous seas quickly abating, but the wind seeming to increase as we turned into it. The *Pilot Book* gave directions to the pass and warned of the current that invariably flowed out of it. The wind was also against us and we wondered if we had enough power to make way against their combined force. With the engine flat out we inched our way in through the narrow gap in the coral. A shark almost as long as *Iota* swam alongside us until we were inside the lagoon.

We headed across the lagoon to a beach towards the southern end of Ongea Ndriti, the smaller of the two islands enclosed in the lagoon.

There was a shallow patch of sand off the beach and we let go the anchor, not quite believing we had arrived.

A large early lunch compensated for the breakfast we had no time or appetite for earlier. As we ate we savoured feelings of relief, relaxation, peace and accomplishment.

We could not have chosen a pleasanter refuge. Ongea Ndriti's precipitous cliffs had been etched away at sea level and eroded by the sea and wind into fantastic shapes. A few trees grew on them from a precarious hold. A sheer-sided archway pierced the large rock that lay off our beach. Birdlife abounded. Bosun birds and frigate birds wheeled around the cliffs; white and grey herons patrolled their waterfront territories pausing frequently to stand motionless on one leg to look for fish. Further inland, smaller birds with persistent cries emphasised the loneliness of the anchorage.

On the low tide ledge we could walk quite a way around the island.

At high tide the beach was only a narrow strip, but when it was low we could walk quite a way around the island on a ledge at the base of the overhanging cliffs. We disturbed orange and green crabs that rattled as they scuttled away sideways. There were many shells – mostly the homes of hermit crabs. Waves pounded unmercifully on the reef. We looked at the wreck we had seen from the sea and vividly imagined her last dying moments with a shudder.

The weather continued foul all the next day, but we were well protected and could relax. When the wind dropped we set off in the dinghy to explore, rounding the north side of the island to see even craggier cliffs, caves and islands. We were on the point of returning when yet another island attracted our attention. As we approached we found to our astonishment a lagoon inside it. We went in through the narrow gap and gazed in wonder. Here was the anchorage to end all anchorages: about three quarters of a mile by half a mile, three fathoms of water in the deepest part, a sandy bottom and an entrance about as wide as *Iota* was long. We sounded the shallow part of the entrance and determined we could get *Iota* in at high tide.

Into our newfound haven we went. That night it blew hard again, the rain lashing us and thunder rumbling around. We felt safe and secure. We heard and saw even more birds, their chorus rising to a crescendo in the evenings. A flock of flying foxes flapped back to their roosts in the morning after a night foraging. The shoreline was fringed by steep rocks or mangroves so landing was difficult, but we managed to scramble ashore at one end and climb up the jagged rocks. Here more surprises greeted us; we found a garden of coconut, cassava and pawpaws. The coconut trees were small so Simon could reach the nuts with the boat hook.

As we breasted the top of the ridge the sun came out and we looked over the northeast side of the island. The lagoon was studded with islands, each green and wooded, sitting peacefully in bright blue sparkling water. We wondered what other wonderful secrets Ongea would reveal to us. For several days we enjoyed the solitude, listening to the birdcalls and the water lapping and gurgling against the overhanging cliffs. The forecast from Nadi gave no indication of settled weather – we were under the influence of a broad stationary convergence. The weather in the convergence zone was not predictable and varied from overcast, drizzly calms to strong, squally wind. It could, however, be relied upon to be, in some way, foul.

We stayed in Ongea for over a week, but the end of Simon's holiday was drawing closer. It was time to leave – converged or not. We went back to our first anchorage where a German ketch, *Typee*, was sheltering. Hans and Lotte were as relieved as we had been when they found refuge on their way west from Rarotonga.

We left together the next morning; the sky had cleared and the wind was blowing at about 25 knots from the east. We surfed along in huge waves sailing fast – well over 6 knots – and passed between the high islands of Totoya and Moala before dark. *Iota* was enjoying herself, but steering was hard work. She managed to toss Simon out of his bunk with one great lurch; he landed with such a bang I thought we had hit a rock.

I took a moon sight to give us an idea of our latitude and it put us about 20 miles south of our course. Since we had anticipated the current would be taking us north we were reluctant to believe it. Simon dispelled the doubt when he sighted the lighthouse on the Astrolobe Reef – we were indeed 20 miles too far south.

We came closer to the wind and aimed for Suva. For yet another hour we saw no land, but, at last, mountains appeared in the haze. A departing ship enabled us to identify the entrance to the harbour. The weather forecast was threatening us with a depression so we hurried in through the reef.

We anchored off the town flying our yellow quarantine flag to await clearance and listened to the strange noise of traffic. It was Saturday afternoon; we were resigned to wait for our freedom until Monday, but became the subject of official attention on Sunday morning. An immigration officer shouted to Simon so he went ashore. Then the health official arrived. Simon had gone ashore before the yacht had been given a health clearance – a dreadful offence. There was a protracted argument so neither officer noticed we had spent a whole week in the Lau group before officially entering – a much worse crime! We were the hundred and twenty-first yacht to arrive in Suva that year and moved to the yacht club to compare notes with other yachts over a welcome cold Fiji beer.

John of *Bonaventure de Lys* and Hans and Lotte of *Typee* we already knew; all of us had experienced difficult weather on the crossing between Tonga and Fiji. We were sitting comparing notes when Beth and Graham, a couple from the trimaran *Lodestar*, joined us.

They told us of an embarrassing moment. 'We were down below having a rest. The windvane was steering and we were sailing along comfortably. All of a sudden there was a loud blast of a ship's siren right next to us. It scared us out of our wits and we shot up on deck. It was a trading boat – she was only a boat's length away from us. The crew and passengers all waved and when they saw we didn't have any clothes on, they cheered!'

Another couple came to our table. They had been touring the islands on a trading boat.

'Anything interesting happen?' Simon asked.

'Yes,' they said. 'We came across a trimaran sailing along with apparently nobody on board. The skipper went close to investigate and blew his siren when we were nearly alongside. Two stark naked people came rushing up on deck. We all cheered!'

~

It rained every day until the end of Simon's holiday. Everything on board was mouldy. We discussed our options – did we want to cruise around Fiji next year? If so, I could go to Lautoka where it would be drier, but there was no slipway or other facilities for yachts, or I could stay in Suva. It was already uncomfortably wet in Suva and the wet season had not even started! The more it rained the less appealing Fiji seemed.

'Okay,' said Simon. 'Let's take *Iota* back to Sydney and think again.'

He enquired about shipping. The *Tauloto* was due in a month's time and could take both *Iota* and me. The decision was made.

We discussed the possibilities for our next cruise. Simon didn't want to go to the Mediterranean – too crowded and anyway he knew it already as he had been born in Cairo and his parents had holidayed there. Maybe it would be fun to explore the French canals, but it would be easier and cheaper to charter a local barge.

'We could ship the boat to Lima and you could find a timber truck to take her as back-loading over the mountains to the headwaters of the Amazon. Then we could sail down the Amazon through the jungle,' he suggested.

'Heavens,' I said. 'That sounds a bit ambitious.'

I thought the chances of transporting *Iota* on rough Peruvian jungle roads so she arrived in a usable condition were not great. I looked at the map and found we would be travelling for over 3000 kilometres through humid, impenetrable jungle, in rivers infested with piranhas.

'I think you've gone too far this time,' I said. 'And I'm starting to think I would like to have a base ashore where I could have some animals – a dog, a donkey and a duck. There isn't enough room on *Iota* to keep them.'

The more we talked about it the more appealing it seemed. We would sell *Iota* and start looking for a place where we could indulge our whim to live close to nature and become self-sufficient.

I waited for the *Tauloto* in the convenient and secure bay off the Tradewinds Hotel. It was close to the home of Jean and Dennis, the couple whom I had met on the *Tauloto*. They were welcoming and opened up their house for showers and laundry. Dennis took me with him when he was visiting inland villages.

Jenny, who had lived on board *Iota* with me in Martinique, wrote to say she was on her way back to Australia and would be passing through Suva. She would spend a week on board with me and then join me on the *Tauloto*.

Several friends from Sydney came on holiday to Fiji and looked me up. They all complained about the weather. Geoffrey and Ruth Goodman came in on *Karloo*. It was the first time the two cruising Waterwitches had met and it was a time to compare notes. We agreed that the yachts had served our purposes well.

The two Waterwitches, Karloo *and* Iota, *meet in Suva.*

The time came to move back to the main harbour. I had plenty of help to prepare *Iota* for shipping. The *Tauloto* came into the wharf and we went alongside. I ate a toffee given to me as a parting gift and immediately my bridge fell out, leaving a gaping hole and two fragile unprotected molars. This I would have to live with for the next three weeks, as the ship was sailing within the hour. Jenny told me she thought one of the boys she had met on a yacht was a dentist. She hastily rowed over to the yacht club and came back with Michael. He inspected the problem, mixed up some glue and fixed it while we were being hoisted aboard.

Jim and Syd were their usual hospitable selves and welcomed Jenny aboard. We were the only passengers to Nuku'alofa. I still had my Tongan driving licence and hired a car to show Jenny around the island. Driving was not allowed on Sunday but, no risk, we thought – we could not be arrested on a Sunday; in any case we thought the police would not have time to catch up with us as we were leaving that evening. Syd joined us and we had the road to ourselves.

We went to the north coast and picnicked, but when we returned to the car found a puncture. Jenny and I changed the tyre while Syd admired the view. Late in the afternoon on our way back to Nuku'alofa we had a second puncture. This time, of course, there was no spare wheel. We sat and looked at each other wondering what to do. We were not far from a village, but knew there would be no telephone.

'There might be one at the airport,' said Syd, 'but it's a good five miles back and it will be dark by the time we walk there.'

Jenny helped me load Iota *for the last time.*

'I could go to the village and ask if I could borrow a horse,' I said. 'I could be there in half an hour.'

We went to the village to ask if they had a horse I could use. The answer was 'Yes, but horses don't work on Sundays.'

Despondently we returned to the useless car and wondered how long it would be before somebody noticed we were missing. No doubt a higher being was punishing us for working on a Sunday. At least we had Syd with us and the *Tauloto* could not sail without him. Just as we had resigned ourselves to a long wait we were amazed to see the king's Chevie coming along the road. It stopped to investigate our plight. The king's driver was showing a newly arrived English couple around the island before the husband started the next day in his job as the financial adviser to the Tongan government; they had government permission to drive on a Sunday. We squeezed into the car and drove back to the *Tauloto* and her anxious captain. She sailed just as soon as she had her chief engineer aboard.

Jim was in good poetic form and spent much of the journey back to Sydney composing a poem for me.

I know of some yachties – skipper and crew
Their passion for sailing they keenly pursue
Through seas gigantic
To islands romantic
Running and reaching for miles o'er the blue.

They solved the dilemma of having to pay
For varnish and slipping – a major outlay.
Upkeep is extensive
And always expensive
But needed to keep all those problems at bay.

The answer to this was a portable boat
That could be shipped as deck cargo to places remote:
Bahamas, New Guinea
The South China Sea,
Lowered into the water and left there afloat.

The crew travelled with her – the boss to await.
She rigged and provisioned, prepared to navigate
To harbours and bays
In the Antilles, Marquaise
Exciting adventures sure to elate.

But after a cruise to Fiji from Tonga
They decided that cruising for them was no longer.
The chickens were laying
The donkeys were braying
The call of the country had now become stronger.

epilogue

I had thought that the decision we made in miserable pouring rain in Suva might waver when we reviewed it back in Sydney, but we were both ready for a change of lifestyle. Simon wanted to grow plants and become self-sufficient and I was yearning for some animals in my life. We wanted some acreage.

'Do you realise that *Iota* has been picked up out of the sea and lowered back in again sixteen times on thirteen different ships and we have sailed her over 12,000 miles around the most attractive cruising grounds in the world while I was still hanging onto my pensionable job?'

'Talking of pensions – there's another thing,' Simon continued. 'We're going to have to get married. Provided I get married before I turn 57 my pension will go to my widow should I die first. Seeing I'm older than you are, and male, it's highly likely I will.'

'Highly likely,' I repeated. 'Well, I have my principles, but they're not worth that much. There's really no choice.'

We were duly married as quietly and unobtrusively as possible. It made only one difference – before we were married, Simon was called Mr Simpson and I was called Jenifer, but after, he was called Simon and I was called Mrs Simpson.

Iota sold almost immediately she returned to Sydney. An enthusiastic young couple wanted to sail her across the Indian Ocean to the United Kingdom. By an amazing coincidence I saw her arrival in Singapore. I was on my way back to Sydney from Europe and had stopped over for a few days in Singapore to catch up with friends. I was in an accountant friend's office on the twelfth floor of a building that looked out over the harbour – such a magnificent view that I wondered how he ever did any work. As I looked, a red sail appeared in the distance and, as the yacht came closer, I realised it was *Iota*. I did not get to see the couple or *Iota* as I had to catch my plane, but later learned that this had been the end of their journey as the wife was pregnant and suffering from seasickness. They sold *Iota* and she lay neglected in Singapore for several years until sold again. Her new owners sailed her to Java, but in bad weather met with disaster on rocks. The crew survived, but *Iota* was lost.

In spite of her marvellous success as our 'portable' boat, nobody has tried to emulate us.

I spent the next few years looking for a place where Simon and I could indulge in happy-ever-aftering once Simon had retired. We searched New Zealand and went so far as to buy a property in the Dordogne in France. But eventually we settled in Australia, in the Hinterland of Queensland's Sunshine Coast. As well as keeping the usual farm animals I bred donkeys and called my first donkey foal 'Iota'.